Praise for YOUR YOSEMITE

In his book, *Palisades, 100,000 Acres in 100 Years*, Bob Binnewies gave us a strong reminder of the responsibilities we all share for preservation of our parklands. He has done so, again, with *Your Yosemite*, a page-turning, insider's story and clarion call never to take our parks for granted. We must protect them for all who will inherit these irreplaceable natural treasures.

–Larry Rockefeller, Conservationist

Yosemite, a crown jewel of our National Park System, faces severe threats to its future from overuse and excessive commercialism. In this heartfelt but always factual book, Bob Binnewies shows us what needs to be done to balance environmental protection and public enjoyment of this stunningly majestic place. As a former Yosemite Superintendent, he delivers his vital message with authority and passion.

–James Risser, Pulitzer Prize-winning Journalist

No one who has visited Yosemite will ever forget it—it becomes their park. Few, however, understand this incredible place and it's complexities with as much depth as Bob Binnewies. Rich in personal details and extensively re-searched topics, *Your Yosemite* chronicles the park as only an insider could. Even the most experienced Yosemite advocate will find new and fascinating insights in this wonderful book.

–Laurel Boyers, Yosemite Park Ranger Supervisor

The immense value of our national parks is in their constant invitation to meet them on their own terms, not ours. In Bob Binnewies' engaging book, *Your Yosemite*, the message is that all of us can take great joy from our national parks, if we give back respect for their naturalness. Yosemite withstands great pressures to change it; more cars, more shops, more clamor; more of everything. This book is a plea to hold the preservation line and to hold politicians and park managers accountable if they try to cross it.

–Yvon Chouinard, Rock Climber and Outdoor Business Person

ISBN-979-8-218-48442-2

Dedicated to:
Fred and Amy Binnewies
Louie and Aggie Gastellum
George and Dete Oliver
Members, all, of the spirited National Park Service family

And to,
David Gaines
Steve Medley
Galen Rowell
Yosemite champions gone too soon.

Designed by Carole Thickstun, Ormsby & Thickstun Interpretive Design

AN EXAMINATION BY A FORMER SUPERINTENDENT

Your Yosemite

Robert O. Binnewies

Contents

Acknowledgments. ix
Contested Ground 1
Yosemite, Why Me! 7
    Peggy Rockefeller's Vision 10
    A Yosemite Commuter 12
    Into The Traces 14
Joseph R. Walker, Busting Through to California 17
    Off The Map 22
    Leonard's Journal 24
    A Clash of Cultures 26
    The Great Barricade 28
    A Search for Escape 30
    Climb Or Die 32
    Discovery? 35
    Salvation 37
Old Ways Collapse 41
    Gold! 44
    Desperate Resistance 49
    Invasion 51
    Surrender 53
    The Sanctuary Discovered 56
    A Name 57
    Conquered 58
    Parole and Calamity 61
An Idea with Staying Power 65
    Threats. 66
    Part Of A Team 68
    A Plan for The Park 74
    What To Do with The Cars? 75
    Olive and Oliver. 76
    My Fingers on the Typewriter 81

The Genesis of The Struggle 85
    Horace Greeley On Horseback 87
    It Pays To Advertise 90
    A Conservation Champion Steps Forward 92
    Olmsted 94
    A Park Guardian 96
    Yosemite Prophet John Muir 97
    Fighting for Ownership 100
    Let The Fire Fall 103
    Conquering Half Dome 104
    Management Hurly-Burly 109
The Plan Is Official 111
    Reagan Succeeds Carter 112
    James Watt 114
    Legacy 118
    A Hesitant Romance 118
    A Very Public Conflict 121
    Fighting to Save Yosemite 123
    An Incomplete National Park 126
    Forceful Citizens Voices Are Raised 128
    Park Ranger .130
    Muir And Harriman 130
    The Legendary Curry's Few Tents 131
Theodore Roosevelt 135
    Muir Meets Roosevelt 137
    One National Park 145
Stars and Stripes in the Valley 149
    A Far Away Earthquake Rattles The Park 153
    John Muir and The Battle To Preserve Hetch Hetchy . . .154
    Hetch Hetchy Saves Yellowstone 162
    A Tribute To Muir 163
Stephen Mather, Man Of The Moment 165
    Establishing The National Park Service 168
    Competing For Commerce 171
    Mather Collapses, But Not For Long 174
    Yosemite, Outdoor Classroom 177
    The Commercial Smoke Settles 178

A Flagship Hotel 181

Bracebridge 184

To'tu'ya Returns 186

Mather Is Gone & The Great Depression Strikes 187

The War 190

Donald Tresidder, Two Hats 191

Visitation Explodes 193

"Mission 66" 194

A Trusted Ally, Alienated 197

The Falcons 201

Climb The Big Walls .204

El Capitan 208

The Aerie 213

The Other Park 217

Wilderness Stewards .219

Women, Too 224

The Great Outback 226

Where To Draw The Wilderness Line 228

On Patrol 233

The Riot And A Loss Of Innocence 239

Walt Castle 244

Big League Commercialism 248

The Odd Couple 251

A Rescue 257

Her Royal Highness, Queen Elizabeth The Ii Of England 268

Mr. Rent-A-Riot 283

Looking For Money 286

Bears and Their Neighbors 297

A Wilderness Quota 302

Not So Great 307

Political Drift 309

Business Upheaval 310

The Flood 316

New Plans Emerge 319

The NPS Taken To Court 320

Legal Grind 323

Old Guard On Guard Again 326

Parks at Risk 328
Trademarks 333
Ferdinand 335
Bibliography 339
Articles 341
Index 348

Acknowledgments

THE LEGACY OF YOSEMITE lies in the historic struggle to preserve it and the obligation of present stewards to hand it on, unbroken, to the next generation. Those who have helped me to deliver this important message, told in my own style, have brought expertise, wisdom, constructive criticism, and encouragement to the task. I bow to them in appreciation.

Linda Eade, Yosemite Research Librarian, did not let diminutive budgets and cramped workspace stand in the way of assuring that a highly refined source of documents and images is available to anyone who wishes to learn more about the prized park. All that is needed is a trace of a computer signal, a visit to the library, or even an old fashioned telephone call. I used all three, while always benefiting from Linda's welcoming counsel. Her staff colleague, Barbara Beroza, nurtures the Yosemite photo archive, a treasure trove available to everyone.

My spouse, Midge, a published author in her own right, is a partner who reaches high and invites me to do the same.

Alice Truax lifted a heavy editing load and rewarded herself by traveling from Brooklyn, New York, to hike Yosemite's fifty-mile High Sierra Loop Trail.

Nancy Slowik brought her excellent technical skills to the manuscript, and greatly strengthened its message. Carole Thickstun provided the design, and guided me through the publication process.

With my gratitude, others whose fingerprints are on this work include Lila Beaumet, Heidi Binnewies, Nick Bleser, Laurel Boyers, Dr. Hal Browder, Ginger Burley, Frank Cabot, Scott Carpenter, Ethan Carr, Walt Castle, Doug Cochran, John Dill, Delores Durando, Gene Edwards, Glen Fredy, Carolyn Gastellum, Jay Johnson, Ron Mackie, Dick Martin, Len McKenzie, Lewis Mitchell, Bob Pavlik, Rick Ridgeway, James Risser, John Reynolds, Dan Rivas, Jim Sano, Norman Savage, Jr., Tom Smith, Jim Snyder, Bryan Swift, Dr. Jan van Wagtendonk, Florence "Buddy" Welles, and Dave Willis.

Bridgeport
395
Matterhorn
Peak
Sawtooth Ridge
Slide Canyon
Spiller Canyon
Matterhorn Canyon
Virginia Canyon
Mt. Conness
Saddlebag
Tower Peak
Thompson Canyon
Stubblefield Canyon
Jack Main Canyon
Kerrick Canyon
PACIFIC CREST TRAIL
Return Creek
GRAND CANYON of the TUOLUMNE RIVER
Pleasant Valley
Piute Creek
Rancheria Creek
Paté Valley
Lukens Lake
TIOGA ROAD
White Wolf
Tiltill Valley
Frog Creek
Falls Creek
Harden Lake
CLOSED IN
Hetch Hetchy Reservoir
Wapama Falls
Tueeulala Falls
HETCH HETCHY
Eleanor Creek
HETCH HETCHY
Aspen Valley
Lake Eleanor
RIVER
ROAD
Tuolumne River
Old Tioga Road
Cherry Lake
PARK BOUNDARY
Hetch Hetchy Entrance
Mather
Evergreen Road
of the Tuolumne River
N E S W
Cherry Creek
Middle
South Fork
Hodgdon Meadow
BIG
OAK
0 1 2 3 4 5 kilometers
0 1 2 3 4 5 miles
Big Oak Flat Entrance
120 to San Francisco
Tuolumne

no Lake
Lee Vining
Mt. Dana
Mt. Gibbs
June Lake
395
to Mammoth
Vining Canyon
20
Tioga Pass Entrance
Koip Crest
Kuna Crest
PCT
Middle Fork of the San Joaquin River
Mt. Ritter
The Minarets
Lembert Dome
Dana Fork
Lyell Fork of the Tuolumne River
Mt. Lyell
RITTER RANGE
UMNE MEADOWS
PCT & JMT
Cathedral Peak
CATHEDRAL RANGE
North Fork of the San Joaquin River
Vogelsang Lake
Mt. Hoffmann
Tenaya Lake
JOHN MUIR
Merced River
May Lake
Merced Peak
Olmsted Point
Clouds Rest
Merced Lake
Mt. Clark
CLARK RANGE
rcupine Flat
Mt. Watkins
TRAIL
Tenaya Canyon
Little Yosemite Valley
Half Dome
mite k
North Dome
Tenaya Creek
Mt. Starr King
Yosemite Creek
Yosemite Falls
Nevada Fall
Illilouette Creek
Buena Vista Crest
Yosemite Village
Glacier Point
Vernal Fall
El Capitan
Sentinel Dome
Ostrander Lake
CLOSED IN WINTER
Cathedral Rocks
Bridalveil Creek
Chilnualna Creek
marack Flat
Bridalveil Fall
GLACIER POINT ROAD
YOSEMITE VALLEY
Badger Pass
South Fork of the Merced River
Chinquapin
WAWONA ROAD
Mariposa Grove
AD
Merced River
ne Flat
Foresta
Arch Rock Entrance
Yosemite West
PARK BOUNDARY
WAWONA
Fish Camp
South Entrance
El Portal
140 to Merced
41
to Fresno

Contested Ground

YOSEMITE IS CONTESTED GROUND, a phe-
nomenal natural landscape wrapped in controversy. In the mind's
eye "Yosemite Valley" conjures an image of a fantastic work of
art sculpted by powerful natural forces, immense in scale and yet
somehow in perfect proportion. Those who first recorded this scene
guessed at the height of the giant granite walls, making estimates
from hundreds of feet to upwards of a thousand. They were far shy
of the three-thousand vertical feet presented by the mightiest of
the valley's rock faces. These walls are animated by waterfalls, most
thundering but some so feathery that the leaping white water evap-
orates into thin air before reaching the valley floor. And beyond the
walls and waterfalls, up in the alpine country, are the sharp granite
peaks of the Sierra Nevada Mountains, so lofty that they avoided the
impact of the glaciers during the last ice age and now attract hikers
and climbers from all over the world.

Use of Yosemite by humans dates back only a few thousand years,
a mere flash of time on the earth's clock. Immediately to the east
of the Sierra Nevada, where the abrupt mountain escarpment
gives way to high desert plains, the Paiute, Shoshone, and Wash-
oe claimed territories and hunting grounds as their ancestral right.
Just to the west of Yosemite Valley, where the foothills of the Sierra
Nevada edge onto the vast interior Central Valley of California, the
Miwuk and Yokut held sway. In between, Yosemite Valley became a
sanctuary for a gathering of refugees from various Native American
ethnic groups, a remote and almost inaccessible place unknown to
many and draped in legend by the few who came in contact with
the valley's inhabitants. According to the etymologist Madison Beeler, the valley's occupants were called the *Yohé-met^i,* meaning in the
dialects of some foothill tribes, "they are killers." Such a fierce reputation, whether deserved or not, could well serve an enigmatic clan.

European explorers of the Pacific coast in the 16th century, like Juan
Rodriguez Cabrillo and Sir Frances Drake, limited their forays to

narrow strips of land by the ocean. Spanish settlement along the coast in the 16th and 17th centuries was similarly confined, leaving interior California to its indigenous peoples. The first hint of momentous change in the traditions and cultures of the Sierra Nevada came in the 1830s in the form of a straggling line of Anglo men intent on seeking new fortune, not in the *glory* of the mountains, but by *surviving* them. The indigenous people of Yosemite, who perhaps sensed the presence of these alien men as they passed by, may have thought that their refuge was touched, but would never be breeched.

But the natural fortress would not stand. Settlers eventually arrived in Yosemite Valley to claim portions of this Shangri-La as their own, paying nothing except sweat equity for the acreage they claimed, or making similar claim through government permit. They cut down trees, fenced in meadows, built roughhewn cabins and lodges, and awaited the tourist trade sure to follow, exhibiting an extraordinary entrepreneurial belief in a place that was still almost impossible to reach without exhausting physical effort. Paradoxically, this isolated valley was so scenically forceful that it was being heralded as a national treasure by the very pioneers who began to swing their axes, shoot and trap wildlife, graze their livestock, pound in the fence posts, and dump waste in the river.

The human anarchy in Yosemite was growing so rapidly that it provoked a national response among politicians and steamship and railroad owners who preferred tourism on their own corporate terms. These leaders, most of whom would never see Yosemite Valley, nonetheless gathered their voices and votes in an unprecedented manner to defend the natural splendor and economic budding of this faraway place, and they put teeth and precedent into their actions by judging Yosemite to be "inalienable," defined in Webster's Dictionary, as "of that which cannot be given or taken away." When Congress, in revolutionary mode on July 4, 1776, approved the Declaration of Independence, it proclaimed the "inalienable right" of every citizen to "life, liberty, and the pursuit of happiness." Almost a century later, President Abraham Lincoln, struggling to keep our nation intact, took a moment from the anguish of the Civil War on June 30, 1864, to approve a federal grant of land to the State of Cal-

Ahwahnee Hotel, circa 1927

ifornia to conserve and manage Yosemite Valley and the Mariposa Grove of Giant Sequoias. These lands, still secreted or nearly so, were granted for "public use, resort, and recreation," and were to be held "inalienable for all time."

When President Lincoln affixed his signature, his action was admirably forward looking, a statement that the United States indeed would survive and that its government leaders should establish a conservation endowment on behalf of its citizens. The Yosemite Grant became an anchor point for the stewardship of public lands that signaled the subsequent establishment in 1872 of Yellowstone National Park. Generations of political leaders have since expanded an inestimable nationwide system of public parks, historic sites, monuments, wildlife refuges, and outdoor recreation areas that have been copied around the world.

But conservation of land for public benefit is rarely easy. Another anchor point for our nation's modern environmental movement is a deep canyon in the Sierra Nevada named Hetch Hetchy. Sculpted by glaciers, its mighty walls adorned by some of the tallest waterfalls in North America, it is a place that broke John Muir's heart. He called the heartbreak "a water tank." In 1913, the US Congress and President Woodrow Wilson approved legislation that allowed for the construction of the O'Shaughnessy Dam, a concrete plug of more than 300 feet in height and 900 in width that choked the flow of the mountain-fresh Tuolumne River and its tributaries to fill an 8-mile-long reservoir. The purpose was to pipe water to the San Francisco Bay area, 170 miles away.

Yosemite Valley and Hetch Hetchy are both within the legal bounds of 750,000-acre Yosemite National Park. This boundary line was ignored when Hetch Hetchy Valley was flooded—the only instance in the history of our nation that such an industrial invasion has been allowed in a national park. Muir's anguish was not enough to save Hetch Hetchy, but others who embraced the Muir environmental philosophy prevented dams from being constructed in Yellowstone. The O'Shaughnessy Dam still stands and functions—still drowns Hetch Hetchy Valley—still is a gross reminder that raids on our national conservation endowment can succeed if citizens are not actively watchful and willing to unite in defense.

Yosemite Valley was invaded, too, first by a force of militiamen during the California Gold Rush who were intent on destroying the small Native American community there, and, soon after, by pioneering adventurers intent on tapping into the commercial potential of such a scenically profound locale. That commercial promise is represented today by the nearly four million annual visitors to Yosemite National Park. The balancing act that confronts Yosemite's stewards today is to allow for this "use, resort, and recreation" without bringing real harm to the native life and human pleasure that the park is intended to perpetuate.

I was honored in 1979 to take on the responsibility of managing splendid Yosemite. As superintendent, I shared in the day-to-day dynamics of the park with rangers and naturalists, maintenance

Your Yosemite: **PROTECTING A PUBLIC TREASURE**

personnel, scientists, and administrative staff who were tasked with providing access and safety for the public while at the same time, always close to the line of contradiction, preserving naturalness. During my management journey I witnessed rescue and wildlife triumphs, agonized over rescue and accident losses, stretched for additional discretionary funds from private sources, found amazing talents among the staff, helped draw a wilderness line, attempted to help dampen law enforcement problems that should never have migrated into the park in the first place, stumbled professionally, and even welcomed the visiting Queen of England.

One of my immediate assignments was to complete a master plan for the park. My predecessor, Superintendent Les Arnberger, in cooperation with a team of National Park Service (NPS) planning professionals, brought the plan near the finishing point. It was intended to guide decision-making well into the future and my priority was to assure that the plan was finally signed, sealed, and delivered as a durable management document.

There was good need for such a plan. Yosemite Valley, only seven square miles in size and a small fraction of the total Rhode Island-sized park, was the seat of the largest commercial operation in any national park, anywhere in the world. Stephen T. Mather, the founder of the National Park Service, was a champion of commercialism, reasoning in the early 20th century that only by providing attractive hotels and related accommodations could enough visitors be attracted to the parks to justify to members of Congress this continuing experiment in conservation.

Mather succeeded, but with care. He chose Yosemite to demonstrate that commercialism and environmentalism, joined together by constraint and quality, could allow the public to have their park and enjoy it, too. The result was the flagship Ahwahnee Hotel. When I arrived at Yosemite, the Ahwahnee was still high fashion, but only one product among the many commercial offerings of the Yosemite Park & Curry Company, a multi-million dollar park monopoly owned by the Music Corporation of America.

Each night in Yosemite Valley, thousands of park-inspired customers could lay their sleepy heads on YP&CC pillows. These customers were joined by thousands more day-visitors and campers who had not the means, inclination, or reservations needed to pay the attention-getting concessionaire overnight prices. All were arriving via thousands of cars. Traffic gridlock had become a challenge for the park rangers, equivalent to screeching your fingernails across a blackboard—jarring in what was supposed to be one of nature's best venues.

The challenge and the opportunity was to "match human wisdom with a matchless place," as Park Ranger Laurel Boyers expressed it, and to make the right choices for Yosemite so that millions more, for years to come, could discover that Yosemite was indeed inalienable, a place of inspiring magnificence safe from human habits that all too often overburden scenic places with bricks, mortar, lumber, blacktop, and advertising.

The planning choices were many; none of them easy. Should commercial services be reduced, tolerated, expanded? Where should the human imprint be when rocks fell from the cliffs or flood waters washed through the valley? How many miles of road were needed to accommodate traffic, and for what destination purposes? Was gridlock okay? If not, how should traffic be controlled? What of the historic Native American presence in the valley—should it be more vividly celebrated, and if so, how? What should be the commercial relationship of the mighty Yosemite business machine to surrounding gateway communities? Where should employees live? Where should utility trucks, machinery, and logistical supplies be maintained and stored? Where should criminals be jailed? What areas of the park should never feel the bite of construction?

And, bottom line, what was the capacity that would match people with a matchless place?

To find answers to such questions, a sense of Yosemite's broad history is imperative. I have interspersed historic milestones with some of my personal experiences as superintendent, inviting readers to share in both with me, not so much to seek an understanding of my motivations and foibles as to learn more about their own choices as owners of Yosemite National Park.

    Your Yosemite: **PROTECTING A PUBLIC TREASURE**

1

Yosemite, Why Me!

EARLY IN THE YEAR 1979, I walked into the office of National Park Service Director Bill Whelan to try to convince him that we, the nation's citizens, needed a Great Plains National Park. I was in Washington, D.C., as a representative of the National Audubon Society, and we were working closely with the NPS on a number of initiatives. I decided to seize my meeting with Whelan to introduce an initiative of my own. I had in hand a map that depicted the Theodore Roosevelt National Park in western North Dakota. This park, which consists of about 70,000 acres, preserves the badlands habitat of the historic Maltese and Elkhorn Ranches where Roosevelt went into the cattle business in the 1880s. Around it lie more than 1 million acres of grassland managed by the United States Forest Service—the largest such federally-owned grassland habitat in the United States.

If the two federal land holdings could be merged into one, I proposed, the result could be what I dramatically referred to as the creation of "America's Serengeti"—a park vast enough to support roaming herds of bison, elk, deer, and antelope, with eagles flying overhead and grouse scurrying close to the ground. A semblance of the Great Plains of old, now glimpsed only in 19th-century paintings and photographs, could be brought back to life. The National Audubon Society was ready to support Director Whelan if he wished to take on the immense political struggle of convincing the North Dakota Congressional Delegation and the Chief of the U.S. Forest Service that transferring to the NPS a huge block of grassland presently devoted to cattle-grazing was a good idea.

Whelan, however, was focused on another tough fight. In collaboration with many environmental organizations, the Audubon Society included, he was deeply committed to the Alaska National Land Interest Conservation Act, which was then making its way through Congress. If successful, this legislation would create fifteen new NPS areas, almost doubling the land base preserved within the boundaries of national parks. Whelan said he simply could not afford to take on another major political initiative at the time despite his agreement that the creation of a Great Plains National Park was a praiseworthy goal. (The following year, the Alaska legislation was, in fact, approved by Congress and signed into law by President Jimmy Carter, adding almost 80 million acres to the national park system.)

I sincerely thanked the director for his time, and reiterated Audubon's determination to work with him on Alaska every step of the way. As I walked toward the door, Whelan followed me, grabbed my arm, and suddenly asked, "How would you like to go to Yosemite?"

I was dumbfounded and immensely complimented when Whelan offered me this job, but also filled with uncertainty about how I would handle such an important post with its large set of responsibilities. The lead management position at Yosemite is a premier career position within the National Park Service, a post that brings with it professional standing at the forefront of the organization. Yosemite is also known as a political hot potato, a tough assignment that demands adept maneuvering between frequently combative interest groups. But saying no to such an offer, even if it meant leaving an organization I loved and uprooting my family, seemed unimaginable. Before I'd stepped out of Whelan's office, dizzy with the offer, I knew I wanted the job and that I would hold on to it as long as I could.

Whelan was asking me to go back to my roots. I had grown up in the National Park Service, both professionally and literally. My father had joined the NPS in 1936, serving as the first Chief Ranger at Mammoth Cave National Park, Kentucky, and my siblings and I had spent our childhoods in various national parks, moving with our parents from assignment to assignment, vagabond-style, a characteristic existence for NPS "brats." The influence of the parks was certainly contagious. All three of us have had lifelong associations with the NPS.

   Your Yosemite: **PROTECTING A PUBLIC TREASURE**

While in college, I worked on a trail crew in Rocky Mountain National Park and was a forest fire fighter in Sequoia-Kings Canyon National Parks. My first permanent ranger job came in 1961 at Yellowstone National Park. At the end of the summer season my wife, Midge, and I were assigned to Old Faithful for the winter. Before snow closed the roads in November, we were required to purchase a six-month supply of frozen, powdered, and canned foodstuffs, supplemented by fresh eggs stored in oats. As newlyweds barely into our twenties, we found the challenge of shopping for a half-year supply of food, on credit, entirely intimidating. Midge is a native of Fresno, California, and attended college in temperate southern California. Her family used to "go to the snow," meaning that they would hop in their car on a January or February day, drive up into the mountains, find a snowbank, throw a few snowballs or slide on sleds, and then drive back down to their home in the snow-free Central Valley. I knew more about snow, the dry, fluffy, sun-bleached kind that, in the cold months, occasionally decorates the Jemez Mountains of northern New Mexico where I spent most of my grade school and high school years. Neither of us knew about the spectacular, domineering, lengthy, and dangerous winters that are a hallmark of Yellowstone.

We were quick to learn. We had no choice. We were lent an ancient truck that we drove to a grocery store in far distant Jackson, Wyoming, to collect and haul back our food supplies, and rented an old ice cream freezer for a dollar a month into which we dumped the perishable stuff. I had pretty decent winter clothes and Midge made do. We both sported rubber insulated boots whenever we stepped outside, "good to thirty below," the advertisement said. That was somewhat true if you did not stand still. Our wintertime Old Faithful community consisted of two rangers and their families, and two "winter keepers" privately employed by the concessionaire. Otherwise we were largely cut off from society for about five months in a frosty environment where outdoor temperatures in January and February regularly hovered at zero or well below, and once touched minus 66°. An over-snow tracked coach operated by Harold Young, who claimed to be a direct descendant of Brigham Young, reached Old Faithful once a week from the village of West Yellowstone, about thirty miles away, carrying a few intrepid tourists, our mail, and an occasional delivery of vegetables and fruit. In January a small group of scientists arrived from New York University-Albany and stayed in a bunkhouse while they studied cloud seeding in the plumes of the geysers and, at night, taught us to play "Liar's Dice." There were no snowmobiles in those days, so no other visitors. Long before spring, our eggs began to taste like oats. When the roads finally opened to tourist traffic in the late spring, our immune systems, having gone into hibernation along with the bears, were little defense against the bad cases of the flu that attacked both of us. And we repeated all the same experiences for a second winter.

PEGGY ROCKEFELLER'S VISION

After the Yellowstone experience and three additional years of further training in Washington, D. C., I was assigned in 1968 to Acadia National Park, Mount Desert Island, Maine, where my work put me in contact with the irrepressible Mrs. David (Peggy) Rockefeller, who was to change the course of my career. There were hundreds of islands off the Maine coast, ecologically fragile, thinly soiled, and up for grabs in the private market place. Almost no zoning laws applied to these islands. Increasingly, new houses were crowding mainland and island shorelines, trees were being felled, and sewage pipes were extending straight out into the ocean. Peggy Rockefeller wanted to protect as many of these islands as she could from injurious development. She thought that private owners could still have their dream vacation homes or cabins nestled out of sight, but without destroying the islands' natural habitat and scenery in the process.

On an early springtime day she invited me to meet with her at her Seal Harbor "garage apartment" to discuss the challenge. With trepidation and considerable curiosity, I arrived for our meeting. Within minutes, her warm manner had put me at ease and we were sipping hot tea and poring over maps of the area, deep in discussion about the need for island conservation.

When I asked Mrs. Rockefeller how she planned to convince owners to limit development on their own islands, she replied, "Bob, we're going to blind 'em with fancy footwork!" In truth, however, she was making a sound case for enlightened self-interest.

Peggy Rockefeller reasoned that owners all along the coast would benefit from a collective effort to assure perpetuation of the natural vistas that prompted them to buy islands in the first place, and her instinct was excellent. She called it "do-it-yourself zoning." If property owners voluntarily donated their development rights to charitable organizations, they could both claim tax benefits and simultaneously assure the gallant beauty of the state's rugged coast. To realize this dream, she formed the Maine Coast Heritage Trust, a not-for-profit organization that specializes in cost-free counseling for landowners on the uses of conservation easements. Today, the Maine Coast Heritage Trust claims the voluntary protection of more than 140,000 acres in Maine, including the total land surfaces of 300 exquisite islands.

Peggy convinced me to take a leave-of-absence from the NPS to help manage the Maine Coast Heritage Trust. One year stretched to five, an unprecedented career detour for any young park ranger. At the end of my tenure with the MCHT, I returned briefly to an NPS assignment in Atlanta, Georgia, but, soon after, I was recruited by the National Audubon Society, whereupon I resigned from the NPS in 1977 and moved to New York. Part of my surprise at being offered the superintendent's job at Yosemite that morning in Whelan's office was that I was no longer officially in the NPS ranks. Fortunately, there was a grace period of two years' time during which meandering NPS employees could be reinstated if the NPS wanted them back.

My only question was why Whelan had selected me when there were scores of senior NPS executives who would have leaped at this opportunity. Whelan later explained to me that he wanted a "nonconformist" in the Yosemite post, someone with strong environmental credentials and weak institutional habits. Being labeled a nonconformist is not necessarily praiseworthy, but coming from Whelan it was. He fit that description himself, having risen in professional rank through the federal Job Corps program, not the National Park Service. He was known as an urban park specialist, and in the early

1970s, while working at Golden Gate National Recreation Area, in San Francisco, he had overseen the tricky process of transferring the notorious prison on Alcatraz Island from the U. S. Department of Justice to the NPS and opening it for public visitation. In this and other initiatives at Golden Gate, Whelan succeeded impressively. In 1977, President Jimmy Carter appointed him NPS Director.

After leaving Whalen's office, I hopped a shuttle flight back to New York, caught the train to suburban Ossining, and walked into the house my wife and I had bought only two years earlier, bursting with my news. I assumed that Midge would be ecstatic. After all, she had been born and raised in Fresno, practically on the doorstep of Yosemite; she would be going west, going home. When I asked her if she was willing, all the costs of such a move seemed to pass across her face; uprooting the kids; leaving her beloved bookstore job; selling our house; moving across the country; taking on obligations, vintage the 1970s, of being a "superintendent's wife" with attendant and assumed social responsibilities. Midge was inclined, far more, to the independence of her own career and personal choices, but after a sleepless night she agreed that we should go.

A YOSEMITE COMMUTER

We arrived in Yosemite National Park in July, 1979, and, practically choking on the lump in my throat, I headed off to work from our new home in the small village of El Portal, about twelve miles from the headquarters office in Yosemite Valley. I drove into the park at the Arch Rock Entrance Station and then followed winding Route 140 for about five miles up through the narrow Merced River Canyon. This portion of the route clings to the northern side of canyon walls that encase the cascading Merced River. Huge boulders trapped in the riverbed are proof that geological and gravitational forces are alive and well up on the steep walls and slopes of the canyon.

At the top of this five-mile incline the canyon walls are barely separated and would be joined in a granite clench except for the slashing river that has demanded an exit from the valley for eons. Here, the road leveled and wound through a stand of trees to reveal the opening valley view (a scene now reserved by a one-way road system as

     Your Yosemite: **PROTECTING A PUBLIC TREASURE**

an exit treat). The river is quieter, white water replaced by a gentle, rippling flow. It hugs the perimeter of historically famous Bridalveil Meadow. Near the meadow, depending on the season of the year, Bridalveil Fall roars or streams feather-like from the heights of a granite wall. The profile of imperial El Capitan looms at a distance, daring travelers to explore beyond it into the very heart of Yosemite Valley. For another six miles various traffic signs and other vehicles using the roadway were the principal signs of human presence. The route passed through stands of pine trees edging against the river. Oak trees dot meadows. Only at the far eastern end of the valley, after Half Dome and Yosemite Falls burst into view, does sizable human development present itself.

My destination was Yosemite Village—no ordinary town. Everyone in it is either serving the park and its visitors, or is one of those visitors. Over the years it had become a real sprawl. The park headquarters, a rustic, two-story building constructed in 1924, fronted on a large parking lot (subsequently converted to pedestrian use during my tenure). Next door is the Yosemite Museum, added in 1925 with funding provided by the Laura Spelman Rockefeller Memorial Fund, and, adjacent to it, the Visitor Center, an example of 1960s architecture that exists uneasily amid its rustic neighbors. Nearby, is the Rangers' Club, built in 1920 with funds donated by Stephen Mather, the first director of the National Park Service.

Just across the street from headquarters was the Girls Club, constructed in the 1930s by the Civilian Conservation Corps as a place of feminine refuge in the male-dominated park. The neighborhood includes a large grey concrete building that houses the National Park Service vehicle repair shop and, on its upper floor, the jail. The industrial-size concessionaire warehouse and laundry facility is just a stone's throw away.

Eastward from park headquarters is the historic Best's Studio, constructed in 1926 and subsequently to become the Ansel Adams Gallery. The neighboring Pohono Gift Shop was full of pseudo-Indian souvenirs but soon became the Art Activity Center, a gathering place for visitors who wish to participate in artist-led workshops. Beyond the Art Center is the two-story post office, dating to 1925, and adjacent to it, Degnan's Deli, a 1956 addition commemorating pioneers John and Bridget Degnan who arrived in Yosemite Valley in 1884 and began baking bread for the intrepid visitors of that era.

Next was the Village Store full of groceries, souvenirs, gear, cameras, books, maps, posters, and just about anything that might tempt a visitor to the cash register. Then there was a bank at the far end of the parking lot near the executive offices of the Yosemite Park & Curry Company. Beyond these offices is the bulky YP&CC maintenance garage and beyond that, the substantial housing area for concessionaire employees.

Scattered around the core of the village are dozens more houses and apartments for concessionaire and NPS employees. On a hillside between the village center and the Ahwahnee Hotel is the hospital/dentist building. In the opposite direction from the village, one-half mile from park headquarters, is Yosemite Lodge, a complex of buildings that accommodates hundreds of guests. To the south, Curry Village offers its tent cabins to hundreds more visitors. NPS campgrounds add to the mix of development.

To a surprising degree these various facilities are screened by trees and topography so that their intrusion on the natural scene is muted, but "village" is the right word. Standing at Glacier Point at night and gazing down into the chasm of Yosemite Valley, hundreds of tightly clustered village lights blaze away, signaling that this robust development imprint is alive and prone to spread.

Yosemite Village, now well into its second century of existence, is a thriving symbol of the complex tension between an extraordinary landscape inscribed by powerful natural forces, and a catalog of human deeds that speak to the adoration of such a treasured place. The basic question is: how much adoration is too much?

INTO THE TRACES

By privilege of office as superintendent, I had become the primary spokesperson and senior government steward for Yosemite, accepting the institutional reality of that sign which famously sat on President Harry Truman's desk: *The Buck Stops Here.* If events proceeded with general success or even remained steadily uncontroversial, I would receive some of the credit. If they did not, I would deserve most of the blame. I was succeeding Superintendent Leslie P. Arnberger, who had served in the position for five years and fought hard to win public approval for the need to corral development within the park in favor of increased preservation of natural resources, and I wanted to add to his momentum. My hope was that I might remain in my post for many years, perhaps even until I retired. It all depended on the buck.

The life of most superintendents is one of institutional musical chairs: moving from post to post, one gorgeous place to another until finally ending up at the close of careers in a city-bound regional office or the head office in Washington, D.C. I had followed that same pattern, moving from Colorado to California to Wyoming to Washington, D.C., to Maine, Georgia, and New York, and then back again, with blindingly good fortune, to California and Yosemite, where I wished to stay. I had my hand on the helm of a robust national park, privileged to represent my employer, the American public. The job promised never to be dull and the aesthetics were breathtaking. I was on a team of professionals whose credentials ranged through intricate science and broad educational services; through public protection and safeguarded wild habitat; through history toward park plans better defined; through wilderness right to the edge of a kind of wildscape suburban management. Yosemite is a compelling environmental taskmaster that promises great personal reward in lifestyle and sense of accomplishment, if most of the pitfalls can be avoided. In short, national parks in general and Yosemite, specifically, invite immense allegiance from their lucky stewards. I felt aligned.

Captain Joseph R. Walker

     Your Yosemite: **PROTECTING A PUBLIC TREASURE**

2

Joseph R. Walker, Busting Through to California

IN THE FIRST FEW DAYS of my assignment, I spent as much time as I could just touring the park, usually accompanied by various members of the park staff who were helping me understand the immense intricacies of Yosemite. I was a tourist in a National Park Service uniform, privileged to have personal, exceedingly well-informed guides. On one of those outings, we were standing beside a trail in Tuolumne Meadows when someone said, "Walker probably passed right by here." I asked, "Who is Walker?" He was, I learned, the symbolic tip of a spear point, a pathfinder who signaled a momentous cultural upheaval like few that have ever occurred on earth. Behind Walker was a hovering landslide of European descendants who were eager to claim their share of land and riches in raw territory open to their power. Ahead of Walker was that raw territory and its inhabitants, native peoples of many languages and traditions but less power, who subsisted on the wild bounty of the land. There was no place known as Yosemite.

In the first decades of the nineteenth century, very few citizens of the fledgling United States were preoccupied with land preservation. Instead, the U.S. government was in the thorny process of conquest and nation-building. Revolutionary War veterans were still reminiscing about their exploits as young men under the command of General George Washington even as the nation's third president, Thomas Jefferson, was presiding over the Louisiana Purchase of 1803. By this purchase, immense territories were annexed to the nation between the Mississippi River and the Continental Divide, a great swath of the North American continent that still remained mysterious and unmapped.

In many ways Joseph Walker, the illiterate beaver trapper who set out to find a new overland route to Mexico-controlled Alta California in 1832 embodied the spirit of courage, adventure, and ambition that so characterized the expansion and exploitation of the American West. Along his haphazard route, entirely by chance, he would come close to one of the most elegant natural art treasures on earth. It is questionable whether Walker ever laid eyes on Yosemite Valley, and unlikely that it would have been of much interest to him if he had. The trapper was not looking for a place to settle but simply a way through. Yet his story is integral to the Yosemite legend.

Washington Irving, in his narrative, *The Adventures of Captain Bonneville, USA*, described the thirty-five-year-old Walker as "about six feet high, strong built, dark complexioned, brave in spirit, though wild in manners." He continued, "He had been for many years in Missouri on the frontier; had been among the earliest adventurers to Santa Fe, where he had gone to track beaver and was taken by the Spaniards. Being liberated, he engaged with the Spaniards and Sioux Indians in war against the Pawnees; then returned to Missouri and had acted by turns as sheriff, trader, and trapper until he was enlisted as a leader by Captain Bonneville."

Benjamin Louis Eulalie de Bonneville and Walker were thrown together by the demands and hazards of the frontier. Bonneville was born in France, raised in America, and educated at the United States Military Academy at West Point. Walker happened to meet him just as the captain obtained a leave from his regular Army duties to organize an investigative expedition into the country west of the Rocky Mountains. Bonneville reasoned that he could best avoid serious confrontations with natives by leading a contingent of frontiersmen rather than soldiers. Clusters of frontiersmen had been wandering ever westward in search of beaver for years, and, with a few hair-raising exceptions, they had been grudgingly accepted by the tribes, whereas soldiers would undoubtedly be seen as invaders.

                    Your Yosemite: **PROTECTING A PUBLIC TREASURE**

The Captain himself was keenly interested in the beaver trade. Practically every man in America either wore or wanted to wear a beaver hat, and the demand for pelts, known as "hairy bank notes," extended to Europe and Asia. Tough-minded John Jacob Astor, the German-born founder and owner of the Pacific Fur Company, had made a fortune by cornering much of the market in western North America. With Astor as his principal backer, Bonneville succeeded in raising funds for his expedition. If he could find beaver, Astor's business contacts guaranteed that a ready-made market awaited Bonneville.

Joseph Walker, equally interested in the beaver trade, agreed to be chief scout and second-in-command of the expedition. He spent two years in Fort Osage, Missouri, assembling supplies and gathering recruits. In May 1832, the Bonneville Expedition, an imposing volunteer force of 110 mounted men, a twenty-wagon supply train, and a large herd of extra horses, headed west.

Most of the men on this expedition would have lacked almost any level of formal education, but they would have been well versed in the skills of survival. They generally wore loose-fitting, well-oiled buckskins, moccasins, and broad-brimmed hats. Most of them carried a .53 caliber Hawken flintlock rifle. The men carried enough lead, gunpowder, wadding, and bullet molds to last for several months barring a pitched battle of some sort. For close work, the rifle was usually complemented by a smooth-bore, single-barrel pistol and a French-made tomahawk, carried in a belt loop just next to a scabbard that secured a scalping knife. A two-bladed swell-end pocket knife was usually tucked somewhere in the buckskins, completing the armament.

Initially, the Bonneville contingent moved through familiar lands, following the Platte River for hundreds of miles across the Great Plains and then angling northwestward along the North Platte River to its intersection with the Sweetwater River. At the slow pace dictated by wagon transport the men threaded along water-nourished avenues through the tribal domains and hunting grounds of the Sioux, Kiowa, Comanche, Pawnee, Crow, and many other indigenous nomadic peoples who, for centuries, had found sustenance in the same vast, wildlife-abundant territory. Finally, they left the grasslands behind in a long, gradual climb to South Pass in present-day Wyoming.

In August 1832 the expedition reached its initial destination along the banks of the Green River. The trappers now found themselves at the edge of the map. Trails and shared information among frontiersmen were sufficient to guide adventurers all the way from the Missouri to the banks of the Green. There, the trails fizzled and knowledge of what lay beyond became hazy. Other trappers had explored the Green River and its tributaries, but their descriptions were vague at best and often topped off with imaginative brag. No one among the new arrivals really knew how wide the country was, whether the Pacific Ocean lay just beyond the next hill or thousands of miles away. Even the Native Americans who inhabited the region shared little knowledge of the land beyond the Green.

There were already two to three hundred trappers in the Green River area when Bonneville and Walker arrived. Many had been tempted to the region by advertisements for trappers that ran in the *St. Louis Gazette and Public Advertiser*: "enterprising young men to ascend the Missouri to its source, there to be employed for one, two, or three years." The rewards could be great; it was rumored that a bundle of sixty beaver pelts could be worth as much as $600 if the pelts were successfully delivered to market. But the costs were also great. The trappers had to push into unfamiliar mountain chasms, find the beaver, spend months in isolated toil, survive the deprivations of winter weather, be ever on the lookout for human enemies and wild predators, cure the pelts expertly and cure themselves if sick or injured, exist on whatever food could be snared, grubbed, hooked, or shot, and haul the pelts out of the mountains where they could barter or sell them, re-supply themselves, and begin the cycle all over again.

Bonneville decided to pitch camp by the Green River to wait out the winter before pushing westward the following spring. A few miles upstream, on a tributary known as Horse Creek, he set his men to work erecting a rude stockade, aptly named "Fort Bonneville," where they settled in for the frigid months to come. The surround-

　　Your Yosemite: **PROTECTING A PUBLIC TREASURE**

ing beaver waters had already been sorely abused, making Bonne-ville and Walker all the more eager to find new sources, but when springtime arrived they decided to linger among the larger commu-nity of trappers and Native Americans that were assembling for the 1833 Horse Creek Rendezvous.

The annual gathering of beaver trappers, known as "the rendez-vous," was famous throughout the Rocky Mountains. General William Ashley, politician and fur trader, had realized that the best way to get beaver pelts to market was to meet the trappers on their turf rather than wait for them to make the long trek across the Great Plains to Missouri. In 1825, Ashley held the first rendezvous at Burnt Creek along the banks of the Green River. Tucked into Ashley's trade goods was a generous supply of whiskey guaranteed to fuel advantageous bargaining that would return a huge profit to this frontier entrepreneur.

By the time Bonneville and Walker arrived on the Green River to settle in for a year and resupply, Ashley had long since departed with a fortune in skins, but other traders had stepped in to dispense a variety of goods, some vital, others irresistible: guns, powder, lead, blankets, knives, hatchets, traps, trinkets, and, of course, hundreds of gallons of whiskey. The previous rendezvous, held in the Grand Teton country, had been marred by an attack by Gros Ventre Indians who took a dim view of incursion by trappers into their domain. The 1833 rendezvous was set for the area near Fort Bonneville on Horse Creek where Shoshone Indians were accommodating. An estimated three-hundred-fifty trappers and five-hundred Indians took part in the annual blow-out, joined by preachers, journalists, spoilers, gamblers, European aristocrats, and the tenacious traders. For five weeks the encampment was alive with horse and foot rac-es, fights, friendships, gossip, news, swapping, gambling, and even nuptials of a sort between some of the trappers and Indian women.

The pelt count at the Horse Creek rendezvous was adequate, but the assumption had always been that one exhausted stream could be exchanged for the next watercourse just over the ridge. Now, when a trapper reached a new drainage, he might discover that someone else was there already, or had been there and gone. There were abundant beaver up north in the Yellowstone country, but also Blackfeet and Gros Ventre who had already proven that they were capable of defending their lands from invaders. To the south, the garrisoned Mexican outpost villages of Taos and Santa Fe and the Sangre de Christo Mountains supported some beaver, but not in worthwhile numbers.

Rumor had it that the young and bold Jedediah Smith, an occasional partner of Ashley, had somehow trekked across southern desert lands all the way to Alta California in 1827. He had returned with stories of a promising land rich in wildlife, mountain beaver waters, peaceful Indians, Spanish imperialists, and large herds of cattle and wild horses just waiting to be rounded up. Unfortunately, Smith was not at the rendezvous to confirm these rumors or explain his route of travel. He had been killed by the Comanche two years before the Horse Creek Rendezvous.

OFF THE MAP

Bonneville and Walker undoubtedly heard of the Jedediah Smith rumors. In a cleverly enterprising moment, they traded some of their used expedition equipment for hundreds of pounds of beaver pelts. Bonneville sent the pelts east to be sold. He issued orders to use the profits to purchase and transport fresh supplies all the way back to the Green River to be stashed at his makeshift fort. These supplies would be waiting for him when he and his men returned from wherever they were going. Then on August 20, 1833, Bonneville and Walker led a column of ninety-eight mounted men toward the vaguely known Great Salt Lake.

Each trapper had extra horses to be used for packing supplies and changing mounts as needed. Buffalo robes were used for bedding, often tossed on the ground under an open sky. For better protection, a deer hide tent was usually erected, but these were not in the style of the grand teepees of the Great Plains Indians. The trappers' tents were small and utilitarian. One or two cooking pots were carried along, as was a strategic supply of trinkets, ribbons, beads, butcher knives, shiny medals, and similar trade goods. The men knew how to use awls, needles, rawhide thread, and fishhooks, how to skin animals and make good use of bone and antler as well as flesh, and how to spark a fire to life using flint and steel. They kept knives and tomahawks sharp with a whetstone strap. Most precious of all were the beaver traps; each man commonly possessed three or four.

To a large degree, the Bonneville/Walker contingent consisted of men who were competent at surviving on their own or in groups of two or three, men who had been hardened by living off the land and depending on their wits. They knew that if they became injured or sick, medical aid would be minimal and administered by one of their companions. An almost unwavering wilderness rule was that a man was expected to keep moving no matter what. Surrendering to trauma could be a self-inflicted death sentence.

The trailblazer Jim Bridger had first encountered the shores of the Great Salt Lake in the winter of 1824, and Bonneville and Walker had a general idea of how to find it by riding toward the western sky and hoping to intersect with the Bear River. They were soon finding the topography that confronted them to be drastically changed. The verdant meadows of the Green River had been replaced by arid hills, sagebrush-strewn plateaus, and dry streambeds with sparse pickings of wild game and forage for the horses. Ahead, the Wasatch Mountains, a western arm of the Rocky Mountains with peaks of over 11,000 feet, stood guarding the approaches to the Great Salt Lake.

Bonneville and company kept to the rolling high ground, probably north of the lake, transiting dry gullies that cut diagonally across their line of march and avoiding the worst of the mountain topography. Somewhere along the way the expedition leaders split their forces. Taking forty men, Bonneville planned to trek northwestward into Oregon territory, to investigate "the level of British influence." With the remaining fifty-eight men, Walker was to head directly west, toward Alta California. The two units planned to reunite at the Great Salt Lake the following summer. Walker took his fair share of extra horses, ammunition, and trade goods. Each of his men was also carrying about sixty pounds of Buffalo jerky to see them through the uncertain months ahead.

Walker also carried with him an important document, a visa secured in advance by Bonneville from the Mexican government that would presumably allow entry into Alta California for Walker's small party of American trappers. The Mexicans, who had only recently thrown off the yoke of Spanish rule, would not welcome forays by U.S. military personnel into their territories, but a handful of civilian explorers sharing information of new trade routes through uncharted land could be advantageous. At the same time, Walker and his company of men understood that they were responsible for their fate. If the mission failed, only Walker would be accountable.

More than a thousand miles of barren topography separated his party from its objective.

LEONARD'S JOURNAL

A first-hand description of the Walker expedition was written by Zenas Leonard, a member of Walker's party, who kept a written account of their journey westward from the shore of the Great Salt Lake. Leonard, too, had faced his share of hardships. Originally from Clearfield County, Pennsylvania, he had been active among the trappers for four years before Walker enlisted him. In one instance, he and a few companions fought off a Blackfeet raiding party. On another occasion he and some fellow trappers were caught out in remote territory by winter storms and survived by eating beaver skins. What made him exceptional on the frontier, though, was his ability to write. For this reason, Walker recruited Leonard, already at Green River when the Bonneville party arrived, to act as the "clerk" of his expedition.

As Walker's party moved west from the Great Salt Lake, even rudimentary knowledge of the ground ahead was sorely lacking. The men only knew that the sun set in the direction in which they rode. A string of purplish mountains far off to the south seemed to parallel their course. Their eyes continually scanned the horizon, trying to learn quickly of potential danger. Trees of any size were scarce and wild game even more so. The last wild animal of any note had been an unfortunate buffalo, found wandering incongruously along the shoreline of the Great Salt Lake. Otherwise, the occasional rabbit seemed all that the miserly landscape had to offer.

Only four days out on their singular trek, the Walker party began to encounter Indians, some of whom Leonard referred to as "Bawnack." When the Indians learned of Walker's intent to seek a way west to the Pacific, they counseled that the trappers should take "much meat" into the empty lands that lay ahead. They also suggested that the trappers follow Indian paths from waterhole to waterhole until they came upon small streams at the base of a snowcapped mountain. Then they were to follow the largest stream until it merged with others to form a river. The river, they said, should lead the expedition onward toward Alta California, but none of the Indians knew for sure, having never themselves made the journey.

The Walker party typically measured distance in days, not miles; the number of days traveled from the Green River and the days estimated yet to come. The scruffy desert plateaus over which they rambled changed very little in scene, and the breezes were similarly monotonous, strengthening to a steady wind by midday. The men might find themselves in the midst of blowing, stinging sand, but most of the time the push of the dry wind induced a mind-numbing tedium until evening temperatures finally softened. Then it was jerky for dinner. Luckily, thanks to Indian guidance, the party was beginning to pick up signs of an explorer's fondest wish, a river that might lead them through the wilderness, giving them succor along the way.

The Humboldt River is a strange watery trail of almost three hundred miles that rises in mountains of northeastern Nevada, wanders southwestward into the desert for about half its length, then swings northwest until it disappears without fanfare into the Humboldt Sink, a geologic oddity about fifty miles east of present-day Reno, Nevada. There is no outlet to the sea for the Humboldt, no mightier river to join. Its unceremonious submergence leaves behind a mere puddle of a lake, homely wetlands attractive to migratory waterfowl, and a silent capitulation to the aquifer hiding under the desert plain. When Walker and his party encountered the Humboldt it was nameless, at least by their standards, so they declared it to be the "Barren River." As Leonard later wrote, "you may travel for many days on the banks of this river without finding a stick large enough to make a walking cane." The men made cold camps along the riverbank; not enough wood could be found for campfires.

A CLASH OF CULTURES

The Humboldt irrigates a jade trail of grasses that runs parallel to the main channel, in some places forming meadows more than a half-mile wide. These watered lands were an obvious magnet for life—birds, plants, beaver, and, most notably, indigenous peoples. Walker and his trappers were on a quest to break open a "new" trade route across a high desert region, but along the course of their proclaimed Barren River they were finding plenty of company.

Unlike their counterparts to the east, the Shoshone who occupied the Humboldt River basin had never seen a white man or the paraphernalia he carried with him. They watched from a distance as Walker's men unpacked their traps to try to catch beaver. As the trappers backed off in their practiced manner to allow beaver to approach the traps, some Shoshone men crept forward. They were described by Leonard as small in stature, on foot, and mostly naked except for rudimentary costumes of reeds and marsh grass.

The trappers tried to shoo the Shoshone away, but each time the trappers backed away, the Indians would creep forward again. Leonard judged that they were simply curious, but a few of the frontiersmen assumed that the Indians were trying to steal their traps. Eventually a few "discontents," as Leonard described them, unlimbered their Hawken rifles and fired. According to Leonard, "two or three" of the Shoshone were killed. The following day, three more met the same fate.

Walker was off scouting and not present when these acts of violence occurred. Although the lives of Indians were not highly valued on the frontier, the trappers involved knew that their leader would be angry if he knew what had taken place. They tried to hide the killings, but without success. When Walker learned of their secret, he "disciplined" the men responsible, according to Leonard, who gave no details about exactly what this meant. Walker knew revenge might follow such thoughtless conduct. He ordered his men to move on immediately.

After a rapid and lengthy march, the Walker party reached an area of small lakes where there was "an abundance of fine grass" for the horses. But the corps of men had not ridden far or fast enough. "A little before sunset," Leonard wrote, "on taking a view of the surrounding waste with a spy glass, we discovered smoke rising from the high grass in every direction." On foot, Shoshone had tracked and surrounded the trappers. The expedition horses were promptly rounded up and put on picket lines. Using the shoreline of a nearby lake as a rearguard defensive line, Walker's men hastily piled up saddles and equipment in an attempt to construct an improvised fortress. "Before we got everything complete, however," Leonard reports, "the Indians issued from their hiding places in the grass, to the number, as near as I could guess, of eight or nine hundred, and marched straight toward us, dancing and singing in the greatest glee."

At about one-hundred-fifty yards, the Shoshone stopped their forward movement except for five of their number who advanced more closely. Leonard assumed these men to be "chiefs" who, through sign language, beckoned the trappers to come out from behind their barricade to join in the smoking of pipes, or so Leonard guessed. Walker judged this to be an obvious trap and refused. Instead, he decided to demonstrate a show of force by directing some of his men to fire at a few ducks floating in the lake. The sound and fury of the rifles caused many of the Shoshone to drop to the ground. They had probably never before witnessed the firepower of a gun. But they had the advantage of greatly superior numbers and were apparently not persuaded by this show of force. Slowly the Shoshone stood up from their hiding places to continue the confrontation.

In a highly creative attempt to demonstrate his group's power, Walker next sent out a handful of men to erect a beaver skin target. Amazingly, some of the Shoshone wandered over to help. Riflemen proceeded to fire into the target, peppering the skin with holes and again attempting to deliver a palpable message to the Shoshone that very deadly weapons rested in the hands of the trappers. Evening light was fading into darkness when the target demonstration concluded. The Shoshone withdrew into their grassland hiding places.

At dawn, the Walker party mounted once more to flee their new enemies, but they were surrounded again. The Shoshone were "in the grass, in front, rear, and either side of us," reported Leonard. A group of eighty to one-hundred Indians could also be seen ahead, visibly attempting to block the trappers' way forward. The lead trappers hurriedly changed mounts to assure that they were on the best and strongest horses. Then Walker ordered a charge.

The result was violent, one-sided, and appalling. Thirty-nine Shoshone lay dead or severely wounded; a few trappers dismounted and used the Shoshone's own weapons to finish off the victims. The trappers named the region "Battle Lakes."

THE GREAT BARRICADE

The chronicle of Walker's journey into history has lengthy gaps suggesting that, except for the calamity with the Shoshone and moments of unanticipated hardship, much of the trek was fraught with tedium. For several weeks, the men traversed the rolling high-desert land of what is now known as the Great Basin Desert in Nevada. The land was dotted with solitary mountain clusters that resemble immense islands anchored in a static plain of desert scrub brush. These clusters were easily bypassed by maneuvering on the plains that surrounded them, but not so the next formidable alpine opponent, the eastern escarpment of the Sierra Nevada Mountains.

This mountain chain stretches four hundred miles north to south on what is now the eastern boundary of California. On average, the Sierra Nevada is forty-five miles wide east to west. The east-facing wall of the mountains is formed by an immense block of the earth's crust that is being forced upward by tectonic upheaval. Geologists estimate that the crest of the Sierra is gaining altitude at the rate of two inches per century. The main battlement of the Sierra is a one-hundred-fifty mile wall of sharp peaks capped by 14,491 foot Mount Whitney. These peaks are decorated with small glaciers, permanent snowfields, boulder slides and slick rock, knife-edged summits, hundreds of lakes, cascading streams and waterfalls, precipitous canyons, and secreted velvety meadows.

To the lasting regret of historians, Walker made no map of his route, left no telltale sign for others to follow, and added no annotations to the writings of Zenas Leonard. Assuming that the Humboldt was the likely pastoral thoroughfare for passage across the desert, a rough idea of the Walker route can be envisioned, but Leonard's vague descriptions of people, places, and events offer only anecdotal clues. One of the most significant is his description of a lake reached by the expedition in late October, 1833. "The water in this lake," he reported, "is similar to lye, and tastes like pear ash. There is also a great quantity of pumice stone floating on the surface of the water, and the shore is covered with them."

Leonard's portrayal immediately eliminates Lake Tahoe which sparkles with freshwater in its mountain nest. Leonard's comment best matches eighty-square-mile Mono Lake, the remnant of an inland sea that lies in a basin just to the east of present-day Yosemite National Park. Mono Lake is an anomaly. Small mountain streams tumbling down from the Sierra provide inflow into the lake, but the only outlet is evaporation. Dry desert air blows across the lake's surface, pulling enough moisture into the atmosphere to offset replenishment from the inflowing streams and occasional rain and snowstorms. Mono Lake is also unusual in that it is a chemical mix of salts, calcium, and magnesium that is twice as salty as ocean water and eighty times more alkaline. The lake supports no fish, but it is a vigorous incubator of other life forms. Billions of tiny brine shrimp and alkaline flies thrive in its ecosystem, providing a rich source of food for birds, including thousands of phalaropes, grebes, and—incongruously—California gulls. Ninety percent of the gulls that patrol the ocean beaches of California are hatched at Mono Lake and return to hatch their offspring there. The hatchlings, once airworthy, fly away across the mountains to their ocean habitat. This cycle of transposition from desert to ocean and back again has been repeated for centuries.

The pumice stone to which Leonard referred is abundant at Mono Lake. Symmetrical volcanic cinder cones, rising five- to six-hundred feet, guard the lake's southern shoreline. This area is surreal, almost otherworldly in appearance, and cluttered with obsidian, clinkers, and pumice spawned by an active region of volcanic mischief that spreads along a thin segment of the earth's crust where the up-thrusting Sierra is trying to break clear of the gripping desert.

Looming above the trappers on the Sierra skyline to the west of the lake would have been Mounts Gibbs and Dana, Gaylor Peak, White Mountain, Mount Conness, and North Peak, all unnamed at the time but eventually to become major landmarks in the Yosemite wilderness. They were part of an enormous wall of alpine resistance facing the trappers.

A SEARCH FOR ESCAPE

That waning autumn, the curiosities of Mono Lake would have been little appreciated by Walker and his men. They urgently needed to discover passage over the Sierra Nevada. If none could be found, the options were ugly. Entrapment during winter on the east side of the mountains would quickly become a harsh struggle against freezing temperatures, high desert blizzards, and starvation. The supply of buffalo jerky was all but gone. The expedition was in alien territory blocked by untold miles of soaring granite walls to their front and the callous desert they fervently wished to be rid of behind them. To backtrack with food supplies all but exhausted, hostile Shoshone perhaps waiting in ambush, spent horses, and the danger of blizzards out in the barren region they already had traversed must have been unthinkable, especially with nothing to show for the risk; no beaver pelts; no rounded up herd of cattle and wild horses; no knowledge of where the trail ended; no success of any kind, just suffering.

Despite their quandary, Walker's men were not alone in this rough country. As had been the case almost from the beginning of their trek, they were sharing the landscape with native peoples. Along the eastern base of the Sierra, bands of Paiute lived in scattered encampments, having long since learned to subsist on sage hens, grouse, squirrels, rabbits, pine nuts, fish, wild rye, acorns, and the occasional deer, antelope, or bear. They lived in yurt-like shelters of bent willow and tightly packed bundles of grass that could withstand the worst winter weather and the hottest summer sun.

Had Walker examined the indigenous way of life more closely he might have noted that one food item stood out from all others: the acorns that were a staple of the Paiute diet. Even a cursory glance at the surrounding landscape would confirm that no oak trees grew in the region, but abundant supplies of acorns were coming from somewhere. That somewhere proved to be beyond the jagged spine of the High Sierra. Paiutes routinely traded obsidian and other treasures from their region for the nutritious acorns and other items from the west, confirming that humans could find transit through what otherwise appeared to be an unassailable stronghold.

Walker perhaps attempted to enlist pathfinders from the Paiute community to help find the way forward, but ethnic relations quickly deteriorated after the trappers returned the generosity by stealing a young colt and another animal that Leonard referred to as a "camel." Instead, Walker sent out scouting parties of trappers in land that was a riddle to him. On one of these scouting forays, Leonard reported that several trappers rode high onto the slopes of the Sierra, searching for passage. When the angle of ascent became too steep for the horses, the men dismounted and attempted to gain more elevation on foot. A trapper named George Nidever, who was participating in the effort, got separated from the others and was left behind far down the slope.

Unknown to the trappers, two Paiute had been shadowing the party and crept unseen between the scouting party and Nidever. When the men gave up their attempt and turned to begin descending, the

Paiute, fearing discovery, ran downhill ahead of them. "Nidever, who at once supposed they had been committing some mischief with us, fired, and, as they were running one behind the other, killed them both at one shot." Back in camp that evening, Nidever confessed to Walker that he was "very sorry," probably worried that his reckless action would spark conflict with the Paiute that might find the trappers mortally outnumbered.

CLIMB OR DIE

Luckily for the frontiersmen, one of the other scouting parties had been more fortunate, finding an Indian path that led to a mountain pass. It was a significant avenue of commerce, a trading route used by Indians that was defined at the lower elevations by a thread of scarred earth created over the ages by the impact of countless feet. If men on foot could cross the Sierra, the trappers hoped that they might be able to ascend along the same trail on their horses, choking down the fear that they might be forced at some point to leave their mounts behind and scramble for survival with only the clothes on their backs and the meager supplies that they could carry.

As dawn broke on October 16, 1833, the Walker party began its concerted ascent into the Sierra Nevada. Even in summer, crossing above the Sierra timberline on horseback can be a daunting experience. The powerful topography, the unsteady gait of the horses trying to find footing on rock, the constant physical exertion necessary even from the saddle, and an abiding sense that the smallest error or equine panic can cause sudden grievous injury or even death, are challenges that continue to this day. But the Walker contingent had no choice. The men had to attack the granite battlement late in the year, riding their horses upward on a steep pathway directly into an icy, exacting, indifferent realm.

Half a hundred men started up the trail. Leonard wrote of the "toilsome journey" and "poor speed" of the expedition members. The lower reaches of almost any trail into the Sierra are temptingly benign, giving little warning of the confrontation soon to come.

 Your Yosemite: **PROTECTING A PUBLIC TREASURE**

Most passageways through the few openings hidden along Sierra's toothy spine require elevation gains of thousands of feet. These are punishing climbs that suck energy from man and stock animals alike.

The principal route used by the Mono Lake Paiutes, the route Walker is assumed to have taken, was up a gash in the mountains that came to be known as Bloody Canyon. Leonard described the view confronting him and his comrades as being one of "peaks generally covered with rocks and sand, totally incapable of vegetation, except on the south side where grows a kind of juniper or gin shrub."

After an exhausting daylong ascent, Walker's men found their mounts on flat rock at a breach in the mountain wall. The path ahead angled downward, signaling that they had reached a stony mountain pass. After months marked by hunger, fear, and doubt, this must have been a moment of triumph for the men. The expedition's chronicler looked back to take in a bird's eye view of the scene, the folds and undulations of the Great Basin desert running far off to the distant eastern horizon. A four-thousand-foot drop lay just behind him and the baseline of the Sierra, far down by Mono Lake, was probably softening in evening shadow. Leonard pronounced the view "awfully sublime," but any celebration was short. Until now, the men had been traveling in autumn, but gaining the pass had thrown them right into the grip of winter.

If there was any sense of history in pitching camp that night it was not recorded by the expedition clerk. Leonard noted that "we had not suffered much from cold for several months previous to this, but this night, surrounded as we were with the everlasting snows of the summit of this mountain the cold was felt with three-fold severity." In morning light, "it was with no cheerful prospect that each man prepared for traveling as we had nothing to eat worth mentioning—as we advanced in the hollows sometimes we would encounter prodigious quantities of snow. When we would come to such places a certain portion of the men would be appointed alternately to go forward and break the road to enable our horses to get through, and if any of the horses would get swamped these same men were to get them out. In this tedious and tiresome manner we spent the whole day without going more than eight or ten miles."

After yet another miserable nighttime camp, Leonard reported that, "This day's travel was very severe on the horses, as they had not a particle to eat. They began to grow stupid and stiff." His terse wording provides only a hint of the torment that confronted the expedition members. They were exhausted, cold, and starving, struggling forward at an altitude that stripped away their last remaining energy. Still, progress demanded a continuing and strenuous effort, and there was no certainty of where the men were or how far they had to go to escape their suffering. All they knew was that a harsh mountain ascent lay behind them and that combat with other waves of mountains lay ahead.

Perhaps unsurprisingly, it was here that some of Walker's men began to talk of mutiny. Revolts are a supreme test for any leader. Luckily, Walker managed to hang on to the allegiance of most of his cohorts, enough so that he could deny horses and ammunition to those who threatened retreat. In the end, no one deserted.

"Two of our horses were so much reduced that it was thought they would not be able to travel in the morning at all," Leonard reported. "It was agreed that they should be butchered for the use of the men," who ate "this black, tough, lean horse flesh as if it had been the choicest piece of beefsteak." David Smith, a historian at San Jose State University and a specialist on the Walker expedition, has concluded that twenty-four horses were lost during the trek, seventeen of them shot and butchered for food. Leonard compared the condition of the expedition's horses to "old and feeble men." As these once-valuable animals failed, they became an ominous sign of defeat.

Despite these privations, the trappers and what remained of their horses continued their descent toward the western horizon. Unlike the sudden ascendant sweep of High Sierra faced by anyone who wishes to make the crossing from Mono Lake, the mountains tilt downward from the crest toward western lowlands at a less precipitous, but still daunting angle. The slanted topography and trapped soil result in richly diverse life zones compressed into a handful of miles, providing for the traveler a brisk change in climate and scene that otherwise could be witnessed only by journeying hundreds of miles from northern to southern climes.

The treeless heights at the crest give way to white bark and lodge pole pine, then, further down the gradient as life zones change, to red and white fir, sugar, Jeffery, ponderosa pine, oak, and chaparral. Mixed in are well over a thousand species of plants, ultimately documented in precise terms by Stephen J. Botti, illustrated by Walter Sydoriak and designed by Carole Thickstun in their botanical opus, *An Illustrated Flora of Yosemite National Park*, published in 2001. For Walker's men, trekking through such biodiversity meant only that their chances of survival were increasing.

DISCOVERY?

Did Walker's men reach the cliffs of Yosemite Valley? Leonard's tantalizing descriptions suggest that they passed close by, perhaps even within a mile, and that some of the men may have explored the possibility of descending into the valley itself. Here is Leonard's account, dated November 13, 1833:

"We began to encounter in our path many small streams which would shoot out from under these high snow banks, and after running a short distance in deep chasms which they have through the ages cut in the rocks, precipitate themselves from one lofty precipice to another, until they are exhausted in rain below. Some of these precipices appeared to us to be more than a mile high. Some of the men thought that if we could succeed in descending one of these precipices to the bottom, we might thus work our way into the valley below, but on making several attempts, we found it utterly impossible for a man to descend, to say nothing of horses."

There are many deep canyons in the Sierra Nevada, but only two places that most accurately fit this description: Yosemite Valley and its smaller cousin, the Hetch Hetchy Valley. The ridgeline route from Mono Lake through the mountains touches the northern periphery of the greater of these two valleys. Leonard's description, inspired even as he was struggling to stay alive, stands as testament to the exciting and accidental discovery of supreme natural places; in this case, probably Yosemite Valley.

(In his book, *A Way Across the Mountain*, historian Scott Stine makes an educated guess that Walker transited the Sierra Nevada far north of the Yosemite area, labeling claims that he "camped at Yosemite" in 1833 to be a "myth." My speculation takes the claim by Walker and members of his party at face value. Debate about the Walker route never will be clearly resolved; there is no hard evidence pointing the way.)

Soon after, the trappers moved on to yet another overnight camp, this time in a grove of giant trees that Leonard estimated to measure "from sixteen to eighteen fathom round the trunk." A fathom is equivalent to six feet, so Leonard was suggesting that the trunks of the trees he saw were about one hundred feet in circumference. Most historians assume that Leonard is describing the Giant Sequoias (*Sequoiadendron giganteum*), the largest living entities on earth. Both the Tuolumne and the Merced Groves of Giant Sequoias in Yosemite National Park are strong contenders for the honor so attended by Leonard's succinct description. Many years later, George Nidever, the remorseful slayer of two Paiutes on the east side of the mountains, contended that the crossing of the Sierra Nevada took the trappers along a ridgeline "between the Merced and Tuolumne Rivers." If so, the corps of men would have passed just to the north of Yosemite Valley, putting them on course toward the Sequoias.

In later years, Walker held firmly to the supposition that he and his men had been in proximity of Yosemite Valley. He never claimed, though, that he had looked straight down into the abyss. Had the expedition leader done so, he would have seen a domain encased by three-thousand-foot vertical cliffs that seem to favor falcons and render human effort insignificant. He might also have seen waterfalls, those clusters of white "comets," as John Muir described them, plunging into that deep pool of airspace. And in the late autumn of the year, if Walker had been on his belly in the snow to peek over the edge, he would have glimpsed evidence of a different season altogether, another climate, a paradise of pastoral beauty free of snow and seemingly unpopulated, except, perhaps, for a few telltale wisps of smoke that might have suggested some kind of human habitation after all. Certainly he could not have failed to notice, across that mile-wide lagoon of air, nature's most distinctive Yosemite monument, the grand and colossal Half Dome.

The mighty trees at the men's campsite earned mention in Leonard's account but did not slow their escape. They continued downward as rapidly as energy and track would permit, leaving snow and gray rock behind, hurrying into the oak woodlands and grassy knolls that greeted them, finally breaking out into the welcoming sweep of California's Central Valley, an immense 42,000 square miles of what would become some of the most productive agricultural land on earth.

SALVATION

Seven days after leaving Yosemite, the men reached the largely uninhabited San Francisco Bay region. Turning south, trying to find a Mexican habitation of any kind, the expedition reached the shoreline of the Pacific, where, to their amazement, they saw in the distance a sailing ship anchored offshore. Members of Walker's party grabbed blankets and started waving and shouting. Boats were dispatched from the ship and the flabbergasted trappers soon found themselves aboard the *Lagoda*, courtesy of their host, the equally startled Captain John Bradshaw out of Boston. The crew of the *Lagoda* had been loading cowhides, a Mexican commodity and lucrative cargo that would bring a degree of wealth to the captain, crew, and their sponsors if the ship survived the harrowing voyage back to Boston around Cape Horn at the tip of South America.

Bradshaw tapped a keg of California brandy to celebrate the fluke rendezvous between the overland and seafaring Americans, fed the half-starved Walker men, deposited them back on shore, and pointed them toward the Presidio at Monterey, the Mexican seat of government in Alta California. (The flag of Spain had been raised at Monterey in 1770. In 1821, the flag of Mexico, symbol of revolutionary triumph, replaced it.)

The shabby trappers set out for the Presidio but found instead the impressive Mission of San Juan Bautista, first established in 1797 by a Spanish corporal and five soldiers, but expanded over the succeeding decades so that it now sat among orchards, vineyards, and farms. Trickling in on what was left of their wasted horses, Walker's bearded men must have been a curiosity to the Franciscan friars, Hispanic residents, and Indian servants who populated this small, vibrant community. Here the frontiersmen were quizzed about their ordeal and allowed to camp as guests during the winter months. In spring of 1834, Walker and his men hit the trail once more, riding east toward the planned rendezvous with Captain Bonneville. They were not empty-handed. The Walker expedition herded along 315 horses and forty-seven head of cattle, and was followed by a pack of dogs.

Walker had no intention of assaulting the Yosemite region again. Instead, he maneuvered south along the base of the Sierra foothills, probably following a course suggested by Mexicans or Indians. Following the South Fork of the later-named Kern River, Walker and company rode along a gradually ascending boulevard of splendid meadows framed by groves of cottonwood. The upper reaches of the river drainage introduced them to a slump in the Sierra sprinkled with Joshua trees, marking an abrupt ecological transition from grassland to desert.

Compared to the Sierra crossing, the trappers must have found the Kern River route forgiving, an easy ride up to the summit pass and a relaxed amble down into the desert in a benign season of the year. But Walker was again in trackless territory and once again paid a price, this time by wandering for many days through the dry and desolate landscape, losing many horses and most of his cattle before finally rediscovering the life-giving Humboldt River. Nevertheless, by following the river course east, Walker successfully made contact with Bonneville on the Bear River in the vicinity of the Great Salt Lake on July 14, 1834, almost one year after the two expedition leaders separated. Walker reported that beaver pickings had been slim in Alta California. This news and the decimation of the horse and cattle herds greatly displeased Bonneville, who is said to have been "bitter" about Walker's lack of success.

Walker would return to Alta California in 1845, this time as guide and scout for John C. Frémont. Just a year later, Frémont would lead the Bear Flag Revolt to wrest control of California from the Mexican government. Zenas Leonard did not return with Walker. Instead, the scribe found his way back to Fort Osage, Missouri, to establish a successful trading post that provided supplies and sage advice to the rising flow of westward-bound adventurers.

Walker and his beaver trappers were fortune hunters. Their passage across the Sierra Nevada was inspired by commerce, not by a grand exercise in discovery. But the very same year these men made their way westward, the first stirrings of a belief in the value of land conservation were beginning. In 1832, the same year that Walker headed out from Camp Osage, President Jackson signed legislation that set aside four sections of land in Arkansas as the Hot Springs Reservation. The purpose of the legislation was to assure that the health-giving quality of the thermal springs bubbling from the base of Hot Springs Mountain at a rate of half a million gallons a day would remain under control of the federal government "not to be entered, located, or appropriated for any other purpose whatsoever" except as a bath spa available for the enjoyment and medicinal benefit of the public. This was a first glimmer of a national park conservation agenda.

Walker is not known to have championed the concept of preserving rare places of superb natural quality. In fact, the beaver-trapping industry was exploiting a natural resource to the point of annihilation. Certainly Walker never would have guessed that the untamed, seemingly uninhabited and extremely remote landscape that almost killed him would one day become a volatile testing place for the concept of wildland preservation. Fame eventually found Yosemite and then it circled back to encompass Walker. Of his many exploits, it is his presumed accidental encounter with Yosemite for which he is known. Place names in the Sierra Nevada region attest to his passage; Walker Pass, Walker Lake, Walker River. In the Alhambra Cemetery in Contra Costa, California, there is a gravesite headstone that reads:

Capt. Joseph R. Walker
Born In Roan County, Tennessee
December 13, 1798
Emigrated to Missouri, 1819
To New Mexico, 1820
Rocky Mountain in 1832
Camped At Yosemite November 13, 1833
Died October 22, 1876

3

Old Ways Collapse

JOSEPH WALKER made no known contact with native peoples living in Yosemite Valley, said by Park Archeologist Scott Carpenter to have represented a continuum of human habitation in the Sierra Nevada of 3,000 to 4,000 years. Still, Walker had successfully crossed through a region that, until then, had been the domain solely of Indians who had found refuge, seclusion, and sustenance there far from the turmoil of worldwide colonization. Unfortunately for the Native Americans, the notions about conquest and exploitation that motivated frontiersmen like Walker were the biases that would prevail in California in the 19th century. Walker's arrival in Alta California presaged a trickle of westward migration by fortune seekers that would turn into a flood of destruction of the traditions and life-sustaining habits of native peoples.

There are many areas within our National Park System that honor cultural remnants, most of them preserved in silent celebration of the ruins and artifacts left behind by disappeared people—some hidden in mystery, others known to have moved on or been forced out to settle elsewhere. These areas (Mesa Verde in Colorado, Chaco Canyon in New Mexico, Canyon de Chelly in Arizona, Ocmulgee, Georgia, and many others) are touchstones that invite our understanding of a multifaceted human history predating European "discovery" of the Western Hemisphere.

Yosemite is different. At the time that Yosemite began to emerge into the modern public consciousness, there was nothing hushed and disappeared about its native residents; they were right there, living. Early in my tenure in the park, I came to greatly admire my staff colleagues, Jay Johnson, Les James, Ralph and Dr. Julia Parker, and others of Native American descent. These colleagues, represented particularly by eloquent and principled Jay Johnson, wanted an Indian Cultural Center to be located in the valley so that the story of the Miwuk and Paiute who lived there could be fully presented to the public. They wanted, too, a place where their spiritual inheritance, a deep respect for nature's gifts, could be a formative part of the environmental legacy of the park. I was conflicted by the rightness of their cause versus the urgent need to reduce development in the crowded valley, but if there ever was to be more development, only the Indian Cultural Center qualified.

The Spaniards who settled in California in the 1700s confined their military outposts and Catholic missions to the coastal province between San Diego and San Francisco. Ranchos in adjacent foothills supported herds of cattle and horses. Native peoples in the vicinity of these settlements came under the sway of the church and were classed by the Spaniards as "neophytes" if they converted to Christianity or "wild" if they did not. Neophytes often became the colonizers' servants, tending to agrarian and domestic needs, and oppressed by strict discipline to remain peaceful. Those among them who found the yoke of Spanish rule too onerous had only one obvious choice: to flee inland and attempt to find safety among the tribes and clans in the great Central Valley.

The pursuit of escaped neophytes occasionally took Spanish soldiers into the interior, but the soldiers apparently probed no further than the foothills of the Sierra Nevada, leaving unmolested the mountains and their myriad places of concealment. In the early 1800s, a Spanish expedition explored in the Central Valley with the intent of founding a mission there, a plan soon abandoned due to vulnerability in such an isolated region where help, if needed, would be too far away. The native peoples who lived in the sequestered Yosemite region remained generally unaffected by the Spaniards although apparently aware of them. (In 1978, a visitor to Yosemite Valley found a Spanish coin dated 1781. It was most likely a trade item.)

North of the Spanish settlements, tsarist Russia maintained a coastal trading post at Fort Ross, about sixty miles north of San Francisco. Russian voyagers crept down the Pacific coast from Alaska to stake this claim and maintained a presence there from 1812 to

1841. Unlike the British, French, and Americans, who made concerted attempts to control Canada and the Pacific Northwest, the Russian custodians of the fort made little effort at conquest of new territories.

In fact, the Russians' thirty-year presence at Fort Ross might have become no more than a footnote in the history of the American West if it had not precipitated an outbreak of smallpox in 1837. Native peoples had little immunity to this highly contagious disease, and within months thousands of Indians were dead. It is difficult to imagine a military campaign that could have yielded more devastating results. The native population in the Central Valley was cut by more than half. As a result, interior territories that had been largely controlled by Indian ethnic groups fell open for the taking. The defenses that had existed for the native peoples, primarily their superiority in number and the combined strength of cooperative communities, collapsed. Centuries-old traditions and lifestyles crumbled. But not all clans were equally affected. Indians living in Yosemite Valley were too remote to be impacted by the smallpox epidemic. The shock for them would be indirect, a disintegration of the old ways among neighboring tribes and an opening into nearby lands for assertive newcomers.

Two of these newcomers were Swiss-born John Sutter (1803–1880) and Ohio-born James D. Savage (1817–1852). Accompanied by nine settlers of European descent, ten Kanakas (Hawaiians), and a young Indian boy, Sutter found the place he was looking for at the confluence of the American and Sacramento Rivers, fifty-four miles upstream from Yerba Buena (later renamed San Francisco in 1847). The remnants of Indian clans in the area offered no resistance. Mexican officials, interested in profitable activities in lands they had largely ignored, duly granted Sutter a claim that allowed him to construct and operate a small flourmill, raise wheat, and tan hides. In turn, Sutter sought and won Mexican citizenship.

The initial years of the Sutter operation were difficult, but as more immigrants and adventurers turned up in the region, the enterprise slowly gained momentum. Arrival at Sutter's Fort, as the compound came to be known, was a cherished achievement for those who had braved the long overland route to California. Business was good enough that Sutter decided to build a larger flourmill. To provide lumber for the project, he also constructed a sawmill facility along the South Fork of the American River where, in a valley nestled up against the base of the Sierra Nevada foothills, trees could be readily harvested.

James Savage was an immigrant from Ohio who arrived in California in 1846 after a harrowing overland journey that claimed the lives of his wife and only child. Promptly recruited by those who joined John C. Frémont in the Bear Flag revolt of that same year against Mexican authority, Savage was soon suspected of rustling cattle. A reputation for playing by his own rules followed Savage from an early age. In *One Hundred Years in Yosemite*, Carl Russell quotes an Ohio woman who had known Savage before he moved west at age 29: "Jim was smart as a whip, shrewd, apt in picking up languages—he was vigorous and strong—loved all kinds of sports. Sometimes Jim would come to church, but, oh, he was such a wag as a youth. More often than not, he would remain outside, and when he knew time had come for prayer, he'd flick the knees of his horse and make him kneel, and then wink at us inside. We couldn't laugh of course, but we always watched for this trick." Shortly after the Bear Flag revolt, John Sutter's foreman James Marshall hired Savage to join the crew at Sutter's new sawmill in Coloma Valley.

GOLD!

In January, 1848, Sutter was on a business trip to newly named San Francisco when Marshall and his workers discovered gold in the raceway at the site of the Coloma Valley sawmill: Marshall rode as fast as he could to the distant hamlet to inform his employer. When Sutter heard the explosive news he tried to keep it quiet, probably hoping to stake as many claims as possible before others arrived on the scene. But secrecy proved impossible. In a flash, "Gold discovered at Sutter's Mill" became a clarion call heard across the continent. The result, so well documented in the nation's history, was that thousands of would-be prospectors crashed into California, destroying the slow pace of colonization that, until then, had seemed to match the mood of such a gentle and abundant land.

By May, only five men remained in San Francisco. The rest stampeded into the Coloma Valley to try their luck, soon followed by an army of fortune seekers from the east coast. Some came by wagon, on horseback, or on their own two feet while others scrambled for passage on sailing ships. The long and dangerous voyage around Cape Horn was still the quickest way to the west coast. Still another approach was to ship out to Panama, cross the risky, disease-ridden isthmus on foot, and attempt to board a northbound ship on the Pacific side. Before gold was discovered, about 1,000 individuals of European descent lived in California. In a matter of months, this population swelled to more than 300,000. Thirty-five thousand people came overland, and 230 ships sailed into the bay, creating a jumbled forest of masts. When the ships finally arrived, many were simply run aground as captains and crewmen abandoned their posts to join passengers in the rush for gold. The small unit of U. S. Army troops stationed at San Francisco was hit so hard by desertions that it became all but inoperable.

For John Sutter the gold rush was a disaster. His land claims were overrun by trespassers and the glimpse of gold at his mill had been merely a trace of deeper sources, further up in the foothills. Sutter's workers disappeared to search them out. Customers vanished, too. Deciding he had no choice but to follow, Sutter gathered together a force of 100 Indians and 50 Kanakas, transferring what was left of his enterprise to his son before his departure.

For the vast majority of gold seekers the dream of ready fortune became a nightmare of debt and dashed hopes. Sutter was no exception. He and his men found some gold, but the instant culture of gambling dens, saloons, and price-gouging for supplies in the gold camps made short work of any real profit. Sutter lamented that the famed California Gold Rush caused him "heavy loss." Even his son, left behind to guard the family venture, proved to be a disappointment. The father had wanted his territory to be named Sutterville, but the son chose the name Sacramento instead.

Savage, too, joined the chase for gold, but he proved to be unusually adept at it. While most prospectors saw the native peoples as an obstacle, Savage had an innate understanding of frontier commerce, skill with languages, and an ability to recruit Indians to help him. He reasoned that Indians knew secrets of the land that frantic gold seekers might easily overlook. He learned Indian dialects and "married" several Indian women. His wives, estimated at a dozen or more, allowed Savage a degree of acceptance among some of the native peoples in the foothills unmatched by any of his gold-seeking contemporaries.

Tall and blue-eyed, Savage wore red shirts as a kind of flamboyant statement, and he quickly developed a larger-than-life reputation as rumors of his skill circulated through the foothills. One admirer said of Savage, "No dog can follow a trail like he can; no horse endure half so much. He sleeps little, can go days without food, can run a hundred miles in a day and night over the mountains and laugh for hours over a campfire as fresh and lively as if he had just been taking a little walk for exercise."

With his crew of Indian helpers, Savage made a gold strike by panning in the streams high up in the foothills. This location, later named Big Oak Flats, was only a few short air miles from concealed Yosemite Valley, but those who poured in to grab their share of the gold-laden stream gravel had no incentive to explore further. Savage stayed in the area for about a year, but friction between his Indian compatriots and other gold-seekers finally led to violence in which one white man and several Indians were killed. To avoid a larger conflict, Savage packed up hurriedly and left, moving with his Indian helpers further into the Sierra foothill wilderness.

The confrontation at the diggings was symptomatic of racial attitudes among the gold-seekers. One miner said, "the native was, in the general opinion, a dangerous animal which it was lawful to destroy. So whoever had occasion to kill one did not avoid it, and thought he had done a useful and praiseworthy deed." Common words to describe native peoples included "savage," "thief," "beggar," "murderer," "drunkard," "plunderer," "predator," "witch," and "whore." Lafayette Bunnell (1824 –1903) of Rochester, New York—

journalist, historian, and self-taught medical practitioner—was both a witness to and participant in events in the foothills, and claimed that the Indians were causing "depredations" and making "murderous assaults" on the avalanche of armed men who were scrambling by the hundreds into traditional Native American hunting and camping grounds.

Years after the gold rush, the Indians unsuccessfully petitioned the federal government, seeking financial reparation for transgressions visited against them and contending that the gold-seekers "brought among us drunkenness, lying, murder, forcible violation of our women, cheating, gambling, and wrongful appropriation of our lands."

In hidden Yosemite Valley, the enigmatic Ah'wah'nee'chee residents were not initially threatened by the tumultuous influx of adventurers. Shielded by the citadel-like topography and their reputation among neighboring Indians for wielding supernatural powers and using poisons to confront enemies, they remained

Lucy Telles

unmolested. The gold-seekers had no knowledge of the existence of the Ah'wah'nee'chee or their valley.

Still, a threat was building. When James Savage retreated from his diggings at Big Oak Flat, he and his Native American companions passed through the boomtown of Mariposa, a hodgepodge of tents and muddy lanes, and found their way into the deep and rugged canyon of the Merced River, following the river's course up to its confluence with its South Fork tributary. Here, in remote country never before claimed by white men, Savage set up camp less than twenty miles from Yosemite Valley. Between Savage's camp and the valley, the Merced River dances downward in a fierce cascade through a jumble of immense boulders wedged into place by sheer cliffs. Nature had concocted an almost impenetrable barrier to the valley's entrance that challenges the best engineers, even today. There is no evidence that Savage made any serious effort to overcome this barrier; he was intent, instead, on securing his newfound claim.

He cobbled together a log-and-canvas trading post intended specifically for the purpose of bartering with native peoples. Bringing in supplies that the Indians wanted, Savage was confident that they, in turn, would find gold for him. Lafayette Bunnell, who had joined the human stampede to the golden Sierra Nevada foothills and brought with him rare literary talent and skills of observation, remarked that Savage "exchanged goods for enormous profit" in his dealings with Indians. But Savage unknowingly had set up his camp in the traditional wintering grounds of the Ah'wah'nee'chee, and these secretive, watchful people knew almost instantly that a gold-seeker was in close proximity. They knew, too, of the harsh treatment the Miwuk and other foothill Indians had received who stood in the way of prospectors' gains. Ah'wah'nee'chee warriors appeared, seemingly from nowhere, and began to severely threaten Savage's presence. The trader's knack for frontier survival and his alliances with some native peoples were not enough to mount a purposeful defense against this mysterious adversary. Outnumbered and in an exposed position many rough miles from help of any kind, Savage retreated to the relative safety of the gold camps further down in the foothills.

He built two new trading posts, one on the Fresno River near present-day Oakhurst and another at the Agua Fria diggings only a few miles from Mariposa. By so doing, the industrious Savage placed himself among a handful of merchants who, in the midst of the gold frenzy, were actually getting rich. One ounce of gold was said to buy a can of oysters; five ounces would buy a shirt; one pound, boots or a hat. While most of the prospectors lost what assets they had and could not find enough gold to make up the difference,

     Your Yosemite: **PROTECTING A PUBLIC TREASURE**

still the hopefuls kept coming. Savage was there to sell them what they needed.

For the local tribes, the waves of armed strangers flooding their land must have been bewildering. For centuries, they had shared common ground, defended tribal spheres, maneuvered with the seasons, traded—even with enemies—and governed themselves. Whereas the prospectors had often traveled for thousands of miles, the Indians had traveled almost nowhere, save for the occasional hunting or trading foray into a nearby region. Gold seekers brought with them a new kind of force and avarice that stunned the native peoples. The gulf between cultures was immense. Meanwhile, thousands of miles away in Washington, D.C., the abrupt celebrity of California had caught the attention of politicians who quickly saw the wisdom of bringing this resource-rich territory into the union. In September 1850, President Millard Fillmore signed legislation that established California as the 31st state.

DESPERATE RESISTANCE

Seventy-four men organized themselves into a militia, electing Sheriff James Burney as their captain. James Savage was appointed scout. The general mood among Burney's men was that chasing after Indians, guilty or otherwise, was "a fine chance for the boys to have a frolic." In the skirmish that followed, the gold-seekers claimed to have killed forty Indians while losing six of their own volunteers. The Indians, having no guns, had to depend on guerilla tactics, using surprise when possible and hiding or trying to escape when confronted by the superior weaponry of the militiamen. In a second engagement near what is now known as Fresno Dome, the gold-seekers, this time led by Savage, claimed to have eliminated another twenty Indian warriors. They christened the spot Battle Mountain. These highly skewed violent encounters came to be known as the Mariposa Indian Wars.

In January, 1851, California Governor John McDougal, himself a gold miner, gave the adventurers official sanction by authorizing the formation of the Mariposa Battalion, a unit of two hundred men.

Savage, having proven his leadership skill, was made commander of the battalion and promptly elevated to the rank of Major. But the campaign against California's Native Americans was no longer simply military; it was now one of national policy. The U. S. Congress approved the Indian Appropriations Act in 1851, overseen by Federal Commissioners, with the clear intent of confining Native Americans everywhere in the nation to reservations, and, if possible, converting them to Christianity. Eventually, 310 reservations would be established throughout the United States. The events in the Sierra foothills in 1851 marked an assertive beginning to this nationwide policy of "benign" incarceration. Savage's first order of business in his new post was to entice or coerce as many foothill Indians as possible to relocate to reservations in the Central Valley.

One of the main targets of this effort was a Native American chief named Bautista. Many years earlier, Chief Bautista, an orphaned and frightened eleven-year-old of uncertain tribal affiliation, had been captured by Mexican soldiers near the Mission of San Juan Bautista. Raised by the friars as a neophyte, Bautista learned Spanish, became a skilled horseman, and may even have been living at the mission when Joseph Walker and his beaver trappers passed through. As a young adult, Bautista married a Miwuk woman and joined the Indian community in the Sierra foothills. He brought with him the stylish manners he'd learned from the Mexicans and soon became recognized among his adopted people as a talented leader.

Bautista was a principal suspect in the attack on the Fresno River trading post. Rather than track him down, the commissioners sent word by Indian runners that he would be afforded safe haven if he appeared at a treaty ceremony. The Federal commissioners and James Savage thought of Bautista as a formidable opponent who might be able to unite foothill Indians into a structured force. Bautista's signature on a treaty would be a strategic victory for the commissioners. When word was returned that Bautista agreed to come in, the whole proceeding was delayed pending his arrival. He was the last chief to arrive and the first invited to sign the treaty, attesting to his particular importance as an Indian leader.

     Your Yosemite: **PROTECTING A PUBLIC TREASURE**

At an assembly point on the Las Mariposas Grant, owned by John Frémont, a number of chiefs and head men made their marks on the Treaty of Camp Frémont in March 1851. In so doing, they acknowledged that they and their peoples were under the jurisdiction, control, and authority of the United States and that they relinquished, forever, all right, title, claim, or interest in any lands in the State of California that once had been their domain. The lands at issue, vaguely defined, theoretically stretched from the shoreline of San Francisco Bay to the crest of the Sierra Nevada Mountains.

In return for giving up their ancestral lands, the chiefs and head men would lead their followers onto rancheria (reservation) lands between the Tuolumne and Merced Rivers near the present-day Central Valley town of Snelling. Each year, the Indians would collectively receive one hundred cows and one hundred sacks or barrels of flour. They would be taught to farm, a vocation contrary to the practices of hunting-and-gathering learned from their forebears. The Indians were being asked to give up all that they had known—their way of life and traditions, the graves of their ancestors, their status and pride. They would live on rancherias in the Central Valley near other native peoples with whom they often had traded and sometimes fought. They would be monitored by white men and expected to live in peace, segregated from the Anglo migrants who were fast surrounding them to claim productive agricultural land. A compelling reason for the native peoples to accept such a one-sided agreement seemed to be that their traditional homelands, once offering security and nourishment, had been shattered by powerful, dangerous invaders.

INVASION

Thirty-nine x's appeared on the treaty, representing a much larger group of Native Americans. Bautista represented only a small contingent of native peoples, and no chief representing the Ah'wah'nee'chee was present. Even so, all Indians in the territory were supposed to abandon their encampments and surrender. Those who did not would be hunted down. On the very day that the treaty was signed, James Savage assembled his Mariposa Battalion and went in search of the hidden Indians of Yosemite, whom he believed had attacked his Fresno River trading post.

Major Savage's volunteers, recruited primarily from the gold encampment at Agua Fria, had no formal military training. For the most part, their uniforms were the clothes on their backs, their armaments the rifles, pistols, and knives they already had at hand, their transport the horses and mules already owned or borrowed. Savage divided his citizen-soldiers into three companies. One company would trek south along the foothills in pursuit of resistant Indian holdouts. The other two companies, seventy-five men in all, were kept under Savage's personal command. Their mission was to march into uncharted mountain terrain where they could easily be ambushed by Indian forces. There was some speculation among the men that they might confront warriors numbering in the hundreds. Accompanying Major Savage was "Doc" Lafayette Bunnell who signed on to provide medical services.

Savage and his men moved upward into the dark folds of pine and cedar, where snow still marked the winter season. At the end of a long day of riding, the men camped in a meadow on the shores of the South Fork of the Merced River. They were now inside what would become the southern boundary of Yosemite National Park, about a mile from the present-day Wawona Hotel. The nameless campsite offered reasonably level ground and grazing for the horses.

Savage's scouts soon confirmed that about two miles downriver from the battalion bivouac there was a small assembly of Indians, later identified as *Noot'chu*. Savage decided to reconnoiter the Indian camp for himself and planned to take along only one man to avoid the possibility of detection. The ever-curious Bunnell decided to follow and soon caught up with the Major and his companion. To test the doc's stamina, Savage increased his pace almost to a trot, causing the third man in the party to fall behind, but Bunnell stayed right on Savage's heels. When the Noot'chu encampment could be discreetly observed, Savage and Bunnell dropped to the ground to conceal themselves. And Savage complimented his medical officer, saying, "Bunnell, you play it well." While the other man crept up to join them, they took stock of activities in the camp and judged by

     Your Yosemite: **PROTECTING A PUBLIC TREASURE**

the tranquil mood of the place that the Indians remained unaware of white men nearby.

While Savage and Bunnell remained hidden, the third man was sent back to camp with orders for Captains Boling and Dill to bring the militiamen forward, quietly, on foot. On arrival at Savage's hiding place, the battalion was formed into a skirmish line and emerged from the woodland cover, taking the Noot'chu by surprise. The amazed Native Americans made no attempt to resist. No shots were fired. Savage knew a few of the Indians, recognizing them through trading contacts, and, using a combination of Miwuk words and sign language, made known to them that the Noot'chu were captives and that the camp was to be abandoned. After gathering whatever belongings they could carry, the Noot'chu were made to set fire to their bark-and-pole structures and marched to the Mariposa Battalion encampment.

Using a time-honored frontier tactic, Savage immediately selected young Noot'chu men to act as runners, their assignment to alert other Indian groups in hiding that the Mariposa Battalion was near and intended punitive business unless these bands surrendered promptly. Over the next several hours more Indians cautiously began to approach the battalion camp. These proved to be Pohono'chees, who, like the Noot'chu, had hoped that they were far enough into the mountains not to be pursued by white soldiers.

SURRENDER

The following day, another Native American appeared, an elder of modest physical stature wrapped in a robe of rabbit skins. He was weaponless and stood alone on the periphery of Savage's encampment. This man carried with him the emotional burdens of his people and represented the pitiless impact that cultural collision often brings. He was Tenaya, Chief of the Ah'wah'nee'chee. The moment James Savage stepped forward to meet Tenaya, a page was turned. History would guard the slight imprint left by native peoples on the Yosemite region, but a new era was at hand.

Tenaya apparently intended to negotiate the surrender of the Ah'wah'nee'chee so that there would be no need for the battalion to go in search of his people's valley stronghold. The Chief may have believed that if white men entered the valley, spiritual protection for his people would be broken. More assuredly, Tenaya knew of the deadly threat posed by well-armed militiamen. According to Bunnell, the Chief hoped that if his people went to a rancheria, time would pass, the hostilities in the foothills would quiet, and the Ah'wah'nee'chee would eventually be allowed to return to their home. Tenaya had no illusions about reservation life, which he described as being "yarded like horses and cattle," but he seemed willing to take the chance.

Bunnell gave his version of the verbal exchange. Although the language barrier must have been difficult for both men, Savage apparently confronted Tenaya by wasting no time on niceties: "Your people must go to the commissioners and make terms with them," he said. "If you do not, your young men will again steal our horses; your people will again kill and plunder the whites." In response, Tenaya said, "It is useless to talk to you about who destroyed your property and killed your people." He added an impassioned plea, "We do not want anything from white men. Our women are able to do our work. Go, then, let us remain in the mountains where we were born, where the ashes of our fathers have been given to the winds. I have said enough."

Savage was not swayed. To the Major and his men, Tenaya was not a chief, he was a "Satan." The battalion commander made clear that Tenaya and his people were going to peacefully come out of the mountains or that Savage and his men were going in to get them. Surrender was demanded.

Tenaya promised to bring his people to the militia encampment. When challenged about his honesty, Bunnell claims that he said, "I am old and you can kill me. Why would I lie?" The Ah'wah'nee'chee were rumored to adorn themselves in black and yellow war paint and had a reputation for unusual prowess on the battlefield. Savage chose to take no unnecessary chances. Tenaya was allowed to disappear back into the woodlands just as he had come, silently and alone. The battalion commander would wait at least for a day or two to learn the result.

Late the next day, Tenaya reappeared on the fringe of the soldier's encampment, but without any of his followers. Was this a trap? Were black and yellow warriors surrounding the camp, waiting to fill the evening air with a blizzard of arrows? More than one man among the volunteers must have been fingering the trigger of his rifle. But the lone Chief claimed that his people were following at a much slower pace, struggling on foot through deep snow toward the bivouac. Savage was skeptical, but Tenaya assured him that the Ah'wah'nee'chee would soon arrive and offered himself as hostage. After another day passed, still with no confirmation that Tenaya's people were surrendering, the Major formed his battalion into rank and asked each man to step forward if he was willing to confront the perils that might lie ahead. No man hesitated. All took the symbolic step into the unknown. Savage assigned a few men to remain behind to guard the captive Noot'chu and Pohono'chee. The following morning, Tenaya was herded to the front of Savage's mounted men and told to lead the battalion into the realm of the Ah'wah'nee'chee.

Progress was steady at first, but Tenaya's warning proved to be true; when the battalion crested a high ridgeline, the horses were suddenly struggling in snow several feet deep. The lead rider would aggressively urge his mount forward, busting trail until the animal tired, at which point the next rider in line would do the same. The distance from the Wawona bivouac site to Yosemite Valley is about fifteen miles. In the course of three days, Tenaya had walked in steep terrain and tough winter conditions from his hidden valley to Savage's encampment, returned to the valley, trudged back again to the battalion camp, and then returned to his valley home yet again, a true commentary on Tenaya's endurance and desperation.

As the battalion members were descending from the ridgeline, the first of the Ah'wah'nee'chee appeared, a silent string of women, children, and older men struggling uphill in single file through the snow. The head count was seventy-two Indians, none of them armed for battle. Tenaya tried to explain that the people straggling past Savage accounted for all of the Ah'wah'nee'chee except for a few young men who had fled into a labyrinth of mountain canyons, fearing for their lives. Savage suspected that the warriors had in fact fled nowhere, but were waiting somewhere down the trail to spring a trap. The Major insisted that Tenaya be placed under guard and sent with his people back to the distant bivouac. Pressing into service another Ah'wah'nee'chee man to replace the Chief as pathfinder, the commander kept his forces moving down slope toward an uncertain and perhaps very dangerous objective.

THE SANCTUARY DISCOVERED

Not long afterward the battalion broke from the forest cover and emerged onto a steep rock-strewn gradient overlooking the veiled dwelling place of Tenaya and his people. They were probably on Turtleback Dome above what is now known as the "tunnel view" (or "inspiration point"), so named when a highway tunnel was chiseled through solid rock in a manner that abruptly flings the full spectacle of the valley into the arriving motorist's line of sight. Savage and his comrades may have been the first white men ever to stare into the chasm from this vantage point. Bunnell captured in his own words the masterpiece of natural splendor that suddenly opened before him: "None but those who have visited this most wonderful valley can even imagine the feelings with which I looked upon the view. I found my eyes in tears of emotion."

That evening the battalion pitched camp in a lush meadow not far from Bridalveil Fall near the western entrance to the valley. In the waning light, Savage dispatched several men to search for a fording place that would allow riders to cross to the north shoreline of the snowmelt-swollen Merced River. The Ah'wah'nee'chee prisoner who was serving as their reluctant guide had indicated that travel along the northern shoreline would be less difficult. Darkness fell before they could find a crossing. Sentries were posted and campfires began to glow as the men settled in for the night.

Doc Bunnell, still impressed by what he had seen, found in his companions by the fire a ready audience for his idea of exercising European-style right-of-discovery by choosing a name for this concealed jewel of the Sierra Nevada Mountains. In his account of the campfire dialogue, Bunnell explained his reasoning: "It would be better to give [the valley] an Indian name than to import a strange and inexpressive one; that the name of the tribe who had occupied it would be more appropriate than any I had heard suggested. I then proposed that we give the valley the name Yo-sem-i-ty, as it was suggestive, euphonious, and certainly American; that by so doing, the name of the tribe of Indians which we met leaving their homes in this valley, perhaps never to return, would be perpetuated."

A few members of Bunnell's audience were not convinced. One man argued that any stronghold of "thieving heathens" should not be honored by an Indian name. Another proposed the name Paradise Valley. The debate, though, was short-lived. A "rollicking Texan" named John O'Neal shouted "Hear ye, hear ye. A vote will now be taken to decide what name shall be given the valley." On voice vote, the name Yo-sem-i-ty was affirmed.

Bunnell was under the impression, and so assured the men around him, that the name in translation meant grizzly bear. The etymologist Madison Beeler, however, explains that Yosemite is a derivative of *yohmologis*, a southern Miwuk word referring to the fearsome reputation that the Ah'wah'nee'chee had among surrounding tribal groups. According to Beeler, the Miwuk word for grizzly bear was *iwūmat i*. Bunnell's attempt at interpretation seems to have inventively mixed portions of Miwuk words, not uncommon in the Wild West where Native American languages and dialects were almost entirely incomprehensible to English-speaking people. The doc's improbable word campaign nonetheless left his lexicon stamp permanently on a dazzling place.

By first light the men were again on the move, having found a place where their horses could safely splash across the river. The battalion column was divided, most of the riders moving to the north shoreline with a few staying along the south bank to block a possible escape route. Compared to the mountain slopes and snow pack the battalion had navigated to discover the valley, the flat ground leading into the deep interior of the glacially stone-worked basin allowed the men to move forward with relative ease. The scale of the place was difficult to comprehend. Men made estimates of the height of the walls, some suggesting that they might soar as high as eight-hundred to fifteen-hundred feet. They were missing the mark by half. If an army of Ah'wah'nee'chee warriors had been standing atop the verge of El Capitan they would have been invisible to the men below. But there was no army of warriors.

About midway along the seven-mile course from Bridalveil Meadow to the abrupt eastern terminus of the valley, Savage's men began to discover abandoned Indian shelters. Positioned to capture the warmth of winter sunshine, these shelters were made of pine poles tightly bound with wild grape vines and walled with slabs of cedar. Suspended high above ground on sturdy poles were the granaries filled with bushels of acorns gathered from the black oaks that graced the valley floor. Acorn flour was a staple of the Ah'wah'nee'chee diet, part of an abundant natural larder that also included deer, rabbit, and squirrel, wild berries, fish, and edible roots. In the shelters, the granaries shared space with rabbit and squirrel-skin blankets, musical instruments, perhaps a deer horn hammer, fish spears, fire sticks, soap stone, and baskets made of materials gathered close at hand, their designs telling stories of spirits and legends.

Evidence gathered in modern times by archeologists suggests that these clusters of shelters had been the center of existence for perhaps two hundred or more people, but the Mariposa Battalion's arrival had frightened away their occupants. For the invaders, the compounds had the eerie feel of an Indian ghost town abandoned in haste.

Savage was taking no chances. Battalion members probed into boulder-strewn talus slopes and crevices, expecting at any moment to raise their weapons and begin firing. Two of Savage's men even climbed up past Vernal and Nevada Falls at the eastern limit of the valley, but they found no one. In the hours of searching only one Ah'wah'nee'chee was finally discovered, an old woman nestled under a rock overhang, wizened and almost immobile. Obviously harmless, she had been left behind, perhaps by her own choice, because she was too weak to follow her people out of the valley. During an attempt to manhandle the woman onto a mule, perhaps in a misguided attempt to rescue her, the old woman died in the hands of alien men.

Savage was confronted by twin dilemmas; the enemy had vanished (and might still pose a threat), and clouds were gathering in the sky above. He wanted to exit the valley before a winter storm trapped him there. Bunnell found Savage sitting on his horse, looking west past Yosemite Falls toward El Capitan. "This affords the best prospect of any yet discovered," he exclaimed to his medical officer. "Just look—splendid!" Bunnell thought that Savage had finally gained some appreciation for the view, but the Major quickly corrected him. "My remark was not in reference to the scenery," he said, "but to the prospect of the Indians being starved out." In the distance, smoke was rising from locations that marked the various Ah'wah'nee'chee compounds. Savage had given the order to burn the shelters and everything in or near them. The granaries provided the most spectacular fireworks. An estimated eight hundred bushels of acorns were torched and lay crackling on the ground.

By the following evening the Mariposa Battalion was back at Wawona, where about three-hundred-fifty Indians were still being held captive. Food was running short so hasty preparations were made to escort the prisoners down through the foothills to the Fresno River where they could be turned over to federal commissioners. The commissioners would be responsible for forcing the Indians the rest of the way down into the Central Valley to rancheria confinement. Progress was painstakingly slow with so many on foot. A few successes at shooting wild game by Savage's men were insufficient to meet the needs of the hungry troops and their captives.

On impulse, the Major assigned Captain Boling and just nine men to a guard detail while he and the rest of the battalion hastened ahead to the commissioner headquarters. They were greeted with enthusiasm and rewarded with an abundant supply of food and drink. When Savage was questioned about the meager complement of guards he had left behind, he contended that the Indians "could not be driven off" because he had promised them presents of trade goods when they were placed in custody. As far as he was concerned, "hostilities were at an end," the forays had served their purpose and the Indians were soundly defeated.

Only a few miles upslope, Captain Boling had settled his captives for the night. One of Boling's guards had managed to shoot a deer, so the captain, guards, and an Indian boy who had helped haul in the carcass rewarded themselves by roasting slabs of meat and gorging themselves. Satiated appetites, fatigue, and the warmth of the campfire brought on a deep sleep. When the guards awoke at dawn they were startled to discover that only one Indian remained at the campsite, the young boy who had helped them with the deer and fallen asleep by their side. The Captain and his nine men, obviously outnumbered by adversaries who had regained the tactical advantage of stealth and ambush, were in no mood to pursue them. On hearing the news, Lafayette Bunnell, affirming the general attitude among his peers, complained that "we had been outwitted by these ignorant Indians."

Not until late spring did an expeditionary force of thirty-five volunteers, this time under the command of Captain Boling, return to Yosemite Valley to deal with Tenaya and the escapees. In a reversal of roles, James Savage acted as scout. The Boling contingent was detected by Ah'wah'nee'chee sentinels as it approached the valley. Warning reached Tenaya in time to allow him to gather his followers and rush to an escape route, probably where a forceful stream plunges down a cleft in the valley wall near Mirror Lake, a small wetland tucked into a tight canyon between Half Dome and North Dome at the eastern extremity of the valley. Unlike the unencumbered frothy fury of most of the valley's waterfalls, this watercourse, known today as

Snow Creek, stair-steps down in a series of interlaced cascades, in essence creating a precipitous ladder of hand-and-footholds that the Ah'wah'nee'chee had long used for access to the High Sierra. Left behind to spy on the attackers were five young warriors. They were quickly detected by the troopers, run down, and captured.

Some of Boling's men were able to track the Ah'wah'nee'chee to the base of Snow Creek and started to scramble up the almost perpendicular trail. "The first intimation that they had of the Indians being near was a shower of huge rocks which came tumbling down the mountain, threatening instant destruction," Boling reported. Some of the men were knocked down and one man's rifle was ripped from his hands and sent spiraling by a heavy stone projectile. Boling's men retreated, but not before "pressing the Indians closely," as Boling reported in an official dispatch, and capturing "the old Yo-semity chief, whom we yet hold as a prisoner."

The Captain called a halt to further pursuit until a mule train packed with supplies reached the valley. When the men leading the mules finally arrived, they were accompanied by thirteen Noot'chu warriors. In the Wild West a common ploy was for white men to recruit Indians to track and fight other Indians. Competition and antagonisms between the tribes could play to the advantage of a savvy military commander who needed the skills and knowledge that native peoples had at their fingertips. Boling and Savage took full advantage of this opportunity, playing the Noot'chu against the Ah'wah'nee'chee. Resupplied and with reinforcements at hand, Boling led his company of men on foot up and out of Yosemite Valley, using the steep Snow Creek Trail. Aided by the Noot'chu trackers, he was able to proceed rapidly toward his quarry and surprised thirty-four of Tenaya's people who were camped at the alpine lake known to the Ah'wah'nee'chee as Py'we'ack (Lake of Shining Rocks) and subsequently renamed Tenaya Lake by Doc Bunnell.

PAROLE AND CALAMITY

After yet another long march under guard from Yosemite Valley to the lowlands of the Central Valley, Tenaya and those with him were incarcerated on a grassland rancheria where summertime temperatures routinely reached 100 degrees or more. After months at the rancheria, the defeated Ah'wah'nee'chee begged to be allowed to go back to the mountains. By the spring of 1852, the federal commissioners considered the Ah'wah'nee'chee to be harmless and allowed them to be paroled to return to Yosemite Valley. This reprieve proved to be brief. Gold fever still was at epidemic levels in the Sierra Nevada. Prospectors were pushing further into the mountains in search of their glittering dreams. In late May, not long after Tenaya had returned to Yosemite Valley, eight of these gold-seekers worked their way into the valley and pitched camp at Bridalveil Meadow. This time Indian warriors were nearby. The gold seekers were attacked. Two of the men were killed and a third man went missing. According to hearsay, one Indian was also killed. The rest of the prospectors escaped back down into the foothills to again sound an alarm of Indian hostilities.

James Savage was quick to the saddle, leading a company of men in search of the "murderers," but he was unable to find any renegade Indians in the rough country where the attackers were suspected to have fled. The punitive task then fell to Army Lieutenant Seymour Treadwell Moore, a West Point graduate. Moore led a company of soldiers into Yosemite Valley in June and confronted a small band of five adult male Indians. Otherwise, the valley seemed to be abandoned. There was no sign of Tenaya. Lieutenant Moore then set spurs to horse and led his troopers in further pursuit. They found no trace of the chief.

In the end, Tenaya's cleverness at avoiding capture only prolonged his ordeal. With what was left of his followers after fleeing the valley, the chief hunkered down for a time on lands of the Mono Paiute. Tenaya, who had been born in the Mono Lake basin, counted a number of Paiute among his Ah'wah'nee'chee people. Over the years, the Ah'wah'nee'chee had routinely traded with their Mono Paiute neighbors.

In the rough-and-tumble of gold rush California, Savage was far away from Tenaya's troubles, having been appointed to act as an Indian agent for a Central Valley rancheria on the Kings River, near present-day Fresno, which was a bit like serving as mayor for the reservation. In this capacity, Savage, the off-and-on-again champion or disciplinarian of Native Americans, confronted two white men he accused of needless violence against the Indians under Savage's jurisdiction. In addition, he laid blame on them for attempted theft of some of the lands assigned by the government for rancheria purposes. One of the men, a county judge identified in the historic record as Major Harvey, sought out Savage at a trading post and demanded a retraction and apology. Instead, Savage lunged at the man and slapped his face. This assault dislodged a pistol tucked into Savage's waistband; the gun went clattering to the floor and slid out of reach. Seeing that Savage was suddenly unarmed, Harvey drew his own pistol and began firing repeatedly at close range. Savage died almost instantly in the volley.

Tenaya never knew of Savage's death. In a twist of fate, he, too, soon died violently. Sometime in the summer of 1853, his reluctant Mono hosts became angry at the Ah'wah'nee'chee. The exact cause, place, and date of Chief Tenaya's death are lost in the haze of history. There is reasonable anecdotal certainty that he was killed by avenging Native Americans, and that the weapons used were stones thrown at him until his body lay crushed and lifeless. Ironically, both Tenaya and Savage died at the hands of members of their own ethnic groups, but the victor was never in doubt in the larger cultural clash that each represented.

In a microcosm of the agonies and glories of land conquest where old customs are no defense against greatly superior strength-of-arms, the newly arrived Anglo invaders had cleared Yosemite Valley of a centuries-old claim by Native Americans. Now the victors would spend decades fighting over Yosemite among themselves.

The raw edge of conflict and grief between new immigrants and indigenous peoples that dramatizes much of America's Wild West history in the nineteenth century tends to overshadow the much deeper chronicle of times gone by when indigenous peoples found their own spaces on the land and celebrated their own customs and beliefs. At Yosemite, the drama of the moment when James Savage confronted Tenaya is an entry point to better understanding and appreciation of the old ways and the full scope of the park's human history juxtaposed with its natural history. This is the ongoing job of archeologists, ranger-educators, and of the Native Americans themselves. The task is not so much to tell of the drama of the Mariposa War as to see the war for what it was, a moment, repeated in history all over the world, when people are demonized and misunderstood simply because they are strangers, speak a different language, live in a different style, dress differently, worship differently, have a different skin color or different eyes, and occupy lands that others want. Left behind at Yosemite by the Ah'wah'nee'chee was evidence of a culture of art, survival, sustainability, asylum, and grace with the land that park visitors should come to know as a fundamental part of the park story. One of the beauties of national parks is that this story, and others like it, can be told in detail—a reach toward understanding that is an essential NPS obligation and service to park visitors.

4

An Idea with Staying Power

THE NATIONAL PARKS have been popular since their inception, not only with millions of visitors, but also with many Americans who greatly value the fact that these great expanses have been preserved for them whether they are ever able to visit them or not. The author and educator Wallace Stegner has famously called our national parks "America's best idea," a perception that was first expressed early in the twentieth century by British Ambassador to the United States, Lord James Bryce, a close friend of President Theodore Roosevelt, and more recently by the film makers Ken Burns and Dayton Duncan in their PBS television series of the same name

One test of national parks' popularity has been their growth over the last century. There are now more than 400 "units," as they are called, in the U. S. National Park System. They stretch from the tiny Saint Croix Island International Historic Site which touches the Canadian border in northeastern Maine to the American Memorial Park on the island of Saipan in the Northern Mariana Islands, a United States Territory far out in the western Pacific Ocean. The largest of the national parks is 13.2 million-acre Wrangell-St. Elias in Alaska. The smallest is the Thaddeus Kosciuszko National Memorial, a .02-acre dot in Philadelphia.

Our "best idea" has also been adopted across the globe. At least ninety-eight countries now host national parks, sharing a common allegiance to the concept of nature conservation in an international arena otherwise filled with pronounced cultural and political differences. South and North Korea have national parks. African national parks are great tourist attractions (Kenya alone boasts thirty-four parks.) Belgium has three national parks, but is outdone by the four in Kazakhstan. Australia established the first of its 516 national parks in 1879. Canada followed with the first of its forty-two in 1892. Denmark claims the largest of all national parks, a 24 million-acre giant in northeast Greenland that is slowly revealing itself from beneath protective ice sheets forced into retreat by global warming.

Passion for areas of the National Park System in the United States has grown with each generation. Yosemite alone attracts millions of visitors each year, and many return again and again, making the park a vacation tradition. In part, the popularity of our national parks has resulted from the promise of spectacle and entertainment; that first awesome step to the rim of the Grand Canyon, the majestic sound and dance of Old Faithful Geyser, the striking desert brilliance of Bryce and Zion in southern Utah, the plunge of Yosemite Falls. In part, it has been due to an increased environmental awareness of our vanishing wilderness spaces and a desire to protect what remains. And it also stems from the profoundly democratic notion at the heart of the parks' existence; that the nation's natural and cultural treasures should belong to all of us. As Ansel Adams put it, "National parks represent those intangible values which cannot be turned directly to profit or material advantage." And yet this is also what makes our parks so vulnerable, as Adams also understood: "It requires integrity of vision and purpose," he warned, "to consider such impalpable qualities of the same effective level as material resources."

THREATS

These "material resources," in fact, continue to make our large national parks lightning rods for controversy and heated dispute, and are why parks like Yosemite and Yellowstone exist in a low-grade state of siege. Those who see the parks as an obstacle to private gain fervently insist that vast tracts of land under federal stewardship, especially in the western United States, should at least be "de-regulated" and at best be done away with entirely. The mantras are "wise use" and "multiple use," and they are employed by a variety of organizations and individuals to advance priorities for mining, logging, drilling, cattle grazing, and off-road motorized use on public lands, and, if possible, to reclaim great swaths of those lands for private ownership, preferably with few if any restrictions on "use." And there are those who value the national parks only for their profit-generating potential which often runs counter to their long-term survival. In 1988, in Reno, Nevada, a Multiple-Use Strategy Conference drew a cross-section of activists who supported various goals for reconfiguration of federal land management practices, including "opening all public lands, including wilderness and national parks, to mining and energy development" and "expanding national park concessions under the management of private firms with expertise in people-moving such as Walt Disney."

Although there is little likelihood that drill rigs will soon be arriving in Yosemite Valley or that a theme park will replace the natural scene, pressures to commercialize the park continue to be intense. Visitors bring their wallets and expectations of service—of food, lodging, souvenirs, camping supplies, books, maps, and clothing. They also respond to whatever opportunities are presented to them—to rent a horse, buy a martini, pay for tour and guide services, and generally enjoy a spectrum of resort-style offerings provided by privately operated commercial companies. Provision of these services is very much part of the ongoing development pressure on Yosemite. There is a constant push by commercial vendors for more profit centers and a constant resistance by park administrators and environmental advocates to further development.

Finally, the very popularity of the park becomes a threat to both its survival and its appeal. Looking at Yosemite Falls on a beautiful springtime day is the stuff of indelible memory. Looking at Yosemite Falls over the heads of several hundred other spectators is a bit less memorable. Spending an hour or more stalled in traffic on a valley road or turned away because the campgrounds are full is a memory of a different sort. Park stewards must balance demands for use against responsibilities for preservation in the face of both human foibles and considerable political mischief.

Visitors take their parks for granted, and they should be able to do so. They should be confident that they can bring to parks their own choices of how to share space and time in a naturally timeless place, to sit quietly and listen, to wander and observe, to test muscle against the landscape, to leave behind, even for a moment, the asphalt, cacophony, packaged entertainment, hurried steps, electronic gadgets, and organizational boxes of robust, demanding life in contemporary America. But visitors must also be alert for adversaries to our parks' survival, and be ready to rise in defense of them when they judge that a corporation or individual is too anxious to bend the park environment farther away from conservation and more toward cash registers or quirky ideological presumptions. To meet this objective it is important to recognize more fully the role of this country's national parks in providing quiet scenic recreational opportunities for its citizens as well as visitors from other countries, and not let these opportunities slip from our grasp.

PART OF A TEAM

At the forefront of this need are the professional park staff members themselves. They are on the front line, drawn to careers in captivating places, well informed of the details, and obligated to communicate as clearly and objectively as they can about the values they protect. This was certainly part of my mandate when I arrived at Yosemite. A new superintendent is usually afforded certain grace by the park staff to navigate existing management priorities, connect names to faces, and scramble to learn the details of his or her fresh responsibilities. I knew virtually no one on arrival at Yosemite except Assistant Superintendent Bill Burgen, who I had teamed with on a rescue operation while we were serving as park rangers in Yellowstone, and Bill Dingler, a park naturalist I worked with in Acadia National Park, Maine. Even more, I had briefly visited the park on only one previous occasion, to attend the wedding of my brother on the lawn at the Ahwahnee Hotel. In terms of knowing about the cultural and natural history of Yosemite, I was a raw novice, typical of management transfers within the NPS, and knew that I would have to scramble fast to learn.

The park staff was a characteristic slice of humanity, men and women of all persuasions, biases, and hopes working together under the influence of the responsibilities vested in them to guard and nurture Yosemite. My immediate colleagues who shared in the daily pace and surprises of my office were Assistant Superintendents Bill Burgen and John Byrne, both with excellent NPS credentials, and Karen (Donaldson) Blinn and Yvonne (Bustillos) Radanovich, experts in the art of administrative calmness.

The park administrative structure was divided into management categories that included visitor protection, maintenance, interpretation (a catch-all name for a variety of educational services), concessions management, personnel, and resource management. Each of these categories was further refined to include specialists in many fields; search-and-rescue experts, medical technicians, botanists and archeologists, librarians, law enforcement rangers, ranger-educators, warehouse supervisors, mechanics, heavy equipment operators, structural and forest fire fighters, research scientists, those who kept the water-driven power plant whirling 24-hours-per-day, 365-days a year; even jailers and a locksmith.

One of the staff members I would come to know and greatly admire was Walt Castle, a veteran of the Korean War, superb horseman, natural leader, and Yosemite's Animal Packer Foreman. He had first come to the park, saddle in hand, on the advice of an old-time cowboy who said, "if you think you're a packer, go to Yosemite." Castle won a job but abruptly received a leathery lesson from his new boss, Bob McGregor. When he asked McGregor, "What do you want me to do," McGregor gave Castle a steady look and said, "If I got to tell you what to do, I don't need you." The message was clear; saddle up, throw harnesses and pack saddles on the mules, and get out there and do the job. And take care of those animals! When McGregor retired several years later, Castle succeeded him.

Trail Crew Foreman Jim Snyder worked in the park's distant outback. His place of business was so remote that I heard about Snyder months before meeting him. Snyder was a student of park history and an ardent believer in the theory that people deserved wilderness, and wilderness deserved the best succor that human wisdom could provide. His dented hardhat and blossoming sideburns framed a very sharp intellect. His belief was that trails could be an avenue of fabulous personal experience for thousands of park visitors so long as the trails were safe, durable, and touched the wildscape ever so lightly. He disdained heavy machinery in favor of hand tools and fulcrums, and used dynamite like a surgeon. Snyder talked with his crewmembers about the "totality" of the park, suggesting that the entire ecosystem, including human visitors, past and present, should be understood as an interconnected whole—that preservation of Yosemite's values rested in a thorough understanding of its history, vulnerabilities, and purpose. His crews formed allegiances of lifetime staying power based on team-spirited hard work, visible on-the-ground results, and shared pride in rough country subsistence.

Laurel (Munson) Boyers was another staff member hard to track down. Like Snyder, she was doing her job in the enormous wilderness that reaches far out to the edges of the park, helping to blaze the way for equal status between women and men in what traditionally had been the male-dominate ranks of uniformed park rangers. Boyers was working with science and management colleagues in search of an ever-delicate balance between use and guardianship of Yosemite's natural charm. She had every right to claim her place in the stewardship of the park; she was born in Yosemite Valley, the daughter of parents who had been hired by the concessionaire to manage the old Glacier Point Hotel. Boyers had other career choices, but none that attracted her like her own backyard. In her spare time, she and park naturalist Ginger Burley would lead hiking groups into the backcountry, letting their "inner children play," as Burley put it. They gave the impression that, for them, freeze-dried food and a tent beside a glimmering mountain lake were far superior to a hamburger at the mall or dining on fine china.

Among the many others I came to know and appreciate, I referred to Jay Johnson as "Yosemite's Secretary of State." His Native American parents had come to the park during the Great Depression as employees of the concessionaire, recruited like others of their ethnic background to work at the lowest level jobs. They lived in "Indian Village," a cluster of small houses segregated from the larger community. Johnson was born in the valley in 1931, and, as Ah'wah'nee'chee children had done before him in an earlier century, he roamed the valley, playing and exploring. Boarding school in Nevada was his next destination. In the early twentieth century, many Native American kids from throughout the west were sent to such schools where they were expected to learn to better fit into American society. Johnson was a good student, but if social engineers of the era thought that they would suppress his heritage, they were mistaken. During this period he gained caring respect for his ancestors and their principles.

When Johnson finally returned to Yosemite after boarding school, and following his military service, he joined the forestry crew and advanced years later to become the park's Chief Forester. He also became a champion of Indian spiritual beliefs in the complex relationship between humans, their antecedents, other life forms, and the earth itself. He sought, and seeks still, the establishment of an Indian Cultural Center in Yosemite Valley and tribal recognition for the Southern Sierra Miwuk Nation. His was a selfless, determined leader who formed a strong alliance with Park Archaeologist Scott Carpenter to bring forward for better public awareness the fullness of Native American reverence for the land and customs of daily life.

Outside the government ranks, but in close partnership, was Henry Berrey, Executive Director of the nonprofit Yosemite Association. The Association was a small publishing house that provided a superb collection of park-related books, maps, and related materials for sale to park visitors. The Association's profits were spent primarily in support of research, museum curatorial needs, archaeological investigations and the arts at Yosemite, priorities that were usually beyond the reach of the park budget. Berrey, I learned, was a curmudgeon with a very big heart, a keen eye for talent, a low tolerance for imperfection, and absolute fidelity to Yosemite. He was matched in commitment by Rusty Rust, the postmaster, Jim Wurgler, the resident doctor, and Chuck Woessner, the dentist, three stalwarts of the Yosemite community who stood on the middle ground between a big government presence and an even more imposing concessionaire operation.

Ansel Adams and his wife, Virginia, no longer were fulltime residents in the park when I arrived. They had moved to Carmel on the California coast, but returned occasionally to Yosemite. On one of their visits soon after my arrival, they graciously invited me for a drink in the small living quarters they used behind the Ansel Adams Gallery. I had grown up in New Mexico, a locale especially appealing to Ansel's artistic impulses. It was there that he clicked the camera shutter on *Moonrise over Hernandez,* one of his most famous photographs (even though his son, Michael, happily claims to have set up the tripod and aimed the camera before Ansel did his part). So, we talked mostly about New Mexico. On another occasion, I happened to come upon Ansel strolling near his gallery on a bright autumn day. He invited me inside for a look at some of his amazing work and, in a gesture of easy camaraderie, offered to give me two small autographed photos of Yosemite scenes, a habit he had of sharing his skills with many of his park neighbors. I declined the gifts, explaining the conflict-of-interest that such gifts would impose between a Park Superintendent and concessionaire, reasoning that he readily accepted with a twinkly smile. I have been wondering ever since just how pleasant those photos would have looked hanging on my wall. Adams's connection to Yosemite and his creative work was profound. He claimed that, "I knew of my destiny when I first experienced Yosemite."

Across from my office, about 100 yards away, was the Yosemite Park & Curry Company executive office presided over by Ed Hardy. Hardy's staff was even larger than mine, posing not only the challenge of learning a great many more names and faces, but also signaling the obvious; that competition for Yosemite's destiny, measured by commercialism versus scenic gain, would be robust, as usual. Over decades at Yosemite, commercial activities had moved progressively from assorted mom-and-pop ventures to dominating corporate might. From a theoretical business perspective—all environmental concerns aside—Yosemite could be perforated with lucrative commercial enterprises, a kind of shotgun blast of commercialism in all the accessible scenic locations. Through the years people had tried everything from a hotel atop Half Dome to expansive chalet settlements in the backcountry. Over the decades the balance scale had shifted away from the shotgun approach to a more concentrated zeroing-in of profit-making facilities in the eastern end of Yosemite Valley, with outliers primarily at Wawona and Tuolumne Meadows. Hardy's responsibility was to maximize profit for his corporate em-

Oliver Lippincott at the controls of his Locomobile, Yosemite Valley, 1900

ployer; mine was to maximize preservation for my public employer; the balancing scale on which our conflicting agendas rested was unsteady.

The most compelling task when I arrived at Yosemite was to finish the work of my predecessor, Superintendent Les Arnberger, by completing a master plan for the park that would guide future management decisions for decades to come. Such a plan had been envisioned since the days of Muir and Olmsted, but never fully achieved. The idea of finally putting a plan on paper was to define rational stewardship guidelines that a strong majority of the public would favor. Throughout the park's history, various interest groups had claimed to speak for the "true owners of the park." The contentious line between development and preservation remained hot.

In what became the largest single instance of public involvement in planning in the history of the federal government, Arnberger and an NPS planning team, led by John Reynolds, had solicited opinions from thousands of people who visited Yosemite or were concerned about national parks in general. More than 65,000 people took time to fill out and submit their responses to a lengthy workbook about park purposes, promises, and threats. Arnberger and members of the planning team also traveled around the nation in the late 1970s, holding well-attended public hearings on the subject. The resultant public response was very clear: The foremost need at Yosemite was to preserve the natural environment. All other activities, commercial, administrative, and utilitarian, should be subordinate to this sterling purpose.

At the time, the Yosemite Park & Curry Company was a subsidiary of the Los Angeles-based Music Corporation of America. Company officials, sensing that future development initiatives in the park might be blocked as a result of the planning team findings, had also elicited feedback from 100,000 of its park customers, urging them to ask for and fill out the workbook and send it to the NPS planning team. Twenty-seven-thousand of the concessionaire customers contacted by MCA responded to the company's invitation, but the results did not suggest widespread support for increasing development.

As *Backpacker* magazine reported, "If MCA was looking for a wide diversity of opinion in support for expanding the 'level and extent' of facilities, such as replacing tent cabins with motel-type accommodations and permitting conventions to be held in the park, the plan backfired." Only 13% of the concessionaire-encouraged respondents favored motel units as a replacement for tent cabins; only 17% supported expansion of facilities. The numbers among general respondents were 7% for motels, 9% for expansion. A subset question to allow snowmobiles into the park was opposed by 75% on the concessionaire list, and 84% were in opposition on the general list. The idea of hosting conventions in Yosemite landed with an equally resounding thud.

The results of the NPS's questionnaire allowed Arnberger and Reynolds and his planning team colleagues to identify, in accordance with public expectations, five principal goals for Yosemite:

1. Reclaim priceless natural beauty.

2. Markedly reduce traffic congestion.

3. Allow natural processes to prevail.

4. Reduce crowding.

5. Promote visitor understanding and enjoyment.

These five goals, a total of twenty words, spoke volumes about the struggle to lift Yosemite to the highest level of conservation, a place where modern human enterprise and distinctive environmental values are truly matched in harmony. The document that followed, entitled *General Management Plan,* was a modest 81 pages in length, but it had been backed by public support at an unprecedented level. New to the job and with solid backing from NPS Director Bill Whelan, I felt empowered to get the plan finalized and approved so the NPS could begin working to make its goals a reality.

WHAT TO DO WITH THE CARS?

The General Management Plan (GMP), called for carefully targeted reductions in visitor accommodations and campsites "to avoid flood plain and geologic hazards." It also identified various administrative structures, employee houses, warehouses, offices, maintenance facilities, and an obsolete sewer plant to be removed entirely from the valley. The big elephant-in-the-tent, however, was what to do with automobiles. Visitation to Yosemite was increasing every year and had reached 2 million per annum. Yosemite park rangers, many of whom had chosen their profession for the appeal of living and working in natural settings, were increasingly finding themselves serving as traffic cops.

Puzzling out solutions to such bureaucratic problems on paper is one thing. Being on site is another. Soon after I assumed my new responsibilities, Chief Ranger Bill Wendt asked me to go for a walk with him to Taft Toe, a secluded glade tucked under the south rampart of the valley's big walls. With large Ponderosa pines guarding the periphery and a slight breeze audible in the tree canopy, the place offered a pleasing sense of shelter. Our walk had taken us not far from the main entry road into the valley, but the hum of traffic had already faded, and birdsong replaced the sound of tires on blacktop. Taft Toe undoubtedly had seen its share of livestock grazing in the pioneer days, but time and seclusion had healed old wounds. The softly sheltered glade at the foot of the powerful cliffs is just the kind of habitat that parks are established to protect.

"We're standing in a 500-car parking lot," Wendt said. The NPS planners, struggling with the vexing questions on how to reduce traffic congestion in Yosemite Valley, had singled out Taft Toe as a possible transportation hub due to its strategic location about midway between the east and west limits of the valley, across from El Capitan. The new parking lot would be a collection point for day visitors. They would park their cars, get oriented in the information kiosk to be built at the site, and climb aboard shuttle buses for the remainder of their excursions. Visitors with overnight reservations at concessionaire facilities or in the campgrounds would be allowed to motor on past Taft Toe and park in spaces at their assigned accommodations.

OLIVE AND OLIVER

Wendt and I also were standing in the avalanche of transportation history at Yosemite. Just two generations prior, during the lifetime of my grandfather, Olive Logan had decided to visit Yosemite in

     Your Yosemite: **PROTECTING A PUBLIC TREASURE**

1870, and she wrote about her experience in an article entitled *Does It Pay To Visit Yo Semite?*

Logan was an actress, author, and self-described "wandering easterner" who took it upon herself to warn unwary visitors about the rigors of the trip to Yosemite: "I think it not unwise to tell a plain unvarnished tale of what awaits the Yo Semite pilgrim; for of the dozens of persons who have written about Yo Semite, I have never known one who gave anything like an accurate description of the perils and tortures attendant upon the journey thither."

After arriving by train in San Francisco, Logan discovered that everyone she met was enthusiastic about her plan to see the famous park, but that none of them had yet made the expedition themselves. After reaching Stockton with relative ease, she was stuffed into a stagecoach with other passengers. On the dry summertime road she discovered that sixteen pounding hooves can stir a mighty cloud of dust: "I put my head gasping out the window to see the driver. He was gone: so were the horses. The crack of a whip was still heard, and some of the locomotive power was impelling us forward, but through the dust who should say what it was?"

When Logan could see, her view was of receding civilization, the detritus of the gold rush, and Chinese railroad laborers left to fend for themselves. She reports jouncing "past deserted mining towns with the dried-up sluices and ruined huts; past Chinese and Chinese and yet again Chinese, and after that Chinese gambling and Chinese mining and irrigating and planting." At one stop "a jolly little Italian and his wife and babies" squeezed in among the already crowded assemblage of passengers. "He was chatty and merry, smelt of onions and wore gold rings in his ears." The family stayed aboard the coach only for a few miles, getting off at their "little ranch running wild with luscious grapes."

By the end of the first fourteen-hour day in the stagecoach Logan complained, "you are coated with dust, your eyes are smarting, your tongue clogged, your hair caked, your limbs are sore, your flesh is inflamed, you want to go home!" She was informed that the coach would be on the road to the Yosemite trailhead the following morning by 4:00AM. On that memorable second day, the driver "went jolting over rocks, goading his horses down the hollows only to run up the opposite side at an insane gallop, sending the battered inmates to the roof where their heads are banged and beaten." Finally Ms. Logan and her fellow inmates arrived in mid-afternoon at the end of the stage road where mounts were saddled and waiting for them.

"At first the change to horses was pleasant; this was the theory; it was groundless." A cold mountain rain and approaching darkness did not bother the riders so much as did a pack mule that their guide, Ferguson, was driving ahead of the string of horses. "Every ten minutes or so, it runs off and has to be followed on the keen gallop by Ferguson—all our horses, being accustomed to drive mules, turn out and gallop after the offender, causing their weary riders to perform involuntary circus feats which bring tears to their eyes." At last a small log cabin came into view, the overnight stop. "All of us, men, women, and children, married and unmarried, friends and total strangers lie down in the one and only room and pass the night in blissful disregard of civilization and modesty."

Up at dawn and in the saddle once more, Logan and her intrepid companions did not arrive at Hutchings' hotel in Yosemite Valley until late in the day. Speaking for the females, she writes, "Hutchings lifts us off our horses—inert masses of what were once tolerably strong-minded and particularly strong-bodied women. Hutchings pours wine down our throats. He tells us we were all doing well, as most ladies faint." Logan's memories of the valley continue in this vein; the moment she almost stepped on a rattlesnake; the discovery of a tombstone in memory of a man who had been kicked to death by his horse and her dread of the return trip to San Francisco.

For better or worse, Logan's account made no discernible dent in the arrival of new settlers and tourists to the area, especially after the rail lines were extended through the Central Valley in 1871. Trail systems into the region were being upgraded into proper wagon roads, including a road championed by Park Commissioner George Coulter that reached all the way to Crane Flat near the north rim of Yosemite Valley, leaving only a short horse-trail plunge of about thirteen miles to Bridalveil Meadow. Road access to the valley was inevitable, awaiting only the funds necessary to stabilize the precariously narrow lane angling down steep slopes to the valley floor.

Meanwhile, Yosemite Valley was steadily becoming a mini-boomtown, with shacks and structures popping up everywhere. The forest cover was under assault to provide for building materials and firewood. These intrusions included piggeries, trash dumps, saloons, stores, a butcher shop and laundry, and were soon to be joined by a bakery, stables, studios, outhouses, irrigation ditches, bridges, horse trails, meadows fenced off for livestock, and, of course, hotels.

In 1900, Oliver Lippincott, also decided to visit Yosemite. He was a photography dealer from Los Angeles who decided to use his trip as a publicity stunt, arriving in Yosemite Valley in one of the first automobiles to ever reach that sequestered chasm. His vehicle of choice was a gasoline-and-steam-powered Locomobile that sported a two-cylinder, ten-horsepower engine. Lippincott was a man of exceedingly generous proportions, and the sight of this boxy contraption, with the 300-pound-Lippincott behind the wheel, was an arresting sight as it bumped along the stagecoach road from Wawona to the valley at a blinding speed, topping out at ten miles an hour. Lippincott had wisely brought along a mechanic, Edward Russell, to keep the burdened vehicle functioning, and they made the trip of about eighteen miles from Wawona in only three hours, approximately the pace of a good horse.

 Author and historian Hank Johnson reported in his book, *Ho For Yo-Semite*, that Lippincott had to be cautious about frightening the teams of harnessed horses and mules used for routine passenger and supply services. One wagon master, probably speaking for all of his colleagues, shouted, "What in hell do you want to bring such a nuisance up into this country for? You city people, with your contrivances, are always making trouble!" During his two-week stay, Lippincott took pleasure in his celebrity status by motoring around at all hours. "At night in the valley the mere sight of the Locomobile's two headlights and the sound of its shrill electric bell were sufficient to secure right-of-way over every other vehicle, for horses were willing to jump over the bank or climb a tree to make way for us," the plump driver reported.

Lippincott gave permission to Henry Washburn, one of the brother-owners of the Wawona Hotel and Yosemite Stage & Turnpike Company, to borrow the vehicle and mechanic for a side trip to Glacier Point along the wagon road built to that destination in 1882. The dealer and a group of spectators arrived first, via horse-drawn coach, in order to greet Washburn and Russell on their after-dark arrival. "Nothing would do the next morning," wrote Lippincott, "but that the Locomobile must go out on the overhanging rock where only the most fearless and level-headed have ever dared to stand." Washburn recruited several men, including a "stout" young man named Babe Burnett, destined to be the football captain for Stanford University, to maneuver the 650-pound automobile out onto the overhang using ropes, log treads, and muscle power.

Lippincott gleefully reported that the overhang was "fairly suspended above the valley—while below yawned an abyss of over 3,500-feet," and continued, "the Locomobile was inclined at such an angle that it seemed ready to roll over at any moment—Washburn and Burnett, both with ropes tied about their waists, were sure to go with it if it should start." With the vehicle in position, a chunk of wood was shoved under a rear tire to keep the car from rolling forward. Once an American flag and a pretty lady had also been placed in the frame, Lippincott climbed into the car and posed for a picture. Half Dome is visible in the distance.

After his adventure, Lippincott observed that "there are some advantages and some disadvantages connected with the propulsion of the machine amid the wilds of nature." How right he was. Standing in opposition to what would become a mechanized deluge of automobiles into Yosemite were the valley's stage coach and freight wagon operators who contended that their methods of transport were far superior and more dependable, a traditional service and livelihood that should be vigorously defended. Noisy, smelly, mechanically unreliable playthings for the well-to-do had no place in the mountains, they said.

For a short time the coachmen and freighters won, but the invasion of Yosemite Valley by automobiles was imminent, startling, and uncontrollable. Cars putt-putting here and there in the meadows, blatting and grinding up and down the roads caused animals-in-harness to prance, buck, and try to run away. In a momentary bow to old practices, motorized vehicles were banned in Yosemite Valley from 1907 to 1913, but, inevitably, horse drawn vehicles gave way to vehicles measured by engine horse power. In good ways and bad, this transformation would thoroughly change patterns of use and visitation in the national parks.

MY FINGERS ON THE TYPEWRITER

The 20-acre Taft Toe site where Wendt and I were standing was being offered as a victim to the avalanche of cars that started as a Locomobile pebble and now swept millions of visitors each year into the valley. The site was screened by guardian trees and, except when visitors were arriving or departing, would be largely out of sight and mind. The overall result seemed worthy, corralling hundreds of cars each day to reduce traffic congestion in favor of shuttle buses used for group transportation and sightseeing purposes. Wendt certainly knew the traffic problems in Yosemite Valley better than anyone and might be expected to support just about any solution to the quandary. Nevertheless, the chief ranger thought that the sacrifice of Taft Toe was a very bad idea. He was not willing to stand by without sounding an alarm.

At my desk several days after the Taft Toe visit, I let my "fingers do the talking" and wrote, "Yosemite now is at a crossroad. During a century of public custodianship of this great park many decisions have been made, all well intended, which have resulted in a march of manmade development in the valley. Today, the valley is congested with more than a thousand buildings—stores, homes, garages, apartments, lodging facilities, and restaurants—that are a reflection of our society. The valley floor is bisected by approximately thirty miles of roadway which now accommodate a million cars, trucks, and buses a year. But the foremost responsibility of the National Park Service is to perpetuate the natural splendor of Yosemite and its exceedingly special valley. The intent of the National Park Service is to remove all automobiles from Yosemite Valley and the Mariposa Grove and to redirect development to the periphery of the park and beyond. Similarly, the essence of wilderness, which so strongly complements the valley, will be preserved. The result will be that visitors can step into Yosemite and find nature uncluttered by piecemeal stumbling blocks of commercialism, machines, and fragments of suburbia. Implementation of this general management plan will be the first step in carrying out this intent and a distinct turning point in the management of the park."

I did not mention specifics in this preamble, but I had joined Wendt in opposing the Taft Toe option, and we were not alone. Even members of the planning team had grave reservations about the site. The dilemma was how to substitute public transportation for automobile warfare without urbanizing Yosemite Valley even more. For example, NPS Director Whalen's predecessor, Gary Everhardt, had favored the construction of a multilevel parking garage at the valley's western entrance, in Bridalveil Meadow. To convince Everhardt that this would be a disaster, Reynolds and his team developed an artist's rendering of what the parking lot would look like from the overlook at Inspiration Point (Tunnel View) where thousands of visitors are treated to their first memorable panorama of Yosemite Valley.

The director took one look at the photo and that was enough. The idea was dropped. Reynolds proved to be a discerning environmental ally on Taft Toe. Yosemite's Assistant Superintendent John Bryne, who worked closely with the team, was particularly persuasive. The Taft Toe concept was sidelined, hopefully to disappear entirely from future choices to be made about Yosemite Valley.

Another prospect for reducing traffic congestion was to establish a reservation system requiring visitors to plan ahead for entry into the valley during the popular summer months. The park was configured for this type of reservation system with entrance stations at each road access point. On the busiest days, only visitors with the necessary reservations could enter the valley. Those without reservations could visit less well known areas of the park—Wawona, the Mariposa Grove of Giant Sequoias, Glacier Point, and Tuolumne Meadows—or simply cross through the park on the Tioga Road. Many veteran visitors to Yosemite make this choice voluntarily, bypassing the valley crowds during the high travel season in favor of less pressure-packed destinations in the park. The road system cooperates nicely, allowing easy choices of route and scene.

Unfortunately, automobiles are considered the lifeblood of commerce at Yosemite. The idea was met with a pronounced lack of enthusiasm when brought up in informal discussion with concessionaires and their counterpart vendors in the nearby gateway communities. There was, though, a different reason for hope. The GMP pointed toward the need for accommodating more visitors and park personnel in the surrounding gateway communities with fewer in the park itself. This would mean both a reduction of commercial, logistical, and housing pressure in Yosemite Valley and a gain for local businesses, school programs, real estate values, and neighborhood growth outside the park.

Residents of the gateway communities did not need an NPS General Management Plan to remind them of the obvious connection between their towns and the big Yosemite trade engine. Many entrepreneurs were already grasping this opportunity. A reduction in development in the park, as called for in the GMP, would reinforce this transition. Perhaps a reduction in automobile congestion in favor of modern, attractive public transit from gateways to waterfalls could follow.

Thomas Ayers

     Your Yosemite: **PROTECTING A PUBLIC TREASURE**

5

The Genesis of
The Struggle

TO KEEP IN PERSPECTIVE the need to plan with great care for the future stewardship of Yosemite, a careful look back in history is required. Too often a new decision-maker will launch forward without looking back along the pathway that brought him or her to a point of judgment in the first place. This is a risk for any new superintendent. I certainly was so inclined, wanting to prove to Director Bill Whelan that he had not made a mistake, hoping to gain quick acceptance among my staff peers, and eager to demonstrate to Ed Hardy, who already had been in his post for six years, that I was a contender. Like so many who visit Yosemite, or know of it, my impression of park history started and stopped with the legendary John Muir. I had much more to learn.

Almost as soon as Native Americans were forced from Yosemite Valley in the heartrending Mariposa Indian War, the tug-of-war for its commercial promise began. Among the vanguard of adventurers who struggled into the valley along dim trails were tourists, journalists, homesteaders, visionaries, and entrepreneurs. James Mason Hutchings (1820–1902) would prove to be all five.

Twenty-nine-year-old Hutchings arrived in New York from England in 1848 and then, like so many young men, struck out on an overland course that took him first to New Orleans and then, on hearing of the gold strike in California, caused him to join the rush into the state in 1849. After losing most of his money in a failed banking venture, Hutchings decided to pursue his habit of writing about his western adventures. He had heard about the discovery of Yosemite Valley, at the time more rumor than fact, and decided to go see for himself. In 1855, after returning from a horseback trip to Oregon territory, Hutchings was guided into Yosemite Valley by two Miwuk men and accompanied by Walter Millard, Alexander Stair, and Thomas Ayers. Ayers, an amateur artist with a knack for sketching landscapes, had been recruited especially for the trek by Hutchings.

Hutchings and his small party was only the second group of tourists to enter the valley. A group led by Robert B. Lamon made the journey the previous summer, but brought back no written or pictorial record of what they had seen. Hutchings was determined to document his findings. He astutely included Ayers to guarantee that anything he asserted in writing about this supposed mountain Shangri-La would be supported by illustrations. Ayers would be the first of many artists to attempt to capture the essence of Yosemite.

The five days Hutchings spent there on this first investigation changed his life. He immediately wrote an article about his trip for the *Mariposa Gazette*, the nearby boomtown newspaper founded in 1854. Then, once he was back in San Francisco, Hutchings put his efforts seriously into publishing and in 1856 began marketing *Hutchings' Illustrated California Magazine*. The lead article in the first edition was titled *The Yo-Ham-I-Te Valley and Its Waterfalls*. "Yonder a water-fall of two-thousand-five-hundred feet; as it rolls over the edge of the precipice, its quivering spray is gilded with the colors of the rainbow." He referred to the "Giant's Tower," (El Capitan), the "Cascade of Rainbows," (Bridalveil Fall), and the "Twin Domes, (Half Dome and North Dome).

Ayers' fine sketches accompanied the article and in due course newspapers and magazines in Boston and New York City started picking up the story. The message was that the Wild West was filled with exciting and gloriously untamed places that were just waiting for sightseers, especially for those who could afford the cost and time and were daring enough to try. Hutchings is quoted in Dr. Jen A. Huntley's book, *The Making of Yosemite, James Mason Hutchings and the Origin of America's Most Popular National Park*, as saying: "the Yo Semite, at the time, was as a sealed book to the general public, … it was our good fortune to be instrumental in opening its sublime pages to the public eye, that it might be known and read by all men."

Sadly, Thomas Ayers' contribution to this opening would be brief. He returned to Yosemite Valley in 1856 to sketch more scenes and

     Your Yosemite: **PROTECTING A PUBLIC TREASURE**

was subsequently invited to exhibit his artistic work in New York City. Returning west again after the exhibit, he was on a passenger ship in 1858 bound from southern California to San Francisco when tragedy struck. The ship floundered and sank in roiled seas; there were no survivors.

HORACE GREELEY ON HORSEBACK

One of those inspired by these reports was the redoubtable Horace Greeley (1811–1872), publisher of the *New York Tribune*, who in 1859 decided to make the journey out west and write about his experiences. Yosemite Valley was his primary destination. The 49-year-old Greeley was rotund, bald, patrician, and near-sighted, but he was also intrepid.

In mid-August, Greeley reached Stockton, California, a city of about fifteen thousand people. From Stockton, he endured a long carriage ride to Bear Valley, site of the John C. Frémont ranch. (Three years before, Frémont had been the first candidate for President of the United States of the newly formed Republican Party, losing to James Buchanan. Greeley was an early champion of the party). After a short visit, Greeley said farewell to his host and, transported by wagon, headed for Yosemite Valley. By noon, at the end of a wagon road twelve miles beyond Mariposa, Greeley, accompanied by a fellow adventurer and two locally recruited guides, reached the trailhead to Yosemite and traded the luxury of the jolting wooden wagon seat for saddle horses.

Greeley and his crew were roughly following the path taken by the Mariposa Battalion up into the foothills and reported that "we rose along the southern face of the ridge overlooking the Chowchilla Valley until we seemed to have half California spread out before us like a map." Greeley could see Tule Lake far away in the southern basin of the Central Valley and, on the western horizon, the Coastal Range that rimmed the Pacific Ocean. Beyond the ridgeline to the east, Greeley reported that "on this side the descent is far steeper, and we traversed for miles a mere trace along the side of the mountains where a misstep must have landed us at least a thousand feet below." Eventually, the party "bade adieu to daylight at Grizzly Flat, a spot noted for encounters with the monarch [nearby Giant Sequoias] of our American forests."

Greeley was very favorably impressed by the landscape as he approached Yosemite. "The Sierra Nevada lack the glorious glaciers, the frequent rains, the rich verdure, the abundant cataracts of the Alps," he admitted, "but they far surpass them—they surpass any other mountains I ever saw—in the wealth and grace of their trees. Look down from almost any of their peaks and your range of vision is filled, bounded, satisfied, by what might be termed a tempest-tossed sea of evergreens, filling every upland valley, covering every hillside, crowning every peak but the highest with their unfading luxuriance."

There was some discussion among the riders about making nighttime camp, but Greeley insisted that he had to reach Yosemite Valley, spend the following day investigating, and then press on to the next stop on his extensive itinerary. The men descended the precipitous trail into the valley by moonlight. By the time the riders reached the valley floor, they still had several miles to go to reach their destination, a rustic log cabin built by James Lamon, the brother of Yosemite's first tourist explorer. "How many times our heavy eyes were lighted up by visions of that intensely desired cabin," Greeley said on their arrival at 1:00am. Lamon, the "astonished landlord," was one of Yosemite's first homesteaders. As well as constructing the cabin and planting an orchard and garden, he had appropriated 160 acres of the valley floor, his land claim bolstered by his bold initiative and hard labor. Many like him would follow, but on the night of Greeley's visit, Lamon's home was one of only two shelters in the entire valley. "To my dying day I shall remember that weary, interminable ride," Greeley wrote. "We had been on foot since daylight; it was now past midnight; all were nearly used up, and I in torture from over twelve hours' steady riding on the hardest trotting horse in America."

The next morning, however, Greeley was up and exploring the valley. He was not without his criticisms, pronouncing Yosemite Falls a "humbug" due to the August dribble that paled in comparison with the falls' lively springtime runoff, and complained about "all the

     Your Yosemite: **PROTECTING A PUBLIC TREASURE**

foolish names which foolish people have given to different peaks and turrets." In all, though, Greeley felt that the valley more than lived up to its reputation. He proclaimed it "the most unique and majestic of nature's marvels," concluding, "I know of no single wonder of nature on earth which can claim superiority over the Yosemite."

Greeley foreshadowed the complicated role that the media would play in the future of Yosemite and so many other natural wonders around the world. A nationally known newspaperman and reformer who would eventually run for president, Greeley commanded a huge reading audience. By urging people to visit Yosemite he was to some extent hastening the region's transformation from secluded mountain shelter to tourism target. At the same time his declaration of landscape values, echoing the messages of James Hutchings, helped begin to change people's perspective from the dismissive nineteenth-century attitude of pathfinders like John Savage. Greeley championed a more appreciative assessment of natural splendor, urging readers to think beyond exploitation and to seek out the land's intrinsic riches, rewarding themselves with moments and memories of sheer elation in the galleries of nature's best works. He found for himself just such a place in the Sierra Nevada and pronounced Yosemite Valley to be not merely a local geological curiosity, but a scenic treasure of national stature well worth protecting for the ages. Greeley's message would resonate, particularly, along the eastern seaboard, its residents already feeling the pinch of crowding and the constraints of urban and industrial barricades that walled them off from the land.

Meanwhile, James Hutchings had not forgotten his earlier encounter with Yosemite. After his publishing initiative floundered, he and his wife, Gertrude, established their own presence in the valley in 1863 by purchasing a rude two-story frame hotel from another pioneering speculator, Gustavus Hite, and claiming a 160-acre parcel of land near the base of Yosemite Falls. In essence, Hutchings was gambling what was left of his capital and credit on tourism in one of the most isolated sightseeing destinations in the nation, hoping that Greeley's promotional article would be followed by many more like it.

Hutchings' timing was favorable. Despite the traumas of the Civil War, politicians and tycoons were thinking ahead to the day when California could be firmly tied to east coast business enterprises. There seemed to be no end in sight to the cycle of speculation, settlement, and opportunity that had been sparked by the gold rush.

IT PAYS TO ADVERTISE

In his effort to attract visitors to Yosemite, Hutchings found an unlikely ally in the person of a frail Unitarian minister from New York named Thomas Starr King (1824–1864). King had arrived in San Francisco in 1860 at age 36 to assume his duties at the First Unitarian Church, having already established a reputation in New England for his oratorical skills and his love of natural grandeur, a passion he had articulated in a popular book entitled *The White Hills, their Legends, Landscapes, and Poetry*. Just over five feet tall, King made up for his small size with a "golden" voice that enraptured audiences throughout the California towns and camps he visited. An ardent supporter of the Union and Abraham Lincoln's bid to be President, King was an equally fervent opponent of slavery.

His arrival in California came none too soon. State residents were torn between casting their lot with secessionist states or keeping faith with the Union. In addition to his anti-slavery stance, King argued at many citizen gatherings for a strong federal government that would bring economic benefit to California farmers and, in commerce, take full advantage of California's strategic business location on the Pacific Coast. The nationwide vote in 1860 that put Lincoln in the White House included a crucial affirmative margin in California of 711 votes. King was dubbed the "orator who saved the nation."

King's zeal for his country's governance was matched by his enthusiasm for its natural landscapes. Soon after his arrival he joined the intrepid few who had found their way to Yosemite, and began sending dispatches to the *Boston Evening Transcript*, describing his findings. "I have visited the Big Trees of Mariposa and have descended into the jaws of the Yo-Semite," he reported. "Great is granite and Yosemite is the prophet." Historian Arliss Ungar, in *Nature Writings*, quotes

Yosemite Valley Night Scene by Albert Bierstadt, 1864

King as saying about his hike from the valley up toward the base of Half Dome: "The first great reward in this notch is the fall of Pi-wy-ack, abused by the Yankees with the name, Vernal, and which it is said the true Indian title means shower of sparkling crystals. A tide sixty-feet broad, it purrs here some three-hundred-feet over the perpendicular." King's time in California was brief, only four years. He died of diphtheria before the war's end, but left his mark politically and in journalistic joy for natural beauty. Four geographic sites are named in his honor: a lake, meadow, and dome in Yosemite, and a mountain in New Hampshire.

Such tantalizing reports as King's were reinforced in 1862 when Carlton Watkins (1829–1916), a student of the new technology of photography, visited and made the first black-and-white images of Yosemite Valley with his cumbersome box camera. His photos, later sold at Groupil's Art Gallery in New York City, added to the mystique of Yosemite among many eastern seaboard residents. The following year, Alfred Bierstadt, the renowned Hudson River School artist, made his initial visit to the Sierra Nevada in 1864, spending seven weeks making sketches and drawings, primarily in Yosemite Valley. His extravagant use of gossamer light juxtaposed against deep shadow and his habit of expanding natural scenes into visionary landscapes earned Bierstadt high praise and lucrative sales. King, Watkins, and Bierstadt were delivering a powerful message, making an early and influential connection between the arts and places of great picturesque quality that, unknown to them at the time, would become national parks. The aesthetic association that captivated the attention of many of their equally talented peers of the era would grow and span the generations.

Although picture and word images being produced by artists, photographers, and journalists were not enough to assure the financial survival of the handful of entrepreneurs in Yosemite Valley, America's industrial revolution was rapidly changing the face of the country after the Civil War, as King had predicted, and would surely impact them. The strategic initiatives to build railroads, strengthen shipping, and expand the national footprint with new communities, farms, and businesses were pulling Yosemite ever closer to a reckoning with the outside world. Advocates for the Central Pacific and Union Railroads rightly guessed that, once a steel track spanned the nation, tourists would clamber aboard trains to confirm for themselves the dazzling reputation of the Wild West.

A CONSERVATION CHAMPION STEPS FORWARD

Captain Israel Ward Raymond (1811–1887) followed in the footsteps of Hutchings, Greeley, and King, and came away convinced of the magnetism of what he had seen. But Raymond did not have to wait for the railroads to profit from Yosemite's growing popularity. His company was operating at least twenty-three steamships, including one named the *Mariposa*, on the long, circuitous route between the east coast ports and San Francisco. A successful businessman with New York roots and a determination to thrive in California's new markets, Raymond was an executive of the newly formed Central American Steamship Line, a maritime enterprise that hoped to benefit from tourist trade. He was first-and-foremost trying to make a profit for his company, but at Yosemite he embraced an equally compelling priority: to try to be gentle in the conduct of business in this vulnerable place.

Raymond was particularly impressed with the tree-adorned valley floor, but he worried that most of the trees would soon be cut for building materials and firewood in order to clear the way for gardens and livestock grazing. The historian Dr. Alfred Runte, in his important book, *Yosemite: The Embattled Wilderness*, reports that Raymond was well aware of the "Shame of Niagara," a popular phrase of the era that referred to the unbridled commercialism that had so damaged the American side of the celebrated waterfalls. Sir Richard Bonnycastle, a British visitor, dryly observed after visiting the falls in 1849 that, "it requires little to show that patriotism, taste, and self-esteem are not the leading features in the character of the inhabitants of this part of the world."

On his return to San Francisco from his visit to Yosemite, Raymond promptly sought out John Conness (1821–1909), a gold-rush veteran who had recently been appointed by the California Legislature to the United States Senate and subsequently gained favor with President Lincoln as a straight-talking, down-to-earth politician. Raymond convinced the senator to introduce a bill into the U. S. Congress that would "let the wonders of Yosemite be inalienable forever."

Raymond's choice of the powerful word "inalienable," which evoked the language of the Constitution, signaled his belief that protection of Yosemite Valley and the Mariposa Grove of Giant Sequoias was of profound legal and moral importance. On the other hand, the written congressional testimony suggests that Senator Conness was somewhat underwhelmed. He said of the legislation to his colleagues, "this bill proposes to make a grant of certain premises located in the Sierra Nevada Mountains, in the State of California, that are for all public purposes worthless, but which constitute, perhaps, some of the greatest wonders of the world." Ironically, it was probably the presumed "worthlessness" of the territory that made Raymond's efforts to protect it prevail.

In June 1864, as Federal troops were laying siege to Richmond, Virginia, a disparate collection of bills reached President Lincoln's desk. The Congress had authorized funding for the construction of two floating batteries that were intended to pulverize Confederate coastal defenses. It had also overturned the draconian Fugitive Slave Act of 1850, and settled by treaty various agricultural disputes with Great Britain in the regions of Hudson Bay and the Puget Sound. Perhaps most surprising, without controversy or serious debate, the Congress had approved legislation that allowed for a grant of federal lands to the State of California comprised of Yosemite Valley and the Mariposa Grove of Giant Sequoias. The legislators directed, moreover, that these lands be held "for public use, resort, and recreation," and that they be "inalienable for all time." On June 30, 1864, the president signed the legislation into law.

OLMSTED

Another improbable figure in this chapter of the region's history was Frederick Law Olmsted (1822–1903), the landscape architect best known for designing and supervising the creation of New York City's Central Park with Calvert Vaux. In 1863, though, the forty-one-year-old Olmsted was nowhere near New York City. Like so many others, he was trying to make a living by following the money to California. He found his way to the ranch in Bear Valley formerly owned by John C. Frémont who had sold out in the same year, 1863, and was far away, serving as a Major-General in the Civil War. The new owners, primarily interested in further development of the gold mines on the property, hired Olmsted as their manager, an atypical job for the landscape architect but one that he performed from 1863 to 1865.

When California Governor Frederick G. Lowe appointed a board of park commissioners to manage the nearby Yosemite grant, Olmsted, who was championed by Raymond, stood at the head of the list. The other appointees, representing a wide range of viewpoints, were State Geologist Josiah Whitney; William Ashburner, who worked with Whitney on a geological survey of California; E. S. Holden, a railroad promoter; Alexander Deering, an attorney; George W. Coulter, one of the lucky few who'd struck gold; and Yosemite homesteader Galen Clark. Governor Lowe served as a ninth ex-officio member.

According to historian Charles E. Beveridge, Olmsted was at first not particularly impressed with the Yosemite scenery, but he gradually fell under its spell as he became more accustomed to the region's aridity and stark beauty that were very unlike the rolling hills and damp hardwood forests of his home turf. Rising quickly to the task, one of Olmsted's first actions as commissioner was to hire geologists Clarence King and James Gardner to draw an accurate survey of the Yosemite Grant, judging that good stewardship required precise knowledge of the resource. Olmsted predicted that Yosemite might become the "far noblest park or pleasuring ground in the world," but worried about its vulnerability, cautioning that it could not be seen simply as a collection of spectacular cliffs and waterfalls, but needed to be understood as a balanced and harmonious whole.

Despite the isolation of Yosemite, Olmsted foresaw an attraction that ultimately would trigger millions of visits. In a prescient statement that haunts park managers to this day, he wrote, "An injury to the scenery so slight that it may be unheeded by any visitor now, will be one of deplorable magnitude when its effect upon each visitor's enjoyment is multiplied by these millions." True to his experiences as a landscape designer, Olmsted argued for careful and aesthetically thoughtful development, suggesting, for example, the judicious placement of a carriage lane that would allow visitors to see the Valley's sights without trampling the meadows. At the time, however, he was shouting into the wind. His fellow Commissioners and many others who agreed with the park's potential to attract tourists were strongly aligned on the side of speedy development and therefore deaf to Olmsted's plea. Charles Beveridge contends that Olmsted's thinking on regional landscape design was refined by his experience at Yosemite, which ended with his resignation from the Commission in 1865 to return to New York, and would guide much of his future work, but his Yosemite report would languish, almost forgotten, for many years.

A PARK GUARDIAN

The member of the commission with the most intimate knowledge of the Yosemite country was Galen Clark (1814 –1910). He is credited with being the first confirmed Anglo visitor to the Mariposa Grove of Giant Sequoias, an accidental triumph that resulted from his fight to rid himself of tuberculosis. In 1853, when Clark found his way into the Sierra Nevada Mountains, doctors had given him little hope of surviving his illness for more than a few months. He settled in at his "ranch" in Wawona in 1857 and began welcoming the early visitors on their way to Yosemite Valley. One such visitor described Clark as "handsome, thoughtful, interesting, and slovenly."

Protecting the giant trees became Clark's life project. He worked with Raymond and others to guard the Sequoias from the ax and to assure that these forest behemoths were included in the Yosemite Grant. Soon after the commission convened, Clark was proclaimed "guardian of the grant." In essence, this solitary mountain man became Yosemite's first park ranger, and what he sacrificed to this endeavor in terms of financial earnings he gained in years lived, surviving until the age of ninety-six.

One of the first challenges for the Yosemite Commissioners was to dispute the land claims of Lamon, Hutchings, and two other petitioners who were attempting to claim homesteading rights on the floor of Yosemite Valley. The cloistered Lamon seemed content to tend to his orchard and garden and deal with visitors only when they sought him out. By this time he had extended his legal claim to include an additional 218 acres. Hutchings was less ambitious in terms of acreage, but much more determined to tap into the tourist trade. He had laid claim to one of the most desirable locations in the valley near Yosemite Falls, an excellent spot for welcoming saddle-sore visitors. Neither man had paid anything for his land. The commissioners contended that Hutchings and Lamon had no legal right to territory owned by the public-at-large and pronounced the two men to be squatters. Meanwhile, as Hutchings had predicted, the tourists kept coming, and his rickety Upper Hotel (renamed the Hutchings House) began to expand. In 1866, Hutchings built an addition called Cedar Lodge, which included the Big Tree Room, particularly memorable to visitors because of a cedar tree eight feet in circumference where it emerged from the lobby floor. The living tree exited through the roof, soaring 175 feet above the lodge.

The steamship executive Israel Raymond worked hard to reach a compromise with Hutchings, agreeing that providing accommodation for visitors to Yosemite was essential. Mindful of the importance of tourism, the commissioners offered 10-year permits to Hutchings and Lamon in recognition of their pioneering presence in the valley. Both men declined and readied themselves for a protracted contest of wills, with Hutchings leading the way.

YOSEMITE PROPHET JOHN MUIR

In 1869, with the Hutchings/Lamon controversy still unresolved, the thrilling promise of cross-country rail travel became a reality, thanks to the golden spike that connected the Central Pacific and Union Pacific Railroads. Raymond and his steamship enterprise would suffer the consequences. For many Americans, the chance to race across the continent in a matter of days was irresistible and became the obvious mode of preferred travel. In less than two decades, Yosemite had gone from being a hidden valley to a reachable tourist destination.

In anticipation of the increase in tourists that would accompany stagecoach access, James Hutchings and others had been expanding their hotel facilities. Since he and his pioneering neighbors would need building materials, Hutchings concluded that a sawmill would be a practical investment. In 1869 he hired a thirty-one-year-old odd-jobber named John Muir (1838–1914) to construct and operate the mill.

Muir, born in Scotland but raised in Wisconsin, was a prodigious wanderer and explorer of his own inventive ideas, some practical, most philosophical. Before coming west he had already rambled on foot for hundreds of miles, as far north as Canada and southward through the eastern hardwood forests from Indiana all the way to Florida. He had intended to travel on to South America, but after a bout of malaria he decided to explore California instead.

He brought with him an intellectual curiosity sharply honed during his years as a student at the University of Wisconsin. At age twenty-two, and largely self-taught, he had taken some of his practical inventions to the 1860 Wisconsin Agricultural Society Fair. There, he met Jeanne Carr, wife of Professor Ezra Carr. Mrs. Carr, an amateur botanist, was immensely impressed with Muir, subsequently describing him as a "genius," and she and her husband became his mentors during his four years as an off-again, on-again student at the university. Muir held equally high regard and affection for Jeanne Carr and proclaimed her to be his "spiritual mother."

Mrs. Carr would stay in contact with Muir the rest of her life, often exchanging correspondence with him after he left the university and eventually catching up with him when her husband received an appointment in 1869 as the first agricultural professor at the newly established University of California, Berkeley. This proximity to her cherished student-wanderer would give Mrs. Carr an opportunity to introduce Muir to many members in the budding academic society of the San Francisco Bay Area, and, eventually and happily, to act as matchmaker for him.

A year before the Carrs moved west, Muir had arrived in San Francisco after a forty-three-day voyage around Cape Horn. He paid little attention to the city of gold rush fame, instead setting out almost immediately on horseback and foot to investigate the places that, by repute, had stirred his restless interest—Yosemite Valley and the Mariposa Grove of Giant Sequoias. Muir fell in love with the High Sierra instantly, and cast about for some job that could keep him there.

By this time, his experiences were many and varied. He'd labored in a factory that produced broom handles and rakes and in a carriage

          Your Yosemite: **PROTECTING A PUBLIC TREASURE**

factory where he almost lost his eyesight in a job-related accident. He tinkered with his various inventions and learned to be a capable sketch artist and bird-watcher. He trained horses, operated a ferryboat, and of course rambled before picking up a job in the High Sierra herding sheep.

Sheepherding and running a sawmill seem at odds with the image we have of Muir today, but at age thirty-one, riveted by the High Sierra and almost penniless, he needed money to live in the valley year round. Muir toyed with the idea of becoming a doctor before realizing that his true interests were in botany and geology. The Yosemite wilderness would prove to be an excellent instructor. Gaunt, bearded, and blue-eyed, Muir became part Pied Piper and part prophet, eager to share his knowledge of the region. He became passionate about rallying others to the concept of maximum protection for the natural resources he was discovering.

The association between Hutchings and Muir is a fascinating moment in the history of Yosemite—one man trying his best to fence in and claim a favored slice of the valley for his private purposes while the other was drawn to a personal crusade to prevent exploitive human practices. Although Muir and Hutchings would continue to cross paths for years to come, their professional association lasted less than two years and ended in acrimony (matters perhaps exacerbated by a flirtation between Hutchings's lonely wife and Muir). Hutchings fired Muir and took control of the small cabin Muir had lived in, turning it into a tourist accommodation. Muir, who had begun taking visitors on nature walks in Yosemite Valley, again took up the wandering life and began to write articles advocating wilderness preservation in the High Sierra.

"Here," he wrote, "with bread and water I should be content. Even if not allowed to roam and climb, tethered to a stake or a tree in some meadow or grove, even then I should be content forever. Bathed in such beauty, watching the expressions ever varying in the faces of the mountains, watching the stars, which have glory that the lowlander never dreams of, watching the circling of the seasons, listening to the songs of the waters and winds and birds, would be endless pleasure. And what glorious cloudlands I should see, storms

and calms, a new haven and a new earth every day, aye, and new inhabitants—I feel sure I should not have one dull moment. And why
should this appear extravagant? It is only common sense, a sign of
health, genuine, natural, all-awake health."

FIGHTING FOR OWNERSHIP

Meanwhile, Hutchings's and Lamon's appeal for ownership title
to land in the valley wound its way through the courts, eventually
reaching the U.S. Supreme Court. In 1872, two years before the first
road was forced through the mountains into the valley, the claims,
by unanimous consensus of the Supreme Court Justices, were denied. The case, *Hutchings v. Low* (82 U. S. 77), reinforced an earlier
court finding in *Frisbee v. Whitney* that federal lands could not be
claimed by states or individuals unless so ratified by Congress. Justice Stephen J. Field wrote the opinion, stating that in the cases of
Hutchings and Lamon "no such ratification has ever been made,
and it is not believed that Congress will ever sanction such a per-
version of the trust solemnly accepted by the State (of California)."
An important precedent was strengthened that, in decades to come,
would serve to protect federal lands from illegal piracy. Hutchings
was reduced from presiding as presumptive landowner of 160 acres
of some of the most prized scenic real estate on earth to being a
tenant functioning under permit at the pleasure of the Board of
Park Commissioners. But this stalwart trailblazer was not left empty handed. He was compensated by the State of California for the
structures and bridges he had constructed, receiving $24,000 and
the right to continue to operate his hotel as a public benefit, a decision that set the stage for concessionaire services in national parks
that continue to this day. His neighbor, Lamon, and the two other
claimants in the suit were similarly rewarded.

Hutchings's fight to claim ownership of land in the Yosemite grant
was a close contest. Had he prevailed, the budding concept of national parks may have suffered a quick demise, even though he intended
no such result. Nonetheless, his attempt was not lost on those paying
attention. Horace Greeley's *New York Tribune* was editorially aghast at
the politicians and judges who sided with Hutchings and Lamon.

"Certainly, we do not think we make too large a claim when we ask of Congress, in the name of the whole country and of the world of civilized men, to refuse this petition," said the editors, adding in blunt terms: "Barbarian or half-civilized States do not so respect great natural wonders, nor propose to devote them to the enjoyment of the world. If Californians do not see their own interests more clearly, and if they will not respect the rights of the whole country, it is the bounden duty of Congress to protect us in the possession of this most splendid of Nature's gifts. . . ."

Taking the opposite view, a committee report in the House of Representatives suggested that "as regards the question of a plea-sure-ground, it only concerns the comparative few who will have the means and leisure to visit the valley, and these could see and enjoy quite as much if its thousands of acres were carved up into smiling homesteads whose owners would probably guard the valley as carefully as any official appointed by the State."

This battle line, public custodianship of parks versus private sover-eignty, was drawn in Yosemite Valley and still stands as a point of conflict whenever the need to preserve natural ecosystems is de-bated. In this debate the word "environmentalist," once a respected term, has been used by many to marginalize or stigmatize those still defined in Webster's Dictionary as "devoted to protecting the ecological balance on earth."

Hutchings took his stand in Yosemite and lost. At the very moment he was so engaged, another momentous political event was taking place far from Yosemite in Yellowstone country.

In 1872, legislation to establish Yellowstone as a public park moved through the Congress without undue controversy except for a brief debate about the scale of the project, over two million acres to be set aside for preservation and public use. Yellowstone was extremely remote and buried in deep snow for a good part of the year. Most members of Congress who cast their votes in the affirmative viewed it as a curiosity that might someday draw a few intrepid visitors and assumed that, like Yosemite, it was of no apparent commercial val-ue. President Ulysses S. Grant signed the legislation into law.

In response to the ongoing controversy at Yosemite, the legislation allowed for ten-year permits to develop tourist accommodations within Yellowstone, but also made clear that none of the land could be claimed for private purpose. No state existed in the Wyoming and Montana Territories, so administrative authority was vested in the Secretary of the Interior. Yellowstone thereby became the nation's first federally established national park.

Hutchings had lost his land bid at Yosemite in the same year that Yellowstone National Park was established, but he continued to push aggressively for what he judged to be privileges of rank that just about any person who broke new ground in the wilderness might assume. This sentiment reflected the spirit of the Wild West where possession, legal or otherwise, was considered nine-tenths of the law, at least by those who got there first. At the same time, the Board of Park Commissioners was faced with the demands of a growing number of frontier entrepreneurs who wanted a piece of the commercial action in Yosemite Valley. Hutchings continued to maintain a kind of fortress posture on his non-owned 160 acres, until the commissioners finally had enough and evicted him from the valley in 1875. After his eviction, Hutchings did not venture far from the park, becoming an innkeeper in the nearby foothills. In 1902, on a trip into the valley, his horse became frightened, reared, and stampeded in panic; the ninety-two-year-old Hutchings was thrown from his buggy and killed. He is buried in the pioneer cemetery in Yosemite Valley.

By 1875 several hotels and related businesses were operating in Yosemite, including the Cosmopolitan Hotel operated by C. E. Smith, which was known for its saloon, billiard hall, and baths. Among the drinks served in the saloon were "Sampson with the hair on," "rattlesnakes," and "corpse-revivers." Road access had improved and tourists were arriving in ever larger numbers. A guest register maintained at the valley's Cosmopolitan Saloon and Bathhouse between 1873 and 1884 contains the signatures of more than 18,000 visitors, including those of Ulysses S. Grant, Rutherford B. Hayes, James Garfield, Rudyard Kipling, William (Buffalo Bill) Cody, Lillie Langtry, and William Randolph Hearst. The register was not available in

1871 when Ralph Waldo Emerson spent time there with John Muir. Emerson later said that Yosemite "was the only spot I ever found that came up to the brag."

Other parts of the park remained difficult to visit, reachable only by challenging trails, if trails existed at all. The panorama at Glacier Point, for example, was known to be spectacular. Half Dome dominates the airspace nearby, Yosemite Falls forms a brilliant white exclamation point on the far north wall of the chasm, and the Merced River peeks up from the impossibly reduced meadows and forest canopy on the valley floor, carrying the eye toward monumental El Capitan off to the west. In short, Glacier Point was an excellent scenic destination, but there was no tourist-friendly trail that reached it. One enterprising person decided to grab at the opportunity. Instead of trying to find space for another hotel in the valley, James McCauley, a sailor-turned-entrepreneur, approached the Board of Commissioners in 1871 about building a toll trail up to Glacier Point. If he could hang a trail on the sheer valley wall and snake it upward on a rocky trajectory to achieve the necessary elevation gain of more than 3,000 feet, McCauley reasoned that he would be guaranteed to make money.

With permission granted, he hired John Conway and a crew of nine men to perform the work, investing two summer seasons and about $4,000 in the task, most of which he had raised in loans. The Four-Mile-Trail, later modified and lengthened, was an immediate, gravity-defying success. For $1, hikers and horseback riders could reach one of the grandest viewpoints ever created by the combined forces of plate tectonics, glaciers, exfoliation, and the slow but forceful erosion of rock by the roots of the vegetation clinging to the cliffs' surfaces.

LET THE FIRE FALL

In 1872, McCauley was camped at Glacier Point, perhaps to celebrate the completion of his trail. Legend has it that he had a campfire going, but rather than douse hot coals when he was ready to bed down, he just kicked the embers over the edge. McCauley's first impromptu Fire Fall was a meager display, but eight years later, when he and his family were proprietors at the Mountain House at Glacier Point, he made the Fire Fall into a regular, flaming event. McCauley had acquired a ten-year lease from the Board of Commissioners to house guests in his rustic, one-story structure. He found that pushing a cascade of burning red cedar bark over the cliff's edge after dark was wildly popular with guests, those who stood nearby at Glacier Point to watch the burning bark disappear into the void and others who looked up from the valley floor to witness the thrilling pyrotechnic display. The distance down the cliff face was so great that the embers would consume themselves and blink out before setting anything on fire in the valley.

This performance would be repeated and embellished over many decades, with drum beats and chants floating up from the valley floor to "let the fire fall," until 1968 when National Park Service Director George Hartzog, Jr., ordered the stunt permanently discontinued. One can still see where lichens were scorched off the cliff face by the descending hot bark, the scar a silent witness to a nineteenth-century Yosemite showman.

CONQUERING HALF DOME

While McCauley oversaw the completion of his trail and watched Glacier Point begin to develop commercially, Captain George C. G. Anderson (1835 –1884) had a similar objective in mind, only in his case the target in question had been examined by the expert eyes of geologist Josiah Whitney, who proclaimed that it "never would be trodden by the human foot." Anderson, a Scottish emigrant like John Muir, wanted to build a toll-trail to the summit of almighty Half Dome, and polish off that improbable feat by building a hotel on top.

Anderson found his way into Yosemite Valley in 1867 after experiencing nothing but disappointment in his search for gold. The rough roadways that allowed foot, horse, and mule traffic to lurch in and out of the valley were much in need of improvement. Described as a "brawny, powerful man with tattooed arms, a splendid specimen of manhood, a Viking of a man" by Gertrude Hutchings, Anderson was able to put his prospecting skills to use as a trail builder. He began to eke out a living by hiring himself out to extend and smooth the persistently expanding trail network. In his spare time he began "trodding" around the park, exploring the intriguing delineation where the valley floor meets the boulder-fortified talus slopes and the imperial vertical walls. Most people who visit Yosemite are happy to stand with their feet planted on the flat ground and look toward the heights. But there is an eclectic subculture of humans who are irresistibly drawn to the walls, not to observe them but to climb them. Anderson was among the first of this faction to test himself against upright Yosemite.

Over the millennia, Half Dome has been sliced, smoothed, rounded, and chiseled by glaciers, the subtle wedging power of ice crystals, the lubrication of water, lightning strikes and wind storms, snow pack, blistering sun, and gravity; irresistible forces that sculpt nature's seemingly immovable objects. The exfoliated northwest face of the dome is three thousand feet of almost perpendicular granodiorite rock. The bulk of the monolith is egg-shaped in appearance, steep at the base then arching gracefully toward the summit, a reasonably flat 16-acre surface that in Anderson's day was available only to birds, rodents, and insects. In 1875, after several years in the park and with the ebbing of the season's work, Anderson set out to change this.

He approached Half Dome from a high saddle on its easterly flank where the distance from base to top was least intimidating. Access from a smaller dome attached, hip-like, to the giant dome allowed a scrambling approach to the point of final assault, a static wave of smooth granite flowing upward as if designed to rebuff all human ambition. But Anderson came prepared. He would assault the rock using a hammer, bradawl, miner's drill, eye-bolts, wedges, rope borrowed from trail builder John Conway, and his own considerable physical strength.

Although Anderson appeared to be driving a large nail into solid granite, there was a careful precision to his method. With each blow of the hammer onto the head of the drill, he simultaneously twisted the drill shaft to produce a fierce cutting force that the rock could not withstand.

Blow after blow, twist after twist, he shattered and cut away bits of rock to make a hole deep enough to allow a wooden wedge to be pounded into it. Then he hammered an eye-bolt into the wedge, forming a solid anchor.

By spacing the holes at intervals of about five feet, Anderson gave himself the advantage of best angle-of-attack for his hammer blows, ensuring that each bolt would become part of a symmetrical continuum. The bolts had to be strong and secure enough to hold his weight and to accommodate a single-strand daredevil ladder made up of sailor's knots tied in the rope. No store existed nearby for the purchase of enough rope so Anderson made part of it out of strands of flimsy twine. He used a forge at his cabin to make the bolts and made round-trip journeys to the dome as needed—fifteen miles of rugged trail with an elevation differential of over 4,000-feet—or camped near his work site when he could.

Had Anderson made a blunder anywhere along his climb, by trusting a loose bolt or an improperly fastened rope or losing his grip, footing, or balance, the result would have been swift and lethal. But on October 12th, 1875, Anderson stood triumphantly on the summit of Half Dome waving an American flag. Then he hurried back down to weave together a better rope with proper sailor-knot handholds, packed the rope by mule to the base of the dome, hauled it up to the topmost bolt, tied it in place, and descended, fastening the rope to his series of bolts as he went. The rope climb was ready for customers.

Before snow closed the route that year, eight people used Anderson's rope-and-bolt marvel to reach the summit. They included Park Guardian Galen Clark and Sally Dutcher, who was working in the valley for the photographer Carleton F. Watkins. Dutcher was the first Anglo woman to record a climbing victory in Yosemite. True to the contemporary dictates of women's fashion, she wore a long dress, making her exploit all the more impressive. The last of the eight to summit Half Dome in November of that year was John Muir. Others would follow in succeeding years, paying for the privilege, until most of Anderson's ladder was swept away by avalanching sheets of ice in the winter of 1883-84. Anderson, who had hoped to replace the rope with a wooden ladder and build his hotel atop the dome, died of pneumonia the same spring that his rope climb was destroyed, his ultimate vision of development atop Half Dome unfulfilled.

In 1884, Alexander Phimister Proctor and Alden Sampson arrived in the "semi-Mexican" town of Los Angeles. Proctor was a native of Canada who claimed to be well versed in the ways of the wilderness and bragged that he was a foster child of Little Wolf, a famous Cheyenne Chief. Outfitted in a beaver hat, fringed buckskins, a scalping knife, and a revolver holstered butt-forward, he had the carefully orchestrated appearance of a mountain man or gun fighter, but in fact he was an artist. He and Sampson had been roaming the west sketching scenes, hunting, and exploring. Sampson's background was a bit less glamorous than his companion's; he was a street-savvy New Yorker.

On hearing of Yosemite, the two young wanderers decided that the place beckoned them. They purchased five horses named Spider, Buck, Pinto, Pink, and Rattlesnake and set out on a rambling ride toward their destination, passing through a tiny village of six adobe houses known as Pasadena.

Yosemite Valley proved to be all that the two men had hoped for, and Galen Clark's description of the grandeur visible from the summit of Half Dome left them tantalized. Clark speculated that some alpine climbers from Switzerland might hear of the Half Dome challenge and be lured across the Atlantic to replace Anderson's ropes. The twenty-four-year-old Proctor had a better idea; he would do the job himself.

The fact that the rope route was gone and that the two adventurers had no rock-climbing experience did not discourage them. In a booklet later written by Proctor, he confessed that they decided not to inform anyone that they were going to try for the summit, reasoning that if they withdrew no one would be the wiser, if they died their gallantry might be honored, and if they succeeded they would be heroes.

On a summer day, the artists stood at the base of the loafed shoulder of the dome inspecting the bits and pieces of the Anderson route still visible and in place. They were poorly equipped. Each had a rope, but no hammer, drill, or bolts. The ropes were sturdy, but nowhere near long enough to form a continual nine-hundred-foot thread to the top. Still, against heavy odds, youth sometimes is served. Proctor decided to lasso his way to the dome's summit.

He made a loop in his climbing rope and began tossing it aloft until he snagged one of Anderson's remaining bolts. With a few firm jerks to confirm that the loop had tightened around the bolt, Proctor hoisted himself up, hand over hand, until he was within arm's length of the bolt. Grasping the bolt, he then jackknifed himself up until his foot was high enough to come down on top of his fingers. "When I reached the pin," he said, "my method was to climb up on it, always leaning against the wall of the mountain, and hook my big toe over the pin." Seeking support against the wall with his free hand, the rope dangling and forgotten for the moment, Proctor would lift himself until his whole body weight was precariously balanced on the bolt. "When I was balanced all doubled up, I would straighten myself up slowly and throw for the next pin. I was standing on a two-inch pin with my big toe the only support between me and the valley below." The fact that Sampson chose to follow is a true commentary on friendship. At the end of the first day, the two novice alpinists were only partway to their objective. They found a narrow ledge just large enough to sit on, tied themselves to a nearby bolt, and spent a cold, fitful night.

The second day, Proctor spent more than an hour throwing his loop at a particularly vexing bolt about thirty-five-feet above his head. Finally the lasso connected, or so the artist hoped. In one of those do-it moments when daring triumphs over logic, he climbed the rope. The remaining bolts were more obliging until, near the top, footing and hand-pressed friction against the stone allowed the two survivors to catwalk, then slowly to uncoil, stand erect, and step forward. Proctor later said of the victory: "Those two days on Half Dome were for me the divide between careless youth and serious manhood. Those hours of anxiety and danger, trying to accomplish something which in itself was of little value to the world, had crystallized in my mind the ideals that had vaguely been floating in it."

Proctor might have been speaking for the legions of rock climbers who have, over the generations, found the Yosemite ramparts to be a testing ground, vertical puzzles to be solved at exceedingly high risk, a challenge to physical coordination, conditioning, willpower, and trust. Proctor and Sampson made a gesture that was suggestive of what was to come. When they descended to the base of the dome, they coiled their ropes and left them for whoever might be next. Only a few accepted the invitation.

Not until thirty-five years later, in 1919, was the Anderson route modified and strengthened by members of the Sierra Club. Still later, parallel steel cables attached to waist-high iron stanchions were substituted for the rope-and-bolt concept, thus opening the summit of Half Dome to thousands of park visitors. Today, the number of cable climbers is limited to four hundred per day on weekends and holidays. Climbers are required to obtain a permit from the National Park Service in advance, at a cost of $1.50. There is no hotel on top to greet them.

MANAGEMENT HURLY-BURLY

As the numbers and variety of sightseers grew, the demands of managing Yosemite grew as well. In fact, in the last two decades of the nineteenth century, the Board of Park Commissioners was in political turmoil, a blur of changing personalities and biased loyalties. The commissioners had abruptly relieved Galen Clark of his duties in 1880, replacing him with none other than James Hutchings, the park evictee, who was subsequently dismissed in favor of two successors who were then also released under acrimonious circumstances. Eventually, Galen Clark once again assumed the guardian responsibility nine years after being deposed, and served in the position for an additional eight years until he retired at the age of eighty-three.

At the same time, business enterprises were popping up throughout the valley and on the travel corridors that connected Yosemite to the outside world. The Washburn brothers from Vermont erected the stately Wawona Hotel in 1879, using their knowledge of charming New England architectural and construction techniques to create what became an exemplar of tasteful commercial development in national parks. A nearby whitewashed covered bridge invited ready passage over the South Fork of the Merced River, thanks to Galen Clark who had constructed the original span in 1868. The Washburn brothers seemed to have an artist's sense that judicious and attractive design was good for business. By contrast in Yosemite Valley, for every tolerable hotel, such as the Stoneman and Sentinel, the sprawl of lesser structures that disrupted land and scenery was becoming epidemic.

6

The Plan Is Official

I WAS LEARNING THIS HISTORY and much more about my intriguing new place of residency and work as my first year at Yosemite was drawing to a close. Then, without warning, a threat to all planning efforts to guard the great park from overwhelming use struck from an unexpected direction. NPS Director Whelan was fired. Lee Bowman, reporting for the *Pittsburg Press* on April 25, 1980, said "After three years of battling to keep the nation's parks from becoming parking lots, NPS Director William J. Whelan is out of a job." Bowman continued, "Interior Secretary Cecil Andrus said he had removed Whelan because 'I believe it is best for the service, for the department and for Mr. Whelan's health.'"

According to the reporter, Whelan "remains puzzled over his sudden dismissal, which came several months after the furor over his attempts to reduce traffic at California's Yosemite National Park by moving most concession stands to the edge of the preserve had apparently subsided." In fact, Whelan himself had told me as much. He said that he had been dangling by a thread, but that he had tied a knot to the end of it and was hanging on. Then, just as the peril seemed to have passed, the thread broke.

Whoever advocated Whelan's removal probably assumed that the plan for on-going Yosemite stewardship would also hit the circular file. Fortunately the Carter Administration was still in place and Whelan was succeeded by Russell E. Dickenson, a highly experienced, thorough park professional. There was also simply too much public momentum behind the effort. After thousands of people had willingly participated and trusted the process, no last-minute, behind-the-scenes political maneuver was going to stop it in its tracks. On September 16, 1980, I signed the final version of the Yosemite General Management Plan.

I felt that we were keeping faith with those we worked for, the millions of visitors who wanted their park accessible, but not disgraced. The plan was not perfect; no plan is, but this one was a marvel. It was clear, precise, compact, and celebrated by many who had participated. It was a design for the way forward in Yosemite that could prove useful to concessionaires, business people in the gateway communities, the public, and park managers alike. If we all knew the rules, our combined collaboration could strengthen all nurturing aspects of this treasure of the Sierra Nevada. Assistant Western Planning Team Manager Kenneth Raithel, Jr., added his signature, as did NPS Western Regional Director Howard Chapman. The plan was official, a template intended to have staying power and bring results.

Immediately, we began looking for ways to implement the new plan. One of the easy first steps was to close the nine-hole pitch-and-putt golf course on the grounds of the Ahwahnee Hotel. Public approval for doing away with this bit of manicured lawn, dating back to World War II, had been overwhelming. Closure was confirmed when nine flags plucked from the greens were personally delivered to my office by huffy Ed Hardy who was not pleased, but grudgingly willing to cooperate.

Soon after, an abandoned and intrusive bakery building erected in 1900 by John and Bridget Degnan was dismantled, its oven transported to Wawona to be put on display among structures at the pioneer history exhibit. An unused lodge in the Mariposa Grove of Giant Sequoias was taken down after Ed Hardy hosted one last party there, as was the dilapidated old sewer plant in the west end of Yosemite Valley. At the same time, plans were advancing for new housing and maintenance facilities at the El Portal administrative site. The GMP was alive.

REAGAN SUCCEEDS CARTER

Meanwhile, Ronald Reagan's bid for the presidency against Jimmy Carter was gaining momentum. Everyone at Yosemite tried to feel reassured that Reagan's familiarity with the park would help protect it if he prevailed in the forthcoming election. While serving as governor of California, he had made a trip into the Yosemite backcountry with his spouse Nancy, her aide Nancy Reynolds, his son Ronald Reagan, Jr., Norman "Ike" Livermore, the Administrator of the State of California Resources Department, and two security guards. The host for the trip was Johnny Jones, a legendary packer in the Sierra Nevada. Jones was known for the high professional standards he required of himself and his employees. The packers often said that Jones was a "small man who cast a large shadow."

Jones had been working in the mountains for thirty years when he got a call from Bob Barnett, head wrangler for the Yosemite Park & Curry Company, asking that he take a special party into the Moraine Meadow region in the remote southern portion of the park. Jones was not interested, but Barnett, also a highly respected packer, convinced him of the importance of this particular adventure. On the appointed day, at the end of a dirt road near the Chiquito Pass trailhead on Yosemite's south boundary, dusty limousines pulled up to rendezvous with Jones and his packers. Out stepped the Reagan party. In his book, *Following the Bells*, Jones wrote that Reagan "just loved the mountains, loves horses, loves people." He confirmed, too, that Reagan was a "terrific rider," high praise indeed from Jones who was known among his peers as a discerning expert in the judgment of equestrian skills.

Jones described Reagan as "tough, rugged and woolly," a good camp partner who was "willing to work, to go out and do things for you." When Jones wandered out of camp early one morning to check on his horses and mules, he was astonished to discover the governor of California skinny-dipping in a mountain stream. "God," exclaimed Jones, "it's too cold to take a bath!" But Reagan just smiled and said that he was enjoying the clean mountain water. This visit, which quickly became part of Yosemite's local lore, made us warily hopeful after Ronald Reagan defeated President Carter in November. A sigh of relief traveled through the ranks when NPS veteran Russell E. Dickenson was retained as NPS Director in the Reagan Administration, the only political appointee in the Department of the Interior to endure the transition. Soon afterwards we received the news that James G. Watt had been appointed Secretary of the Interior.

Watt was founding president of the Mountain States Legal Foundation, a law firm specializing in pro-business activities on western public lands that had gained notoriety for fighting with evangelical zeal against initiatives to conserve wildlife and forest habitat, save endangered species, and assure clean water resources. Financial support for the firm was provided, in part, by Joseph Coors of the Coors Brewing Company, a co-founder of the conservative Heritage Foundation and an active member of Reagan's "kitchen cabinet," an unofficial advisory group of wealthy business people who had access to the President. The kitchen cabinet recommended ideologically aligned individuals to be appointed to key positions in the Reagan Administration. Watt was among them. On environmental issues, Watt's extremism made the President look like a Democrat. The optimistic mood at Yosemite and throughout the National Park Service evaporated.

Watt became a lightning rod in the Reagan Administration soon after the President took the oath of office in 1981. As it turned out, the President's delight in backcountry rambling did not factor into policy-making at the Department of the Interior. Soon after taking his post, Watt attempted to eliminate the Land and Water Conservation Fund, a federal program that had been in existence for sixteen years and stood on a foundation of strong bipartisan political support. Federal revenues gained from offshore oil and gas drilling activities, motorboat fuel taxes, and entry fees collected at national parks

'Surely,' says I, 'not *the* James Watt, folk-hero and famous wilderness rapist!' 'That's me,' says he. And I says, 'Not the renowned despoiler of our precious national heritage!' 'Right,' says he. So I ate him.'

and fish and wildlife areas may be reinvested to provide increased and improved outdoor recreation opportunities at all levels of government. Federal, state, and local agencies have access to the fund to enhance many resource-based activities including hunting, fishing, boating, camping, hiking, horseback riding, picnicking, winter sports, wildlife preservation, and educational programs. In essence, the fund is a revolving investment account; income flowing in from some federally sponsored natural resource activities and flowing out to others. Nonetheless, Watt made an attempt early in his tenure as Secretary of the Interior to do away with it. His effort met with quick and firm resistance from members of Congress, forcing him to drop the idea, but Watt's style and agenda were clearly evident. He was going to dismantle as much of the federal government's environmental legal structure as he possibly could. The Sierra Club began referring to Watt as "public enemy number one," and the club's membership began to skyrocket.

The virulence of Watt's position was a shock to many Americans on both sides of the political aisle after a decade of bipartisan effort to protect the environment and provide increased guardianship for our water, air, wildlife, and habitat. During the Nixon Administration, the National Oceanic and Atmospheric Administration and the Environmental Protection Agency had been established, the Endangered Species Act and the Clean Air Act had been passed, and the Federal Water Pollution Control Act had been strengthened. In the following Carter Administration, the Department of Energy was established. Cecil Andrus, the former Idaho governor who was Watt's predecessor as Secretary of the Interior, had helped shepherd the Alaska National Interests Lands Conservation Act through Congress, creating 15 new national parks and strengthening protection for the Arctic National Wildlife Refuge.

Watt declared his intent to severely cut the budget of his own Department of the Interior, open federal lands to aggressive oil, gas, and coal extraction, and even "dispose" of some of this land at bargain prices for industrial development. His beliefs, combined with the abruptness of his appearance on the political scene and the breadth of his power, left environmental advocates reeling. Among the Secretary's critics was Ansel Adams, who referred to Watt as "one of the most dangerous government officials in history."

I met Watt the year after he was appointed when, during a trip to California, he decided to visit Yosemite. En route to the park, the Secretary stopped at the San Luis Reservoir on the far west side of California's Central Valley. During a press conference held at the reservoir, Watt was quoted as saying, "I don't believe in Republicans and Democrats. I believe in Americans and liberals."

On his arrival the next day in Yosemite Valley, Watt held a follow-up press conference at which reporters fired questions about whether the Secretary really believed that those citizens who did not agree with his political views were un-American. Watt, on the defensive but always smiling, verbally jousted with the reporters about the comment he had made at the San Luis Reservoir, resulting in no questions asked by the press about Yosemite or his agenda as steward of the nation's land, mineral, and wildlife resources.

After the press conference, Watt made clear that he always wanted me by his side when photos were taken during the park visit. He knew of the good image that park rangers had nationwide and wanted to be so associated, but only for the photo opportunities. This was confirmed when, out of hearing range of the reporters, I tried to summarize the details of the *General Management Plan* and to remind the Secretary of the strong public role in its development. Watt quickly cut me off by saying, "the more hotels, the better—fill up the whole valley."

Watt stayed that night at the Ahwahnee Hotel. Under the cover of darkness, rock climbers found a smooth face of granite midway up the wall adjacent to Yosemite Falls and attached a bed sheet that flapped in the wind with the message "DUMP WATT." The resultant news photos that recorded his visit to Yosemite were not of the Secretary of the Interior with me, in my cameo appearance standing at his side, but of the bed sheet.

Watt's tenure as Secretary of the Interior came to an abrupt end in the autumn of 1983. He created a firestorm of criticism while speaking at a U. S. Chamber of Commerce event. Referring to the U. S. Commission on Fair Market Value Policy for Federal Coal Leasing

    Your Yosemite: **PROTECTING A PUBLIC TREASURE**

that functioned under his authority, he shocked the audience and news reporters by saying of the Commission members, "I have a black, a woman, two Jews, and a cripple." Action was initiated in the U. S. Senate to force his dismissal, but he resigned instead. My moment with James Watt was a harsh reminder that our national parks exist only at the pleasure of an informed political majority.

Regardless of history and precedent, the parks and all environmental preserves are nothing more than laws or executive orders on paper. They can be changed. Watt wanted to open all wilderness areas to mining and fossil fuel extraction. My impression was that he cared nothing about Yosemite National Park—was contemptuous of its very existence. His attitude was a signal of a hard-right, anti-environment turn by some in the nation's political arena who, in increasing volume, use ridicule and scare tactics to advance a zealous view that natural resources exist only to be conquered. They twist the word "freedom" to mean environmental anarchy. Those who cherish the innocence of nature and worry about its vulnerability are attacked verbally, and sometimes physically, as opponents of "freedom."

Ironically, in 1984, and despite the Watt moment, President Ronald Reagan signed the California Wilderness Act which safeguards three million acres of spectacular habitat throughout the state, including 90% of Yosemite's landscape. In one of environmental history's many paradoxical twists, the man who elevated James Watt to such high government office also proved to be a champion of the wilderness. President Reagan signed forty-three similar wilderness bills, putting under special protection more than ten million acres nationwide. He joined in construction of America's environmental house. The national parks are at the foundation of this effort, and to appreciate the obligations we have to protect them and the privilege we have of trying to hand them on in good health to the next generation, we need to understand the continuum between visionaries like Muir and political stewards of our nation's resources, like Reagan.

LEGACY

John Muir wrote many articles about Yosemite which painted word-pictures of scenes, rambles, glaciers, rocks, floods, weather, wildlife, plants and forests, geology, and even "A Paradise in Clouds," which would increasingly captivate readers across the nation. He had a knack for combining his scientific observations and personal wilderness exploits with arresting word imagery.

From the start, Muir's early writings were well received. The mystery of Yosemite served as a magnet for the imagination of his growing audience of readers. Seventeen of his articles were published in the *Overland Monthly* before it ceased publication in 1875. Muir then continued to write about California's natural riches for the *San Francisco Evening Bulletin*, the *Sacramento Union, Harper's New Monthly* Magazine, and *Scribner's Monthly* describing other adventures. Muir's personal life was driven by his robust intellectual might and curiosity, predominate over basic lifestyle needs like a fulltime job. His writings produced wages of a sort, allowing him to find meager housing in the San Francisco Bay Area where he had chosen to live after the conflict with James Hutchings. He may, though, have teetered on the edge of vagrancy before his mentor and mother-figure, Jeanne Carr, came to the rescue.

A HESITANT ROMANCE

After their shared days at the University of Wisconsin, beginning in 1860 when Muir was a twenty-two-year-old student, and continuing in California, Mrs. Carr was watchful of Muir's well-being. She was a cheerleader for her prized student, undoubtedly aware of Muir's tenuous financial circumstances and wanderlust habits, and likely suspecting that he might be on a path to chronic rootlessness. She began an active, encouraging correspondence with him that eventually included a particularly tantalizing letter. In 1874, Mrs. Carr wrote to Muir of her "dearest friend in California," a refined and attractive twenty-seven-year-old woman named Louisa Strentzel, and arranged for Muir and Louisa to meet at the Carr home in Oakland.

Louisa's father, Dr. John Strentzel, was an immigrant from Poland who, like so many others in his newfound nation, had come west with his wife, Louisiana, during the 1849 gold rush, traveling overland by wagon from Texas territory with their two-year-old daughter and ten-month-old son. The son died of diphtheria, a dreaded disease that took many children during this period. The Strenzels settled in 1853 in a small valley near the Carquinez Straight in the upper reaches of San Francisco Bay where the soil was rich and the climate proved ideal for planting orchards.

By the 1870s, Dr. Strentzel and his spouse had become well established in Bay Area society. Their daughter was well regarded in her own right for the skills she had developed as an orchardist and classical pianist. Jeanne Carr had chosen wisely for Muir, but the naturalist was no Casanova; it would take five years of continual encouragement, primarily by the persistent Mrs. Carr, before Muir asked Louisa to marry him. His timing was less than perfect. He finally proposed and Louisa accepted the day before he was to leave on a voyage to Alaska. The bride-to-be was tolerant of the voyage, but this incident hinted strongly at how their married life would proceed.

After the wedding on April 14, 1880, Muir settled on the Strentzel ranch and began to assist his father-in-law. He also stayed active with like-minded friends in the Bay Area who shared his passion for wild landscapes. The men would occasionally meet to reminisce about past experiences and discuss possible future outings. Alaska and the appeal of natural places worldwide were much on Muir's mind, but always secondary to his passion for the Sierra Nevada and Yosemite.

In between orchard chores, and apparently with the consent of Louisa and her parents, he regularly found precious time to wander away from the ranch and continue his adventures. In the Sierra Nevada, he began to explore further south of Yosemite, paying particular attention to the Giant Sequoia groves in what is now Sequoia National Park. The nearby South Fork of the Kings River, which had cut an incredibly deep canyon in the western flank of the mountains, was judged by Muir to be another of nature's masterpieces, easily in league with the Merced River's Yosemite Valley and the Tuolumne River's Hetch Hetchy Valley. He wrote in one of his articles, "in the Sierra Nevada are many Yosemites."

Muir worried about the impact of logging on the Giant Sequoias. In an article for *Harper's New Monthly Magazine*, he wrote, "The sequoias are the most venerable-looking of all the Sierra giants, standing erect and true, in poise so perfect they seem to make no effort, their strength so perfect it is invisible. Trees weighing one thousand tons are yet to all appearances imponderable as clouds, as the light which clothes them." His underlying message challenged the assumption that man should be allowed to brutalize and destroy these natural marvels. He warned that when Sequoias were felled by axe-men, the brittle wood "breaks like glass." Sequoia wood generally was sold for low-quality building projects, including use as fence posts. Muir's articles raised awareness and began to reach an ever wider audience.

In an article in 1877 for the *American Association for the Advancement of Science*, where his theory on glacial impact in the Sierra found an appreciative audience, he also wrote of the need for the "most watchful attention of government" to preserve natural resources. By 1880, the year Muir finally married Louisa, his writings had earned him the status of a cerebral wilderness hero.

In the following decade, Muir played a less active political role as he embarked on his new responsibilities as a husband, father, and cultivator of fruit trees. But the concerns he raised about the Sierra continued to spread among an increasingly diverse number of constituents. He cautioned that extensive sheep and cattle grazing and logging in the Sierra Nevada was becoming not only an ugly intrusion on a delicate habitat, but was also dangerous. Grazing and logging threatened to destabilize the gigantic west-tilting watershed that released billions of gallons of snowmelt water each year into the lower foothills and flatlands of the Central Valley. Without the filtering and sponge-like quality of meadows and forests, this annual springtime runoff could become a destructive torrent. Mine operators and ranchers in the Sierra foothills and farmers in the Central Valley, not necessarily attuned to Muir's philosophy of preservation, nonetheless heard his message and began to fear the impact of deforestation in the mountains. They started to urge the Yosemite Commissioners, who had been vested with authority for the Yosemite Grant in 1864, to push for federal expansion of the grant to curtail and control logging.

This idea of expansion was appealing to the chronically underfunded commissioners because it might allow them to expel freelance loggers in a wide section of the Sierra Nevada and substitute selective timbering of their own to help pay the bills. Beyond the specific concerns of flood threat and the pecuniary needs of the Yosemite Commissioners there were still others, much more in step with Muir's thinking, who were becoming accustomed to the idea that a federal grant meant the Yosemite region belonged to all Americans. If the California commissioners entrusted with its care were not up to the task, a better means of preserving this great natural resource must be found.

A VERY PUBLIC CONFLICT

Charles Dorman Robinson settled in the Bay Area with his wife, Kathryn, in 1876. Both were successful artists. After making his first trip to Yosemite Valley in 1880, Robinson was smitten, and he would return for twenty-three consecutive summers to paint scenes. In 1885, Robinson decided that he wanted to build a permanent studio in Yosemite Valley and received permission from the Yosemite Commission to do so. Soon afterward his permit was summarily rescinded, probably because other local art vendors who had better lobbying access to the commissioners did not want the competition. Robinson was enraged. Familiar with the politics of cronyism in the valley, in 1888 he brought twenty-two counts of misconduct against the commission. The denunciation by such a prominent Bay Area artist was duly trumpeted in the *San Francisco Examiner*, William Randolph Hearst's newspaper, prompting an investigation by the California Legislature. The scrutiny came to naught, but Robinson's complaints proved to be the tip of the iceberg. The political profile of Yosemite had been raised in the public eye, never to recede.

The journalist George G. MacKenzie appeared on the scene just as the Robinson squabble was reaching its height, arriving in California in 1886 and soon finding his way to the great valley. Like Robinson, he quickly fell in love with what he saw, hiking the trails and byways, exploring in the nooks and crannies, and taking careful notes. The result was his guidebook, *Where To Go and What To Do*, that offered touring options around Yosemite Valley. He saw the role of those who loved the valley as being one of stewardship rather than exploitation, and he found himself increasingly furious with the Yosemite Commissioners. Before long, like Robinson, he would go publicly ballistic with his concerns.

In 1889, as the MacKenzie storm was brewing, Robert Underwood Johnson, associate editor of the New York City-based *Century Magazine*, joined John Muir on an eight-day pack trip into the Yosemite country. At the time, *Century Magazine* enjoyed a circulation of more than 200,000 subscribers and was among the nation's more influential periodicals, specializing in Civil War history and counting Mark Twain among its regular contributors. On horseback and by foot, the two men visited the Mariposa Grove of Giant Sequoias, Yosemite Valley, and Tuolumne Meadows, where Johnson could see for himself the impact of sheep grazing on the region's mountain meadows.

Despite flood concerns, an estimated 90,000 sheep were being herded into the High Sierra each grazing season in flocks of two to three thousand. Each flock was attended by three to five men and their dogs. The environmental harm spoke for itself, meadows reduced to muddy expanses by overgrazing, fragile plants destroyed, and streams turned brown by erosion. Muir referred to his former wooly charges as "hoofed locusts," and Johnson later described the scene as "barren soil fairly stippled by the feet of countless herds of sheep." The editor became an eager convert to the need for preservation of the Yosemite high country and better control of slapdash commercial development down in the valley.

Legend has it that, sitting in the glow of a campfire at Tuolumne Meadows, Johnson proposed to Muir that the two of them join forces to push for establishment of Yosemite National Park, spurred on by grievances about how the Yosemite Grant was being managed by the State of California Commission. Muir was initially reluctant. His aspirations had been more modest. He hoped for an expansion of the present grant, but had not been inclined to challenge the Commissioners' role outright. Johnson, however, contended that federal protection was needed if anything was to remain of the High Sierra wilderness and its prized valley. The federal government had proven an able steward of Yellowstone, sending in the U. S. Cavalry to assert control. Johnson wanted the same for Yosemite, and he was determined to add the power of his journal to the cause. He urged Muir to become a contributor. Muir agreed.

FIGHTING TO SAVE YOSEMITE

In the January 1890 issue of *Century Magazine*, under "Topics of the Times," Johnson and his editors launched their campaign against the commissioners. The editorial was called "The Care of Yosemite Valley," and it complained that commissioner leadership was "fatuous," the grant poorly cared for, and that "a crisis in its management is near at hand." The editors reminded their readership that "a citizen of New York is as much one of the owners of the Yosemite as a citizen of California, and his own right to be heard in suggestion or protest is undoubted." And yet even concerns politely and privately raised were frequently "denounced by certain members of the commission in the most violent and parochial spirit." It concluded by saying that even many in California would support a bill for the park's "recession" to the federal government with the assurance that it would be capably administered, as Yellowstone Park now was.

The magazine also printed several letters on the subject, including one from George MacKenzie mentioning the commissioners' hopes that the federal government would expand the amount of land presently under their protection. Why would anyone consider such a thing, MacKenzie asked, when the commissioners did such a poor job of managing the grant already under their care? On the other hand, he pointed out, it was extremely difficult for the commissioners to do their job properly, given their situation: they had no professional training for the responsibilities vested in them, visited the valley rarely, were paid nothing for their services, relied on only one guardian to monitor thousands of acres, and were not given

State funds necessary to manage the park properly. Implicit in all the *Century* pieces was the notion that if the commissioners could not manage the job entrusted to them, the time had come for them to step aside.

In March, 1890, California Congressman William Vandever (1817 –1893) joined the debate by introducing legislation to declare the High Sierra a protected forest reserve. Vandever represented California's 5th Congressional District, a vast area extending from San Diego through Los Angeles and far into the Central Valley and Sierra Nevada Mountains. His constituents included business associates with close ties to the Southern Pacific Railroad. Southern Pacific executives, like their peers in the steamship companies of earlier decades, had a vested interest in promoting California tourism, especially by tempting east coast travelers to journey west rather than to Europe. Vandever was well aware of the interest of railroad executives in the potential for business profits that a tourist magnet like Yosemite might yield, and in the halls of Congress he acted accordingly.

In the meantime, George Mackenzie's crusade against the Yosemite Commissioners gained traction, resulting in truly caustic articles that appeared in *The New York Times*. A July 20, 1890 article was boldly headlined, "The Neglected Yosemite, Some Inexcusable Faults In Management; Despoiling The Yosemite, An Official Report That Is Full of Falsehoods; The Commissioners Decide to Continue Their Ruinous Policy—Congress Should Take Action."

MacKenzie contended that "the antics of California's Yosemite Commission continue to bring disgrace on that body of incompetents," that the Commission was a "bullying plutocracy," and that visitors to the valley received the "least possible service for the greatest pay of the Yosemite stablemen and hotel keepers." In an earlier piece, the journalist had lamented the loss of wildflowers to hay fields and overgrazed pastures in Yosemite Valley, and, like Muir, the messy use of wildfire to clear land. In response, J. P. Irish, a member of the Commission's Executive Committee, dismissed these criticisms as misguided advice that "flower gardeners" are needed to improve the valley, adding, "what nature has wrought here is on a scale too grand to adapt itself to the skill which is exhausted in planting sweet peas and trimming private hedges." The commissioners were not only incompetent, MacKenzie claimed, but rude, as well: "There you have the answer made by the men entrusted with the charge of the Yosemite to the accusation that they have converted the flowery meadows of the valley into hayfields, and that the parts not used for such unworthy money making have been pastured by starved horses and mules until the soil of the valley is scarcely more than a sandy waste."

Another commissioner, M. H. Hecht, said in a letter to the *New York Times* (July 28, 1890) that he had been assigned to the Commission's Committee of Complaints, but that no complaints from park constituents had been presented to the commissioners during a three-day summertime meeting in the valley. Hecht's letter prompted a response from Robert Underwood Johnson in the very next issue of the *Times* in which he referred to his Yosemite visit with John Muir and then proceeded to list all twenty-two charges of commission wrongdoing that had been "made under oath by Mr. Charles D. Robinson before the California Assembly Committee on Investigation."

Meanwhile, Vandever's first legislative effort to protect the Yosemite region met with considerable opposition. The commissioners, many of them California Legislature members, joined by local residents with stake-holds near the valley, opposed this first attempt to establish a federal presence adjacent to the state grant. Instead of backing down, however, the congressman withdrew this first version of the legislation only to resubmit it with amended language on a much more ambitious scale. Vandever doubled down in a sense by also introducing a separate piece of legislation in response to Muir's pleas to establish Sequoia National Park further south in the Sierra Nevada.

Robert Underwood Johnson went to Washington, D. C., to lobby for the legislation, enlisting among others Frederick Law Olmsted. In succeeding months Vandever's legislation moved through the congressional process, winning wide support. An important modification was made in the legislative language, changing reference to the area to be protected from "federal forest reserve" to "national park," reflecting the Yellowstone precedent.

That summer, Muir stepped forward as promised. *Century Magazine* published two Muir articles, "The Treasures of Yosemite" and "Features of the Proposed Yosemite National Park." He urged support for Vandever's legislative initiative by highlighting the charm of the region. Of Yosemite Valley, Hetch Hetchy, and other Sierra Nevada chasms, Muir wrote, "Though of such stupendous depth, the canyons are not raw, gloomy, jagged walled gorges, savage and inaccessible. With rough passages here and there, they are mostly smooth, open pathways conducting to the fountains of the summit; mountain streets full of life and light, graded and sculptured by the ancient glaciers, and presenting throughout all their courses a rich variety of novel and attractive scenery—the most attractive that has yet been discovered in the mountain ranges of the world."

He also warned his readers of the lumbermen who threatened the groves of Giant Sequoias: "Were the importance of our forests at all understood by the people in general, even from an economic standpoint, their preservation would call forth the most watchful attention of the government," and worried that, "every kind of destruction is moving on with accelerated speed." He described the technique used by "sheepmen" to burn forest cover to improve pasturage: "The entire belt of forests is thus swept by fire, from one end of the range to the other." Muir devoted only a few words to the core purpose of the articles, but they were powerful words: "Steps now are being taken towards the creation of a national park about Yosemite, and great is the need, not only for the sake of the adjacent forests, but for the valley itself." He said that the surrounding mountain ecosystem and Yosemite Valley were integrally connected, like "the fingers to the palm of the hand—as the branches, foliage, and flowers of a tree to the trunk."

When the articles appeared, Johnson made sure that they were strongly reinforced by graphic illustrations of Yosemite scenes to drive home the point that Yosemite was worthy of the nation's most purposeful conservation efforts—a place so unique that anything less than full federal attention to this resource was unacceptable.

Within weeks, the much changed and expanded Vandever legislation was passed by the House of Representatives and the United States Senate, reaching the desk of President Benjamin Harrison. On September 25, 1890, the President established Sequoia and General Grant National Parks. Then, on October 1, 1890, he signed the bill to establish Yosemite National Park.

The Yosemite legislation was a paradoxical compromise, much more in many respects than Muir and Johnson could ever have hoped for, and yet infuriatingly less in a crucial aspect. The newly created national park around Yosemite Valley encompassed a mind-boggling sweep of more than 900,000 acres of Sierra Nevada wilderness, but a crucial 39,000 acres, consisting of Yosemite Valley and the Mariposa Grove of Giant Sequoias (the original Yosemite Grant) had been left in the hands of the California Board of Park Commissioners.

In essence, a new national park now surrounded the valley and grove, but the state grant remained a beleaguered island unto itself, separated lawfully from the national park and managed by the commissioners as an enclave forbidden to federal representatives. Nonetheless, advocates for the greater protection of the region had achieved a huge conservation success. Federal authority became a vivid reality when Troop I of the Fourth U. S. Cavalry was dispatched from its base at the Presidio in San Francisco. About a mile downriver from the Wawona Hotel, the troopers pitched a camp of tents lined up in orderly rank, cleared a parade ground, planted a flagpole, and assumed patrol duties that placed the cavalrymen in an immediate contest of wills with sheepherders and poachers in an immense, craggy, and uncharted alpine territory.

The U.S. Army presence in Yosemite brought a degree of much needed protection to the High Sierra. When troopers found trespassing sheepherders, they would drive the flocks out of the park in one direction and escort the herders for many miles in the opposite direction, sometimes with creative physical encouragement. But the cavalry was not welcome in Yosemite Valley or the Mariposa Grove. These precious and popular tourist sites remained the turf of the commissioners who made known to military officers in command of the cavalry that soldiers were free to pass through in conjunction with their patrol duties, but should not linger, and definitely should not interfere with commission prerogatives.

While the ground at Yosemite shifted, politically speaking, Muir maintained active contact with his cadre of friends and associates in the San Francisco Bay area. Among the participants at informal gatherings was Warren Olney (1841–1921) who had been born in Iowa territory, served in the Union Army during the Civil War, and subsequently gained his law degree at the University of Michigan before making his way, newly married, to California in 1868, the same year that Muir arrived in the state. A well respected lawyer and political leader in Oakland and San Francisco, Olney was also an enthusiastic outdoorsman. He wanted to make the wilderness a regular part of his life by repeatedly visiting favored places in the High Sierra.

FORCEFUL CITIZENS VOICES ARE RAISED

By the 1890s, a number of faculty members and students at the University of California, Berkeley and the recently-established Stanford University were also taking advantage of their proximity to Yosemite and the High Sierra. Joachim H. Senger, a philologist and Professor of German and Greek at Berkeley, was especially keen on the need for preservation of the Sierra Nevada and had organized a reference collection of maps, scientific information, and writings about this alpine range. He began to promote the idea of forming a club in defense of the mountains, probably inspired by the Appalachian Mountain Club founded in 1876 in Boston.

When Professor Senger decided to organize a coalition of like-minded academics, scientists, and community leaders into a formally chartered outing club, Muir, Olney, and William Keith, a landscape artist well known in the Bay Area, were enthusiastic about the idea. Olney developed the necessary Articles of Incorporation and by-laws. In May 1892, twenty-seven signatures were affixed to the Articles of Incorporation to officially establish the Sierra Club. The mission of the club was "to explore, enjoy, and render accessible the mountain regions of the Pacific Coast; to publish authentic information concerning them; to enlist support and cooperation of the people and the Government in preserving the forests and other natural features in the Sierra Nevada." The Sierra Club would lead annual expeditions on foot or horseback to camps set up in select high country locations. These trips quickly became the popular basis for the club.

Before long, 182 charter members were listed in the by-laws; many of them important figures in the social and political life of the new state. Muir was elected president and Olney first vice president. In addition to Muir, Keith, Olney, and Senger, the members included Robert Underwood Johnson and wealthy businessman Adolph Sutro, later to become mayor of San Francisco. United States Senator George Perkings and Chief Justice William H. Beatty of the Supreme Court of California were charter members. Dr. Joseph LeConte, a medical doctor turned geologist who had helped organize the University of California signed on as did David Starr Jordan, the President of Stanford. Employees of the U. S. Geological Survey were on the charter member roster and, in an important outreach to Yosemite pathfinders, so, too, were Park Guardian Galen Clark and entrepreneur James Hutchings, Muir's former employer and oft-time antagonist. As a commonsense extension of interest in wilderness camping, members of the newly formed club began raising citizen voices in defense of the newly designated 900,000-acre Yosemite National Park, still under assault by livestock operators.

George MacKenzie was not listed as a charter member of the Sierra Club, perhaps because he was too combative, but he had continued separately to demand change in the management structure of the Yosemite Grant. Just prior to formation of the Sierra Club, another of his articles appeared in the *New York Times*, this one headlined, "Defending Grave Abuses, The Yosemite Commission Makes a Report, Bitterly Attacking Corrections and Intelligent Critics of Their Management—A Queer Lot of Apologies." MacKenzie was scathing in his commentary. He charged that "the antics of California's Yosemite Commission continue to bring disgrace on the body of incompetents." Implied, and finding an increasingly sympathetic audience, was that the Yosemite Grant and the newly formed national park should become one and the same.

PARK RANGER

While this policy debate was underway, protection was disrupted at Yosemite when regular cavalry units were pulled out during the 1898 Spanish-American War. Left behind were a few civilian "Forest Agents" who had been employed by the army. This handful of agents would be no match for the sheep men who had continued over the years to secret themselves in the mountains despite the best efforts of the cavalry to weed them out. In 1899, Captain Joseph E. Caine and his First Utah Volunteer Cavalry arrived at Wawona to take up the chase again where earlier military units had left off. He kept the Forest Agents as part of his force, but Caine did not think that Forest Agent best described the duties of this civilian contingent. He changed the title to Park Ranger.

MUIR AND HARRIMAN

In the meantime, Muir's sphere of influence outside the park continued to grow in unexpected yet critical ways. In 1899 he was invited to join a two-month, 9,000-mile scientific voyage along the coast of Alaska that was sponsored by the railroad magnate Edward H. Harriman (1848–1909). Harriman described the expedition "as a summer cruise for the pleasure and recreation of my family and a few friends." In fact, Muir was one of 126 passenger and crew members, and the guest list included twenty-three invited scientists, artists, and taxidermists, including the famed Hudson River Valley naturalist John Burroughs.

The ship, the *George W. Elder*, made its unhurried way along the coast of Alaska, stopping frequently to allow shore parties to collect specimens of flora and fauna, study glaciers, and make a photographic record of the expedition. The *Elder* sailed past the Pribilof Islands and Cape Fox into the Bering Sea and all the way to the Siberian coast where Harriman wanted to leave his footprints before reversing course. More than 5,000 photos were taken, and "thirteen genera and six-hundred species new to science" were added to the scientific register. Muir and Harriman came to know and respect each other during the expedition, a crucial point of personal contact that would prove to benefit Yosemite.

Curry Tent Camp

THE LEGENDARY
CURRY'S FEW TENTS

By the turn of the century, a new breed of stagecoach and carriage-born visitors to Yosemite Valley was well separated from the very early days of saddle-born agony on narrow, rough trails that had been the price paid to reach the sequestered destination. Improved wagon roads available to these "second generation" visitors created a demand for more and better accommodations in the park. Among lodging choices, the Sentinel Hotel, a group of buildings much modified and improved at the old Hutchings Hotel site, offered fine dining and music during dinner for the steep price of four dollars per day. For many who stayed at the hotel, their visit to Yosemite was a once-in-a-lifetime experience, but what of those who could not afford such a steep price for lodging?

David A. Curry and his wife, Jennie, heard about Yosemite while gaining their teaching credentials at the Indiana University. They were trekkers who had led fellow students on outings into Yellowstone National Park during their summertime breaks from school. When the couple found their way west to teaching jobs in California, and eventually to Yosemite Valley, they quickly realized that a rustic camping experience might be very popular there. In 1899, while the *Elder* sailed in Alaskan waters, they erected a few tents in an unlikely location, hard up against the base of Glacier Point on the shadowy, cool side of Yosemite Valley where visitors could stay for half the price of a night at the Sentinel Hotel. Before the first year was out the tent count had risen from seven to twenty-five. They had established a successful business venture, one that would permanently transition them from teaching to the hospitality trade.

In succeeding years, the Currys created a mini-village in Yosemite Valley, almost all of it made from canvas, including bathhouses, a bakery, a fruit stand, a barbershop, and a candy and cigar store. They provided a swimming tank, tennis, croquet, and a pool hall. In support of the operation were vegetable gardens, an orchard, sawmill, a hen house, and pastures for beef cattle and milk cows. Camp Curry became a destination-of-choice for many park visitors year after year, weaving an annual visit into family tradition. David Curry presided over the venture as the grand host, shouting "WELCOME!" to arriving guests and "Let Er' Rip Galleger!" when announcing the Fire Fall from Glacier Point that became a mainstay of nightly amusement for his clientele.

In 1916, a young fourteen-year-old boy named Ansel Adams stayed at Camp Curry on his first visit to Yosemite. His parents had recently given him a Kodak Box Brownie camera. One of the first pictures Adams took in Yosemite was fondly labeled "my upside-down photograph of Half Dome." The boy snapped the picture as he was falling from a tree stump that crumbled under his feet. Regardless, he was pleased with the result, just as he was with other images the camera produced. Adams called David Curry the "Stentor of Yosemite," referring to a herald in *The Iliad* who spoke with a powerful voice. He remembered that "after dark" the Stentor would "bellow for the fire to fall from the great cliff of Glacier Point—whereupon someone up there would push the glowing embers of pine-bark fire over the cliff while a soprano sang a thrilling song. Even at that age I knew it was an insult to Yosemite."

Although the law clearly stated that the Currys' right to run their business rested in the hands of the commissioners, David Curry quickly adapted a fiercely proprietary relationship in the valley. He became known for regularly entering into tactical and verbal combat with both his business competitors and the Yosemite Grant administrators. When David and Jennie Curry began to put their stamp on the park, however, their timing was close to perfect.

Your Yosemite: **PROTECTING A PUBLIC TREASURE**

7

Theodore Roosevelt

TENSIONS AROUND THE MANAGEMENT of the Yosemite region showed no signs of diminishing by the turn of the century. There were powerful constituents on either side of the debate. Generally speaking, on the one side, where money was being made, there were the lodging owners, stage coach operators, and vendors, and further afield, the still persistent stockmen and loggers. This constituency was joined in loose alliance with the much criticized Yosemite Grant Commission. On the other side, where preservation was favored over profits, the Sierra Club continued to grow in numbers and influence, and Muir continued to write elegant articles about the beauties and delicacies of the wild.

This debate was at a kind of low grade fever level when events far away took precedence. In 1901, President of the United States, William McKinley, a popular Republican serving in his second term, was assassinated by anarchist Leon Czolgoz. Suddenly thrust into the highest office in the land was the 42-year-old Vice President, Theodore Roosevelt (1858–1919). Roosevelt had been born into wealth in New York City and attended Harvard University, but he always had a profound appreciation for the outdoors. An early indication of his taste for adventure was when he managed to climb the Matterhorn during his wedding trip to Europe. Personal family tragedy struck four years later. On the same day, February 14, 1884, at the Roosevelt home in New York City, his wife, Alice, died of Bright's disease and his beloved mother, Martha, died of typhoid fever.

Roosevelt coped with his intense grief by leaving the city to become a part-time rancher and deputy sheriff in Dakota Territory. Out on the Great Plains, he threw himself into the hardscrabble life of ranching, gaining the respect of taciturn cowboys through his

President Theodore Roosevelt and traveling party at base of Grizzly Giant,
John Muir just to his left, 1903

willingness to share their work and do it well. Roosevelt became a highly skilled horseman, western style, and a determined lawman. He would later say that his time on his ranches, the Maltese and Elkhorn in present-day North Dakota, "took the snob out of me."

The splendor of the plains appealed immensely to Roosevelt. He was concerned that machines and tools could in a matter of days destroy primeval natural habitat that had existed for centuries, but lay helpless in the path of disruptive human settlement. Years later, writing of the continuing need to conserve such places, Roosevelt said, "It is also vandalism wantonly to destroy or to permit the destruction of what is beautiful in nature, whether it be a cliff, a forest, or a species of mammal or bird."

On his return from Dakota Territory in 1886, Roosevelt resumed a political career that had included brief service in the New York State Assembly prior to his adventures in Dakota Territory. He succeeded in becoming President of the New York City Board of Police Commissioners; basically top cop. During his policing days in the city,

Roosevelt sometimes would cross the Hudson River by rowboat and scramble up the cliffs of the New Jersey Palisades to roam and hunt for small game in the wildland forest that decorated the heights. In a continuing political progression, he was serving as Secretary of the Navy during McKinley's first term only to give up the safety of his desk for the hazards of combat during the Mexican-American War, leading his Rough Riders and himself to instantaneous national fame in the hills of Cuba. Returning in glory to New York, Roosevelt was elected Governor in 1898 and then joined the McKinley ticket for the national election of 1900.

MUIR MEETS ROOSEVELT

Roosevelt's service to the nation intersected with Yosemite's destiny in 1903 when he visited California to strengthen political contacts. He took advantage of the opportunity to include a side trip to the famous park. Although the Yosemite portion of his California visit was ostensibly for pleasure, Roosevelt very likely was aware of the stressful dividing line between the state-managed Yosemite Grant and the surrounding federally-managed parklands. There was ample reason for the commissioners to be uneasy about his visit. In his first year as President, Roosevelt had signed legislation to establish Crater Lake National Park in Oregon. A few months before his trip out west, he had done the same to preserve Wind Cave in South Dakota. Obviously, he was inclined toward federal conservation protection. In addition, although he had never met Muir, Roosevelt requested that the self-taught naturalist serve as his escort to Yosemite.

For Muir, the timing was not good. He had agreed to join in a globe-circling expedition with Charles Sargent, Director of the Arnold Arboretum at Harvard University, to collect plant specimens. But when Sargent learned of the naturalist's chance to participate in the Yosemite outing with Roosevelt, the arboretum director promptly suggested that the global excursion be postponed. Sargent had an ulterior motive. He disliked the President, whom he considered light on scientific knowledge and long on bombast, but Sargent wanted letters of introduction from Roosevelt to the Czar of Russia and Emperor of China. He thought Muir probably could secure the coveted letters while camping in the mountains with the President.

Sargent's encouragement to Muir to accept Roosevelt's invitation prevailed. At 10:00 pm on May 14, 1903, as instructed, Muir climbed aboard a Pullman railroad car nestled on a siding in Oakland. When the naturalist asked a porter where he was to sleep, the porter responded, "Mr. Muir, it is not advised that guests retire before the President arrives." When Muir asked when the President was expected, the porter told him that Roosevelt was at the Commonwealth Club in San Francisco and would probably not arrive until about midnight. "Then it is to bed with me," said Muir, and insisted on being directed to his berth. When Roosevelt reached the Pullman with his traveling party well after 1:00am, he asked whether Muir was aboard. When told that his special guest was asleep, the amused Roosevelt said, "I'm glad the cheeky fellow didn't crawl into my bed."

The special train, consisting of a locomotive, the Pullman car, and a combination passenger/baggage car, chugged across the Central Valley, switching tracks along the way until it followed a spur line to the foothill community of Raymond, the jumping-off point for stagecoach access to Yosemite. In addition to Muir, the President's traveling companions included California Governor George Pardee, President of the University of California Benjamin Wheeler, President of Columbia University Nicholas Butler, the Secretary of Navy William Moody, Surgeon General Dr. Presley Rixey, the President's private secretary William Loeb, Jr., two Secret Service Agents and, after their arrival in Raymond, a squad of soldiers.

Significantly, no members of the Yosemite Commission had been invited to join the President's party. They had to content themselves by awaiting his arrival in Yosemite Valley. In Raymond, the Roosevelt group was met by two eleven-passenger coaches operated by the Yosemite Stage & Turnpike Company. The company's best coachman, Bright Gillespie, held the reins of the four-in-hand team of horses harnessed to the lead stage. A mounted company of thirty cavalrymen sat astride matching dapple-grey horses, ready to escort the President. The cavalrymen were the personification of the units that had been rotating in and out of the park for years, ambassadors of government when possible, policemen when necessary, and soldiers always.

Roosevelt was dressed for the occasion in shirt, sweater, baggy pants, leather puttees, and sturdy shoes. He sported a cowboy hat, bandanna around his neck, and wore a rugged Norfolk coat, just right for out-of-doors travel. The bearded Muir wore a dark and wrinkled suit of seemingly long-abused duration. For an asthma sufferer like Roosevelt, the dust kicked up by a stagecoach could have been troublesome, but he had picked a good month for his visit. In the springtime, the soil moisture held down the dust in the Sierra foothills and nourished green grasses and wildflowers.

The uphill stagecoach journey from Raymond to the Mariposa Grove of Giant Sequoias took a modest six hours, with stops to rest horses and passengers at Summit House and Sell's Ahwahnee Tavern, way-stations that catered to Yosemite's growing waves of tourist adventurers. When the party reached the Mariposa Grove, they were met by park rangers Charles Leidig and Archie Leonard. Animal packer Jack Alder had at the ready a string of horses and mules to be used in the next phase of the President's outing.

At the Mariposa Grove, the President ordered his distinguished traveling companions to be on their way to the comforts of the nearby Wawona Hotel. The cavalry troop and Secret Service Agents were to accompany the larger group while he stayed behind only with Muir, the two park rangers, and the animal packer. The plan was that Roosevelt and his trail companions would rendezvous two days hence with the larger group in Yosemite Valley. The Secret Service Agents were nervous about leaving the President unguarded, given events of the recent past, but he waved them along with a cheery "God bless you."

Soon after the others departed, Roosevelt discovered that his "wahh bag," a valise containing his personal toiletries and extra clothing, had been accidentally carried off to the hotel. "His jaws snapped together like a coyote," reported Muir, "and the flow of language made even the packers listen with admiring attention." Roosevelt's outburst was short-lived. He was where he wanted to be, enjoying the first of four prized days of "rest" in Yosemite in the company of sturdy companions.

Leidig assumed the responsibilities of camp cook and that first night served up fried chicken and seared beefsteak accompanied by potatoes and corn, biscuits or bread, black coffee that could hold a spoon upright, and perhaps something medicinal. Reminiscing years later about his night in the Mariposa Grove, Roosevelt wrote: "The majestic trunks, beautiful in color and symmetry, rose round us like the pillars of a mightier cathedral than ever was conceived by the fervor of the Middle Ages. Hermit thrushes sang beautifully in the evening, and again burst forth of wonderful music at dawn." To Leidig, the President expressed an entirely different, more practical desire. "I am tired and want to rest and sleep," he announced, and so there he was snuggled in a heap of blankets provided by his hosts, a tarp propped up over his head on two sticks anchored by rocks.

The next morning, camp coffee, bacon, and biscuits were waiting courtesy of Leidig, who had started the cook fire before dawn. By 6:30am the dishes had been scrubbed with ashes and the remaining campfire embers mixed with snow. Roosevelt's small party of experienced mountain men broke camp efficiently. Soon, all equipment was packed on mules and the men were mounted and ready for a day in the saddle. Although best known for his rambles on foot, Muir, the former bronco buster, was an excellent rider, a fact surely appreciated by Roosevelt who greatly respected the craft of fine horsemanship.

Leidig led the way. In the Yosemite country, trails are narrow and almost always constricted by a combination of rock, precipice, slope, timber, brush, pocket lakes and stream-freshened gorges. Riding is single file, the pace generally at a steady walk. The route chosen by Leidig, in keeping with the President's directive to "outskirt and keep away from civilization," was to follow a trail network that took the riders to about 9,000 feet in elevation, passing through Empire Meadow on the ascent and Westfall and McGurk Meadows during the descent past Taft Point, ending up at a campsite near Sentinel Dome, only a short distance from Glacier Point. The ride covered about twenty miles through wilderness. Even though it was May,

Leidig reported snow depths up to five feet. At one point the President's mount got "mired down" and "Charley had to get a log to get him out." The log was used as a make-do lever to help the horse regain footing. The men took turns breaking trail. Wind was blowing and snow falling. Roosevelt declared the adventure "delightful."

Leidig's choice of a campsite was sufficiently distant from Glacier Point to avoid the sight of James McCauley's box-like hotel, a jolting example of commercial intrusion that was best kept at arm's length for a few more hours. "Around the campfire that night Roosevelt and Muir talked far into the night regarding Muir's glacial theory of the formation of Yosemite Valley," Leidig later recalled. "They talked a great deal about the conservation of forests in general and Yosemite in particular. They discussed the setting aside of other areas in the United States for park purposes—during the trip, Muir seemed to bother the President by picking twigs for the President's buttonhole—there was some difficulty encountered because both men wanted to do the talking."

Freeman Tilden, in his book, *The National Parks*, said of Muir: "He frequently opened the word faucet and let the flood loose—two adjectives for every noun, a verbal phalanx in which every clause was trained to march straight ahead, fire a tremendous salvo at the end, and disperse the enemy, galvanize the unappreciative, and spread the good news of conservation to the world." Of course, the author might just as well have been describing the President. But if the two men were competing to make their thoughts known, the President was clearly receptive both to the surroundings and to Muir. Later he wrote, "Ordinarily, the man who loves the woods and mountains, the trees, the flowers, and the wild things, has in him some indefinable quality of charm, which appeals even to those sons of civilization who care for little outside of paved streets and brick walls. John Muir was a fine illustration of this rule."

Snow fell during the night while the Roosevelt party slept. Just after dawn the next morning, with the weather clearing, Roosevelt and Muir made their way to Glacier Point. A cavalry unit under the command of Colonel Joseph Garrard, five photographers, and a small gathering of spectators stood ready to welcome the President to the famous overlook and to capture the moment on film. In the brightening morning, Roosevelt and Muir stepped onto Overhanging Rock, the same place where Oliver Lippincott's Locomobile had rested uncertainly three years before. Muir in a dark suit, high-collared shirt, bow tie, and hat, stuck a large sprig of pine in his lapel for the occasion. Roosevelt, still dressed in his casual outdoors clothes, struck his natural pose of command and authority only inches from the rock's edge. Together, the two men symbolized the obligations of governance and the benefits of citizen advocacy; the resulting photograph stands among the most classic images ever to find its way out of a national park.

The President's precious hours of seclusion were now over. A day of reconnection with the public and the anxious commissioners lay ahead. Roosevelt, mounted and in the lead, started down the trail toward Yosemite Valley with Muir, Leidig, Leonard, and Alder following. The cavalry troop, spectators, and photographers took the alternate wagon road route back toward the valley. Leidig and Leonard were dressed for the occasion of meeting up with an expected crowd of well-wishers that they assumed would be waiting for the President at the end of this second day on the trail by wearing their best head gear and finest uniforms, white shirts, dark blue overalls accented by oiled chaps, boots, and shiny spurs. The riders were not using the famous Four-Mile Trail. They followed a different trail from Glacier Point that drops briskly down via a series of switchbacks to Illilouette Creek and then sneaks past the base of well-named Panorama Cliff. It intersects about a mile further on with a trail near Nevada Falls at the threshold of Little Yosemite Valley. From this point the riders would make an almost 180° turn onto a lower trail leading to Clark Point and still steeply downward to the base of Vernal Falls. From there, a short, gradual descent onto the valley floor remained.

Although the total distance of the ride from Glacier Point was only a little over eight miles, the elevation change was Yosemite-dramatic, over 3,000 feet, a steep trail by any measure. But the President and his experienced companions had no difficulty, leaning back in their saddles with feet thrust forward in the stirrups to maintain a teamwork center of gravity with their horses. Less experienced riders on the downhill tend to sit upright or even lean forward hanging onto the saddle horn, throwing their balance ajar, probably to the irritation of the mounts and certainly to the regret of their jolting bodies. On arrival at a prearranged lunch stop at the brim of Nevada Falls, the President and his trail partners were surprised by scores of excited men and women waiting there to greet them. Despite the demands of a strenuous uphill hike from Yosemite Valley to the lunch site, a happily assembled crowd of stylishly dressed men and women, many waving small American flags and sporting the red-white-and-blue on ribbons wrapped around their hats and bonnets, were there to greet the famous man. Ever the politician, Roosevelt rode forward to acknowledge his admirers, then circled back to whisper to Leidig that the stop would be brief. Soon mounted again, the horsemen were followed down the trail by the foot-borne enthusiasts.

Little did Roosevelt know that an even more festive event awaited him when he reached the floor of Yosemite Valley. Leidig later recalled that "Mr. John Stevens, Guardian of the valley under the State administration, and certain of his Commissioners, especially Jack Wilson from San Francisco, had made plans for a large celebration. The Chris Jorgenson Studio home had been set aside for the President's official use. A cook had been engaged from one of the best hotels in San Francisco to serve a banquet. The Commissioners had arranged a considerable display of fireworks." When Roosevelt reached the cluster of tents at Camp Curry, an eager crowd, estimated by the startled Leidig to be about one thousand people, blocked the path. Yosemite Valley was still very remote and the season early, but there they were, onlookers on horseback, passengers in surreys, wagons, and buggies, a few in automobiles, and hundreds more on foot, all pushing forward to have a look at their President.

Leidig, who had been riding just behind the President, was on a spirited horse and carrying a Winchester rifle, his holstered revolver prominently on display. In an instant he galloped past, shouting "Follow me." Leidig raced straight at the front rank of the crowd, only pulling back hard on the reins at the last moment and giving his mount a little spur in the same instant. The horse skidded on its hind legs and reared, front hooves pawing the air. Waving the Winchester, Leidig hollered at the crowd to stand aside. Roosevelt doffed his hat, smiled, and waved to the spectators as his horse galloped through the gap.

John Stevens (who served as park guardian from 1899 to 1904), the commissioners, and Roosevelt's traveling party, having arrived safely from the Wawona Hotel, were awaiting the President at Sentinel Bridge, but the commissioners' elaborately-laid plans for a splendid evening of welcome and revelry were immediately crushed. Roosevelt allowed himself to be escorted by the officials to the Jorgenson Studio where he accepted a glass of wine from the artist and viewed several paintings, but then he announced apologetically that he would have to bypass the banquet. Instead, the five camping companions, again absent the commissioners, headed west toward Bridalveil Meadow, a journey that provided the President with ample opportunities to see examples of the pioneer ramshackle sprawl that blighted the valley.

The final night around the campfire included more talk between Roosevelt and Muir, the park rangers making sure that curious onlookers stayed at a distance. At one point the President and naturalist walked out into the meadow for private conversation, probably on the subject of the bifurcated management of Yosemite. During the meadow walk or otherwise on the camping trip, Muir surely must have encouraged the President to bring the full measure of national park protection to the valley. The next morning, with bystanders still ringing the meadow, Roosevelt was reunited again with his traveling party who once more had stayed the night in hotel accommodations, this time in the valley, perhaps enjoying the banquet that the President deliberately avoided. Roosevelt pronounced the trip to be full of "wonderful relaxation."

Just as the President was saying his goodbyes, Muir suddenly remembered the assignment he had been given by Charles Sargent. The President later recounted Muir's last-minute fumbling: "He informed me that his friend had written him, asking him to get from me personal letters to the Russian Czar and Chinese Emperor; and when I explained to him that I could not give personal letters to foreign potentates, he said, 'Oh, well, read the letter yourself, and that will explain just what I want.' Accordingly, he thrust the letter on me. It contained not only the request but also Sargent's unadorned preface: 'I hear Roosevelt is coming out to see you. He takes a sloppy, unintelligent interest in forests, although he is altogether too much under the influence of that creature Gifford Pinchot, and you had better get from him letters—so that we may have better opportunity to examine the forests and trees of the Old World.' Of course I laughed heartily as I read the letter," Roosevelt reminisced, "and said, 'John, do you remember exactly the words in which this letter is couched?' Whereupon a look of startled surprise came over his face, and he said, 'Good gracious, there was something unpleasant about you in it, wasn't there. I had forgotten.' So I gave him back the letter, telling him I appreciated it far more than if it had not contained the phrases he had forgotten, and that while I could not give him and his companion letters to the two rulers in question, I would give him letters to our Ambassadors, which would bring the same result."

The year after the Yosemite event, Muir did circle the globe studying trees and plants, accompanied for about half the journey by Sargent. This was an important adventure for Muir, but of far less consequence than the meaningful result that flowed from the brief association between Roosevelt and Muir on Yosemite trails.

ONE NATIONAL PARK

For several years prior to Roosevelt's visit, Muir and many of his Sierra Club associates had been promoting the idea of returning the state grant lands at Yosemite to the federal government in the firm belief that such action would improve conservation of natural resources. They had won crucial support for the tactic from California Governor George C. Pardee who judged that the transfer of jurisdiction would rid the state of a troubling expense. The governor had support from newspaper editors in San Francisco, Oakland, Sacramento, Santa Barbara, Fresno, and Los Angeles, the lion's share of editorial backing in California at the time. The Sierra Club was joined in its lobbying effort to void the Yosemite Grant, technically known as re-cession, by several other organizations, most notably the California State Board of Trade. The Yosemite Commissioners, various members of the California Legislature, and some who judged themselves to be deserving stakeholders in Yosemite took a contrary view of the idea. But Roosevelt, Pardee, and Muir had a formidable ally, railroad tycoon E. H. Harriman.

Harriman and Roosevelt had worked together on several conservation and business projects when Roosevelt served as Governor of New York, especially the establishment of the innovative Palisades Interstate Park Commission designed to prevent destruction of natural scenery and to preserve historic sites in the Hudson River Valley. And Harriman knew Muir from the scientific cruise to Alaska in 1899 aboard the *Elder*. The tycoon had subsequently invited Muir to spend a summer at Harriman's getaway lodge at Pelican Bay, Klamath Lake, Oregon.

Harriman's political clout was nationwide based on the substantial financial benefits that his railroad network brought to communities across the land. At the beginning of the 20th century he stood at the pinnacle of transnational business enterprise, sharing this rarified space with only a handful of other multi-millionaires, among them John D. Rockefeller and J. P. Morgan. From secluded Arden House, Harriman's 100,000-square-foot mansion on his 7,800-acre estate forty miles north of New York City, his influence on matters financial and political were always at his fingertips. Most likely, he required little persuasion to become allied with Roosevelt and Muir in the Yosemite cause, undoubtedly seeing the opportunity as a blend of conservation and commerce that fit nicely into his overall business strategy. When Harriman made known to political leaders in California that he was interested in the outcome of the Yosemite matter, the result was dramatic.

The State of California Assembly was first to act, approving re-cession of the Yosemite Grant by a comfortable margin, but trouble lurked in the California Senate. Senator John Curtin was particularly vocal in opposition. In addition to his senate duties, Curtin was a cattleman who grazed his herds in the Sierra Nevada near Yosemite

     Your Yosemite: **PROTECTING A PUBLIC TREASURE**

Valley. On more than one occasion he had come into conflict with U. S. Cavalry troopers who patrolled and protected the surrounding national park lands. Curtin objected to interference by the cavalry with his prerogatives to do as he pleased with his herds and argued against any further expansion of federal authority in the Yosemite region. He started buttonholing his senate colleagues on the issue. His effort to find enough votes to torpedo the re-cession initiative was proving successful.

Holway Jones, author of *John Muir and the Sierra Club*, estimates that only a dozen or so senators were initially on the side of Governor Pardee whereas more than twenty seemed to stand with Curtin. Before the vote was taken, however, intermediaries representing Harriman made known that important railroad interests were at stake and that favorable approval of the re-cession was desired. Message received: When the vote was taken on February 23, 1905, a clear majority supported the governor. About two weeks later, Governor Pardee signed the legislation, signaling the end to more than four decades of Yosemite Valley custodianship by the state-appointed commissioners. The commissioners remained in place for another year pending acceptance of the re-cession by the United States Congress.

On June 11, 1906, President Roosevelt signed into law the necessary legislation that returned authority for the care and management of Yosemite Valley and the Mariposa Grove of Giant Sequoias to the federal government. He also pledged that the government would provide sufficient funding to administer these lands. Almost a half-century after the lands in the Yosemite region were judged to be so prized that they were be held "inalienable" for public benefit, Yosemite National Park had been made legislatively intact. The park encompasses ecosystems varying more than 10,000 feet in elevation, with pockets of perpetual winter hidden in the recesses of treeless peaks on the eastern boundary and lowland vales on the western boundary where summertime temperatures regularly soar beyond the century mark. In between is a profusion of life forms. Cyril and Robert Stebbins, in their booklet, *Birds of Yosemite*, said that, "In a distance of seventy miles between the edge of the foothills and the

Sierran crest, changes in kinds of plants and animals occur that are similar to those found over the vast area between the southern United States and the Arctic tundra."

Roosevelt's enthusiasm for the Yosemite success was no surprise. When the 26th President left office in 1909 he could take credit for inspired conservation achievements that exceeded anything accomplished by other political leaders in either the United States or across the world. On his conservation list are five national parks including Yosemite-made-whole, eighteen national monuments, four game preserves, fifty-one bird preserves, and one-hundred-fifty national forests—a total of more than 230 million acres of protected natural and cultural resources.

Years later, after leaving office, Roosevelt commented that, "The movement for the conservation of wildlife and the larger movement for conservation of all our natural resources are essentially democratic in spirit, purpose, and method."

The early conservation experiment at Yosemite had opened the legislative door for Yellowstone; Yellowstone had then returned the lawmaking compliment to Yosemite. And yet the concept of national parks was still very much in flux, the experiment unresolved, with Yosemite a volatile laboratory.

8

Stars and Stripes in the Valley

ON AUGUST 1, 1906, the newly promoted Major Harry C. Benson (1857–1924) and a company of the Sixth U. S. Cavalry, freed from exile at Camp A. E. Wood up in the mountains at Wawona, rode into the valley to establish "Camp Yosemite." He and his men brought with them the Stars-and-Stripes and the authority that Congress and the President had vested in them. The state commissioners were gone, handing over to Benson all the perplexities of a park experiment now in full thrust.

A tough man in his second army tour at Yosemite, Benson was known while stationed at Camp A. E. Wood for having captured fourteen sheepherders in one week, a cavalry record. He was a West Point graduate, class of 1882, an expert marksman, and a veteran in the campaign against Apache Indians led by Geronimo. On one occasion, Benson was cited for riding ninety miles in nineteen hours while carrying out his duties.

The cavalry camp Benson established in Yosemite Valley consisted of tents on wooden platforms and several durable buildings, including a headquarters, field hospital, commissary, blacksmith shop, and the ever-necessary guardhouse. The cavalry presence in the park was dictated by the seasons. The troopers would be on patrol in the snowless months and then return to the Presidio in San Francisco during winter. Although Benson had received no training at West Point or in field assignments to prepare him for the civilian aspect of his job at Yosemite, he did know the military side. Gabriel Sovulewski, a civilian trail builder working with the cavalry, reported that "officers with detachments set out upon patrols that would keep them away from their base of supplies for thirty days. Many times rations were short and sixteen or twenty hours of action per day, covering sixty miles in the saddle, was not unusual. Constant hammering at the offending cattlemen (and sheepherders) continued for several years."

As acting superintendent, Major Benson faced many challenges, not all glamorous. The late historian Shirley Sargent reported that the soldiers' first assault "was on sanitation, or rather the lack of it. Five public campgrounds, three of them adjacent to meadows where campers pastured their horses and mules, were closed because none boasted so much as a privy." To add to the problem, the local hotel operators were using the Merced River and its tributary streams as a convenient means of washing away raw sewage.

Benson knew, as did all West-Point-trained officers of the era, that poor sanitation could pose severe danger. During the Civil War, soldiers who died of infection and disease numbered more than a staggering 400,000 while deaths by gunfire were less than half that number. Yosemite Valley was small, only seven square miles, and the human population was quickly increasing. Tackling the sanitation problem would win no medals, but inattention could prove lethal.

He also quickly noted that the valley was a "death trap" in another sense: "Practically every person living in the valley kept a rifle, shotgun, and revolver, and any animal or bird that was unfortunate enough to enter was immediately pursued and captured or killed." Benson took a firm stand against the indiscriminate use of guns and traps in the national park, receiving in return the wrath of angry tourists and residents who saw little contradiction between killing wildlife and preserving the park's natural beauty. The fact that Benson did see and act on this contradiction, unguided at the time by any official written policy, is a commentary on his determination to establish practical management standards by which the park values would be preserved.

Among his responsibilities, he was dealing with at least twenty-five permits issued by the commissioners for various commercial activities in the park. Benson was not impressed by most of these activities, reporting in a letter to the Secretary of the Interior that "the place, during the last few years, has come to resemble Coney Island. In my opinion most of these concessions are totally unnecessary

Jack Gaylor, Park Ranger, circa 1906

and should not be renewed," referring to the "cheap buildings" that had sprung up here and there around the valley.

Benson's men were slowly extending trail systems, stocking fish in high country lakes and streams, mapping the territory, and winning their battle against the livestock trespassers in the high country. Containing visitation in the valley, however, was another matter. A spur line railroad would reach El Portal in 1907, just a few miles downriver from the valley's western entrance. Automobiles were chug-chugging along the wagon roads and stagecoaches full of tourists were continually rolling in, announced by clouds of dust. The number of summertime visitors was fast approaching 6,000.

To cope with this flood of people, Benson relied in part on the hand-ful of civilian park rangers that had become auxiliary to the troop-ers. These unschooled men were learning on a daily basis that their official presence became a magnet for visitors who wanted informa-tion, assistance of all kinds, emergency aid, and, when necessary, a police officer. Archie Leonard and Charles Leidig were the first rangers to be recruited, joined under Benson's command by An-drew Jack Gaylor. Like his co-workers, Gaylor had credentials that put him at ease in rugged terrain, but possessed few skills as a host in a national park.

Gaylor was an animal packer working for the military, basically a logistics expert who delivered supplies by horse and mule to outlying Army encampments. He worked in intricate alliance with his stock animals to deliver the goods, sometimes to almost impossible places. The five bullet scars on his body were proof that some of those places had not been on friendly ground. A cowboy from Wyoming territory, Gaylor lived by the motto, "Love many, trust few, and always paddle your own canoe." He had served under Theodore Roosevelt in Cuba and with American expeditionary forces in the Philippines, packing everything to troops in the field from food and medical supplies to explosives and heavy weapons. He was known as an exceptional horseman, but his practical mount-of-choice in rough country was a trusty riding mule. He kept his pack animals fit and fed and roped down well-balanced loads on their backs for the long haul. He contended with all sorts of accidents and surprises, made solitary camp along the trail when necessary, and generally found a hearty welcome from troopers when he reached remote outposts.

Major Benson must have seen something special in this weather-worn, mustachioed, lanky ex-packer. At fifty-one years of age, armed as always with his Winchester carbine and Colt 45 revolver, Gaylor shifted to the chores of "lawman, fish planter, handyman, forest fire fighter, rescuer, protector of wildlife, and wandering information bureau," as historian John Bingamon described the duties of America's first park rangers. Gaylor was at the grassroots level of authority where hooves met the earth. In one instance while on horseback, he literally shot out the tires of a Model-T Ford "tin lizzy" to halt some joyriding teenagers who had failed to stop on his command. He served for fourteen years in Yosemite, reaching the rank of assistant chief park ranger, and died with his boots on at a backcountry ranger station at Merced Lake. His patrol partner, Andy Swartz, packed him out, draped over the withers of a trusty mule. A measure of the professional respect Gaylor gained among his contemporaries is still suggested by the surrounding geography: Gaylor Peak, Gaylor Lakes, and Gaylor Basin, all landmarks in the

High Sierra near Tioga Pass, now tributes to this one man's effort to form profound alliances with the living natural environment, not to defeat, but to defend.

About fifteen miles as the crow flies from Gaylor Lakes, tucked in the heart of the Yosemite wilderness, is exquisite Benson Lake, a memorial to Major Benson. Historian Bingamon says of Benson, "In the early days of the national parks it took more than ordinary energy, enthusiasm and ability to protect them from depredations and misuse. Moreover, it took courage to face the hostility of men, often powerful and influential, whose selfish interests were thwarted by withdrawal of the park lands from exploitation. Many officers and men contributed to this valuable service, but Benson stands pre-eminent among them, not alone because of the long period of his activity in national parks, but because he also brought to his task a prophetic vision." The "long period of activity" to which Bingamon refers included, in 1908, Benson's reassignment from Yosemite to Yellowstone where he served as acting superintendent for two years, fighting pitched battles with gangs of poachers. He eventually retired from military service with the rank of colonel.

A FAR AWAY EARTHQUAKE RATTLES THE PARK

In any national park, some events are well beyond the control of the resident chief administrator. On April, 18, 1906, just weeks before President Theodore Roosevelt signed the legislation to merge Yosemite Valley and the Mariposa Grove of Giant Sequoias with the larger national park, and only about three months before Benson arrived in the valley, a shock occurred in the San Francisco Bay Area that would affect Yosemite with unanticipated political force. The San Andreas Fault rumbled to life.

This fault line, formed by the colossal North American and Pacific tectonic plates, extends for almost 800 miles, angling through California from the Salton Sea near the boundary with Mexico to Cape Mendocino near the Oregon border where the fault line veers away from land into the ocean. At regular intervals, the contest of geologic tension between these plates gives way to abrupt slippage between them, causing earthquakes. In 1906, the epicenter of slippage in the fault line was practically underneath San Francisco. At the time, San Francisco was the largest city on the U. S. Pacific Coast, home to about 400,000 people, a hodgepodge of mostly wooden structures packed closely together and warmed by stoves and fireplaces. The quake struck at a devastating level, later estimated on the Richter Scale to be between 7.7 and 8.25 in order of magnitude, collapsing buildings and dumping fire from hearths that swiftly flared to the level of disaster, sweeping uncontrolled flames through the city and killing thousands. The quake and subsequent fire destroyed about eighty percent of the city's infrastructure.

Yosemite was insulated from the quake by distance. The ripple effect that would hit the national park would not be in the form of falling rock and torn earth, but in the form of a huge man-made concrete structure later to be named the O'Shaughnessy Dam. Upstream from the dam an 8-mile long reservoir, 300-feet deep, would contain 360,000-acre-feet of trapped Tuolumne River water.

JOHN MUIR AND THE BATTLE TO PRESERVE HETCH HETCHY

Even as the earthquake catastrophe struck, officials in San Francisco had been desperate to increase the fresh-water supply to the city. Local wells and streams were inadequate to meet the fast-growing need. Equally of concern, the city's primary water sources were privately owned, a circumstance that made residents vulnerable to price-gouging as demand increased. Even before the fire, engineers had been eyeing the abundant flow of fresh water that poured into the Central Valley from the Sierra Nevada, a source that, if it could be tapped, would prove to be of immense economic and safety benefit to the city. In the urgent scramble to recover from the earthquake, developing an ample source of water for San Francisco became a top priority. The trick for the engineers was to find stable rock in a narrow defile that would serve as a natural anchor for a man-made dam. They were searching for a site that promised minimum construction in return for a reservoir of generous depth and volume.

     Your Yosemite: **PROTECTING A PUBLIC TREASURE**

Many choices existed, but none was so appealing to engineers as Hetch Hetchy Valley, named by Native Americans for the brome, ryegrass, oniongrass, and other plants that produced edible seeds. From an engineering perspective, the site was ideal. Hetch Hetchy is a glaciated valley similar to Yosemite Valley, immense in scenic quality with waterfalls pouring down from precipitous granite walls, wide meadows, and a narrow exit through which river water escaped into the foothills. It also was like Yosemite Valley in another respect: Hetch Hetchy was preserved within the boundaries of Yosemite National Park to be held "inalienable" for future generations.

Advocates for a new San Francisco water source began to argue that Hetch Hetchy Valley was subject to flooding during springtime run-off, plagued by clouds of mosquitoes in summer, so far from popular tourist routes that it was visited by almost no one, and therefore basically useless. They contended that nothing of value would be lost by drowning the place under a massive reservoir. From the perspective of San Francisco officials, the fact that the valley was part of a national park only increased its desirability. There would be no need to purchase land rights if control of the valley could be transferred from the federal government to the city. John Muir, on the other hand, who had visited Hetch Hetchy on his rambles in the Sierra Nevada, judged the valley to be "a grand landscape garden," full of flowering meadow plants, sheltering oak and ponderosa, and rich in wildlife.

The battle was joined. Muir and his allies had hardly caught their breath after the re-cession victory at Yosemite before they found themselves facing off against city leaders who had access to state and national policymakers at the highest level. Muir had his stature, pen, paper, word craft, and stalwart colleagues, Robert Underwood Johnson among them. At issue was the meaning and purpose of national parks. Were they federal storehouses of land temporarily set aside only until other human-defined purposes consumed them, or were they to be honored as inestimable environmental treasures preserved for the ages? There was no question that the earthquake-battered San Francisco Bay Area was in need of a fresh, clean source of water. Muir and Johnson did not protest this reasoning.

They protested that city engineers were unwilling to consider other choices for a water supply from among the many rivers flowing down from the Sierra Nevada in less vulnerable locations. The engineers seemed fixated on making Hetch Hetchy Valley into a "water-tank," as described by Muir, and in the process risking rupture of the hard-fought and still infant concept of national parks.

The majority of residents in the Bay Area were not swayed by the fact that Hetch Hetchy was inside a national park. Even Warren Olney, who had provided such adept legal assistance in the formation of the Sierra Club and had gone on to serve as Mayor of Oakland, aligned himself with the reservoir project, injuring forever his relationship with Muir. The Sierra Club was also torn. A majority of the members supported Muir, but a substantial minority sided with Olney, underscoring the divisiveness of the choice to be made. In the numbing aftermath of the earthquake, few in the city wanted to spend time searching for more acceptable water sources if the city engineers said that Hetch Hetchy was the best option.

The odds were heavily against Muir. No nationwide advocate group stood by his side, and no umbrella agency at the federal level had been legislatively established in oversight of the national parks. Each park was essentially on its own. Although officially a part of the Department of the Interior, that department's envoys in the parks, primarily the U. S. Army, were not in the business of defending them politically. In 1908, the year that Major Benson was transferred from Yosemite to Yellowstone, legislation was introduced in the U. S. Congress that would allow the City of San Francisco to take control of water resources in Hetch Hetchy Valley and in a smaller valley nearby also within the park's boundary for the purpose of constructing reservoirs. Senate and House of Representatives committee hearings on the legislation proceeded. Muir was not present at these hearings, but his opposition to the project was known. His stature at the time among the nation's preeminent nature writers assured high scrutiny and extended debate on the issue.

Months became years while city officials pushed determinedly for Hetch Hetchy approval. Muir vigorously pushed back. In 1912, Muir's book, *The Yosemite*, published by Robert Underwood Johnson's

Hetch Hetchy Reservoir, circa 1923

Century Press, indicted the promoters of the reservoir project, and, by implication, all those who might attempt to molest the integrity of any park. Muir wrote: "That anyone would try to destroy Hetch Hetchy Valley seems incredible, but sad experience shows that there are people good enough and bad enough for anything. The proponents of the dam scheme bring forward a lot of bad arguments to prove that the only righteous thing to do with the people's parks is to destroy them bit by bit as they are able."

The controversy came to a head in 1913, in testimony before the House of Representatives Committee on Public Lands, chaired by Congressman Scott Ferris of Oklahoma. Among those in attendance and ready to testify was Gifford Pinchot (1865–1946), the founder of the U. S. Forest Service and a close political confidant of Theodore Roosevelt. Pinchot had been forced from office as the nation's chief forester in 1910 by President William Howard Taft in

an internal Republican Party dispute over the land conservation policies that Pinchot vigorously championed. Now he was running for
a U.S. Senate seat in Pennsylvania on Roosevelt's Progressive (Bull
Moose) Party ticket. Pinchot's involvement in the hearings, and
by implication Roosevelt's endorsement, represented a shattering
challenge to Muir. While serving as the chief forester, Pinchot had
endorsed the return of Yosemite Valley and the Mariposa Grove of
Giant Sequoias to federal control. He also had championed extension of forest reserves in others parts of the Sierra Nevada, another
cause favored by Muir. But the tables had turned: Pinchot opposed
Muir on Hetch Hetchy.

At the Congressional hearing Pinchot was given deference as a senior
government official and was among the first to make a statement:
"So we come now face to face with the perfectly clean question of
what is the best use to which water that flows out of the Sierra can
be put. As we all know, there is no use of water that is higher than
the domestic use. Then, if there is, as engineers tell us, no other
source of supply that is anything like so reasonably available as this
one; if this is the best and, within reasonable limits of cost, the only
means of supplying San Francisco with water, we come straight to
the question of whether the advantage of leaving this valley in a
state of nature is greater than the advantage of using it for the benefit of the city of San Francisco. Now, the fundamental principle of
the whole conservation policy is that of use, to take every part of
the land and its resources and put it to that use in which it will best
serve the most people. I think that the men who assert that it is better to leave a piece of natural scenery in its natural condition have
rather the better argument, and I believe if we had nothing else to
consider than the delight of the few men and women who would
yearly go into Hetch Hetchy Valley, then it should be left in its natural condition. But considerations on the other side of the question
to my mind are simply overwhelming, and so much so that I have
never been able to see that there is any reasonable argument against
the use of this water supply by the city of San Francisco."

Congressman John Raker of California, chief sponsor of the legislation, asked Pinchot, "Taking the scenic beauty of the park as it now stands, and the fact that the valley is sometimes swamped along in June and July, is it not a fact that if a beautiful dam is put there, as is contemplated, and as the picture is given by the engineers, with the roads contemplated around the reservoir and with other trails, it will be more beautiful than it is now, and give more opportunity for the use of the park?"

This rationale was even a bit too much for Pinchot, who expressed doubt that construction of a dam and reservoir would enhance nature's handiwork in Hetch Hetchy Valley. Raker, then referring to Muir's "criticism" of the legislation asked Pinchot if he knew the naturalist. "Yes, sir; I know him very well. He is an old and very good friend of mine. I have never been able to agree with him in his attitude toward the Sierras for the reason that my point of view has never appealed to him at all. When I became forester and denied the right to exclude sheep and cows from the Sierras, Mr. Muir thought I had made a great mistake, because I allowed the use by an acquired right of a large number of people to interfere with what would have been the utmost beauty of the forest. In this case I think he has unduly given away to beauty as against use."

James Phelan, who had served as Mayor of San Francisco from 1897 to 1902 and, like Pinchot, was an aspiring U. S. Senate candidate, gave a particularly graphic description of how a dam might enhance the landscape. In response to a question from the committee chairman, Phelan described the beauties of California and added: "All of this is of tremendous pride, and even for a water supply we would not injure the great resources which have made our state the playground of the world. By constructing a dam at this very narrow gorge in the Hetch Hetchy Valley, about 700-feet across, we create, not a reservoir, but a lake, because Mr. Freeman, who had studied the situation in Manchester and Birmingham [England], where there is a similar case, has shown that by planting trees or vines over the dam, the idea of the dam, the appearance of the dam, is entirely lost; so, coming upon it, it will look like an emerald gem in the mountains; and one of the few things in which California is deficient, especially in the Sierras, is lakes, and in this way we will contribute, in large measure, to the scenic grandeur and beauty of California. I suppose nature lovers, suspecting a dam there not made by the Creator, will think it of no value, in their estimation, but I submit, man can imitate the Creator—a worthy exemplar."

Whatever the comparison to a dam in England, the scale probably was not analogous. The dam on the Tuolumne River was anticipated to rise 227 feet (later extended upward to 364 feet), its sharply-angled, almost sheer concrete face not particularly adaptable to vine and tree camouflage.

In written testimony, Robert Underwood Johnson tried to counter Pinchot's philosophical argument about the multiple benefits of resource exploitation: "There never was a time when there was a more urgent necessity for our country to uphold its best ideals and its truest welfare against shortsighted opportunism and purely commercial and local interests. In 1889-90 came an awakening, largely through the efforts of John Muir, discoverer of the Muir Glacier, a man combining in himself the ideal and the practical as few men of our day. It was he who awakened the administration of President Harrison to the necessity of conserving the public forests instead of giving them over to the tender mercies of the chance comer." He continued, "What is at stake is not merely the destruction of a single valley, one of the most wonderful works of the Creator, but the fundamental principle of conservation. The time has not yet come to substitute for our national motto those baleful words, 'let us drink, be merry, for to-morrow we die.' The records of the hearing before the Senate Committee on Public Lands two or three years ago show that two official representatives of the city confessed that the city could get water anywhere along the Sierra if she would pay for it. This is the crux of the whole matter. The assault upon the integrity of the park has this purpose—to get something for nothing."

Then, turning to the issue of tourism, Johnson added, "As for the general public of travelers, that take so much money to California in quest of beauty—there would be only a phantom valley, sunken, like the fabled city of Brittany, while the twenty miles of the most wonderful rapids in the world, the cascades of the Tuolumne, would be virtually eclipsed." Johnson pleaded with the committee members to consider that "without a touch of idealism, this sense of beauty, life could only be a race for the trough."

Clearly at issue in these hearings was the theoretical dividing line between Muir and Pinchot. While Pinchot served as the nation's first chief forester from 1905 to 1910, he tried to fold the national parks, then existing, into his concept of tapping into natural resources where commercial promise was found. His premise, known as multiple-use, was for him an optimistic balancing act where activities such as logging, mining, extraction of fossil fuels, livestock grazing, and dam building on public lands could be balanced against thoughtful resource preservation and stewardship.

Up to a point, Muir agreed with Pinchot, most tellingly represented by the forest reserves Muir had sought for those portions of the Sierra Nevada not protected within national park boundaries. But Muir went a step further, defending in both word and deed the priceless quality of wild places so vibrant and exhilarating that humankind's ultimate responsibility was to place them in trust so that people of all ages, for all time, could seek their lessons and enjoy their benefits. Hetch Hetchy Valley, supposedly secure within the bounds of Yosemite National Park, had been designated as one of those matchless places. Muir could not fathom that the park boundary could be viewed so soon by so many as merely a nuisance to be overcome, especially when San Francisco's need could be met in other, less compelling locales more suitable to Pinchot's vision of multiple-use.

The effort by Muir and Johnson to defend Hetch Hetchy proved futile. In 1913, by a vote of 43 to 25 (with 29 abstentions) in the House of Representatives, the "Raker Act" was approved, followed soon by a similarly positive vote in the Senate. President Woodrow Wilson signed the legislation, and Muir was in despair. He wrote, "As to the loss of the Sierra Park Valley it's hard to bear. The destruction of the charming groves and gardens, the finest in all California, goes to my heart. But in spite of Satan & Co. some sort of compensation must surely come out of this dark damn-dam-damnation."

Muir's hope was fulfilled ten years later, just as the O'Shaughnessy Dam was completed. In Yellowstone, attempts were being made to construct dams in the park to provide irrigation water for farmers on adjacent lands, especially by raising the level of Yellowstone Lake and, in a separate project, flooding a broad area in the southwestern corner of the park called Bechler Meadow. The argument to flood the meadow had echoes of Hetch Hetchy. Historian Michael J. Yochim states that "irrigators believed that their dams would not threaten, but would rather enhance, park resources. The Bechler dam will result in replacing what is now mostly an unattractive swamp with a mountain lake.' The swamp had 'no value or scenic beauty, but was infested with flies and mosquitoes during the summer months.'"

The farmers and their political allies tried to use Hetch Hetchy as a precedent for their own initiative, but it backfired. As Yochim explains, "In a way, the country needed a Hetch Hetchy somewhere in the national parks to illustrate what did not belong in them, to demonstrate that national parks should be inviolate. It may be easier to actually see what is wrong in a park than to imagine it; Yosemite provided the illustration of what not to do in Yellowstone."

Among the many vocal opponents to building dams in Yellowstone was the Sierra Club Secretary, William Colby, Muir's confidant in the re-cession battle. The New York City-based weekly magazine, *The Outlook*, that had carried articles by Muir and supported him in the Hetch Hetchy battle, and, beginning in 1909, claimed Theodore Roosevelt as an associate editor, provided an effective voice in favor of national park preservation policies. The key political victory for conservationists at Yellowstone came in 1923 when the effort to approve a dam for Yellowstone Lake was defeated in Congress, thus countering the Hetch Hetchy loss and establishing a precedent that later would serve to defend other parks, including the Grand Canyon. Bechler Meadow also was saved from reservoir flooding.

Muir would not live to witness the Yellowstone events. Described as "isolated and despondent" after accepting that Hetch Hetchy would be flooded, he retreated to his home in Martinez. The impacts of deteriorating health were catching up with the naturalist. At age seventy-six, Muir traveled to southern California to visit his daughter Helen. While on this trip he became ill with pneumonia. Alone in a Los Angeles Hospital, he died on December 24, 1914. In the year he died, concrete was being poured at Hetch Hetchy. The 167-mile pipeline that eventually would transport water from the reservoir to San Francisco is all that the engineers imagined, a gravity-fed marvel, but the "lake," controlled by the City of San Francisco, is strictly off-limits to the public; no fishing, boating, or swimming allowed. Access at this location to northern wilderness areas in Yosemite requires hikers and equestrians to tromp right across the top of the dam.

In theory, The Raker Act also allowed for the generation of hydro-electric power to be distributed by the City of San Francisco at low cost to municipal residents. The city promptly reneged on this legal requirement, instead selling much of the power at wholesale prices to the privately owned Pacific Gas & Electric Company. In turn, the company resells the electricity at retail prices, reaping huge prof-its. This cozy arrangement between the city and the PG & E has been questioned for many years, but today remains largely intact. For the privilege of using the water and hydroelectric resources of the Hetch Hetchy Reservoir, the city pays the federal government $30,000 per year.

A TRIBUTE TO MUIR

The year after Muir's death, in an ironic juxtaposition of govern-ment prerogatives, members of the California legislature, most of whom had supported the Hetch Hetchy project, voted to appropri-ate $10,000 for the survey and construction of a High Sierra trail that would memorialize Muir's visionary environmental leadership. Such a trail had long been imagined by members of the Sierra Club, especially by Joseph LeConte who led several scouting trips into the mountains in search of a suitable route. This money spurred the project forward. Over time, legislators made four supplementary appropriations, totaling an additional $40,000. The John Muir trail system which extends from the Happy Isles Nature Center in Yosemite Valley to the summit of Mt. Whitney in Sequoia National Park was completed in 1938, allowing backcountry adventurers to travel for more than two hundred miles through some of the most spectacular wilderness in the forty-eight contiguous states. This trail and the Hetch Hetchy reservoir form opposing stanchions of the John Muir era; one a "water-tank" off limits to the public that to this day symbolizes the potential vulnerability of national parks, and the other, only a slight scratch on hard rock or in the soil of delicate alpine meadows, that invites communion with the natural world.

Both physical imprints on Yosemite remain very much in place. The John Muir Trail ranks among the great avenues to personal outdoor joy available to anyone who chooses to join in the contest between muscle and dazzling reward. Until recently, the dam and reservoir in Hetch Hetchy Valley were just there, seemingly permanent fixtures shoved off on a side road near a wilderness trailhead, merely tolerated and seen only by a handful of annual visitors to the park. The debate had quieted until Mike Marshall and like-minded activists began in recent years to renew it. The organization, Restore Hetch Hetchy, has been formed. Donations to this nonprofit organization are beginning to increase. Residents of San Francisco and their political leaders are being asked to think about water conservation and viable options affirmed by representatives of the University of California, Davis, the Environmental Defense Fund, and the California Department of Water Resources that would allow for the removal of the O'Shaughnessy Dam while still assuring abundant Tuolumne River water and power resources for the San Francisco Bay Area. Recruited to the cause as advisors were three former Yosemite Superintendents, B. J. Griffin, David Mahalik, and me. In December, 2013, an opinion-editorial statement signed by the three of us appeared in the *San Jose Mercury News*. We said, "A century ago, our nation sought to tame the wilderness with large-scale engineering projects, occasionally with destructive results. Today we should commit to undoing one of the worst examples of that destruction. And tomorrow, we can watch a magnificent valley emerge from the depths. Let's make Yosemite National Park whole again."

9

Stephen Mather, Man Of The Moment

DURING MUIR'S LIFETIME no other nation anywhere on earth had deliberately chosen to establish inalienable guardianship of precious natural places, identify them with legal boundaries, and present them for public benefit generation upon generation. This was the spark of the national park idea; bold in vision; vulnerable to interpretation. The testing had come almost immediately in many forms of trespass and in the loss at Hetch Hetchy, but the idea was strong and growing in acceptance. While tests of park authenticity were underway, a graduate of the University of California, Berkeley, named Stephen T. Mather (1867–1930) joined the Sierra Club in 1904 at age thirty-seven. During his lifetime, this native Californian would bring the fledgling concept of national parks to a new height of institutional stability.

Allegorically speaking, Mather's footsteps continued along the pathway left by Roosevelt on the Hudson River Palisades and at Yosemite. Mather used the Palisades Interstate Park System as a place to learn and to refine his thinking about a network of public parks that would reserve the best of our natural heritage for all to enjoy. He used Yosemite as a testing ground for this concept.

Mather lived for a time in New York City after college, no apparent thought of parks in mind, where he worked as a reporter for the *New York Sun*. Five years later he joined the same company that employed his father, an enterprise founded by a former prospector named Francis M. Smith. Smith had discovered a deposit of sodium tetraborate, otherwise known as borax, in Nevada decades earlier and had become a millionaire. Borax accumulates over thousands of years as soft crystals formed by repeated evaporation of mineral-laden waters in arid lands. The crystals, lacking the glitter of gold, but more abundant and easily excavated, hold great commercial value. They can be processed into a variety of products for use in detergent, water softener, eyewash, anti-fungal medication, flux for soldering metals, fire retardant, enamel glazes and paints, glass, pottery, and leather crafts: truly a marketer's dream mineral. Smith had gained notoriety by finding deep deposits of the crystals and establishing a borax monopoly, thereby becoming known as "Borax" Smith.

Stephen Mather, following his father's example, abandoned journalism to set up an office for Smith in New York City to pursue eastern sales contacts. This successful effort prompted Smith to move Mather to Chicago to open a second office more strategically placed for business purposes. Mather proved to be an extraordinary salesman. A friend of Mather's said, "There was something about his eyes and the way his face changed color when he talked. If he was out to make a convert, the subject never knew what hit him." Looking for an edge in the marketplace, Mather had the idea of packaging borax detergent into small boxes just right for kitchen use and also convinced Smith to use the trade name, 20-Mule-Team-Borax. This idea was spawned by the mule teams (actually eighteen mules and two horses) that hauled wagonloads of borax from Smith's Harmony Borax Works in Death Valley, California, across 165 miles of desert, known locally as "ground afire," to a railhead in Mojave, California. Mather guessed that the picturesque mule teams, suggesting ruggedness and dependability, would bring excellent sales identity to the product.

He was right; sales climbed, but Smith, based in California, continually demanded more of his mid-western sales representative, so much so that Mather cracked under the strain. In 1903 he had a nervous breakdown and spent four months in recuperation. Upon regaining his bearings, he went right back into the borax business, this time, in direct competition with Smith. Mather and his new partner, Thomas Thorkildsen, acquired their own sources of borax and used their business savvy, especially in the eastern markets, to gain quick success. Smith, now seeing Mather as a talented challenger, decided that the best course was to join forces again. He did so in 1911 by buying part of the Mather-Thorkildsen enterprise for $1,800,000 with an added ten-year agreement that he would provide borate ore to Mather's company for processing into sales products. In eight years Mather had jumped from salesman to independently wealthy business owner.

Just as he was going into the borax business, Mather joined a Sierra Club outing to Mt. Rainier in Washington State, for him an especially poignant and meaningful event, coming as it did the year his father died. This mountaineering adventure and the personal emotions it carried with it reinforced in Mather a desire to hike and climb. Annual outings with family and friends became a part of his life's pattern.

In 1912, on a wilderness trail in the Kern River Canyon, far from Yosemite at almost the southern terminus of the Sierra Nevada Mountain chain, Mather happened to meet John Muir. Of the encounter, Mather's longtime colleague Horace Albright (1890–1987) said, "One of the highlights of Mather's life was the opportunity to have a long talk with the legendary Muir, whose whole life at this time was devoted to fighting the Hetch Hetchy dam. To save this twin of the Yosemite Valley from flooding simply to provide a never-ending source of water for the city of San Francisco was the flame of Muir's passion, which caught fire in Mather. Muir had also interested him in another of his vital concerns, the addition of vast majestic Sierra areas to Sequoia National Park, or, better still, the creation of a new park between Yosemite and Sequoia. Mather picked the banner up too."

Fortunately, Mather had both the freedom and the money to devote considerable time to his new conservation cause. He took it upon himself to visit most of the loosely defined and slowly accumulating national parks, each with its congressional underpinnings, but functioning almost as independent government afterthoughts. He did not like what he saw of continuing problems of trespass, the absence of trained staff, and unchecked and harmful development. Adolph Miller, assistant to the Secretary of the Interior, was a fellow Berkeley classmate, and Mather made known to Miller his concerns that the national parks were in jeopardy.

Secretary of the Interior Franklin Lane, also Berkeley-connected, got the message. He reasoned that if Mather was so concerned about neglected parks, the borax entrepreneur should just come to Washington to do something about them. Mather was resistant, but in 1915 he agreed to step away from his business activities to accept an appointment as Lane's assistant to oversee the nation's existing thirteen national parks and assorted national monuments. The parks included Yellowstone, Yosemite, Sequoia, General Grant, Mt. Rainier, Crater Lake, Wind Cave, Mesa Verde, Zion, and Glacier, with Rocky Mountain and Hawaii Volcanoes soon to follow. The monuments included Lassen, Grand Canyon, and Zion, all of which would become national parks.

ESTABLISHING
THE NATIONAL PARK SERVICE

Mather faced three immediate challenges in his new position: to strengthen regulatory control of the various random commercial enterprises taking root in the parks, especially at Yellowstone and Yosemite, to create a single government agency that would administer the parks, and to gain needed federal appropriations to fund the new agency. He was no enemy of commerce in the parks. Mather believed that a robust tourist business would convince members of Congress that the preservation of important natural areas could also be economically beneficial to nearby communities and regional transportation companies. He also reasoned that if thousands of people could be tempted to visit the national parks, the delights to be discovered would convince most to become allies in the cause of preservation. Mather envisioned that this large constituency of visitors, influenced by nature itself, would greatly strengthen Mather's messages to Congress.

He found an influential ally in the person of J. Horace McFarland, a horticulturalist from Harrisburg, Pennsylvania, and president of the American Civic Association. McFarland had supported Muir during the Hetch Hetchy controversy. He also knew and admired Gifford Pinchot, but grieved that Pinchot championed San Francisco's political raid on Yosemite. McFarland knew, too, that Pinchot had wanted to house the national parks in the crop-producing Department of Agriculture, an idea that still resurfaces from time to time. In 1911, the year after Pinchot was removed from his post as Chief Forester, McFarland managed to win introduction of a bill in congress to create a self-standing national park agency in the Department of the Interior, primarily with support from western state congressmen. The legislation did not succeed, but by the time Mather arrived in Washington, McFarland had chalked up additional efforts to reach this goal, all the while strengthening congressional interest.

The departure of the U. S. Cavalry from Yosemite in 1913 helped McFarland's cause. Over the twenty-three years of a military presence in the park, the cavalrymen had done their jobs well. Illegal grazing, hunting, and logging had been greatly diminished by the troopers and their role had changed accordingly. Commanders made the case that military outposts in the national parks, considered to be increasingly soft duty, were no longer needed. Without much fanfare, the cavalry era came to an end, leaving behind a handful of civilians in charge with no central administrative agency to guide them. At Yosemite, ex-cavalryman Gabriel Sovulewski became acting superintendent. He commanded five civilian park rangers, a meager force in a mighty place with no structural government help. McFarland did his best, continuing to remind policymakers that defenses were down in the parks. Mather, although a Republican, found immediate benefit in the momentum that McFarland had achieved in the Democratic Administration of President Woodrow Wilson.

Still, a final push was required. Indefatigable and well-connected, Mather recruited a broad coalition of supporters, including Robert Sterling Yard, a Princeton graduate, journalist, stylish denizen from Haverstraw, New York, and outdoor enthusiast. He also won the allegiance of naturalist Enos Mills, the "father" of Rocky Mountain National Park. William Welch, the chief engineer of the Palisades Interstate Park Commission, joined the cause, as did Gilbert Grosvenor, president of the National Geographic Society and editor of the society's highly acclaimed magazine. Landscape architect Frederick Law Olmsted, Jr. whose father had sounded the alarm so many years earlier about threats to Yosemite, gladly lent his support and name recognition to Mather.

Within the Department of the Interior, Mather found an energetic, highly-skilled kindred spirit in the person of Horace Albright. Born in Bishop, California, on the east side of the Sierra Nevada not far from Mono Lake, Albright was a Berkeley graduate and holder of a law degree from Georgetown University. He would become Mather's alter ego, mastering the administrative details that put substance into the policies Mather chose to pursue.

Within a year of Mather's arrival in the nation's capital, on August 25, 1916, President Wilson signed into law an Act of Congress that established the agency of the National Park Service, to be housed in the Department of the Interior, not consumed by the Department of Agriculture as Gifford Pinchot had proposed. At Interior, the new agency would have a profile of its own. The purpose of the agency, as spelled out in words crafted by Olmsted, Jr., is to promote and regulate uses of national parks, monuments, and similar reservations in order to "conserve the scenery and the natural and historic objects and the wildlife therein and to provide for the enjoyment of the same in such manner and by such means as will leave them unimpaired for the enjoyment of future generations."

These words clearly implied that mining, extensive lumbering, livestock grazing, hydroelectric projects, and similar commercial and industrial uses would be in contradiction to the legally endorsed purposes of the National Park Service. By his careful choice of words, Olmsted, Jr., paid tribute to his father's long-dormant 1865 Yosemite report. The elder Olmsted had written that ". . . Yosemite should be held, guarded and managed for the free use of the whole body of the people forever, and the care of it, and the hospitality of admitting strangers from all parts of the world to visit it and enjoy it freely, should be the duty of dignity and be committed only by a sovereign state." The first visionary attempt to define Yosemite and the basic purposes of parks had echoed across the decades from father to son, taking form as a nationwide mandate. The wording of the legislation entrusts the national parks to the present generation, but legally requires that the parks be advanced as a legacy for generations yet to come, a fundamental concept that underpins the preservation agenda of the National Park Service.

     Your Yosemite: **PROTECTING A PUBLIC TREASURE**

Even before the legislation was approved, Mather and Albright had their hands full with the contentious problem of managing commercial activities in national parks. Mather believed that strong companies functioning under contractual agreement with his NPS agency would assure good service, price, and product for park visitors. Contract privileges would depend on performance. If performance was lacking, these privileges could be withdrawn. Business experience was invaluable. Mather sought alliances with financially proven enterprises capable of functioning far from urban support centers in rural outposts where the vagaries of weather, seasons, and unpredictable natural calamities had to be taken into account.

In Yellowstone the choice was clear. The Northern Pacific Railroad Company served this otherwise remote park and was favored by Mather to provide lodging and food to travel-worn visitors. The short-line Yosemite Valley Railroad, however, was not a respectable contender. This spur line had reached El Portal, twelve miles downriver from Yosemite Valley, in 1907. At this location, passengers shifted from railroad cars to stagecoaches or more novel motorized buses for the final trundle into the park. A railroad hotel was available at El Portal to ease the weary bodies of visitors coming and going from Yosemite, but a parallel purpose of the railroad enterprise was to haul logs out of the mountains to a lumber mill downriver. There was no big Northern Pacific-type company knocking on the door at Yosemite. Instead, there was the bold, combative presence of David Curry.

Curry, who had been operating on year-to-year permits since the days of the California Commissioners, was all for a long-term contract to strengthen commercial services in the valley so long as he was the contractor. Mather and Albright had other ideas. As the proposal for Mather's new agency was still making its way through congress, San Francisco was preparing to host the Panama Pacific International Exposition of 1915 to celebrate the completion of the Panama Canal. The Exposition was expected to flood California with millions of visitors, many of whom were expected to find their way to Yosemite. In preparation, Horace Albright, acting for

Mather, hurried to the park to determine how best to accommodate this expected tsunami of visitors. The last thing Mather wanted was a poor visitor report card at Yosemite just as his management initiative for the national parks was coming together.

David Curry, always confident and assertive, was eager to step up to the challenge. By 1915, Camp Curry could provide overnight services for 800 to 900 lodgers and was counting about 8,000 yearly guests. Albright was not persuaded. He reached out, instead, to D. J. Desmond whose business credentials included feeding and housing the construction crews that built the Los Angeles Aqueduct. Albright convinced Desmond to accept a one-year permit with the added incentive of then receiving a twenty-year contract if, at the end of that first year, Albright deemed that Desmond had suitably performed. Curry, bypassed despite his experience in the park, would be allowed to continue to operate his tent camp only under short-term permits subject to annual renewal.

The Desmond Commissary Company was already positioned to operate food concessions at the International Exposition, likely a factor that persuaded Albright. With the backing of investors Desmond accepted the challenge at Yosemite as well, and scrambled into the park to open lodging and food services at the picturesque but now drafty and wobbly Sentinel Hotel. The hotel had changed little since its construction thirty-nine years previously in 1876. Desmond was also given access to the leftover buildings at the military post near Yosemite Falls recently vacated by the cavalry. Mather and Albright also expected Desmond to complete far more ambitious projects, the speedy construction of a new luxury hotel in the valley, three "chalet" camps in outlying scenic locations at Tenaya Lake, Tuolumne Meadows, and Merced Lake, and replacement of the dilapidated hotel at Glacier Point.

The tee-totaling David Curry, confined to his tent camp, was angered that an outsider was given such wide-ranging access to other real and imagined commercial opportunities in the park. Understandably, he took a dim view of his newest competitor, labeling Desmond a low-life "saloon keeper" due to the rumored sale of alcohol at the Desmond-operated accommodations. On one occasion, Curry and Desmond came to blows, the outcome indecisive.

The federal government's tactical commander on the ground, personally selected by Mather in 1916, was Superintendent Washington B. Lewis, the first civilian superintendent at Yosemite to serve under the mandate of the newly formed agency. Lewis would remain in his post for twelve years, until 1928, a marked change from the revolving door management that had plagued the park from its inception. Mather wanted more constancy in the new agency and got it by handpicking Lewis and his peers in other national parks. During his tenure, Lewis brought distinctive changes to Yosemite, most now taken for granted, including electricity and all-year road access. He grappled with many vexing infrastructure needs and was the on-site host when people of influence visited the park. The biggest challenge, however, was managing the problem of commercial service in Yosemite.

Mather and Albright had favored an experienced businessman when they chose Desmond, but Desmond was on unfamiliar ground in a new market with nightmarish logistics. Curry had been in Yosemite Valley for years, learning from his mistakes and maintaining a simple facility made largely of canvas that could be repaired or replaced at minimal cost. He had also attracted a regular clientele as well as hosting new guests each season. By contrast, Desmond was expected by Mather and Albright to establish himself in the valley almost overnight and to provide far more sophisticated tourist services than Curry had ever attempted. Almost immediately Desmond found himself in great financial difficulty.

After only two years, facing bankruptcy, Desmond retreated from the park at the end of the 1917 summer season, leaving behind new hotel structures at Glacier Point, the beginnings of upgraded facilities in the valley, and tent camps in the high country. His nemesis, David Curry, was not there to pick up the pieces. Curry had suffered an accident apparently by stepping on a piece of sharp, dirty metal that caused him to become grievously ill with blood poisoning. He died in April, 1917. After almost two decades of contending with commissioners, cavalry, and late-arriving civilian administrators while putting his personal stamp of hospitality skills on Camp Curry, the fate of his tents and hard-fought success fell entirely into the hands of his partner and widow, Jennie.

Even before the Desmond meltdown and Curry tragedy, Stephen Mather had faced a crescendo of problems in his new role as Director of the National Park Service. Yellowstone had not been the easy commercial fix he imagined. Nasty political reactions to his move to consolidate visitor services in the park had taken much of his energy and time. He and Albright were also in demand to visit various proposed national park areas scattered across the nation, requiring them to maintain hectic travel schedules. Mather had taken on the task of hosting conferences and gatherings to convince community leaders and elected officials of the benefits of parks and the need to properly fund them. In so doing he won more important allies to his cause, including newsman Lowell Thomas, aviator Orville Wright, George Otis Smith of the U. S. Geological Survey, and George H. Lorimer of the popular *Saturday Evening Post* magazine.

In his typical "whirlwind" style, the director was striving almost non-stop to win high recognition for the splendid park experiment. But Mather's nerves began to unravel again, just as they had a decade earlier when he resigned from the Pacific Coast Borax Company. He was compelled to seek refuge in a sanitarium in Devon, Pennsylvania, the same year that Curry died and Desmond went bankrupt. For more than a year and a half, Mather contended with depression exacerbated not only by events at Yosemite and Yellowstone, but also by the frail condition of his precious and struggling NPS agency. All the while, Horace Albright visited him on a regular basis even as the United States was engaged in the terrible carnage of World War I in Europe. Albright might have been sent overseas to the war, but Secretary Lane needed someone at the helm of the parks while Mather recovered. Out in Yosemite, Superintendent Lewis was contending with his own shortage of personnel due to the drain of men away from their civilian jobs and into Army uniforms. During the

Mother Jennie Curry, circa 1920s

1918 summer season, May to September, he hired eighteen-year-old Clare Marie Hodges who became the nation's first female park ranger. She was an expert equestrian who had first visited the park at age fourteen, returning again in 1916 to take on responsibilities in Yosemite Valley as a grade school teacher. When Lewis learned of her interest in ranger work and found himself short of the men he needed, he promptly hired her. Unlike her male counterparts, Hodges patrolled unarmed on the wilderness trails between Yosemite Valley and Tuolumne Meadows, trusting for success in the authority represented by her ranger badge and her own outdoor skills.

Albright received a deferment from war service and continued to act on Mather's behalf until the director finally returned to his post, coming back "strong," according to author Robert Shankland in his classic book, *Stephen Mather of the National Parks*. "Though his ennui and failure-fantasies vanished, opposite fantasies took their place," said Shankland; "he suddenly began slashing away at national park problems with a battle-ax." Among the challenges Mather faced was to highlight the national park possibilities east of the Mississippi. He had strong support among eastern seaboard residents and journalists for his preservation efforts, but the first national parks had been founded entirely among the public lands out west. In the east, private land ownership predominated. The breakthrough came in Maine. A Bostonian named George Dorr had crusaded for a national park on Mount Desert Island on the Maine Coast using his own funds and those of other donors to begin acquiring the necessary property from private owners. In 1919, soon after Mather had recovered from his illness, Lafayette National Park was established (later to be designated Acadia National Park), and Mather had an agency and a presence that spanned the nation. Within less than a decade, Mather would also see the Great Smoky Mountains and Shenandoah National Parks added to this eastern list.

At Yosemite, Jennie Curry was challenged in much more specific terms. While mourning the unexpected loss of her husband, she was bent on assuring that Camp Curry stay in business. The investors that had backed Desmond also were scrambling. They included K. R. Kingsbury, president of Standard Oil of California, James K. Moffitt, vice president of the First National Bank of San Francisco, financiers M. J. Brandenstein and Stanford L. Goldstein, and the alphabetical A. B. C. Dohrmann. These venture capitalists renamed their enterprise the Yosemite National Park Company, imported new management, and poured additional funds into the accommodation upgrades sought by Mather.

At Camp Curry, Jennie turned to her son, Foster, to run the company. Horace Albright was not impressed, saying of Foster that the young man "did not possess any of the virtues of his father, but all of the faults." Foster hung on as manager of the camp for four years, struggling with Superintendent Lewis and the tourism competition, but fundamentally alienating his own employees and members of his family. In 1921, Foster was expelled from the park by his family for alleged misappropriation of operating funds, causing his mother to lament that "all of the fighters in the company were either dead or kicked out of the park," referring to her husband and son.

YOSEMITE, OUTDOOR CLASSROOM

Mather had high priorities for directing commercial activities in the parks and expanding the agency, but he championed, too, the notion that the parks could foster great scientific and educational possibilities. Dr. Loye Holmes of the University of California and Dr. Harold C. Bryant of the California Fish and Game Commission were recruited by Mather for this purpose. These scientists were searching for a way to make use of the extraordinary promise of Yosemite as an outdoor classroom. The first step was to offer free nature-guided walks for park visitors, picking up on John Muir's long ago intuitive role as self-appointed Yosemite Valley escort and teacher. Holmes' participation in this program was brief, but Dr. Bryant would take the opportunity to heart, giving up his position with the game commission to establish the Field School of Natural History at Yosemite. The purpose of the school was to train recruits in the art of presenting information to park visitors in the form of guided walks, museum displays, and publications based on proven scientific and historic data. The school's attendees, who would become known as park "interpreters," were encouraged to choose NPS careers.

Bryant had in mind that the field school could provide specialized training that would benefit many other parks as well as Yosemite, a concept that proved to be valid. Use of parks as outdoor educational assets for the nation helped to validate the need to protect and preserve them.

Ansel F. Hall, a ranger-naturalist and one of the first field school attendees, became an enthusiastic advocate for science at Yosemite in his own right, and went on to form the Yosemite Museum Association. The "modest goals" he set for the association were to disseminate information regarding birds, mammals, flowers, trees, history, geology, trails, scenic features, and other subjects; to develop and enlarge a first-rate museum collection; to support in every meaningful way ranger-educators; to promote scientific investigations and publications; to maintain a library; and to study living conditions past and present of native peoples. Hall's subsequent devotion to the task was so inspiring that the Laura Spelman Rockefeller Memorial Fund underwrote construction of a building in Yosemite Valley specifically to house museum activities, soon followed by similar Rockefeller grants at Grand Canyon, Yellowstone, and Mesa Verde. At Yosemite, Bryant and Hall were inventively tapping into a rich vein of educational potential that easily spread throughout the NPS system and has been copied around the world.

THE COMMERCIAL SMOKE SETTLES

Inventiveness of another sort was taking place at Camp Curry. With the departure of Foster Curry, the management vacuum was filled by Donald Tresidder and Robert Williams, married to Jennie Curry's daughters, Mary and Marjorie. Unknown to Tresidder at the time, the aid he was rendering to Mrs. Curry would change his life. He was from Tipton, Indiana, and had been a student at the University of Chicago when he and his sister decided during a summertime break to "see the west." In 1914, the two travelers were en route by train through the Central Valley of California when flood waters on the tracks near Fresno brought their journey temporarily to a halt. "With time to kill," said biographer, Edwin Kiester, "the young Tresidders debarked from the train, sought out a stage and headed for Yosemite—it was a momentous journey." The brother and sister found lodging at Camp Curry. Soon after, the lanky twenty-year-old Donald met graceful and attractive Mary Curry. He promptly decided to extend his stay in Yosemite, sending his sister on without him.

Tresidder also met several members of the Stanford University faculty who had made a habit of vacationing with their families at Camp Curry. The faculty members liked what they saw in the young man. He was self-assured, physically fit, intelligent, and eager to assist; just the type of student they favored. Tresidder found himself being persuaded to give up his plan to return to Chicago and instead to enroll at Stanford, an appealing prospect given that the move would make courting Mary Curry far easier, even though during the succeeding academic years she went off to Yale. Tresidder became a proficient scholar at Stanford, working toward a medical degree and returning during summer seasons to work at Camp Curry and continue his romance with Mary. Persistence paid off; in June, 1920, he and Mary were wed, and in 1921, the newly graduated Dr. Tresidder and his spouse were again at the camp, likely thinking of the medical career that lay ahead, when the departure of Foster Curry changed their plans.

As assistant manager at the camp, the first challenge for Tresidder was to win a long-term NPS concessionaire contract, a goal that his father-in-law had never reached. The camp had grown to include forty-eight wooden bungalows with private baths to complement the scores of tents on wooden platforms that ran off in all directions from a central courtyard. The tents were advertised as "modern hotel rooms under canvas." The camp included a studio, auditorium, auto garage, and a "sanitary kitchen with an all-white crew." Tucked

*Donald and Mary Tresidder, Stephen Mather
and his daughter, Betty*

under the giant 3,000-foot Glacier Point wall, the camp was also somewhat dangerous. In the summer of 1921, rocks fell from midway up the wall injuring three Camp Curry customers, a hazard that park officials said they would "study." Mather, Albright, and Lewis took note of the change in management at the camp and agreed to provide Jennie Curry with a five-year operating permit, a tepid gesture of support while these NPS officials continued to search for an entrepreneur capable of building the luxury hotel at Yosemite that Mather envisioned.

Albright thought he had found just the right person to build the hotel in Frank Miller, owner of the Mission Inn in Riverside, California. Miller was tempted, tried to raise investment funds, failed in the effort, and quickly abandoned the idea. Tresidder, seeing a clear opportunity, expressed interest in competing for the hotel project. Albright found Tresidder to be a "fine, clean, upright chap, honest, well appearing, and in general the kind of man that would play the game fair." Still, Mather and Albright seemingly could not make the leap in their minds between a tent camp operator and a stylish luxury hotel purveyor. If Albright could not succeed in bringing in an outsider like Miller, there was always the Yosemite National Park Company, mediocre in performance, but perhaps more savvy and financially promising than the Curry contingent. In the eyes of Jennie Curry and her family, Mather was on the verge, again, of giving unfair advantage to a business competitor.

In the autumn of 1921, the contending parties were called to Washington, D. C., to meet with Mather, Albright, and Secretary of the Interior Albert Fall to settle the matter. Donald Tresidder and the Curry Camping Company attorney argued that the Yosemite National Park Company had been given broad license to control transportation to the park and provide various commercial services within the valley while the Curry Company was limited by short term permits to serve only its registered guests. Jennie Curry wanted to open a delicatessen, grocery store, and gas station in the "general vicinity" of Camp Curry. Yosemite National Park Company representatives objected, worried that the almost captive audience they served would be eroded. In a bit of government oversight hardball, the Yosemite business competitors were directed to retire

    Your Yosemite: **PROTECTING A PUBLIC TREASURE**

to private discussion and settle their differences or else they would lose their contract and permit privileges and would have to leave the park. Albright was delegated to act as facilitator and ombudsman.

The result was not immediate, but the outcome was startling. Two years after the session in Washington, D.C., the Curry Camping Company and Yosemite National Park Company were defunct. In their place stood the merged Yosemite Park & Curry Company. Tresidder, the business successor to two school teachers who started with seven tents, a campfire, and nine paying customers a quarter-century earlier, was named president of the newly formed company.

Suddenly, Tresidder had in hand the Sentinel and Glacier Point Hotels, Camp Curry, the Big Trees Lodge in the Mariposa Grove of Giant Sequoias, Yosemite Lodge at the old cavalry camp site, six camps up in the High Sierra, all transportation services, garage and fuel services, laundry, print shop, general store, meat market, and even a small lodge over at the Hetch Hetchy reservoir. In 1925, when he took over, the new company could lay 2,000 weary heads on pillows each night in its various accommodations. Except for a few art galleries, a bakery, stables, and the Wawona Hotel, which was built on private land, Tresidder basically had a monopoly in what would become the largest business operation in any national park, anywhere.

A FLAGSHIP HOTEL

As part of the deal, the timeworn Sentinel Hotel would be torn down. Nearby, a luxury hotel would rise. New investors saw opportunity and joined in, including Harry Chandler, owner of the *Los Angeles Times*. Some of the old-guard speculators remained on board, particularly A. B. C. Dohrman. With this increased financial strength the prospect of "the finest hotel in the National Park Service," as Mather put it, became a reality. Only the Old Faithful Inn in Yellowstone might claim equal stature, but this huge, artfully-designed log structure was only open during summer months. The new hotel in Yosemite Valley would be a year-around asset and distinctively urbane.

Mather favored what has become known as "park architecture," buildings of rustic charm in natural settings that favored natural materials; log and stone in forests and mountainous settings; adobe and rock in arid climates. He demonstrated this interest by dipping into his own pocket to pay for construction of the "Ranger's Club" in Yosemite Valley, a Swiss-chalet-type structure of log siding and steeply sloping roof lines that has remained continually in use.

For the luxury hotel, Mather and the Tresidders selected a site at "Kennyville," once the location of pioneer James Lamon's cabin that had morphed into a collection of barns and corrals used for saddle-horse rentals. Visitor preference for automobiles had sent the horse business into decline, but there was nothing wrong with the view. From the site, Half Dome, Glacier Point, Yosemite Falls, and a section of the valley's north wall known as Royal Arches were readily observable, a visual asset that would please any architect. The architect selected for the job at Mather's recommendation was thirty-five-year-old Gilbert Underwood, Harvard-educated and a consulting architect for Union Pacific Railroad with his office in Los Angeles. The NPS Director was pleased with Underwood's recent design work: attractive, site-appropriate lodges at Bryce Canyon and Zion National Parks and the handsome two-story log-and-stone post office constructed in 1925 in Yosemite Valley. To handle the job, Donald Tresidder hired James L. McLaughlin, a robust contractor of good reputation based in San Francisco. On seeing the design, McLaughlin estimated that he could build the new six-story hotel for $525,000 and finish the job in six months.

The reason for the contractor's optimism was that Underwood had ingeniously designed a fairly simple steel-framed concrete structure, leaving the design magic to the detailing. On the exterior, stone veneer and textured concrete, mimicking wood, were intended to harmonize with the surrounding vegetation and soaring granite walls of the valley. The hotel would contain one-hundred guest rooms.

Construction began on April Fool's Day, 1926, and McLaughlin almost immediately began to encounter problems, not the least of which was that Tresidder and Underwood kept tweaking and changing the blueprints. Park Superintendent Lewis was keeping a careful eye on the project to assure that no rock went missing for construction purposes from the nearby talus slopes. Trucking was in its infancy at the time, but all materials—steel, concrete, stone, glass, pipes, wire—had to be hauled by truck up the narrow all-weather access road through the Merced River Canyon into the park. Flat tires and stalled engines were common.

Keith Walklet, author of *The Ahwahnee, Yosemite's Grand Hotel*, confirms that 680 tons of steel and 5,000 tons of stone arrived at the work site by the determination of weary truckers. The six-month estimate for completion of the job came and went, and costs soared. Tresidder and his private investors considered firing McLaughlin, but the Irishman was quick to point out that the always changing and evolving blueprints had his crew standing by idly, awaiting further precise clarification of construction details in addition to the fact that an additional 18,000 square feet had been added to the overall project. McLaughlin stayed on the job and on July 24, 1927, just a little more than a year after ground was broken and about 100% over budget, the doors to the Ahwahnee Hotel swung open. The first to sign the guest register was Stephen Mather. Room rates ranged from $15 to the princely sum of $50 per day. Over at Camp Curry, the average daily rate was $4.50.

By the time the Ahwahnee opened for business the park had become a place for everyone. There were many well-heeled visitors who did not blink at paying the high cost for staying at the Ahwahnee or the slightly lesser fees for other lodging accommodations, but they shared sightseeing space in Yosemite Valley with the canvas crowd at Camp Curry and the campgrounds, day-trippers in their cars, backpackers on their feet, and sore-seated riders in the saddle. This mix of visitors, reinforced by worldwide travelers and organized tours, remains generally intact to this day, except that campgrounds now accommodate mobile "recreation vehicles," some of them more stylish than a room at the Ahwahnee. Horse and mule outfitting has not markedly changed. The pack animals still get to carry everything into the backcountry, including the kitchen sink.

Not everyone was impressed with the final Ahwahnee result. When Ansel Adams saw the new hotel's exterior, he observed, "the architect tried to compete with the environment, and lost." But time was on the side of the Ahwahnee. Weather began to soften the exterior walls and vegetation healed the construction scars. Inside, immense windows framed classic Yosemite Valley views and Tresidder, in a worthy stroke of rebellion against the era's typically popular hunting lodge approach to interior decorating—ponderous leather furnishings and stuffed heads of dead wild animals on the walls—opted instead for art nouveau.

He retained the services of artist decorators Henry Howard and Jeanette Spencer to ornament the walls and beams in bright graphic designs representing the valley's Native American heritage and the abundance of living wild creatures and plants that the national park had been established to protect. Paintings of Yosemite scenes by Swedish landscape artist Gunnar Widforss, whose patron was Stephen Mather, were added to the mix of rugs, Native American baskets, inlaid floor mosaics, stained-glass windows, soft wall paint, and fabric-covered furniture; all merging in delightful combination to celebrate the special status of the Mather/Tresidder flagship hotel. Revising his earlier opinion of the project, Ansel Adams judged the interior of the Ahwahnee to be of "extraordinary beauty."

BRACEBRIDGE

Even as Tresidder was welcoming more and more guests at Yosemite Park & Curry Company facilities, he was looking beyond the traditional summer travel season to tempt additional people into the park in what otherwise were the slack seasons of autumn, winter, and spring. He founded the Winter Club to encourage skiing, sledding, and ice skating. Thinking, too, about how to entertain guests when the sun and outside temperatures went down together, Tressider retained the services in 1927 of Garnette Holme, a Pageant Master, to help bring theater to the Ahwahnee.

The chosen theatrical vehicle was Washington Irving's fictional account of *A Christmas at Bracebridge Hall*, a story of merrymaking by British nobility at a country manor house. The story of jolly personages, comings and goings, subplots, and festive celebration seemed a good fit for the almost royal mood of the Ahwahnee. Holme wrote a script loosely based on Irving's work and added music, song, and elegant costuming. The simple plot is that the Squire of Bracebridge Hall welcomes with gusto, pomp, circumstance, and a delectable feast a visiting squire and his entourage who have traveled hard miles through the countryside to reach the destination. For the first presentation on Christmas Eve, 1927, Tresidder cast himself and his wife, Mary, as Squire and Lady of Bracebridge Hall and invited NPS Superintendent W. B. Lewis to be the "visiting Squire." He imported an all-male chorus of friends from the Bohemian Club in San Francisco. Members of the chorus got into the mood by fortifying themselves with generous doses of bourbon to prepare their vocal cords.

With grand flourishes, reinforced by a seven-course dinner, the Tresidders welcomed the visiting Squire and his Lady to the head table and complimented all those in attendance (meaning all the paying dinner guests seated in the Ahwahnee's great dining room) on their arduous journey through the mountains to attend such an imperative event. Ansel Adams was in the first cast, playing the part of the jester, Lord Misrule. Due to the unexpected death of Holme in 1929, Adams was encouraged to step forward to take on the responsibility of Pageant Director, did so, and continued in that role with great success for forty-six years, through the 1973 Christmas season. Tresidder and Holme had struck a winning theme, refined artfully by Adams who had become a stalwart member of the Yosemite community. The year before he became Bracebridge Director, Adams had, in 1928, after a six-year courtship, married Virginia Best whose widowed father, Harry Best, owned an art studio in the valley (later to become the famous Ansel Adams Gallery).

In a way, Bracebridge is an outlier, having nothing, really, to do with Yosemite except that, historically, it helped spark to life the public perception of a lively year-round park, glorious in the winter months as it is stunning in the other seasons of the year. The dinner is so popular that reservations now are awarded by lottery, the performances sold out through the December holiday season. Construction of the Ahwahnee and the Bracebridge celebration mark a moment in the evolution of the park experiment when the official push by the NPS was to tempt as many people as possible to visit. The stress of too much popularity at the more famous parks had not yet become a threat, but Yosemite was standing right on the pathway of collision between use and abuse.

TO'TU'YA RETURNS

In the summer of 1929, as Ansel Adams was beginning to find his way toward fame and Donald Tresidder was trying to build a customer clientele, a poignant moment very different from theatrics at the Ahwahnee occurred when Mrs. H. J. Taylor hosted a visit to the park by To'tu'ya, the last surviving member of the Ah'wah'nee'chee. To'tu'ya had been a ten-year-old girl when she and her people were herded from the valley at gunpoint. In seventy-eight succeeding years To'tu'ya had been living in the foothills about thirty miles outside the national park, but, until encouraged by Mrs. Taylor, had never returned to the site of the sad upheaval that left her a refugee.

"From the meadow she looked up at the rock walls of the valley," wrote Taylor in her book, *The Last Survivor*. "The monolith stood unchanged. The waterfalls drawing their substance from the eternal source of rain and snow spoke to her as they had spoken in her childhood. Looking at Yosemite Falls she cried, 'Chorlock! Chorlock no gone!' She saluted Tu'tock'ah'nu'lah, now known as El Capitan. Her own Indian village had stood in full view of Loya, now Sentinel Rock. It seemed very dear to her. A momentary silence, then in quiet supplication she said, 'Loya, Loya; long time go.' For us the wonders of Yosemite took on new and deeper meaning as the names so full of Indian lore fell from her lips. What a loss to posterity and to history that these names have not been preserved. Bridal Veil, Vernal Fall, Mirror Lake, Sentinel Rock, Half Dome—these names are found throughout the world. Yosemite alone has a Pohono, a Py'we'ack, an Ah'yi'yah, a Loya, a Tis'sa'ack. In these names there is tradition and meaning that expresses the life of the people who originally possessed Yosemite."

On her visit to the park, To'tu'ya was a celebrity, surrounded by curious visitors. Arrangements had been made by park rangers for her to demonstrate some of her skills learned so long ago. From a pile of acorns she was preparing traditional food when a tourist offered her a nickel for an acorn. To'tu'ya, making one last commemorative gesture of resistance against intruders, declined the nickel and kept the acorn.

MATHER IS GONE &
THE GREAT DEPRESSION STRIKES

The partnership between Stephen Mather and Donald Tressider was a fortuitous one. In some ways this period could be thought of as the golden age of relations between the concessionaires and the NPS in Yosemite. The tensions between park administrators and early entrepreneurs, personified by Hutchings and Curry, and the corporate failure of Desmond, had been replaced by a spirit of cooperation. Mather and Tresidder shared a common goal, to bring commercial quality as close as humanly possible to scenic quality, with park visitors the overall winners. Unfortunately, this partnership was unexpectedly cut short. In 1928, only one year after the Ahwahnee opened, Mather was felled by a devastating stroke from which he would never recover. He lingered on and died in 1930.

Gilbert Grosvenor, president of the National Geographic Society, who had trekked with Mather in the Sierra Nevada, said at the time of Mather's death, "many hands have joined in common effort to build up our unparalleled National Parks system. But the untrammeled vision, steady purpose, and indefatigable labor of one man stand out above all else. To Stephen Mather, father of our National Park Service, the people of the United States owe a lasting debt of deep gratitude. The National Parks system that Mather brought about is an American innovation. No other country, not even Switzerland despite its world-renowned scenic splendor, had attempted to develop areas for public use along such lines. Many other countries have in recent years copied the American plan for National Park reservations."

No doubt Mather had seen Yosemite as living proof of all of his assumptions about the need for careful use of the public estate, but his thesis was to be tested anew when, in October 1929, the stock market crashed and the entire country collapsed into the Great Depression. By the early 1930s the national unemployment rate hit 25 per cent. Crop prices in the mid-western farm country dropped by as much as 60 per cent. Demand for raw materials all but vanished. Depositors watched helplessly as many banks simply closed their doors and went out of business. Tresidder and other park concessionaires were exceedingly hard hit by the economic doldrums that followed. Barely making ends meet from the dwindling number of visitors, he used his own funds to help keep the doors open in Yosemite. Fortunately for Tressider, a firm allegiance by those who had made a practice of returning to the park year after year ensured that business did not dry up entirely. Indeed, Yosemite National Park, overseen through most of the Depression years by Superintendent Charles G. Thomson, reaped unexpected benefits from the Depression.

Horace Albright, successor to Mather as the NPS Director, recognized in the deflated land values an opportunity to add lands to the national parks. John D. Rockefeller, Jr., who had made a trip to the west in 1926 in a private Pullman railroad car, complete with a French tutor for his children who were sharing the adventure, admired the national parks, and forged a trusting work relationship with Albright. Rockefeller would become the principal force in the establishment of Grand Teton National Park, Wyoming, and would contribute significantly to other park projects around the nation, especially the expansion of Acadia National Park in Maine.

In 1930, Albright convinced Rockefeller to contribute $1.6 million, to be equally matched by federal funds, for the purchase of 15,570-acres of prime Ponderosa and Sugar Pine habitat to be added to the Yosemite holdings. Donald Tresidder mirrored the Rockefeller charitable grant in worthy purpose if not in size of purse by paying half the cost for an additional 380 acres to be added to the park. George Ball of Muncie, Indiana, who had advanced from producing glass canning jars to the railroad business, contributed half of the purchase cost for 640 acres. In 1932, federal government funds available through a depression-era welfare program for distressed landowners were used to acquire 8,765 acres in the southern section of the park, including the Wawona Hotel, which had been operated privately since 1879. This classic hotel was turned over under contract to the Yosemite Park & Curry Company.

Other unanticipated consequences of the Depression ricocheted through Yosemite when Franklin Delano Roosevelt was sworn in as President of the United States in 1933. Roosevelt immediately set out to create jobs through government programs at a pace and scale never before imagined. A year later, after laying the political groundwork, he kept his pledge. In just ten days of legislative action, a bill creating the Civilian Conservation Corps was passed and signed into law. The result was that 250,000 young men were promptly recruited into the CCC ranks. Eventually more than three million workers would find employment in this quasi-military organization. An even larger works initiative, the Works Progress Administration (WPA), followed in the wake of the CCC, providing a behemoth eight million jobs. Drawn into these programs were engineers, architects, crafts and trades people, artists, foresters, farmers, medical personnel, administrators, teachers, writers, photographers, scientists, and plenty of journeyman laborers.

As the CCC program quickly expanded, ten military-style camps under the command of Army officers were established at Yosemite, each accommodating at least 200 workers, a subset of the 600 camps established throughout the entire National Park System. During the life of the program at Yosemite about 6,800 CCC enrollees passed through the park, planting trees, working on trails and structures, fighting forest fires, attending educational and training programs, and learning to account for their $30-per-month in pay, most of which their bosses required them to send home.

In the midst of this flurry of activity, in life-goes-on fashion, Mary Curry Tresidder found time to contribute to the park's educational services by publishing a booklet in 1932 entitled *Guide To The Trees* in which she highlighted a "world class display of conifers" including sequoias, sugar pines, yellow pines (ponderosa and Jeffery), lodgepole and white bark pines, red firs, white firs, incense cedars, oaks, and other species that so richly decorate the Yosemite ecosystem. In 1938, Ansel Adams, always an enthusiast for his chosen locale, invited his friend, Georgia O'Keeffe, to journey over from her refuge in New Mexico to go on a pack trip with him into the High Sierra wilderness. Fourteen mules carried the camping equipment and supplies.

The CCC men were free to explore the park in their limited off-time from work, probably testing their strength like so many before them against the "un-climbable" walls of Yosemite. In 1934, they probably stood in amazement along with other park residents when a young and robust member of the Sierra Club named David Brower organized a rock-climbing group that resulted in the ascent of Cathedral Spires in Yosemite Valley by Jules Eichorn, Richard Leonard, and Beston Robinson. These men proved that at least some of the walls were climbable if enough adrenaline, skill, and luck were invested in the task.

The CCC and WPA work programs continued apace in national and state parks through the 1930s. Many of the structures produced by careful design and a highly trained workforce remain intact and admired to this day. An icon of this program at Yosemite is the Ostrander Lake Ski Hut that provides an invitation to meet the park on its wintertime terms. The hut bears the name of a Yosemite pioneer family and was the last major project completed at Yosemite by the CCC before the program was disbanded in 1942. In a matter of months, CCC crews constructed the two-story stone-and-log hut, winning for their efforts the repeated phrase, "beautifully crafted." Perched near a backcountry lake at an elevation of 8,500 feet, the hut is accessible in winter over a ten-mile, cross-country ski/snowshoe trail. A hut keeper is in residence to assist the twenty-five or so nightly visitors who haul their own water from the lake, keep the woodstove going, share dented pots and pans for communal cooking, toss their sleeping bags on the few bunks and mattresses in the hut, or enjoy the comforts of an outside snowdrift if there are too many snoozers inside.

THE WAR

World War II marked the end of the Depression-era activities in Yosemite. Many of CCC enrollees traded in their tools for the weapons of the wartime Army and Navy. The Yosemite Field School of Natural History also was closed. The Ahwahnee Hotel was converted into a convalescent ward for U. S. Navy personnel, or, more accurately, into a facility to house psychiatrically disturbed sailors, but the isolated valley proved to be a poor location to treat emotionally and mentally disturbed patients.

The Navy adjusted course, bringing in patients simply in need of recovery from disease or injury. At any given point in time from 1943 to 1945 about 800 patients were housed at the hotel and nearby temporary facilities. More than 6,700 sailors rotated through the convalescent program, regaining strength through recreational and vocational activities. One detail, perhaps not universally applauded by the sailors, was that a bar at the Ahwanhee was converted for the duration into a chapel.

DONALD TRESIDDER, TWO HATS

Even while he was coping with wartime events at Yosemite, Donald Tresidder, ever the diligent Stanford alum, and twenty-nine years after first meeting some of the university's faculty members at Camp Curry, was selected in 1943 as Stanford's fourth president. He accepted this esteemed obligation with eagerness, but he also kept his hand on the helm of the Yosemite Park & Curry Company and launched himself into the tricky and grueling task of balancing two major executive responsibilities. After the war, he continued to juggle these dual workloads as the pent-up desire of citizens to travel launched an upward spike in visitation to Yosemite. At the same time, Stanford was feeling the pressure of education-hungry returning veterans, and, as always, needed money. Dr. Tresidder was staying at the St. Regis Hotel on a fundraising trip to New York City, when, in January, 1948, he was suddenly felled by a heart attack. Mary Curry Tresidder, raised in Yosemite Valley, a Yale graduate, bride at twenty-seven, said to be "intensely shy," and successor to her mother in 1938 as manager of Camp Curry, abruptly found herself in charge of the entire Yosemite Park & Curry Company conglomerate.

Ahwahnee Hotel, circa 1940s

10

Visitation Explodes

DURING THE DECADES PRIOR to World War II, Stephen Mather and Horace Albright struggled with the question of whether the national parks, far from metropolitan centers and tricky to reach on unimproved roads or by spur line railroad service, would ever become popular enough to justify steadfast congressional budget attention. After the war, visitation at Yosemite, which, a decade earlier, had been counted in the thousands, was now quickly rising toward the millions. Across the nation, travelers were flocking to the national parks. People had heard and read about such attractions as Old Faithful Geyser, Half Dome, the mile-deep abyss of the Grand Canyon, the alligator-infested waters of the Everglades, and many other natural attractions held in the public estate. They wanted to see the real thing. Automobile technology had vastly improved during the war. Cheaper, faster, more dependable cars were available to the average consumer and gasoline was $0.10 to $0.25 a gallon. Earlier speculation about the appeal of national parks was swiftly and irreversibly being confirmed. Many families began planning their annual vacations to include return visits to favorite parks, or to make a circuit to include several.

In midcentury, Mary Curry Tresidder stood at the epicenter as public demand for the national parks grew. As a child of six, she had watched her parents erect those first few tents that would become Camp Curry. Now, she was living in the "Tresidder Suite" on the sixth floor of the Ahwahnee Hotel, assured of her privacy by a special key-activated elevator switch. She was presiding over a company that could readily accommodate over 3,000 overnight guests. In addition to the hotels, lodges, and tent camps her company included restaurants, stores, gift shops, golf courses, the Badger Pass Ski Area, swimming pools, tennis courts, garages and gas stations, horse stables, buses, warehouses, and housing for hundreds of employees,

Mary Tresidder became the park's preeminent hostess, gaining allegiance from old-hand staff members who had found their own coveted lifestyles in Yosemite, while contending with the demands of the park's burgeoning popularity. Her company's facilities were frequently overburdened during the high travel season and in need of constant maintenance and repair. For visitors, just finding a vacant bathroom in Yosemite Valley on a summer day could be a challenge. Service to YP&CC customers was dependent on a resort-style workforce; a small hierarchy of permanent supervisors outnumbered by maids, kitchen help, laborers, hosts, cashiers, bar tenders, waitresses, laundry crews, and trades-people who were hired in late spring or early summer and laid off when visitation dropped off after Labor Day. A combination of increasing demands, erratic business cycles, and untested employees were reflected in visitor descriptions of Yosemite's concessionaire facilities as "shabby."

"MISSION 66"

From afar in Washington, D. C., Conrad L. Wirth (1899–1993), who became Director of the National Park Service in 1951, three years after Mary Tresidder took charge of the YP&CC, observed the crush of visitation and asked, practically, whether the national parks were in danger of being "loved to death." If some of the concessionaire amenities in Yosemite and other parks were not as well presented as they could be, many of the NPS offerings were abysmal or lacking altogether. Park Rangers in some areas literally were living in tarpaper shacks. Visitors were struggling on road systems left over from the wagon days and welcomed by far more outhouses than modern conveniences. Information services were spotty and haphazard. In *Preserving Nature in the National Parks*, historian Richard West Sellars explains that Wirth believed that new and vigorous development in the national parks was needed not only to accommodate visitors, but also to control them: "From this new perspective, Wirth argued as urgently as had Mather that development would save the parks." Yellowstone's Superintendent, Lon Garrison, portrayed the dilemma faced by Wirth as the "paradox of protection by development."

Historian Bernard DeVoto, who served as a member of the Advisory Board on National Parks, had a similar point of view. He expressed himself bluntly in an article for *Harper's Magazine* in October, 1955, entitled "Let's Close the National Parks," pronouncing that facilities in the parks were "true slum districts," and urging that the parks be temporarily closed to their fifty million annual visitors until adequate funding to upgrade them could be squeezed from Congress.

In a moment of nimble timing, Wirth took action. The nation's economy was robust, and an unlikely NPS ally was sitting in the White House, the former Supreme Allied Commander in Europe and now President of the United States, Dwight D. Eisenhower. One of Eisenhower's favorite hobbies was fly fishing. He was known to enjoy the sport immensely, often cooking his catch over an open campfire and enjoying all the associated pleasures of rustic outdoor living. The President had carefully inspected several free flowing streams in national parks, fly rod in hand. Wirth's boss, Secretary of the Interior Douglas McKay, arranged for the NPS Director to make his case for salvaging the national parks directly to Eisenhower, just as Muir had delivered a similar plea to Theodore Roosevelt more than fifty years earlier.

In January 1956, Director Wirth and a few members of his staff were invited to meet at the White House with Eisenhower and his Cabinet. Wirth was given his moment and came prepared. He appealed to the goal-oriented President with a tactical program to upgrade the parks within a set time frame and, in military style, labeled the program "Mission 66." The director reminded Eisenhower and the assembled Cabinet members that the 50th anniversary of the establishment of the National Park Service would be celebrated in 1966. He reviewed the basic mission of the agency, its growth and obvious public appeal, and urged a bold ten-year "funding package" to improve buildings, utilities, roads, and trails in the parks designed to protect the landscape while meeting the nation's obligation for park stewardship.

During his presentation, Wirth asked that the lights be dimmed in the Cabinet Room so that he could use a tried-and-true NPS educational technique, the audio-visual show. Up on the screen came images of creaky facilities, poor roads, dejected park housing, and antique utility systems juxtaposed with scenes of visitors trying to enjoy the parks despite these obvious operating problems. Just before the lights came up, Wirth asked, "Where else do so many Americans under the most pleasant circumstances come face to face with their Government? Where else but on historic ground can they better renew the idealism that prompted the patriots to their deeds of valor? Where else but in the great-out-of-doors as God made it can we better recapture the spirit and something of the qualities of the pioneers?" Then the director answered his own questions: "Pride in their Government, love of the land, and faith in the American tradition—these are the real products of our national parks."

The President was convinced. Eisenhower gave his approval for Mission 66 the same year he launched his much more ambitious interstate highway system project. Mission 66, pegged at an investment level of $1 billion, proved to be immensely successful. More than 2,000 new structures, including 100 modern "visitor centers," were constructed in the parks. The Gateway Arch in St. Louis, famously designed by Eero Saarinen, was completed; so, too, the 469-mile Blue Ridge Parkway that connects Shenandoah National Park, Virginia, with Great Smoky Mountains National Park, North Carolina/ Tennessee. Training centers for NPS employees were constructed at Grand Canyon National Park, Arizona, and Harpers Ferry National Historic Park, West Virginia. Four significant new areas of seashore were also added by Congress to the National Park System: Cape Cod, Massachusetts; Point Reyes, California; Fire Island, New York; and Padre Island on the gulf coast in Texas.

This crash program raised the spirits of park professionals who had long struggled in the backwaters of the congressional budget process, but it also sparked considerable controversy. The plan's emphasis on "contemporary design" was a radical shift away from the "park architecture" of old. In part, this shift was driven by budget considerations. The modern buildings coming off the drawing boards at the NPS design centers were cheaper to build than the old-fashioned structures that required fine craftsmanship, use of environmentally appropriate construction materials, and rustic designs adapted to the surrounding landscape. New housing for NPS employees, far superior to the "shacks" in which many of them had been living, was of cookie-cutter design, essentially boxes with replicated floor plans. Rangers and their families transferring from one park to another would often know exactly where the bedrooms and closets were in their newly-assigned house; they had seen the same thing before in a previous park. Some members of the public began to react in horror to this new aesthetic, charging that the parks were becoming "urbanized" and marred by fancy structures in the wrong locations, roads that bored through wilderness, and even carnival-like structures most prominently symbolized by the "sky post," a modernistic viewing platform of spiraling concrete balanced on the summit of Clingman's Dome in Great Smoky Mountains National Park.

A TRUSTED ALLY, ALIENATED

At Yosemite, Mission 66 focused primarily on two projects, the Tioga Road that crosses the park right over the spine of the High Sierra and accommodations in the valley at Yosemite Lodge, the old cavalry post. The Tioga Road project immediately raised the hackles of David Brower, the Executive Director of the Sierra Club and his fellow club director, Ansel Adams. Until then, the Sierra Club had been a dependable ally of the NPS in Yosemite, more of a teammate than a watchdog. Brower grudgingly conceded that the road was in need of improvement, but one 3.3-mile section of the overall alignment would prompt a caustic disruption in the dynamic between the NPS and Sierra Club. Standing in the path of the alignment at Tenaya Lake were rock barriers located adjacent to the shoreline of the lake, and, nearby, a massive dome of glacially polished granite subsequently to be named "Olmsted Point." The new road alignment was proposed to be blasted straight through these rock obstructions, bringing the world of the automobile to the water's edge at Tenaya Lake.

The idea of realigning the road in the lake area had been discussed for years prior to Mission 66. One alternative route would have diverted the road further away from the lake into more benign terrain, but this option, not favored by NPS engineers, would add to expense of the project and invade largely untrammeled territory. Adams, though, felt that insistence by the engineers, empowered by the momentum of Mission 66, to force a more direct route through rock, courtesy of cases of dynamite, typified a "bulldozers of bureaucracy" mindset that was checkmating preservation. He urged his fellow Sierra Club members to join in vigorous opposition to the project and threatened to resign from the club and fight on his own if the members did not sufficiently respond.

Brower and many of the members quickly engaged, officially placing the Sierra Club on record in opposition to the NPS. But, as in the earlier Hetch Hetchy battle, some members disagreed, most notably William E. Colby, one of the club's founding members, who was troubled by the club's demand that, to avoid Tenaya Lake, a new road segment should be sliced into wilderness terrain. A second alternative suggested by the club, to build a new road at the base of the Olmsted Point dome rather than blasting through at mid-slope was rejected by the NPS due to safety concerns. The Adams/Brower preference for the alternate wilderness route prevailed among a majority of Sierra Club members, causing Colby to resign in protest from his position on the Sierra Club Board of Directors. He stayed active in the club on other issues until his death in 1964, but a raw philosophical wound persisted.

Adams, who passionately cherished the Tenaya Lake scene, honoring it through the lens of his camera as well as his activist role with the club, wrote to then Secretary of the Interior, Fred Seaton, emphasizing that, "I have never opposed appropriate improvement of the Tioga Road, but in 40 years' experience in national park and wilderness areas I have never witnessed such an insensitive disregard of prime national park values." Brower and Adams tried to head off the project with articles in *National Parks Magazine* and the *Sierra Club Bulletin*, but won only an on-site meeting with NPS Director Wirth and John Preston, Yosemite's Superintendent from 1952 to 1961, that resulted only in a very slight design modification and a brief delay.

The momentum of Mission 66 triumphed; the road project was completed in 1961. In this particular instance, no solution was ideal.

Unfortunately the NPS's unwillingness to choose an alternative at Tenaya Lake made the agency appear in the eyes of many Sierra Club members to be environmentally high-handed, stubborn, and penny-pinching. The dynamite left not only a gash through the dome near Tenaya Lake, but also left a sense of injury and suspicion between the park administrators and their most influential private advocacy group.

In Yosemite Valley, a much less controversial Mission 66 project was underway. In 1956, construction began at Yosemite Lodge to upgrade the decrepit facility. The NPS and YP&CC collaborated on a series of multi-tiered dark brown square buildings offering more than 360 overnight guest rooms, accompanied by additional dormitory-style buildings to house YP&CC employees. Mission 66 funds were used to provide utilities, roads, and parking lots. The company paid for the buildings. The location is superb, very near Yosemite Falls, but NPS officials, Mary Tresidder, and park visitors may have wished for a better result. In appearance, the upgraded accommodations were similar to a mid-quality motel. In addition, about half of the facility was in the flood plain of the Merced River. The lodge was among the first and largest of the Mission 66 commercial projects, another symbol of good intentions gone awry for the sake of quick and expedient results.

One clear Mission 66 success for Yosemite was the acquisition of a 1,139-acre "administrative site" in the Merced River canyon just outside the park boundary at El Portal. This broadening in the otherwise constricted canyon had been an Ah'wah'nee'chee wintering ground and, later, the terminus of the Yosemite Valley Railroad that stopped operating in 1945. Until El Portal was acquired, all options for commercial and managerial infrastructure were necessarily centered on Yosemite Valley. El Portal was meant to be a relief valve for development pressure in the park. During Mission 66 a handful of stucco houses and a four-classroom grade school were constructed at the site, foreshadowing a hoped-for major reconfiguration of the administrative profile at Yosemite. A cluster of privately-owned cabins and dwellings, left over from the railroad days, offered additional housing, enough so that the combined community made up primarily of NPS and concessionaire employees generated sufficient business to support a small general store.

This is where my family and I settled in 1979 when I arrived at the park. Nothing much had changed since Mission 66 ran its course. The site still held promise for accommodating new administrative offices, maintenance yards, and housing, but not everyone was impressed. The YP & CC president, Ed Hardy, was fond of referring to El Portal as a "hot, dry canyon down a snaky, narrow road." His view was shared by many other executives and employees, NPS and concessionaire alike, who were lucky enough to live in Yosemite Valley. El Portal had become a kind of second-class village. Residents referred to their more "elevated" valley associates, but often with a smile, especially in winter months when the valley was cold and dark, and El Portal was basking in warm sunshine. The local El Portal Market, operated by Hugh and Lou Carter through an NPS concession contract, was a combination grocery, hardware store, and lively meeting place where neighbors exchanged information, sometimes known as gossip. The charm of small-town America was alive and well in El Portal.

My choice to live at El Portal was deliberate, a gesture toward the still unfulfilled expectations that institutional inertia congealed at Yosemite after Mission 66 could be shaken, in not entirely trounced. The unstated rule was that superintendents should live on-site as close to the heart of parks as they could get. This had been the style for decades. But where better to rattle the mold than at Yosemite? If a superintendent could live nearby and still perform his or her duties then why not leave the heart of the park to visitors and essential employees who provided for their safety? Fortunately, NPS Director Bill Whelan felt the same way.

Not everyone was so inclined or agreed with the rationale. I was not surprised to learn soon after my arrival that, high purpose or not, my choice of housing location was dimly viewed by some among the hierarchy in Yosemite Valley who expected the superintendent to occupy Residence # 1, an elegant structure set in exclusivity on the edge of a meadow with a bold picture window view of Half Dome. This wonderful old home had accommodated all of my predecessors, including cavalry officers, and had been a center for many cocktail gatherings among the local social elite. But I had other priorities and so, too, did my wife, Midge. She would largely detour past the hostess role to pursue her own professional career in education and I would try to help jump start El Portal. Already resident with their families in El Portal, and for the similar reason, were, among others, Assistant Superintendent John Byrne, Chief Scientist Jan van Wagtendonk, Chief Forester Loren West, Chief of Maintenance Terry Gess, Concession Specialist Wayne Schulz, Real Estate Specialist Tom Kirn, and Warehouse Manager Don Haig. The administrative site was beginning to function as intended. By contrast, all YP&CC executives lived in Yosemite Valley, seemingly budge-proof. Ed Hardy argued that he was called out at all hours, day and night, to deal with guest and operational problems, as were most of us. He also enjoyed his own exclusive picture window view of Half Dome from his house on "concessioner row" not far from the Ahwahnee. The test would be whether the entrenched executive hierarchy in Yosemite Valley could be relocated over time to El Portal, either by choice or demand.

THE FALCONS

The Peregrine Falcons roosting high above Yosemite Valley on the El Capitan wall were not paying attention to the NPS/concessionaire contest down in the valley or the history of human intrusion into their domain. They were much more interested in a successful nesting effort. The near extinction of the peregrines in the Sierra Nevada mountains was an especially sinister example of how threats far beyond national park boundaries can erode the web of protection that the parks are established to provide, even for species that historically have bred in such safeguarded topography.

Ornithologists believe the peregrine is indigenous to the river canyons of the Sierra Nevada, and that three hundred or so nesting sites once existed in the mountain chain. Between 1949 and 1978, though, a span of almost three decades, not a single nest was recorded by scientists near Yosemite or anywhere else in the Sierra Nevada. This was no fault of the falcons. They are aerial marvels, hitting speeds of close to 200-miles-per-hour in a dive, claiming the fastest velocity among all of earth's feathered species. Hurtling almost straight down, the peregrines trap their unsuspecting victims in mid-flight, generally favoring cliff swallows, but they have also been found to consume a diverse number of birds that frequent the Yosemite ecosystem. With a choice of fairly abundant foods combined with predator-proof nesting sites tucked into rock clefts far up in the vertical world, the falcon's prospect of survival seemed as assured as anything can be in the natural world. But despite their lofty habits of safety and reproduction, and as science would confirm, the falcons were linked dangerously to a contaminated avian food chain.

Rachael Carson sounded the alarm in 1962 about the lethal threat of DDT and its associated brands of synthetic pesticides, but the widespread and often casual use of DDT was not banned by the government until 1972. By then the grand Central Valley of California, an agricultural cornucopia unmatched anywhere on earth, and only a few air miles from Yosemite, had become a virtual sinkhole of DDT toxicity. Birds flying east from the Central Valley into the Sierra Nevada carried cumulative loads of pesticides in their body fat, which was passed on to their predators. The most significant impact on the falcons was that DDT poisoning made the shells of the eggs they laid abnormally thin and fragile. When either of the adult peregrines, who mate for life and share duties attending the nest, would sit on the eggs, the shells would break. No chicks hatched. The overall population of Peregrine Falcons in the Sierra Nevada precipitously declined as did the peregrine population throughout California.

In 1973, partially in response to the nation's heightened awareness of the ecological interdependence of life forms, the U. S. Congress approved the Federal Endangered Species Act, signed into law by President Richard Nixon. This act allows natural resource stewards to take concerted action to attempt to save flora, fauna, and avifauna that are scientifically proven to be in dire jeopardy. (Today, more than one thousand species are endangered nationwide; two hundred on the list in California.) As for the peregrines, scientists had been looking in vain for active nesting sites in the mountains, fearing that yet another magnificent wild species was in grave jeopardy. Then, in 1978, climbers Jim Bidwell, Dave Diegelman, and Dale Bard reported the exciting news that they had discovered an active peregrine aerie high on the wall of El Capitan. In 1981, a second aerie was confirmed on the walls above the Hetch Hetchy Reservoir.

This seemed incredible, only two active nests in the 750,000-acre park, and the only known aeries in the entirety of millions of acres in the Sierra Nevada. The following year, in 1982, Brian J. Walton, coordinator of ornithologists at the California Predatory Bird Research Group based at Santa Cruz, California, arranged for a meeting with me to discuss the future safety of the birds. By then, the falcons had made a slight shift of their aerie to a location on El Capitan in an area known to climbers as the Horse's Shoulder, but observers of the nesting activity, using powerful telescopes and telephoto lenses, had reached a disheartening conclusion. The adults were laying eggs, but no hatchlings were in evidence. If, however, the live eggs could be collected before they were broken by the weight of attending adult peregrines, the scientists explained to Chief Naturalist Len McKenzie and me, the eggs very likely could be successfully incubated. The ornithologists knew how to manipulate the nesting process and fool the adult peregrines, a tactic they called "nest augmentation," a method of using fake eggs to keep the peregrine adults busy at the nest site while the live eggs were safely collected and hatched. Then, according to the Bird Observatory representatives, the hatchlings could be returned to the nest, the fake eggs removed, and all would be happiness in the peregrine household.

This sounded very logical and promising to us except for the details of how to reach an aerie located almost 2,000 feet straight up on an immense span of granite, how to bring such a fragile cargo to ground, how to get the eggs to Santa Cruz and the hatchlings back, a four hundred mile round trip, and then how to return these avian babies to the heights. When the ornithologists turned to us with this challenge, Yosemite park rangers suggested that we turn to Camp 4. The camp, known at the time as Sunnyside Walk-In Campground, is a legendary site conveniently removed from other campgrounds used by families, senior citizens, and the general park visitor popu-lation. Camp 4 is where climbers from around the world assemble to prepare themselves for the big walls. Its inhabitants primarily are young men and women with limber bodies and fine athletic skills. They are casual acquaintances, mostly, but also kindred spirits who are seeking to prove themselves in a sport that promises exhilaration, peril, and deeply personal pride of achievement. The pool of climb-ing talent at Camp 4 on any given pleasant day is second to none.

CLIMB THE BIG WALLS

If the falcons had a story of times past in Yosemite, so, too, did the annual, random collection of adventurers in the climber's camp-ground. They need only look back into the more recent history of the park to find inspiration for their sport. In 1957, Royal Robbins, Mike Sherrick, and Jerry Gallwas stood with their pile of equipment looking up at the 2,130-foot northwest face of Half Dome. Big wall climbing was still on the ragged edge of human capability despite successes on various lesser walls of the valley, and equipment, by today's standards, was primitive. Pundits in the world of rock climb-ing predicted that many of the great Yosemite walls, especially the faces of Half Dome and regal El Capitan, would never succumb to humans. Climbing was generally confined to brief forays, the few practitioners carrying out experiments with pitons, rock drills, ropes, and anchor bolts, and climbing higher in their efforts to solve the more lenient rock challenges.

To reach the summit of Half Dome other than by the historic cable route, Robbins and his companions were confronted by the chal-lenge of the immense northwest face including a dangerous over-hang of rock known as the Visor that loomed at the dome's highest edge. Somehow the climbers would have to find a way to bypass the Visor, if they got that far. Two years earlier, Robbins, Gallwas, Don Wilson, and a land surveyor named Warren Harding had made a similar attempt. Spending five days on the wall and rappelling back down to the base each day, a height of 500 feet was reached, with 1,630 feet left to go.

Half Dome Cable Route

This time, the new team planned to bivouac on the wall preferably by finding a narrow ledge on which to doze during the dark hours or by just anchoring themselves against the wall if they had to using their climbing gear, methods that promised only fitful sleep, if any, but saved precious climbing distance. If Robbins and his partners could achieve the summit of Half Dome the hard way, the entire regimen of rock climbing would change; the seemingly unattainable becoming the ultimate objective. For this attempt and others to follow, Robbins coined the word "rockcraft," descriptive of the basic problem of solving life-threatening puzzles on surfaces completely alien to Homo sapiens. Ever since George Anderson wedged his bolts and strung twisted twine onto the forgiving east shoulder of Half Dome, Yosemite had become irresistible to a certain class of humans who could not bring themselves simply to stand on solid ground gazing skyward while the tantalizing perpendicular world beckoned.

The basic rockcraft challenge is that a dense falling object, absent aerodynamic conveniences like wings or a parachute, accelerates at a speed of 32-feet-per-second. The object will accelerate at 32 feet in the first second, 64 feet in the next second, 128 feet in the third, and so on until, in a flash, a velocity of about 135-miles-per-hour is reached. A falling climber, assuming that he or she is attached to a rope, can instantaneously snap about 3,000 pounds of pressure onto the rope and bits of metal hardware that have been pounded, wedged, or bolted into rock as safety anchors. Climbing rope is designed with elasticity to absorb some of the shock, but if the rope or hardware fails, the climber becomes a traumatic statistic.

Robbins, Sherick, and Gallwas probably looked like walking hardware stores when they approached the base of Half Dome for their daring ascent. Missing from their equipment were modern chocks,

Jeff Widen on Thank God Ledge, Half Dome

ascenders/descenders (metal grips used to inch up and down a dangling rope), and fancy sticky-soled shoes that eventually would find a place in the inventory of successor climbers. The three men undoubtedly lugged a generous supply of hammers, drills, bolts, pitons, and carabineers. The inventory would not have been complete without climbing ropes, slings, harnesses, hammocks, some kind of warm weatherproof clothing, perhaps sleeping bags, medical supplies, cords and nylon straps of varying dimension, food and water, and probably goggles, hardhats, and headlamps. The essential climbing paraphernalia, called the "rack," was carried by each climber in a shoulder sling that allowed the rack to dangle on the climber's hip within easy reach. The rest of the equipment would have been stuffed in "haul sacks" to be pulled up behind the climbers. Carbonate of magnesium chalk used by modern climbers to improve their grip on rock was not available to the Robbins trio.

The weight of equipment, or more correctly, the absence of weight was crucial. Some climbers are known to have drilled holes in toothbrush handles just to reduce weight by a tiny fraction. Most climbers simply do not carry superfluous weighty objects like toothbrushes. Reducing the eight-pound-plus weight of a gallon of water is not possible, so climbers sip and conserve. If luck is with them, they might find naturally occurring dribbles of water here and there on the rock face. If they are unlucky and a storm hits, water, sometimes in the form of snow and ice, becomes a slippery, threatening menace.

Climbers try to keep three parts of their body in contact with the rock at all times. A variety of configurations may include two hands and a foot, two feet and a hand, a back and two feet, sometimes a head, hand, and foot or a shoulder, elbow, and foot, a butt and two knees. The result is an exercise in intense concentration, use of physical strength and stamina, nimbleness, contortion, and a certain cold-blooded self-confidence. Teams of climbers work on "pitches." One member of a climbing team will inches upward while a partner, secured to the rock by hardware, "belays" the safety rope intended to catch the lead climber in flight if he or she falls. At intervals, the safety rope is run through carabineers attached to pitons, bolts, or, more recently, chocks placed by the lead climber so that the momentum of any fall is theoretically short and can be quickly arrested. Pitches are limited by the variables of rope length, rock surface, ability, and terror. For the human specks attached for hours or days to sheer rock, the personal rewards are theirs alone to savor. There are no crowds of cheering fans, no trophies, and few opportunities to be rewarded financially. Rock climbing is sport in its purest sense.

Stewart M. Green, climber, journalist, and photographer, said in his 1957 article, *First Ascent of Half Dome*: "The first day they climbed five-hundred-feet to the previous highpoint where they spent the night. The next day they worked up the wall, hand-drilling seven bolts, doing the longest pendulum yet attempted in Yosemite, and had Royal Robbins lead the famous 'Robbins Traverse' between crack systems. By the fourth day of climbing, the trio was exhausted and suffered in the mid-summer heat as they ran low on water. That day, Jerry Gallwas led the zigzag pitches toward the beetling summit overhangs, which they dreaded. On the fifth day, Gallwas discovered 'Thank God Ledge,' a horizontal foot-wide ledge that traversed left and allowed an easy escape past the Visor. That afternoon, after twenty-three pitches, they reached Half Dome's broad summit. On the summit, Warren Harding (who had come up the cable route) met the climbers and toasted them with glasses of red wine. Harding, however, was extremely disappointed to miss out on the first ascent of this landmark climb."

Afterwards Robbins said, "We feared the enormity of the wall—we dreaded having to reach so deeply within ourselves and maybe find ourselves lacking." The team had made the most difficult climb yet recorded in the United States.

EL CAPITAN

The success on Half Dome left only the great monarch of all rock walls in Yosemite Valley to be attempted, the ominous face of El Capitan. El Capitan is as high as three Empire State Buildings stacked end-to-end. It is the ultimate monolith, a battlement of sheer granite that many thought would never be attained by mere humans. Warren Harding, the wine steward for the Robbins team, thought otherwise. In July, 1958, he and several climbing partners launched Operation Bootstrap. Joining Harding for various stages of the climb were Wayne Merry, George Whitmore, Richard Calderwood, Mark Powell, Bill Feuter, Wallace Reid, and Al Steck. Unlike the Half Dome exploit, Harding's strategy was not to make the attempt in one single, mighty effort, start to finish. El Capitan would be overcome in segments, climbers scaling pitches, bivouacking on the wall when they could, and leaving bolts and fixed ropes in place so that they could rappel back down to the base to recuperate, re-supply, and attend to jobs and family. By leaving the ropes in place the climbers could return efficiently to the highest pitch and continue the ascent.

On many days, no members of the Harding team were on the wall, but persistent effort was paying off. The thread of ropes extended ever upward until finally, on Halloween Day, four months after Bootstrap began, Harding, Whitmore, and Merry judged that the time had come for a final, all-out push to the summit. By then, 2,000 feet of ropes dangled on the wall just west of the "nose" of El Capitan. Hours of climbing were required just to reach the highest of the pitches already established. This was at a ledge designated by the team as Camp V, a kind of haul-bag supply depot nestled under the remaining 1,000 feet of wall above which rock ended and sky prevailed.

On reaching Camp V, Harding, Merry, and Whitmore had no intention of rappelling all the way back down to the valley floor. Their course would be straight up for the next thirteen days with small ledges providing occasional respite. Merry reported that on one of the ledges, about six feet wide, Harding became so excited by his ability to actually stand, unencumbered by ropes and hardware that he started to "run around, throwing his arms wide." Merry noted, too, that on those days when progress was slow or the weather miserable the three climbers would reach a bivouac on whatever ledge they might find, sit in their rocky surroundings, and "just glare at each other." He said that what he missed most was the "feel of terra firma, the more firma, the less terror."

As the climbing team inched up from below to the very brink of El Capitan, they encountered an unavoidable, menacing overhang of rock looming above them as if a final insulting challenge to the audacity of humans. On November 11, with weather deteriorating, Harding took the lead to attack the overhang. To do so, he climbed to the sheltered inner junction where the overhang met the main vertical surface of El Capitan. Then, using bolts and a hand drill he began an odyssey outward toward the overhang's lip. Harding was hanging by slings and carabineers with his back to yawning airspace and his face almost kissing the rock ceiling. And so he continued for almost twenty-four-hours, using headlight illumination at night, fighting against cold and immense fatigue. Harding later commented that scaling the overhang was like climbing along the inside of a giant pitched roof.

Finally, at 5:15am, the five-foot-six, 135-pound Harding hoisted himself onto the topmost edge of El Capitan, stood up, and stepped forward onto gravity-friendly terrain. Whitmore and Merry followed, using the bolts that Harding had secured on the overhang, joining him about an hour later. At the very apex of El Capitan, up-slope from the edge of the cliff and accessible by backcountry trail, the climbers reached a register box placed there by park rangers to record visits to the location by hikers. Harding made the entry: "November 12, via south buttress, 46 days, 675 pitons and 125 expansion bolts, Warren Harding, Wayne Merry, and George Whitmore." He forgot to mention all those ropes still hanging on the big wall.

News of the El Capitan triumph was broadcast around the world. When asked by reporters if others might attempt the climb, the three men speculated that probably no one else would try. In this assumption Harding and his teammates were hugely mistaken. Royal Robbins, teamed with Don Lauria, made the climb the following year, scaling the wall in seven days. Frenzied climbers in the modern era can romp up El Capitan in a matter of hours, doing so with a legacy of tested technique, refined equipment, and detailed knowledge of routes established by predecessors. El Capitan remains a kingdom of peril, marked now by more than eighty different routes to the top named by those climbers who first pioneered them—Magic

Marek Raganowicz, solo climber, Zenyatta Mondatta route, El Capitan

Mushroom, Lurking Fear, Wings of Steel, Salathé Wall, Excalibur, New Jersey Turnpike, Mescalito, Born Under A Bad Sign, Lost In America, and the Realm of Flying Monkey, to name a few.

After Operation Bootstrap, however, the El Capitan Nose needed attention. Chief Ranger Oscar Sedergren was just as impressed as anyone by the team's accomplishment, but he also was the keeper of climbing protocol in Yosemite. The Chief Ranger required that Harding and company return in the springtime to remove as much of their leftover gear as possible from the face of El Capitan. Sedergren's purpose was twofold; to eliminate potential safety hazards consisting of hardware and ropes that otherwise would deteriorate over time and perhaps give way if some other climbers tried to use them, and to protect the natural character of the El Capitan wall. By "top-roping" down the wall, Harding estimated that tidying up could be accomplished in one weekend, and he was right. He rappelled down pitches in a matter of minutes that had taken grueling hours to climb. Ropes and pitons that could be pried lose disappeared from the route, but many of the expansion bolts could not be removed.

The Sedergren protocol was prescient. In years to follow, rock-busting bolts and pitons have disappeared from climbing activities on Yosemite's big walls, replaced by an amazing variety of chocks and wedges designed to fit into just about any crack or crevice in the rock surface, thread-width to several inches wide. "Clean climbing" is a technique championed by the NPS in concert with leaders in the climbing community, Royal Robbins included, that guards big wall routes from deterioration. Chocks and wedges can be jammed into fractures in the rock to provide safety anchoring on the climbing pitches, then plucked out and carried up to be used on the next pitch, thus cleaning the route in the process and causing only slight or no damage to the fractures, leaving an unblemished route for climbers yet to come.

An even more modern variation on clean climbing are the "stonemasters," the daredevils who have learned to specialize in free and solo climbing, leaving behind most or all of the typical safety gear, often climbing alone, and depending on intense mental focus and athletic ability to survive. Author John Long is a preeminent practitioner of the art. He and companions Jim Birdwell and Billy Westbay are celebrated for the "Nose-in-a-Day" climb of El Capitan in 1975, roughly following the Operation Bootstrap route. The best of the speed climbers have reduced ascents on El Cap to a mind-boggling five hours or less, and no wall in Yosemite, including the northwest face of Half Dome, is immune to their exploits. Most are driven by a confidence that they can push ever harder, stretch ever further, and risk ever more to achieve a goal that binds them to vertical rock.

      Your Yosemite: **PROTECTING A PUBLIC TREASURE**

John Bachar, one of the founding stonemasters, admitted that his chosen extreme sport was "addictive." On one occasion he offered a $10,000 reward to anyone who could stay with him for a day on difficult Yosemite routes. No takers. At age fifty-two, while climbing near Mammoth Lakes on the east side of the Sierra Nevada, Bachar fell to his death.

When Harding died in 2002 at age seventy-seven (of natural causes), a remembrance in the *Los Angeles Times* chronicled the "remarkable longevity for a man who consumed untold quantities of rotgut red wine and drove fast cars with wild abandon." Readers were reminded that Harding "was criticized for using siege tactics on El Cap, establishing a series of camps linked to the ground, much like an Everest expedition, and using excessive numbers of expansion bolts to make progress in spaces devoid of cracks and handholds." But Harding was the first and El Capitan the mightiest. In his autobiography, *Downward Bound*, Harding claims his place in climbing lore and identifies himself cheerfully as the founder of the Lower Sierra Eating, Drinking, and Farting Society.

THE AERIE

The mother lode of talent that we turned to at Camp 4 to retrieve the falcon eggs could be traced right back to Robbins, Harding, and their daring partners. Communication between NPS rangers and the Camp 4 denizens was frequent and usually easy. A give-and-take relationship had organically come about because, technically, no one was supposed to live at the camp for longer than two weeks. Rangers worked to enforce the time limit, on occasion by having footraces through the trees with recalcitrant campers, but also turned a tolerant eye to those in Camp 4 who assisted in search-and-rescue missions, giving them slack on the time limit in exchange for their talent. These "rockcrafters" brought welcome backup strength to the small staff of ranger rescue experts who were tasked with bringing injured and stranded climbers off the big walls to safety.

At the time of the peregrine challenge this variable team of Camp 4 volunteers included Yvon Chouinard, John "Yabo" Yablonski, Victor Apanius, Ron Kauk, Werner Braun, Rob Ramey, Peter Croft, Dave

Diegleman, Rick Ridgeway, Alan Bard, Kurt Stolzenberg, Walt Shipley, and Ken Yager, all devotees of the "ditch," the climbers' nickname for Yosemite Valley. The enterprising Chouinard, a French Canadian, crafted innovative climbing gear and was known to sell it in the parking lot at Camp 4 if no one in authority was looking. When the rangers asked if these men were willing to participate in "nest augmentation," the pending bird rescue attempt, the climbers stepped forward, or, more precisely, stepped upward.

In the summer of 1982, the adult falcons must have been startled when climbers rappelled down from the lip of El Capitan to the nest site. The avian parents, frightened but determined to protect the nest, flew back and forth, staying close in nearby airspace, while the climbers carefully lifted four precious unbroken eggs from the nest, substituting fake eggs in their stead. The stolen eggs were placed with extreme care in a specially-padded container designed to provide safety and warmth during the lengthy descent from the aerie down to horizontal ground. Once safely on the valley floor, the climbers handed off the cargo to waiting scientists who set off immediately on a four-hour road race to the ornithology lab at Santa Cruz on the California coast. A few anxious days later, we on the park staff learned that this unique egg relay had succeeded. Three of the four eggs were hatched in an incubator at the lab. One of the hatchlings was kept in Santa Cruz for protection and further study. The other two vigorous chicks, one male, one female, were quickly transported back to Yosemite.

Yvon Chouinard was one of the climbers who returned the chicks to the nest. Remembering the event years later, he said, "We were worried that the parents would think this was very odd and they would not bond with them. But as soon as we rappelled down—after exchanging perky nestling chicks for the fake eggs—we looked through our spotting scopes and saw one parent fly into the nest, looking at the fledglings and cocking her head side to side as if thinking, whoa, that was quick! She then flew off to get some food and progressed to feeding them." The hatchlings fledged thirty-eight-days later, instinctively taking wing in the wild habitat, the accustomed home of their species. Nest augmentations continued

　　　　Your Yosemite: **PROTECTING A PUBLIC TREASURE**

on El Capitan, in the Hetch Hetchy Valley, and finally at a third location, Lake Eleanor on the northwest edge of the park.

The peregrine rescuers at Yosemite and their park ranger and scientific teammates had a precise objective, but a much larger issue was also at stake. A park devoid of indigenous species and without a nurturing habitat to sustain them becomes, in an analogues sense, yet just another broken shell. In this case, the falcons, struggling to survive, were sending out an alarm signaling that humans were poisoning them. But in this instance the rescuers prevailed. Breeding pairs of falcons continued to spread slowly throughout their historic Sierra Nevada habitat as well as to locales elsewhere in California. The Peregrine Falcon was removed from the endangered species list in 1998.

The climbers who participated at Yosemite in the falcon rescue also followed other equally impressive pursuits. Chouinard founded Patagonia and became, like Royal Robbins, a highly successful purveyor of outdoor equipment and clothing; Ridgeway became an acclaimed outdoor adventure photographer, film maker, and author; Bard a respected mountaineer and climbing instructor (as was Wayne Merry); Yablonski, Croft, and Yeager went on to claim a series of bold first ascents and take climbing to daredevil limits; Braun and Shipley became search-and-rescue experts; Kauk a master of extreme routes and an advisor to film actors, including Sylvester Stallone and Tom Cruise; Apanius a research scientist who assisted in recovery efforts for the still endangered California Condor.

Saving the falcons was a continuum of the Yosemite saga; a sparkling moment that seemed to fit perfectly with the whole purpose of the park. It was a rare occasion when action spoke the loudest and a welcome reminder that conservation, rightly targeted, can speed the restoration of wild values that are everyone's right to enjoy. I was just an observer of the assemblage of scientists, park rangers, and world-class climbers who succeeded by tucking two hatchlings back into their El Capitan nest, but, damn, did it make me feel good! This was proof that the best choices for Yosemite lay ahead; that an informed human partnership with the natural environment was essential to the park's secure future, and, on a much more profound scale, to the secure future of the dominating humans themselves.

But this was 1982. The political tides had shifted as personified by James Watt. As the falcons took wing, the Yosemite General Management Plan flew off in a different direction, onto the proverbial shelf. Made clear to me by my superiors was that, except for tweaks around the edges, mostly to improve utility services, efforts to take real steps toward achieving plan goals had descended in priority to low level and would languish there for the foreseeable future.

11

The Other Park

DESPITE CHANGES in management priorities at the political level, most of Yosemite continued to function as visitors should expect thanks to the superb NPS employees, permanent and seasonal, who provided the *service* that is the word-glue between *national* and *park*. During my tenure at Yosemite no one better exemplified this service than Dr. Carl Sharsmith. When I arrived at Yosemite for my first year of duty, Dr. Sharsmith was returning for his forty-eighth summer season on the job. His tenure ultimately would span six decades before he hung up his ranger uniform for the last time at age ninety-one. He was a seasonal employee who spent his summers in a tent cabin at Tuolumne Meadows. The rest of each year he served as Professor of Botany at San Jose State University. Sharsmith reached the park at the beginning of each summer season in his trusty Model A Ford Roadster, "with 200,000 miles on the original engine," he would proudly report. His car was not the only serviceable antique he possessed; so, too, was the ranger uniform that he first put on in 1931. It was sturdy and comfortable, so he just kept using it.

Dr. Sharsmith's main task was to take park visitors on guided walks in the elegant opus of tree-lined meadows, balletic streams, and bold mountains that is the Yosemite high country. In a biography of Dr. Sharsmith entitled *Mountain Sage*, Elizabeth Stone O'Neill describes one such walk:

"Now we are on Dana Plateau, a moonscape of broken boulders 12,000 feet in the sky. We marvel at the pygmy daisies, dappling this alpine desert with purple and gold. 'Try not to step on them' Carl says. Big cumulus clouds balloon over the horizon, grow, swell and combine. By lunchtime we are perched on a rocky promontory with several thousand feet of space sheer below us. We can see storms in every direction: west from the Central Valley, north and south about the great Sierra sea of peaks, and east over Mono Lake, a salt-rimmed mirror in the high desert. The air rings with electricity. When we move, we snap and crackle. Phil poses on a rock cantilevered out over space, and everyone takes his picture with his hair standing eerily straight up. Carl munches his bread and cheese and then he smokes his pipe. Despite his almost eighty years, he doesn't seem tired. After a while he mildly suggests that we come away from the edge where there is the most electricity. A kestrel vaults across the face of the storm.

As the weather worsens, several of the walkers become afraid and suggest that they leave the mountain, but then, Sharsmith points out, they will miss the storm, which would be a pity. He suggests that the group take shelter under an enormous balanced boulder. The walkers huddle together telling stories as the storm flashes and thunders all around

Park Ranger Carl Sharsmith

them, pelting the rocks with hailstones. Sharsmith remains calm; he explains that the hailstones are really something called graupel: frozen pellets of snow. When the rain dies down and a shaft of sunlight breaks through the clouds, the naturalist lifts his pack once more. It is time to move on: Without a word, he heads up through the lowering clouds and the still-falling graupel. A few hesitate. We're cold. Let's turn back. Carl looks at them and his face is transfigured. 'You know what John Muir would say? You can sleep an eternity in your grave. You're only here for a little while.' He turns and heads up again, and we follow. The ground is covered with white several inches deep. Purple daisies, green and gold ivesia and rosy buckwheat are encased in the icy mantle—a white carpet woven with Persian blossoms. The sky is dark and the light like an El Greco painting, the rocks gleaming wet, and we know that it is perhaps the most wonderful day we have ever known."

In his elegant manner Dr. Sharsmith was leaving an indelible message with those who shared nature walks with him. He was not trying to persuade. He was just asking people to more carefully look at, feel, share, think about, and marvel at the environment that is part of their lives and surroundings. Where better to do this than in a place conserved for them, owned by them, and a legacy for their children? He devoted his life to this message. There is now a website, Name4Carl.org, that summarizes an on-going effort to win lasting recognition for this inspirational naturalist by having a peak in the High Sierra named in his honor. The initiative is led by William R. "Bill" Jones, former Yosemite Chief Naturalist, who treasurers the moments during eleven years at the park from 1961 to 1972 when he had the opportunity to work directly with Dr. Sharsmith. Jim Sano, a successor to Jones, says with a smile, "When I first assumed my post as Mather District Interpreter in the 1970s there was a mandatory government retirement age. So, Carl continued to be 72-years-old until the Reagan Administration changed the rule."

The 12,002 peak is not far from Gaylor Peak and Tuolumne Meadows. The Board of Geographic Names, an entity within the U. S. Geological Survey, is the keeper of names for natural features scattered across the nation. Its deliberations are studiously slow when new names are proposed. Jones and his many allies, especially including Sano, are just as steady in their resolve, either to convince the Board or Congress of the validity of this initiative. If the peak is so named, it will be as a celebration of park naturalists everywhere.

WILDERNESS STEWARDS

Trail Crew Foreman Jim Snyder also has made a powerful statement out in Yosemite's backcountry, in this case with his analytical ability, muscle power, and facts on the ground. He first learned his tradecraft from old-timer Bill Sabo, a self-educated, book-loving man from the coal country of West Virginia who found his way into a leadership position in the park focused on maintaining hundreds of miles of the wilderness trail system. When Snyder, as a teenager, first joined up in 1962, Sabo's crew consisted mostly of itinerate recruits from unemployment offices, usually eight to ten men accustomed to hard lives. On hiring day the crewmen were delivered by truck to a trailhead, the entry point for a foot-borne tromp to their work site, often miles into the rugged interior of the park. Occasionally during the weeks to come a packer cowboy and his horse and mule team would arrive at the trail camp to resupply the larder. One mule in particular was always welcome, the "beer mule," a creature found nowhere in NPS operating manuals. The crew was expected to settle in for the duration, meaning weeks in the outback, moving irregularly from work site to work site and only rarely brushing by the front-country pleasures of modern society.

Snyder soon learned that his boss had little tolerance for returning to the same trail section year after year to correct shoddy or haphazard work. Sabo would take his crew out to a section of trail and ask, "What would you do with this?" Sabo was asking the crew to read the terrain, to interpret the topography by determining where the water was coming from, what the plant species were that indicated soil type and drainage, and where rock falls, timber blow downs, wash outs, or wintertime avalanches threatened. Sabo wanted to know from the crew what special techniques, materials, or equipment might be needed to reconstruct, stabilize, and improve the trail section.

The trail crew foreman expected a finished design based on careful thought followed by strong execution that would last for years. These trail segments must be capable of withstanding nature's elements, backpacker steps, and especially the pounding hooves of 1,200-pound equines. Sabo made known that the trail was the lifeline of the wilderness and that he expected vigorous, informed, and successful performance by his crew. The hard-core recruits from unemployment offices usually lasted one season in the backcountry, if they could get that far. Snyder was among those who returned. In the Sabo camp he had found something so personally appealing that he began a professional journey into the trail crew dominion of

Your Yosemite: **PROTECTING A PUBLIC TREASURE**

Yosemite that would extend over the next four decades, succeeding Sabo, carrying on his mentor's traditions, and refining technique.

One example of Snyder's work was when he and his crew built a Roman arch bridge in 1976 on the Tuolumne Meadows/Glen Aulin trail. A swampy spot along a portion of the trail was difficult to traverse in the early weeks of summer when snowmelt was still irrigating the high country. In an earlier attempt to fix the problem, metal culverts had been hauled in on mule back and plopped into the trouble spot, but the culverts were old, rusty, ugly, and half-packed with silt.

Beth Pratt, writing about the bridge project for the Yosemite Association, reports: "to build the arch, they labored after hours to avoid wasting time and money on the unusual project. No one on the crew actually had built an arch, but this didn't deter them in the least. Jim simply read books on 19th century stonemasonry; assigned a mathematically-talented crewmember to figure out the exact geometric patterns, and then they carved the granite by superimposing the patterns over the rock. The metal culverts were packed out to the road by mule while the arch stones were designed and shaped in native materials using traditional skills and hand tools. Getting the materials to the actual site was no simple matter either; they transported the tons of granite over the trail by hand, using dead Lodgepole Pine as rollers."

Snyder later said, "It was incredible that it worked just like in the books; no cement was needed." When the heavy keystones finally were levered into place and the temporary wooden supports removed, gravity and friction became part of the functional design. The entire weight of the structure, from keystones down through the arch, was transferred to the foundation, the earth itself. "That's the way it's supposed to be, in symmetry with the landscape," observed the trail crew foreman. He named the bridge the "Sabo Arch." The small stone bridge is a monument to the ability of humans to applaud Mother Nature rather than slapping her in the face. It is so discreet that almost no one who crosses even notices that the ancient Romans must have been in Yosemite, and that was exactly Snyder's intent.

Trail Crew, 1983, John Schelhas, Bob Binnewies (visiting), Mark Manda, Annie Barrett, Jon Chorover, Lynn Erickson, Doug Binnewies (visiting), John Leonard, Dan Krumholtz, Jim Snyder, Mike Shenton

On the Fletcher Creek Trail between the Merced Lake and Vogelsang High Sierra Camps, Snyder had a different problem to solve. The trail passes through a wide, constantly moist and lengthy meadow. The meadow was being severely eroded as hikers and equestrians maneuvered to avoid furrows cut by pounding feet into the thin alpine ground cover. The furrows would fill with water, prompting passersby to step to the side to find better footing, thus spontaneously beginning the formation of a new pathway that eventually would morph into another watery gutter. Over time, the meadow had become riddled with gutters that disrupted drainage and were destroying the biota of this alpine lawn. Instead of gentle snowmelt irrigation that should spread fan-like over the meadow, the foot-stomped troughs just drained the water away. Water dependent plants were disappearing and invasive species taking hold. Scenically the meadow was just as bad, an insult to the very concept of wilderness preservation. No Roman bridge would suffice here, but Snyder thought he knew how to rescue the meadow. If his crew

Your Yosemite: **PROTECTING A PUBLIC TREASURE**

could put in the fix, other trail crews could do the same elsewhere in the high country.

His strategy was to keep feet and hooves elevated on one functional pathway designed to allow for natural water to flow through portals in a hand-constructed causeway. As with the bridge project, Snyder went back to the books, this time reading the *Draft Horse Journal* and *Draft Horse Primer*, reference materials that described in detail how Amish farmers used teams of draft horses to pull heavy loads. The trail crew foreman also received good-natured advice from two animal-packer cowboys that supplied the camp, Walt Butler and John Moe, about how to work afoot behind the south end of a mule going north. Snyder was given ultimate encouragement when Kate-the-Mule was assigned to the task. Kate was a beautiful and intelligent mule, said Snyder, who "learned to work on a team pulling logs out of an Arkansas swamp."

A flat piece of metal plate bent up at one end to prevent it from digging into soft meadow soil, referred to as a "stone boat," was rigged to Kate's harness. Heavy rocks intended for use as the foundation for the causeway were placed on the boat to be pulled by the mule across the meadow to the work site. As the causeway extended the pull became longer, but Kate, always with a seemingly cheery disposition, seemed not to mind the extra distance. At the end of each workday, Snyder simply turned Kate lose to wander and graze through the night as she pleased. Each morning Kate would show up for work and the apple she knew Snyder had waiting for her.

The trail crew levered the rocks into place in parallel line across a half-mile of meadow while Snyder did the footwork behind Kate, signaling her as necessary with voice commands and the reins. Once the rock walls were complete the next task was to fill the channel in between with dirt and gravel. Kate and some of her mule associates were recruited to haul the fill materials in wooden boxes strapped to the x-shaped sawbuck "trees" of their pack saddles. The haltered mules were led by riders on horseback to a location where a trail crew member, standing on an upslope above the mule, would shovel in dirt to fill the boxes. The distance from the dirt supply to the meadow worksite was about two miles. The mules—four-legged dump trucks just doing their job—would plod back and forth all day.

The first hikers and riders to use the completed causeway pronounced it ideal. The strength of this hand-built conduit is truly impressive. If an elephant happened by the causeway could withstand the impact. Part of the project included filling in the old ruts and troughs that so scarred the meadow. Recovery began immediately, clearly demonstrating that the wilderness environment can be complemented in a manner that still allows for human admittance, enjoyment, and safety. Before-and-after photographs show the result; scars that have healed and Kate's causeway easy on the land, almost unnoticeable.

WOMEN, TOO

When Snyder first began his career at Yosemite, the idea of women in the trail camp was akin to females in a men's locker room; not considered. The women who were beginning to make inroads into the male-dominated work culture of Yosemite were waitresses, secretaries, clerks, cooks, nurses, teachers, a few ranger-naturalists, and dispensers of information at visitor centers, all front-country assignments. Very gradually, though, women began to take on more responsibility and prove their strength, both intellectually and physically.

Still, the backcountry NPS trail camps were about as distant from the cutting edge of gender equality as custom dictated—that is, until Snyder hired Annie Barrett and Sue Brown as trail crew laborers in 1981, allowing them to break through the rock ceiling at Yosemite, so to speak. These two women had been preceded by Nadine Azevedo who filled in as camp cook for one of the NPS crews the previous summer when the man who had been doing the job quit and hiked out of the backcountry. Until the arrival of Barrett and Brown, though, the general assumption, especially among old-timers, was that the all-male culture in the trail camps would proceed uninterrupted, as always. No one gave much thought to women on the crew. When they did, the conclusion was that females were obviously incapable of handling the hard physical labor and keeping pace with the men. And then there was the tricky matter of sex, not in the gender sense but what might go on out there in the bushes and who might fight for the privilege. Some of Snyder's maintenance supervisors down in Yosemite Valley worried about a Sodom-and-Gomorrah out in the backcountry if females were allowed to join the crews.

Snyder, the contrarian, saw no problem. He rightly assumed that the young adults under his command would conduct themselves with good common sense. He was confident in his ability to maintain a kind of craggy mountain discipline among his crew members, except of course for his particular camp cook. No one trifled with Jim Murphy, a former trail crew foreman himself, Irish to the core, and arch-defender of the monarchy afforded to him by his control of the stove. Only a novice in camp might criticize Murphy, to his or her lasting regret. Bruised by an avalanche of blue syntax of artful construction, he or she would make that mistake only once.

When Barrett and Brown joined Snyder's crew they already had experience in trail maintenance. Barrett had worked for the non-profit Student Conservation Association. Brown had similar credentials with the California Conservation Corps. Both of them had worked to repair damage on the Yosemite Falls trail, hiking up to their work site each morning, then back down into the semi-urban valley at the end of their workday. Now the two young women were joining a regular backcountry NPS trail crew far from anything that resembled urban. Snyder worked with them on their first days to teach them the intricacies of constructing rip-rap, a kind of cobblestone treatment applied to particularly unstable trail segments. If properly constructed, rip-rap is capable of withstanding years of pounding by passersby. The procedure involves digging and gathering rocks from nearby areas, carrying them to the work site, and interlocking them in place like a linear jigsaw puzzle. In their first days on the job, both women proved that they could gather, haul, and place rocks in volume. They were quick studies and maintained an impressive work pace. Back at camp at the end of each workday, the women had a leveling effect on what otherwise had been typical male trash talk, except that if pressed they could give back with equal classiness. Snyder learned, too. He secretly believed that women, with their innate planning skills and attention to detail, are better at rip-rap than men.

During his tenure at Yosemite, about 160 men and women worked on Snyder's crews. Most went on to successful careers in education, science, business, the arts, and environmental stewardship, including jobs in the National Park Service. Barrett, for example, became a special education teacher and, as an avocation, a first-rate artist; Yosemite the theme. My sense is that any parents who want young adults to begin finding their own way should encourage them to work for at least one summer, somewhere, on a backcountry trail crew. Lifelong friendships and pride of accomplishment are the potential rewards.

THE GREAT OUTBACK

The prized space in Yosemite that captured the attention of Snyder, Barrett, Brown, and their many strength-worthy team members was informally referred to by those of us in the desk-bound, visitor-crunch arena as the "other park." It is the last domain of horse and mule delivery services, the chosen realm for backpackers; the place where Native Americans and John Muir could still find familiarity.

In a literal sense, all roads lead to Yosemite Valley so the valley is almost always the first discovery for any new visitor. From there, crossing the High Sierra on the blacktopped Tioga Road provides a hint of the astonishing glacial-molded topography that so enthralled Muir. To step away from the blacktop and explore this landscape demands a price. All roads and almost all resort conveniences must be left behind in favor of a return to the basic fundamentals of shelter, endurance, nourishment, and judgment.

Those who choose this path are claiming a precious right vested in them by their national government that is measured not by the number of people on the trail but by an intimate, immeasurable relationship with nature. A single person standing on the summit of a sharp High Sierra peak, arms raised, shouting for the sheer joy of being there and with nobody around to applaud, is a constant reminder that our nation's citizens have chosen to guard such places principally for the shouts yet to come.

In wilderness one can discover a connection to the past, to the times before machines and explosives arrived to dominate the landscape, to scenery unfiltered and natural processes unmolested. One can also reestablish a different sense of time, a different rhythm of being in nature and in ourselves that can be difficult to sustain in this era of high-speed everything; internet, cars and highways, fast food, on-line shopping and dating, smart phones, Twitter, texting, and Facebook.

The obvious rewards of the grand vistas are gradually joined by the subtler pleasures initially unnoticed and closer at hand; an intricate patch of lichen on a rock; a tree boldly inventive in survival; the kaleidoscopic play of untamed tumbling water; form and function of life and topography interlinked. Discovery in wilderness can also be inward, taking us into the very core of who we are, perhaps the best reward of all. A few hours or days or weeks in this altered state, far from the hectic pace of our normal lives, can also suggest new patterns for our future lives, a more informed relationship between humans and their natural surroundings that intensifies respect for both.

The nation formally affirmed the importance of wilderness in 1964 when the U. S. Congress approved the Wilderness Act and President Lyndon Baines Johnson signed the bill into law. The Act requires that wilderness areas be of "sufficient size," which is generally defined as 5,000 acres or more. "A wilderness," said Congress, "in contrast with those areas where man and his own works dominate the landscape, is hereby recognized as an area where the earth and its community of life are untrammeled by man, where man himself is a visitor who does not remain. An area of wilderness is further defined to mean in this Act an area of undeveloped Federal land retaining its primeval character and influence, without permanent improvements or human habitation, which is protected and managed so as to preserve its natural conditions."

This oxymoron, "managed so as to preserve its natural condition," is an obvious bow to the all-consuming presence of humans on earth. Except perhaps for the deepest trenches in the ocean floors, there is no place on the planet that escapes human company. The paradox at the heart of wilderness management is that anything so "managed" is not exactly wilderness in the conventional sense, but a deliberate human effort to preserve aspects of the natural world that, without such intervention, might be lost forever. Wilderness must be monitored and nudged, not simply designated on a piece of paper, to ensure that all life and geologic forms that belong there have precious space to share with human visitors. Jim Snyder called this "understanding the totality of the park."

WHERE TO DRAW
THE WILDERNESS LINE

Wilderness designation of lands within a park boundary is the ultimate level of legal protection provided by the government. That is why, ten years after the Wilderness Act was approved and five years before I arrived at Yosemite, Jim Snyder, squirming in his unaccustomed suit and tie, was sitting in a hearing room in Washington, D.C., trying to convince members of Congress that adding wilderness protection to lands in Yosemite was a good idea.

Snyder was between seasonal jobs in the park, probably the first and only unemployed NPS representative ever to testify before Congress. His presence at the hearing was at the request of the Sierra Club and he was in heady company. Others testifying at the hearing included the governor of California, the director of the National Park Service, the vice chairman of the Yosemite Park & Curry Company, various park superintendents, scientists, and lobbyists— all employed. Snyder was taking a risk. He was at the hearing to offer his opinion, strongly held, about the need for wilderness protection at Yosemite, an opinion that might not necessarily be in synchronization with official NPS policy on the subject.

Snyder had a strong ally sitting at the witness table with him, Dr. Jan van Wagtendonk, former smoke jumper and paratrooper, hiker, holder of a Ph.D. from the University of California, Berkeley, a fire ecology expert, and my eventual neighbor at El Portal. Van Wagtendonk was the resident scientist at Yosemite, specializing in the effect of natural fire on the park's ecosystem. He was a strong

    Your Yosemite: **PROTECTING A PUBLIC TREASURE**

advocate for "prescribed burns," the select use of creeping ground fires deliberately set by highly trained crews to rid forested areas of undergrowth and reinforce natural regenerative cycles. Between the two of them, Snyder and van Wagtendonk could claim to have walked all 840 miles of the Yosemite trail system. They might even have made that claim individually. Both of the men had been on the trails on numerous occasions, probing into the most isolated recesses of the park. They knew the resource and were at the hearing to pass this knowledge to Congressional committee members.

At the hearing, their nemesis was Don Hummel, representing the Yosemite Park & Curry Company. Hummel, a successful attorney and a former mayor of Tucson, Arizona, had served in the Johnson Administration as assistant secretary of Housing and Urban Development and subsequently operated concessionaire business enterprises at Lassen, Glacier, and Mount McKinley (Denali) National Parks. He was highly regarded among his peers and held in good standing among the government elite in the nation's capital.

Hummel's message was that the Yosemite Park & Curry Company was not opposed to wilderness designation that would add a level of supreme protection to portions of the High Sierra sheltered within the park boundary. He applauded this prospect, assuring committee members that concessionaires were strong advocates for the preservation of natural values in national parks and that, in fact, they based their businesses' successes on this very ideal.

He had only two caveats regarding proposed wilderness designation in the Yosemite high country: that nine 30-acre plots should be excluded to allow for the expansion of existing and future commercially-operated High Sierra Camps and that the wilderness line also should be inscribed in a manner to allow for possible future development along the rim of Yosemite Valley. The five trail-accessed High Sierra Camps already located in the Yosemite backcountry were on plots of about two acres each; a total of ten acres overall. Hummel proposed to expand commercial tent camp space by adding another 260 acres to the mix, allowing the tiny camps ultimately to morph into alpine villages of a sort.

Hummel explained to the committee that the Yosemite wilderness, guarded as it is within the boundaries of a national park, was not threatened by "irreparable damage from logging, mining, and other uses," and added that "man's uses, while sometimes thoughtless and not always consistent with our concept of good preservation, are soon healed by nature." He contended that the backcountry trail network in Yosemite was in "miserable condition." To correct this problem, especially to ease access for visitors to the High Sierra Camps, Hummel recommended that mechanized equipment and judicious use of asphalt replace trail crew maintenance. Use of modern technology, he said, "would be less disruptive to a visitor's experience than the prolonged use of hand tools by inordinately large work crews." Referring to the risk of drawing a wilderness boundary line too close to the rim of Yosemite Valley, Hummel cautioned that, "such lines might prevent the Park Service from making decisions that will best enable the people to enjoy both the valley and rim by using that mode of transportation which further study discloses is most effective and least objectionable to the concepts of preservation and use."

When their turn came at the hearing, Dr. van Wagtendonk and Jim Snyder presented statistics to confirm that thousands of people willingly roamed along even the roughest, most remote trails in Yosemite and that this use was expanding. Snyder presented photographs of his eight-person trail crew working on a segment of the John Muir Trail by hand drilling and splitting large chunks of rock that were then moved into place by fulcrum and lever to form a sturdy, lasting trail surface. He testified to the economy, precision, and minimal environmental shock of trail crew work methods, referencing the fact that most of the Yosemite trail network was in place and functioning long before helicopters, bulldozers, jackhammers, chainsaws, all-terrain vehicles, and blacktop were available. The trail network had historic as well as functional value, he added. Snyder did give a bow to Alfred Noble, the inventor of dynamite, by agreeing that explosives in the backcountry tool box were acceptable if used judiciously. Given a choice, though, Snyder preferred the plug-and-feather.

This old-time device consists of a metal spike (the plug) onto which two sturdy wings of spring steel (the feathers) are welded near the tip end of the spike. The feathers flare out from the tip toward the head of the spike. To split a boulder, the plug-and-feather is positioned in a hand-drilled hole and then driven into the hole by sledgehammer blows. Striking down on the spike is the trail crew equivalent of cutting diamonds. Instantaneous compression of the feathers creates a powerful wedging force as the spring steel tries to regain its original form. Assuming that the fault lines and weaknesses of the boulder have been correctly read, the rock will split, a diamond-cutting methodology measured by the ton rather than by the carat.

Snyder and van Wagtendonk argued persuasively that Congress should legally affirm wilderness protection to assure that a major portion of the Yosemite backcountry always would be subject to the nation's highest degree of preservation. They contended that this level of vigilant natural resources stewardship would encourage even more visitation and greater public benefit, a guarantee that a jewel in the crown of America's scenic wonders would always be there for the finding.

Don Hummel counseled that the Congress should take no such action. He pointed out that no overall plan for Yosemite's future management and development had yet been approved by the National Park Service. Until such a plan was in place, he said, the option for wilderness designation should be deferred. Hummel's logic prevailed.

When I approved the Yosemite *General Management Plan* six years later in 1980, Dr. van Wagtendonk was ready. With maps and pen in hand, and firsthand knowledge of the park gathered by so many boot-miles on the trails, van Wagtendonk had plotted with extreme care a possible wilderness boundary. By then, Snyder, long since recovered from wearing a suit-and-tie, was out in the backcountry supervising his crew. Don Hummel no longer had a business association with the Yosemite Park & Curry Company, but was now serving as chairman of the Western Conference of National Park Concessionaires, still watchful of perceived transgressions against commercial vendors in national parks.

Van Wagtendonk and I were reviewing proposed wilderness options for Yosemite one day when we simultaneously reached the same conclusion. Rather than placing the line on the rim of Yosemite Valley, why not reel it right down to the bases of the great walls? Technically, this was possible. Despite the fact that the walls loomed over all the traffic and development on the valley floor they were just far enough removed to be included within the wilderness line. So reel we did. Lines were also drawn around the existing development footprints of the five High Sierra Camps. These popular camps could continue to operate as "non-conforming uses" within the wilderness boundary. Should the day ever come when one or more of the camps become obsolete due to utility failures or for any other reason the camp will be closed and the site restored to a natural condition.

The wilderness line for Yosemite was vetted through the NPS hierarchy in San Francisco and Washington, D. C. It encompasses 94% (about 700,000 acres) of park territory. This was not a stand-alone proposal. Beginning in 1981, Congressman Philip Burton (D-San Francisco) began putting together legislation that would become the *California Wilderness Act*. He already counted as a notable legislative victory the establishment in 1972 of the Golden Gate National Recreation Area, managed by the National Park Service and considered to be a priceless asset for quality of life in the San Francisco Bay Area. His strategy for wilderness preservation was to gather in all such proposals on federal lands throughout California and package them into one major piece of legislation. Despite the recent shift away from environmental concerns when James Watt was appointed Secretary of the Interior, Burton was a political tour-de-force, a master politician adept at persuasion and proficient in winning bipartisan support for his legislative initiatives.

I had one opportunity to speak with him about wilderness protection for Yosemite. He and I were standing on the steps of an office building in San Francisco and Burton was in a hurry, as usual. He needed no convincing about Yosemite. We were in the bill, Burton assured me. Ultimately he gained 36 co-sponsors for his California wilderness bill including then Congresswoman Barbara Boxer, then Congressman Leon Panetta, and Congressman Morris Udall, known among his colleagues as an especially dedicated environmental champion. Sadly, Burton would not be witness to the success of his wilderness legislation. The bill was well on its way to approval when he suddenly died in 1983. He was succeeded by Nancy Pelosi, fortunately a staunch supporter of Burton's initiative. A year later, the California Wilderness Act became law (P. L. 98-425), protecting three million acres in the state, Yosemite terrain included.

ON PATROL

While I was learning of the scale and complexity of the Yosemite backcountry, I also needed to know more about law enforcement challenges in Yosemite Valley, and, so, one evening, I joined Park Ranger Bryan Swift for a nighttime ride in his patrol car. There is stark contrast between a wilderness trail camp barely touching modern-day civilization and the inside of a fully equipped ranger patrol car, radio constantly blatting, armaments loaded and ready, medical equipment at hand, miscellaneous tools, ropes, hardhats, gloves, spotlights, flares, rolls of yellow tape and flagging to temporarily establish restricted zones and mark evidence, measuring tape, camera, perhaps tranquilizing drugs for wildlife, and —now days— computers for tracking suspect vehicles and culprits. The ranger, too, is equipped with a "Charlie Brown" belt that holsters handgun and probably a taser, cuffs, portable radio, mace or pepper spray, and a club-like police baton, all at fingertip position. When I met Swift at his car he was wearing a bulletproof vest under his ranger shirt.

One of Swift's many challenges in Yosemite Valley was to try to stop BASE jumpers. He had been highly trained to deal with almost any law enforcement contingency, but BASE jumping was in a class by itself. The phrase BASE jumping, an acronym for Building-Antenna-Span-Earth, was coined in 1978 by cinematographer Carl Boenish while he was filming in Yosemite. It highlighted the daredevil choices of people who chose to hurl themselves into airspace from the highest manmade or nature-crafted places they could find. Their salvation was the parachute they carried strapped to their bodies, to be deployed when sufficient airspeed was reached, preferably before making explosive contact with the ground below. Yosemite Valley was an obvious choice and the 3,000+ feet of airspace that beckoned from the lip of El Capitan especially so. The basic technique was to run as fast as possible to the lip, dive off, freefall until the moment came to pop open the ram-air parachute, then float peacefully down to the meadow below. Variations on the theme at El Capitan included rumored launches from a handstand, using a pogo stick to hop off, riding a bicycle out into nothingness, skiing off, and jumping at night.

The problem for Yosemite rangers was that many accidents and fatalities occur in the park. They dealt with these challenges and tragedies as part of their professional responsibilities, but understandably had low tolerance for what they viewed as blatant foolhardiness and even less tolerance for picking up the pieces. That meant BASE jumping. When I arrived in Yosemite in 1979, a lively debate was already underway among park officials about whether BASE jumping could somehow be sanctioned and controlled as a safe, though theatrical, activity. At least fifty known jumps were made from El Capitan in 1979 while Chief Ranger Bill Wendt, in particular, struggled with the question of whether a permit system could be designed to assure that safe equipment and qualifying experience of the jumpers could be sufficiently monitored and enforced.

In the meantime, the BASE jumpers turned to the United States Parachute Association seeking an endorsement of their sport. At first, the USPA, the sponsoring organization for skydivers, declined due to concerns about minimum safe altitude for opening a parachute, but then reversed its position as the 1980 summer season approached. I found myself meeting with a group of BASE jumpers, trying as best I could to understand the obvious appeal this spine-tingling hobby had for them, and grappling with mixed messages about whether BASE jumpers were willing to cooperate with the rangers in administration of a tightly controlled permit system. A libertarian attitude definitely prevailed among many of the jumpers who seemed not able to come to grips with the wild abandon of running to the edge of Yosemite cliffs and throwing themselves into space and our need for safety and resource protection restraints. Still, we were willing to try to work with them.

    Your Yosemite: **PROTECTING A PUBLIC TREASURE**

The leaps from El Capitan mushroomed; some of the hundreds of jumpers had permits; many did not. Accidents were occurring and the preferred landing zone, El Capitan Meadow, was taking a beating. This was a classic park management conundrum for me and the ranger staff—where to draw the line between freedom to seek out Yosemite by specialized groups with their own agendas, demands, and attitudes, and the broader purpose of hosting visitors who come simply to enjoy the natural scene. For example, one promoter who sought me out wanted to light up Yosemite Falls at night with powerful spotlights and charge visitors to watch the show while patriotic music blared through loudspeakers and the color of the falls changed to hues of the rainbow until the red, white, and blue grand finale. That was an easy call; no thanks, Yosemite is not a carnival ground.

The summer test in 1980 of BASE jumping in Yosemite simply confirmed that most jumpers found the idea of permits and equipment

Yosemite Horse Patrol Graduates and Walt Castle , circa 1980s

checks to be alien to their idea of wildly free flight. In September, 1980, I made the judgment call and canceled the permit program. Regulations already in place allowed the rangers to enforce restrictions against this activity. My primary reason was that the impact on natural resources, especially the meadow habitat near the base of El Capitan, was too severe. I was also influenced by what seemed to me to be an outlaw mentality among many of the jumpers who made a game out of avoiding ranger scrutiny and safety controls. The United States Parachute Association raised no formal objection, but my standing with the jumpers was zero. Not so among the rangers. Valley District Ranger Dick Martin, who referred to his subordinates as "renaissance rangers" in reference to the variety of challenges they faced each day and their abilities to cope with the unexpected, was strongly supportive of my decision. By then, Boenish was far from Yosemite. He had shifted his filming expertise to the Royal Gorge Bridge in Colorado and, then, in 1984, tragically lost his life in a BASE jump attempt in Norway.

The ban on BASE jumping in Yosemite was followed eventually by restrictions throughout the National Park System after jumpers shifted their attention to Canyon de Chelly National Monument, Arizona, a fragile archeological area, and several other NPS areas. At Yosemite, the ban did not entirely stop the jumpers and continues to be a rescue and enforcement burden for the rangers. For instance, in a more recent protest against the ban, 60-year-old Jan Davis and four other expert skydivers leaped from El Capitan in October, 1999, after planning in advance for a crowd of well-wishers to assemble at the base of the monolith with cameras ready and a live telephone connection to the Associated Press. Their protest was prompted in part by a terrible tragedy earlier that year when Frank Gambalie III made a successful jump, but drowned in the Merced River while trying to flee pursuing rangers. Three jumpers preceded Davis and landed safely. When she jumped, her parachute malfunctioned and she fell to her death.

On the night I took my patrol ride with Bryan Swift we thankfully encountered no illegal jumpers, but he told me of instances when he had to chase them down on foot after they landed in El Capitan Meadow, in some cases maneuvering past friends of the BASE jumpers who tried to block his way. Swift admired the nerve and self-confidence of the jumpers, but he did not admire their conceit, saying, "they seem to think, I'm doing this, to hell with the park environment."

As he routinely worked the late shift, Swift responded to the typical ills of society—grievous automobile accidents, drug and alcohol abuse, drug trafficking, family squabbles, sexual and aggravated assaults, vagrancy, theft, vandalism, and willful destruction of property and natural features. Thousands of visitors are lodged in Yosemite Valley on any given summer night. More than a thousand concessionaire employees are in the mix. Law enforcement problems inevitably result. Swift and his colleagues dealt with the whole gamut, transplanted from afar. He told me that one evening, while he was patrolling through a campground, a frantic mother flagged him down. Her twelve-year-old son was in diabetic shock. Swift grabbed his medical kit and rushed to the boy while pulling insulin glucose from his medical kit. While the mother held the boy's head, Swift pinched shut his nose and shoved a dose of glucose down his throat. The medication worked and the boy already was beginning to recover while Swift transported mother and child to the Yosemite Medical Center for follow-up observation and further treatment if needed. The next evening, he was on patrol in the same campground when he was again flagged down by the mother, this time to agree to pose for a photograph with her grateful and happy son.

On other occasions Swift would encounter backpackers and campers who, for whatever reason, were financially broke. More than once, he dug into his own pocket to lend a few dollars for a bus ticket, a meal or groceries, the transactions made with a handshake and a promise. Sometimes he was repaid. My ride with him that night was quiet, the only adrenaline moment coming when he responded to a complaint at Yosemite Lodge about a disturbance that turned out to be an inebriated concessionaire employee who had stumbled over a trash can and was yelling angrily at no one in particular. Swift booked the young man into the Yosemite jail, obviously for drying-out purpose. Toward the end of the shift, he found four people tucked into their sleeping bags, snoozing away at the edge of a meadow far from any of the designated campgrounds, a minor but illegal incident. When Swift woke them up he encountered a typical problem in Yosemite Valley, a language barrier. As best he could determine, they were on holiday from an eastern European country, their ability to speak English of the highly fractured variety. Swift let them stay where they were, realizing that they had little understanding of park regulations, and passed on a message to the day-shift rangers to lead them to a campground so that they could settle in and continue their visit the legal way.

I was struck by the huge changes in law enforcement professionalism in the national parks between generations. My initial law enforcement training during summertime employment as a Fire Control Aid in Sequoia-Kings Canyon National Parks consisted of having a vintage World War II .38 caliber revolver and a box of bullets shoved across the desk toward me by my boss, Supervisory Ranger Stan Bechtel, with the order, "you are on poacher patrol." That was the style in those days; rangers were more game wardens than police officers. Law enforcement training was casual at best. At the time, I had just graduated from Colorado State University (Class of '59) and was working for a third season on firefighting duty at Grant Grove. I had stayed on the payroll into the autumn after Bechtel's cadre of seasonal rangers departed, most to return to their teaching jobs, so I was recruited. With the gun in the glove compartment of my red-light equipped pickup truck, I drove around on backroads and actually encountered two poachers. They were off-duty airmen from a military base down in California's Central Valley. I stepped out of the pickup, unarmed, and asked them to follow me to the ranger station. They did, claiming they did not know that they were in a national park. Ignorance shared: I had no idea what I was doing. The airmen must have sensed this, but cooperated peacefully, got slaps on their wrists from Bechtel, and returned to their base.

Swift and his peers were many professional levels above this laid-back, almost ancient law enforcement approach. He still had game warden-style responsibilities for wildlife, especially to help maintain a prudent separation between humans who sometimes become far too pushy in their excitement to get close to the home-grown residents of the park. He was adept, too, in the time-honored ranger

　　　Your Yosemite: **PROTECTING A PUBLIC TREASURE**

tradition of being a uniformed information station. He also was equipped and capable of response to any style of law enforcement challenge. In Yosemite, that covered the entire spectrum from urban to bucolic. Swift had the credentials to cope with almost anything that came his way from the underside of society and for good reason in the wake of the horrific Yosemite riot.

THE RIOT AND A LOSS OF INNOCENCE

In the summer of 1970, long before Swift was on patrol, severe nationwide stress found its way across the park boundary into Yosemite. Protests across the nation against the agonies of the Vietnam War sparked to life a widespread counter-culture mood, especially among many young adults. In 1969, a word-of-mouth festival at a dairy farm near the small rural town of Bethel, New York, riveted in lore as "Woodstock," drew an estimated 500,000 participants, there to enjoy three days of popular music by performers including Arlo Guthrie, Joan Baez, The Grateful Dead, Janis Joplin, and Jimi Hendrix. The gathering was reflective of the bold mood of dissent sweeping across America. In the autumn of that year, from east coast to west, millions demonstrated against the war. Hundreds of universities and colleges were shut down by student/faculty strikes. Then, in May, 1970, the tragedy at Kent State University, Ohio, shocked the nation when National Guard soldiers fired into a crowd of protesting students, killing four and wounding nine. Despite this national upheaval no one expected the problems of mass protest and panicked institutional response to spill over into the national parks. The NPS was not prepared when the thunder of dissension came right into Yosemite Valley.

The first hint of trouble at Yosemite came on Memorial Day weekend, 1970, when groups of rebellious young visitors caught the park ranger corps off-guard. Back home, these visitors with chips on their shoulders were probably typical students, family members, and friends who generally stayed out of trouble, but in the park they morphed into free-spirited mutineers, alcohol and drugs involved. Park rangers were startled by the suddenly heightened level of confrontation that seemed to have very little to do with a weekend visit to a national park. On that Memorial Day weekend, rangers scrambled to keep things under control at Yosemite, winning respite only when the three-day holiday came to a close. This interval proved to be the proverbial calm before the storm.

As the July 4th weekend approached, the park became a destination of choice for hundreds of young people intent on exercising their own notions of celebration. The student-run *Berkeley Tribe* campus newspaper described Yosemite Valley as "a place to smoke dope and sing together in the clear mountain air," adding that there was even a hint of a "Woodstock West." Stoneman Meadow, adjacent to one of the valley's major campgrounds near Curry Village, became the unsanctioned assembly point for youthful celebrators.

The meadow had gained a word-of-mouth reputation for being a good place for young people to form impromptu groups, sit around and talk, play guitars, sing, toss Frisbees, surreptitiously explore the personal effects of drugs and alcohol, and feel good about peace and love. Park rangers were trying to tolerate these gatherings up to a point, usually putting an end to the get-togethers before they really got out of control. The rangers did this simply by approaching groups in the meadow and asking them to move on, hoping that they would carry their trash out with them and leave behind only limited damage to the meadow habitat. A few arrests were made when necessary, but the rangers and revelers seemed to share a grudging understanding that usually ended in mutual tolerance and cooperation.

But something alien was building in Yosemite that never before had been witnessed in a national park. The result would be very ugly. Charles R. "Butch" Farabee, former Yosemite park ranger and author of *National Park Ranger, An American Icon*, wrote, "The week prior to the riot, the park was hectic: seven people drowned or died climbing, and rangers issued 151 citations and arrested 57 people, including 37 minors, for disorderly conduct, intoxication, stolen property, and drugs." Stoneman Meadow began to fill on the July 4th weekend with hundreds of young adults, many wandering over from sites they had occupied in the nearby campground, others just showing up, traveling on motorcycles and in cars soon parked illegally along the edge of the meadow. At first, the rangers' response was similar to past incidents in which they sought to use reason rather than force. The numbers, though, had grown in favor of the meadow trespassers.

For a time the rangers maintained a semblance of control. On the evening of July 2nd, they moved into the meadow on foot, advising the occupants that a curfew was being enforced from 7pm to 6am, and watched as most in the crowd accepted orders to leave. Not everyone obeyed. A hardcore resistance was developing among meadow inhabitants determined to stay put. Others walked the short distance to what was normally family-friendly Campground 14 to re-congregate in large groups and noisily continue their partying into the night. Their antics began to disturb and intimidate other campers who felt under siege. Rangers patrolling in the campground had some success in dampening down intrusive behavior, but momentum was building toward intense confrontation.

The following day, July 3rd, saw even more insurgents in the meadow, the crowd now estimated as high as 1,500. Rangers had posted signs confirming the curfew and were ticketing illegally parked vehicles. A few bottles and rocks were beginning to fly toward the rangers. At dusk, the rangers used bullhorns to announce the curfew and demand that the meadow be cleared. Some of the young people left, but many more were boastfully defiant, ready for a war of words, or, more ominously, outright battle. Their weapons included rocks, bottles, clubs, and knives. About a mile away at the government barn near park headquarters, thirteen riders skilled in horsemanship were mounted and ordered toward the meadow. As San Jose State University graduate Laura Avedisian confirms in her carefully researched 1998 thesis on the subject, the men on horseback included four rangers and nine cowboy packers, none trained in riot control. The riders, backed by additional rangers and NPS maintenance personnel on foot, reached a line of trees edging the meadow, formed a "skirmish line," and slowly rode and marched in. Appearing out of the darkness, this latter-day cavalry unit and its foot soldiers had the intended effect. Most of the crowd scattered into the night and for a moment the rangers thought they had regained control.

By July 4th, the revelers were back, the meadow reoccupied. Fireworks were being detonated and intoxication and lewd behavior were clearly evident. The hardcore combatants refused to concede their ground as a CBS news crew arrived to film the confrontation. The rangers, still trying to find a way out of the mess, suggested that the rebels decamp to Sentinel Beach, a secluded picnic area on the shoreline of the Merced River far from the main visitor areas, but got nowhere. Dressed in their gray-and-green uniforms and wearing their campaign-style flat hats, the rangers were symbols of authority. In the mood that existed among occupants of the meadow, authority was the enemy. Many family groups and others at Campground 14 had already packed up in disgust at the antics of the rebels and left the park. The curfew came and went at Stoneman Meadow. The protestors stayed put.

In a repeat performance of the previous night, sixteen riders were on horseback, reinforced by twenty-one men on foot. The riders consisted of rangers, packers, maintenance men, and even some wranglers from the Yosemite Park & Curry Company. Bullhorn orders again were given to clear the meadow. Groups of young people shouted back. As one of the riders later reported, he was "scared," and then someone shouted "charge!" The riders galloped into the meadow swinging ropes and night sticks. All hell broke loose. Rocks and bottles flew; some riders were dragged from their horses. At least one horse, accustomed to the quiet trails of the Yosemite's backcountry, was smashed across the face with a bottle. Rangers used mace. One ranger was confronted by a rioter with a knife and for a brief moment thought he might have to use his gun to defend himself. Patrol cars, pulled up near the meadow, became targets for the rampaging, window-smashing youth. The meadow was in chaos and the heavily outnumbered ranger force was in disarray.

Bloodied rangers and horsemen retreated. Bloodied rioters celebrated. Following the clash, rangers set up roadblocks to arrest rioters who might try to escape by car or motorcycle. NPS maintenance staff and forest fire crews with no law enforcement training were armed with ax handles and drafted to guard concessionaire and NPS facilities at a distance from the epicenter of the riot, but thought to be vulnerable to small gangs of marauders. The rioters established their own roadblock at an intersection near the meadow, building a large fire of branches and logs right in the middle of the intersection, and stopped traffic.

By July 5th, in response to an S.O.S. from the park rangers, law enforcement officers came pouring into the park from the surrounding communities of Mariposa, Merced, and Fresno, and were soon supplemented by U.S. Marshalls and F.B.I. agents. Sheriff Norm Garrett and a deputy from Mariposa County were trapped in their patrol car at the roadblock set up by the rioters. The windows on the car were smashed and the sheriff and deputy, pulled from the car, had to fire shots in the air to escape. Their car was rolled down an embankment and partially scorched by fire. In the waning hours of the day, 146 law enforcement personnel finally regained control of the Stoneman Meadow area, arresting 138 combatants in the process.

The media had a field day. Images of the riot were broadcast on all the major networks. Newspaper headlines were sensational, and recriminations flew. Some visitors sympathized with the rioters and accused the rangers of brutal, police-state tactics. Others vigorously defended the rangers. Superintendent Lawrence Hadley, who, like his contemporaries in Yosemite, had no experience with this level of openly defiant combat, expressed to the media and superiors his full support for actions taken by the rangers to reclaim Stoneman Meadow by force. Nonetheless, he was transferred a few weeks later from his assignment at Yosemite.

The paradigm for law enforcement in all national parks abruptly shifted as a result of the riot. Months later, a Federal Law Enforcement Training Center was temporarily established in facilities near Washington, D. C., to be followed by permanent facilities in other states. Training at these facilities is intense, specialized, and physically demanding. Bryan Swift is among the many ranger graduates. Lost at the riot scene was a certain innocence that parks were guaranteed safe havens where society's larger and potentially harrowing stress points could be left behind in favor of gentle, relaxed association with a beautiful place whose welcoming is a birthright of us all. The Stoneman Meadow riot was an anomaly that has not been repeated. Yosemite has regained its bucolic traction, but its stewards are much more wary and prepared.

WALT CASTLE

Animal Packer Foreman Walt Castle never imagined when he signed on at Yosemite that he would be teaching riot control procedures to rangers on horseback, but there he was one day when I went to the equestrian practice area to watch him in action. Castle's motto was, "no matter what you know about your job, you learn something new every day." The ranger aspirants to the Yosemite horse patrol, many of whom thought they pretty well knew how to handle horses, would unforgettably learn that lesson. Castle handpicked the chestnut-colored quarter horses that he used for patrol purposes in the park. This was not easy. Getting through government red tape and struggling almost always with meager funds, Castle nonetheless had his contacts with horse traders—especially Don Buttrey down in the Central Valley of California—who would work with him to deliver the best possible horses he could get for the money. They did this because Castle was so highly respected among his peers. He wanted horses at least 15.2 hands in height, weighing in at about 1,200 pounds with muscled chests, strong legs, powerful hindquarters, and good overall confirmation. His riding equipment of choice was Keystone Salinas Roping Saddles and Pelham-style single rein bits. The training he designed was for the horses as much as the riders.

Park Ranger Tom (Smitty) Smith, author of the book, *I Am Only A Seasonal*, described his experience as a Castle student: "Our training consisted of running a course on time, jumps over hurdles and running poles, side passing, spins on the forehand, games, traveling over rubber tires and black plastic, simple figure eights, sliding stops, riot and crowd control procedures, rolling inner tubes up against the horse and teaching spur cues—all this and the addition of the occasional firecrackers going off beneath you." Side passing and half passes are used to move equine bulk sideways or at a diagonal against an object, such as an unruly crowd. The forehand turn requires the horse to pivot on its front legs while moving its whole body with its hind legs, just the opposite of what horses instinctively do. The maneuver allows horse and rider to stay face-to-face with whatever is of immediate interest. Horses are naturally attuned to run from danger. Castle required that horse and rider put this habit aside. He wanted the patrol horses not to bolt or buck over some niggling distraction, like a riot. To make the point, the inner tubes and firecrackers used in training were enhanced by simulated crowds made up of park staff members who waved signs, shouted, made wild hand gestures, flapped pieces of cloth, threw pebbles and clods of dirt at the horses, and otherwise made themselves obnoxious. Through a light but purposeful touch on the reins and signaled leg commands from the rider, the horses were taught to accept these odd human antics with studied tolerance.

Castle required of his ranger trainees an understanding that horses can feel pain, hunger, fear, anger, envy, affection, loneliness, curiosity, contempt, frustration, boredom, pride, excitement, cold, hot, wet, lust, love, contentment, and happiness—pretty much a description of the ranger trainees themselves. A basic tenet is that horses, like all domestic creatures, are captives of humankind. They are dependent on their keepers for comfort and wellbeing. They have social, nutritional, physical, and shelter needs that are essential to their health and performance. In the Castle school, neglect of a willing and hardworking horse was unacceptable. The rangers were required to carefully prepare their mounts before climbing into the saddle and to assure cool-down after vigorous exercise. Bits were eased into the mouth; saddles properly positioned and cinched appropriately; definitely not too tight. Use of brute force, punishment of the mount for rider ineptitude, savage spurring, whipping, or stiff jerks of the reins were forbidden. The riders were required to smoothly mount and dismount and always to maintain a "balanced seat" to give the horse the best opportunity to carry its load in relative ease. Equipment was to be kept in excellent condition, hooves picked, coats brushed, saddle, blankets, reins, and halters clean and properly stored.

Castle himself was a constant student of horse technique, taking what he knew of cowboy handiness and western pleasure riding and mixing these skills with classic dressage, intent on developing true collaboration between horse and rider. He had good reason. As Yosemite's Animal Packer Foreman, he was responsible for a government herd of about fifty mules and forty horses, dispatching the ten cowboy packers he supervised on supply and logistical missions to the farthest reaches of the park. His assumption was that he and his crew could pack almost anything into the outback. On one occasion, a heavy and lengthy piece of pipe was required at a High Sierra Camp accessible only by a steep, switchback trail. Castle rigged revolving platforms on the tops of two pack saddles. The pipe was bridged onto the pack saddles between two willing in-line mules. When the mules reached the switchbacks and made the sharp turns, one mule momentarily moving in opposite direction to the other, the pipe pivoted with the motion and was carried without incident to its destination. In the age of helicopters and all-terrain-vehicles, Walt Castle maintained and championed intricate skills that had served in the mountains from the days of frontiersmen and cavalry troops.

The rangers on horse patrol in Yosemite Valley and at Tuolumne Meadows captured this legacy in living-history style, easily becoming as much ambassadors of park ethics as law enforcement officers. As Castle would point out, "I've never met a person who likes a ranger better in a patrol car than on a horse." He also contended that his equine delivery system into the backcountry was much more cost-effective and wilderness companionable than the roar of helicopter blades. He was right, but in 1972 the horse patrol portion of his activities almost came crashing down. A seasonal trail crewman, not associated with the animal packer operation, but apparently mentally conflicted and seeking attention, deliberately set fire to the barn in Yosemite Valley where Castle kept much of his equine stock. Seventeen horses and mules died, including eight patrol horses. In the tense and sad days that followed, Park Superintendent Lynn Thompson, undoubtedly feeling the stress, called Castle into his office and said that the calamity had finished the horse patrol program, at least in the short term. He ordered Castle to release from employment the three packer cowboys who assisted him with the training. Castle was thrown off balance. Quickly rebounding, and with blood pressure rising, he said, "Well, why don't you just fire me, too, and we'll all go down the road together." Thompson in turn was startled, then reconsidered and reversed himself.

Soon after I arrived in Yosemite, I attended one of the horse patrol "graduations." On this occasion, Seasonal Park Ranger Tom Smith was among the trainees demonstrating their skills to the gathered audience. He was riding John Paul, known among the rangers as a "push button horse," so wise, dependable, adaptable, and willing that confidence in his performance was a foregone conclusion— only not this time. Smith and John Paul were loping through a basic figure eight, an easy pattern that they had executed many times. Suddenly, in full view of all those in attendance, John Paul stumbled badly and went down in a heap of flying legs, flapping leather, and dust embellished by airborne Ranger Smith. Smith fell in front of John Paul and the huge horse rolled right over him. Fortunately the ground had been churned up by many performing horses and was cushiony soft. In animal packer jargon, this was a "wreck." John Paul quickly recovered and bounced to his feet, gave himself a shake, and eyeballed Smith as if asking, "what are you doing down there?" The dazed Smith was a little slower getting up. He was coping, half bent over, when Walt Castle rushed by. Smith looked up and saw Castle checking John Paul for injuries. Satisfied that no serious damage had been done to the horse, Castle turned and walked back to the still somewhat bewildered Smith. Assured, too, that Smith was reasonably intact, Castle smiled and said, "hard to find a good horse; I can always find another ranger."

Walt Castle was part doctor, attending to the aches, pains, illnesses, and injuries of many of his four-legged patients, a logistical expert who arranged for timely delivery of all the supplies needed for such a complex operation, a tactician who had to choose priorities in support of a constantly changing list of maintenance and ranger needs, and a teacher. In the slippery world in which we live, when politicians in Washington, D.C., sometimes play harmfully with the government, occasionally pushing it into shutdown mode. People begin talking loosely about "essential" and "non-essential" federal employees, those who might be temporarily furloughed and those who must remain on the job. At Yosemite, Castle and the word "essential" were synonymous.

BIG LEAGUE COMMERCIALISM

In a sense, the innocence at Yosemite was also lost in a manner different from the infamous riot when Mary Curry Tresidder died a year later. Her loss was more than just the passing of a respected person would could trace her roots to the turn-of-the-century pioneering era in Yosemite. She also had carried on the legacy of hands-on local ownership of commercial offerings at the park. She was part of the park community; Yosemite her cherished home and life's work. But, with her death, the extended tradition of home-grown commercial stewardship suddenly was gone. In the next four years, ownership of the Yosemite Park & Curry Company changed hands three times. Loyalists who had worked for the Tresidders for many years found themselves in an unfamiliar topsy-turvy corporate world where management of the company was guided from afar, sometimes by executives who never had or would visit Yosemite. The YP&CC had become a business just like any other, a profit center of considerable potential with a relentless emphasis on the bottom line.

During this commercial upheaval, Richard Nixon was elected in 1972 to his second term as President of the United States. In January, 1973, President Nixon appointed Ronald H. Walker as director of the National Park Service. The Tresidder era had given way to a more impersonal commercial grip on Yosemite and, thereby, on the NPS in general, and now the appointment of Walker upended the era of NPS veterans who stood at the helm of the agency for the prior half-century.

Walker's predecessor, George B. Hartzog, Jr., (1920–2008), was one of those veterans, starting a twenty-eight-year career with the NPS at Great Smoky Mountains National Park in 1945 and then moving up in rank through various assignments, culminating in his appointment by President Lyndon Baines Johnson to the agency's top job.

For nine years he served as NPS Director, the seventh career person to do so since establishment of the NPS in 1916. By contrast, Walker, age thirty-six, had been a staff aid and chief advance man during President Nixon's 1972 campaign, but Walker had no experience with national parks. His appointment reverberated through the ranks of NPS employees, suggesting that the agency might be tilting dangerously toward short-term political expedience and away from long-term conservation purpose. Not long afterward, the concessionaire contract in Yosemite was won by the Los Angeles-based Music Corporation of America, led by Lew Wasserman and Sidney Sheinberg, who, from their executive offices in Los Angeles, assumed corporate command.

The union between the MCA Corporation and Yosemite was a peculiar arrangement. Founded in Chicago in 1928, the company moved to Beverly Hills in 1939 and became the world's dominant show-business talent agencies, claiming among its clients such stars as James Stewart, Henry Fonda, Bette Davis, Alfred Hitchcock, Doris Day, and Ronald Reagan. MCA was known to have good contacts in the Nixon Administration and was aggressive in its acquisitions of entertainment talent and assets. The attraction that Yosemite held for this huge entertainment company at first was perplexing, but then became more obvious. The ever-increasing popularity of national parks as outdoor playgrounds signaled growth potential that fit nicely with a corporate entertainment agenda and promised good return on investment. The benefit for Yosemite was less clear; the contract MCA won required it to pay a franchise fee to the government of only 0.75% of the revenue generated from sales in the park, a pittance by generally recognized commercial contract standards.

The MCA Corporation chose Edward C. Hardy as its on-site chief operating officer. Hardy, a 43-year-old executive, claimed previous successful management experience at Del Webb resorts, the Los Angeles Athletic Club, and the Riviera Country Club, a prestigious members-only golf resort. Despite the lack of NPS experience on his resume, he came to his new post at Yosemite with an understanding that he would be under environmental scrutiny. Hardy acted quickly to establish his credentials by ordering that an old YP&CC junkyard and ugly wood-storage areas that lingered from the Tresidder days be cleaned up, freeing precious Yosemite Valley acreage in the process. This was a good start for the new corporate steward, but the company's highest priority obviously was to bring a healthy return-on-investment to the MCA.

Among the first actions taken by the new concessionaire was to advance the idea of reconstructing the Glacier Point Hotel that burned to the ground in 1969. The old dilapidated hotel, unused at the time, apparently fell victim to faulty electrical wiring. For several years prior to the loss of the hotel there had been speculation about the possibility of connecting the valley floor to Glacier Point via an aerial tramway, allowing customers to be dramatically hoisted through 3,000 feet of airspace amidst breathtaking scenery. The combination of collecting fees for an aerial tramway ride and the sales relationship between tramway customers and a new hotel at Glacier Point was obvious from a business perspective. Hardy suggested that a tramway at Yosemite could be a means to provide "alternate transportation" that would help reduce automobile congestion at the popular view site.

The image of cables decorated by dangling people pods imposed on Yosemite Valley airspace and the associated construction of a new hotel at Glacier Point did not find support from Superintendent Leslie P. Arnberger, many park constituents, or on the editorial pages of influential newspapers. Environmental advocates, already suspicious of the MCA Corporation, lent support to Arnberger and the ideas were dropped.

Still, the influence of Director Walker was reaching Yosemite. in May, 1974, he championed a proposal to replace 150 tent cabins at Curry Village with "modular" motel units. His supervisor, Assistant Secretary of the Interior Nathaniel Reed, an acclaimed environmentalist who was known to have low regard for Walker, drily observed that this proposal might have been "written by the concessionaire." An NPS-hosted meeting in Yosemite Valley on the issue of the tent cabin conversion put Walker under a fusillade of verbal and media fire that damaged his ability to continue as director. President Nixon

        Your Yosemite: **PROTECTING A PUBLIC TREASURE**

resigned due to the Watergate scandal in August, 1974. Walker submitted his resignation in September of the same year. The tent cabin conversion idea was discarded.

An MCA gambit to cash in on Yosemite from another direction also failed, this time in the form of "Sierra," a made-for-television production about crime-busting Yosemite Park Rangers. Overly enthusiastic production crews for MCA-Universal Studios descended on the park to capture the scene and dramatize the fictional story. Real off-duty rangers were hired as bit players in support of professional actors. Two problems resulted. One problem was that "Sierra" was scheduled by its sponsor, NBC, to compete against CBS' "The Waltons." At the time, The Waltons was the most popular program on television, routinely trouncing competitors in the ratings war. Secondly, the production crew, not liking the natural color of some rocks in a scene shot in Yosemite, decided to paint them. The uproar from park users who highly value the natural charm of the park was predictable.

After three months, "Sierra" was pulled from production. Thus, the first efforts by the new concessionaire for commercial advantage in Yosemite bumped along in awkward style, proving more than anything that the park simply could not be treated as a convenient backdrop for profit-center experiments; it was not a set on a backlot at MCA studios. But the MCA was not going anywhere. It held a twenty-year contract in one of the most popular national parks in the world, providing commercial services in a guaranteed captive market that would generate millions in profit. The primary question for Hardy and his staff was how many millions?

THE ODD COUPLE

As I would quickly learn, Ed Hardy was ever alert to his company's media image. Particularly when others were within earshot, he was fond of referring to me as his "leader" and himself as "just a contractor." We were required to make public appearances together at park ceremonies and events, and we juggled media attention between us. The market-savvy Hardy often would say, "I don't care what they report so long as they spell Yosemite correctly." When news reports were critical of concessionaire activities he would shrug them off, saying, "Today's news is tomorrow's fish wrapping paper."

Hardy and I were in the same canoe but attempting to paddle in opposite directions, making it difficult to avoid capsizing. We had to work together and stay away from outright combat if we could. Hardy had an adept business oriented staff, plenty of political muscle through his contacts with government officials and various California business leaders, and the imposing backup power of the MCA Corporation. He had at his beck-and-call the amenities of the Ahwahnee Hotel that he could and did make available to special guests. His residence with its picture window view of Half Dome was a hub of social activity. In his ebullient style he consistently welcomed many of his Yosemite neighbors to the party and was quick to personally engage as a hospitality host with visiting celebrities, especially Members of Congress, Governors, and high level political appointees. He once told Gene Rose, a journalist for the *Fresno Bee*, that he could walk into the White House to meet with members of the President's staff whenever he chose, no appointment needed.

My picture window view in El Portal was of a Manzanita bush and I had no hotel or entertainment budget, just the more customary potluck approach found in most national parks. But I also had the legacy of Yosemite on my side, its prestige as an international exemplar of the highest tenets of conservation and a constituency of thousands of visitors—usually polite and silent—who could react if park values they relished were brusquely threatened. Watchful sympathy of many journalists and editorial writers; the strength of environmental advocacy groups, and the favorable public standing of the National Park Service also were strengths on my side of the conservation divide.

Fortunately, Congressman Tony Coelho, in whose district Yosemite was located, shared friendship with both Hardy and me, but nonetheless stood strongly in the conservation camp. His most prominent demonstration of political leadership on behalf of Yosemite was to succeed in winning National Wild and Scenic River status for the Merced River and its South Fork tributary from the High Sierra to the lower foothills. This effort, begun in 1984, became law in 1987 over the signature of President Reagan and has had lasting positive influence on park management.

With my signature ink barely dry on the *General Management Plan* of 1980, Hardy took a bold and public relations-savvy step in support. He found corporate funds to build a new supply depot and personnel center in Fresno, demonstrating that at least some concessionaire facilities could be effectively located outside the park. This might have seemed standard for any business dependent on good logistics and efficiency, but there had been a hidebound habit for many decades to treat the park boundary as a red line and keep all infrastructure inside, both government and private. Hardy broke this mold and transferred several YP&CC staff members to the new location. I was among those who applauded. I was trying to do my own share of mold breaking by choosing to live at El Portal, but Hardy was much less inclined to do anything similar at the Administrative Site, certainly not move his office there or share the Manzanita view.

Hardy and I were basically stalemated; the political changes that had occurred soon after I assumed my post caused the NPS to go into a holding pattern; facilities in the Yosemite Valley flood plain and talus boulder zones near the cliffs that had been identified for removal in the GMP, many of them concessionaire accommodations, remained anchored in place. So, too, did NPS housing and the cumbersome maintenance yard, also targeted for removal. Steps in the direction of plan implementation were going to be slow at best, dependent on Congressional appropriations, if any, and the backing of Reagan Administration appointees, if any. But there was also a block against any expanded commercial development. The citizen constituency that was on my side would not allow it. Hardy knew this. The stalemate was to his advantage because it assured business-as-usual; no reduction in the pillow count; no requirement for substantial private investment at El Portal. Only on the edges of the commercial imprint in Yosemite Valley could he and I maneuver.

The real commercial action was outside the park, in particular, in the Town of Oakhurst on State Highway 41, the preferred travel route for visitors from southern California to the park. When I arrived at

Yosemite in 1979, Oakhurst basically was a wide spot in the road consisting of a gas station, a grocery store, and not much more. But business people and real estate specialists saw opportunity and were adroitly cashing in on the tourist trade. Oakhurst was beginning to boom. Accommodations in the park usually were at capacity during the high seasons of tourism, thus giving the entrepreneurs in Oakhurst and other gateway communities the advantage of capturing business from the overflow crowd. There was strong evidence, too, that many travelers were deliberately choosing to stay in the cozy motels and eat in the restaurants outside the park, making the park a day-trip destination. I often wondered why the MCA Corporation, with obvious financial strength, did not take advantage of this opportunity at the park's doorsteps rather than nibbling away at the edges of commercial prospects within. The answer probably was that MCA was much more oriented toward entertainment than inn keeper. After those first heady days of the MCA presence in the park when the television series was attempted, the YP&CC must have faded onto the back pages of the MCA's conglomerate ledger book, a small enterprise by comparison to other MCA ventures. Still, it remained what it was, a lucrative business monopoly with Ed Hardy carefully exercising his political muscle when necessary to keep it that way.

I did my best to make sure that Hardy did not over-exert himself, depending as always on public judgment for what Yosemite should be, and what it should not be. Widely accepted—a pillar of strength for the NPS—was that Yosemite always should be allowed to present itself to visitors in its inherent natural form, not to be increasingly checker-boarded by a resort imprint. The long history of development within the park was halted at a stress point of overcrowding that pressed at the edges of visitor satisfaction. Any further aggressive push to expand the existing resort imprint was guaranteed to result in a media and public backlash against the Yosemite Park & Curry Company. Hardy understood this constraint, and, as a matter of habit, I reminded him of it whenever I could.

One worthy effort to cope with crowding in Yosemite Valley was sparked to life in 1970 by NPS Director Hartzog. He earmarked $20,000 in the NPS budget to begin funding a "free, fun, and fre-

     Your Yosemite: **PROTECTING A PUBLIC TREASURE**

quent" shuttle bus system in the valley. In a ceremony at Mirror Lake, long accessible to automobile traffic, Hartzog tied together, rather than cut a ribbon to permanently convert use of this part of the park road system to shuttle-bus-only use. In succeeding years, the NPS paid the YP&CC to operate a fleet of propane-powered shuttle buses, giving visitors the option, free-of-charge, of leaving their cars parked and using this service for transit throughout most of Yosemite Valley. In 1982, a decision was made by the NPS to purchase a new fleet of shuttle buses. These new diesel-powered buses would replace the older double decker and mini buses that the YP&CC owned and operated. Companies, including the YP&CC, were invited to bid on a new contract to maintain and operate the nine NPS-owned buses.

Ed Hardy advised me that the company would not bid. The YP&CC had a lock-grip on maintenance facilities and staff housing in the valley and a corps of experienced shuttle bus drivers. He reasoned that no outside company could compete against these advantages. If no other bid was received, the NPS would have to turn to the YP&CC to continue the subsidized arrangement. But an outside company did bid. ARA Services brought in drivers and mobile maintenance equipment that met contractual specifications. The new shuttle buses were up and running. Then, a funny thing happened, as the saying goes. In the Congressional appropriations process, funds needed to pay ARA for legitimate and satisfactory contract services were denied. The NPS defaulted on the contract. ARA collected its mobile equipment and its drivers and left the park. Operation of the shuttle buses reverted to the YP&CC. There was a political message here; do not rock the YP&CC monopoly.

At almost the same time that the ARA shuttle bus contract was going down, ground was broken in Fresno for the new YP&CC warehouse. Those with shovels, ceremonially pecking at the dirt, included Hardy, Congressman Tony Coelho, esteemed Fresno business leader Lewis Eaton, and me. Construction of a warehouse generally is not newsworthy, a yawn really. In this instance the real news was that the logistic needs for Yosemite could be met from afar, a clear step toward changing old industrial habits within the park. The YP&CC otherwise would stay entrenched, but Hardy nonetheless deserves credit for the symbolism and fact of this accomplishment. The dual realities of the shuttle bus ploy and the warehouse yet again put on display the challenges of containing and redirecting commercial pressures on the park. The opportunity was to keep Yosemite moving forward in stewardship terms toward a superb environmental stature that every visitor would applaud. If this forward motion had to be measured in hesitant steps rather than bold leaps, so be it, I said to myself, so long as the direction is forward.

12

A Rescue

YOSEMITE OPERATES ON A SEASONAL CLOCK; a buildup of visitor services, both NPS and concessionaire, in the springtime, chock full of summertime visitors, a fold down in the autumn, and the wintertime quiet. The high country season is short. Trail passes located on the spine of the High Sierra are sometimes not released by the final snowmelt until late June or early July. As early as Labor Day flurries of heavy, wet snow can surprise the trail crews as they are readying to disband and go their separate ways. The general retreat from the High Sierra begins in earnest by about mid-September as hikers and equestrians decrease rapidly in number and tents are folded and packed out from the High Sierra Camps leaving only skeletal iron-pipe frames behind. Tuolumne Meadows Lodge, also a tent facility, is closed in anticipation of the snow to come that can reach depths of 50 feet or more in some winters. Maintenance equipment and horses and mules are trucked down to Yosemite Valley. High country campgrounds remain occupied only by the resolute few until rangers, as weather dictates, come by and ask them to leave.

Even in the valley, the pace of life slows as the leaves fall, the waterfalls diminish to a trickle, and hundreds of seasonal NPS and concessionaire employees cash their final paychecks for the year. The park is left for those who seek out the fall colors, the sight of snow-decorated valley walls, and skiing and snowshoeing opportunities. Visitors snuggle into accommodations at the Ahwahnee Hotel, Yosemite Lodge, or the insulated tents at Curry Village, or turn on their RV heaters in the campgrounds. At Camp 4, rockcrafters tough it out, lured by autumn's superb climbing conditions, until most of them, too, leave the park as freezing temperatures and the first snow flurries arrive. Out in the wilderness region of the park, the trails become almost vacant except for the most experienced trekkers who deliberately choose to test themselves against terrain and weather that they know can be forbidding.

Every month of the year, though, Yosemite's search-and-rescue experts contend with visitors who get in trouble. Visitors who know too little get lost or injured in an unfamiliar environment where inherent dangers are not given enough cautionary deference. Some experienced visitors think that by personal prowess and sheer physical and mental strength they can contend with just about anything Yosemite can throw at them. In between are the unfortunate park visitors who suffer accidental injury or sudden illness. The percentage of Yosemite visitors in need of emergency assistance is a tiny fraction of the millions who visit the park, but that tiny fraction can amount to numerous "incidents" as they are labeled for record keeping purposes. In fact, more "incidents" occur in Yosemite than in any other park on earth.

On a January day in 1982, when the backcountry was already buried in heavy snow and Yosemite was about as quiet as it ever gets, three people who had no intention of even entering the park became part of a drama that is still vivid in the memories of those park staff members who were involved. A small four-passenger single-engine prop-driven aircraft had lined up for takeoff on a runway on the east side of the High Sierra. Ronald Vaughn, the pilot of this Grumman American AA-5B Tiger airplane, had begun his flight journey in Oklahoma and was on his way to the San Francisco Bay Area. En route, he landed at Mammoth Lakes Airport to take on fuel, check the weather, and file an updated instrument flight plan. With him were his wife, Lee, also a licensed pilot, and his 10-year-old stepson, Donnie Priest.

Civilian pilots have a choice of using visual flight plans, instrument flight plans, or no flight plan at all. Visual flight plans are most common, used in conjunction with Air Traffic Control services when weather is reasonably benign and visibility good. By making a telephone call to Federal Aviation Administration personnel from the airport terminal building to file an instrument flight plan, Vaughan was confirming that he expected poor weather conditions and limited visibility along his chosen flight path. Once a pilot is airborne and "activates" his or her instrument flight plan by establishing radio contact with Air Traffic Controllers, the pilot is given a transponder code specific to the aircraft. This code allows controllers to track the flight on radar, warn the pilot of other nearby aircraft and help steer the pilot to the chosen destination or to the nearest airport in case of emergency.

Pilots of small aircraft who face unusually harsh weather normally do not bother to taxi out for a look, but Donnie Priest's stepfather did. In pilot jargon this challenge to bad flying conditions is labeled "get-home-ites." The flight plan that Vaughn filed with Air Traffic Control indicated that he would fly far north of the Yosemite region toward Reno, Nevada, a distance of about two hundred miles, and then turn west to transit the Sierra Nevada in the vicinity of Donner Pass, a relatively low-profiled region of the mountain chain. The Grumman's altitude capabilities were sufficient to provide 2,000 to 3,000-feet of airspace clearance over that region. That day, Vaughan lined up on the Mammoth Lakes runway, made the go decision, and took off.

The storm striking the crest of the High Sierra was fierce when the Grumman became airborne. Winds tumbling across the mountains from west to east can sweep down the crest to form rotating turbulent air equivalent to horizontal tornados. In such conditions, small aircraft that cannot fly over the storm get slammed around as if being hit by giant invisible hammers. When pilots encounter such acute weather danger they are best advised to make a 180° turn and try to escape. In his last radio contact with Air Traffic Controllers, Vaughn reported severe turbulence and downdrafts in zero visibility. Based on a last vague radar trace, he was in the general vicinity of 9,943-foot Tioga Pass, approximately forty miles north of the Mammoth Lakes Airport, having abandoned the flight plan he filed with Air Traffic Control. He had banked onto a west-bound course either in an attempt to complete a 180° turn back toward Mammoth or to try to escape across the mountain terrain as quickly as possible. Vaughn was trapped in brutal winter conditions, fighting against bludgeoning wind, snow, and dense clouds at the very limits of his aircraft's performance capabilities. Temperature near the crest at Tioga Pass on that day was −15°F and winds were reaching velocities of more than 50 miles per hour. The Grumman disappeared from radar contact.

There was only one silver lining. Search-and-rescue procedures in Yosemite are finely honed based on the deep experience of the ranger experts. The core park rescue staff is on call year around. When the alert was broadcast by Air Traffic Control that a small aircraft might be down in the High Sierra, rescue procedures in the park were promptly put in motion. Among the first rescuers to be alerted to the Grumman's disappearance were Park Rangers Anne and Chas Macquarie, the "snow rangers" stationed for the winter months in isolated splendor at Tuolumne Meadows. The Macquaries, both highly experienced mountaineers, made an immediate attempt to reach Tioga Pass, seven miles from their cabin. They spent hours on cross-country skis fighting wind and deep snow, trying to cross over the pass and reach an area in the vicinity of Helen and Saddlebag Lakes where the Grumman, or what was left of it, was suspected to have crashed.

This search by the two rangers in mountainous terrain under blizzard-like conditions offered almost no hope for success. Still, they continued to risk their own safety to search for the plane before finally being instructed to turn back by their supervisors who were in contact with the Macquaries by radio. No further search attempt could be made for the next three days until the storm finally blew eastward, leaving in its wake clearing skies, below zero temperatures, and gusty winds.

As soon as weather conditions allowed, a combination of fixed wing and helicopter aircraft operated by the Mono County Sheriff's Department, the Civil Air Patrol, and the Fallon, Nevada, and Lemoore Naval Air Stations were in the air. Ten separate sorties were flown along the estimated flight track of the Grumman. Despite turbulence and snow squalls, visibility was rapidly improving. Spotters in the search aircraft had a view of the jagged peaks of the High Sierra outlined by a bright blue sky, white snow, and exposed gray rock so scoured by wind that no snow clung to the surfaces. Down in the bowls and fissures at the bases of the cliffs, snow depth was estimated to be eighty to one- hundred-feet deep.

At the end of that first full day of aerial reconnaissance, nighttime temperature at Bridgeport, a town in the general search area on the eastern side of the Sierra Nevada, dropped to −14°. The elevation at Bridgeport is 6,500 feet. The area where the Grumman was believed to have disappeared was above 10,000 feet where the temperature was surely much lower. Despite good visibility, no trace of the missing airplane was found and bad weather was closing in again. The forecast was for another heavy storm within twenty-four hours.

The searchers were dejected. The chances of finding a victim alive in severe weather conditions drops precipitously from slim to almost none after the first twenty-four hours. The Grumman had been missing now for four days. Some of us on the park staff began to fear that the wreckage might not be found until springtime thaw. The Sierra Nevada is notorious for swallowing up aircraft to be found by happenstance months or even years later, if ever found at all.

Down in Yosemite Valley, search-and-rescue expert John Dill was using a self-invented device he called his "Flintstone ruler" to try to calculate the position of the Grumman based on Air Traffic Control and storm-pattern data. He learned that Vaughn had amended his flight plan via radio contact with Air Traffic Controllers soon after departing from the Mammoth Lakes Airport. Instead of flying north toward Reno, probably anticipating a beating from the storm all along the way, Vaughan decided to attempt a mountain crossing as soon as possible by using Victor Airway 244, an electronic "highway in the sky" that passes over Mono Lake, then just north of Tioga Pass, past the Hetch Hetchy Reservoir to the west, and on to the city of Stockton down in the Central Valley.

In flight distance, the transit over the High Sierra on V-244 is only about sixty nautical miles, but the minimum safe altitude for the transit as defined by the Federal Aviation Administration is 14,500 feet, providing an air cushion of only about 2,000 feet over the peaks that stand across the flight path. The Grumman could not reach this safe altitude. The "service ceiling" for the 180-horsepower Grumman Tiger aircraft, the manufacturer's determination of maximum altitude that the aircraft can reach under ideal flying conditions, is 13,800 feet. Nonetheless, the amended flight plan suggested that Vaughan might try V-244 in an attempt to escape the terrible weather as quickly as possible.

I hold a private pilot license with an instrument rating, and have flown over the Sierra Nevada Mountains several times, usually solo. These were recreational flights for me, the most memorable on a late April day when I departed Mariposa County Airport framed by spring wildflowers, flew up the San Joaquin River drainage and over Mammoth Mountain, where I could look down and see skiers on the snow-covered slopes, then landed at the end of my two-hour flight in summertime heat at the airport in Death Valley. Three seasons in one flight. My flights occurred in clear, calm weather. Even so, for me, from the cockpit of a small aircraft, the mountains were always intimidating. Sitting in my office in Yosemite Valley, trying to track the details of the search for the Grumman, I could only imagine the intense battle Ronald and Lee Vaughan fought at the controls of their aircraft in the furious grip of Sierra Nevada weather on that fateful day.

For Dill, the amended flight plan narrowed the search area significantly. He was finding an anomaly between the assumed flight track along the Victor Airway and the Grumman's last known radar blips which suggested that the Grumman had been blown significantly off course. Dill thought he could come close to pinpointing the location of the downed aircraft if it had crashed soon after the last radar blip was recorded.

Early in the morning on the fifth day of the search, Lemoore Naval Air Station helicopter Angel Three landed in Yosemite Valley to pick up Park Ranger Jim Sano and Yosemite Medical Center Nurse Judy Scholzen. At the controls of the chopper were Lieutenant Dan Ellison and his co-pilot Dave Urban. Also aboard were Crew Chief Jerry Balderson, Petty Officer Reg Barnes, and Navy Flight Surgeon Dr. William Goodin. Dill especially wanted the terrain-savvy Sano as part of the search team. He had flown in Angel Three the previous day on a bumpy and wobbly ride in High Sierra turbulence. Jackhammer air combined with the pungent smell of fuel, oil, and

     Your Yosemite: **PROTECTING A PUBLIC TREASURE**

Park Ranger Jim Sano on spine of the High Sierra

grease in the workhorse helicopter were the devilish companions of crew and passengers.

Dill wanted Sano on the Angel Three chopper because Sano had roamed far and wide in the High Sierra, knew all the important landmarks, and likely had been on foot in the rugged locale where Dill suspected that the Grumman might be found. Sano was a true mountaineer, having first visited Yosemite on a camping trip with his parents when he was seven-years-old. His embrace of the High Sierra and return trips to Yosemite subsequently led him to his ranger duties and stature among his peers as among the most knowledgeable of the maze of alpine peaks, steep cliffs, and hidden chasms that form Yosemite's sharply honed eastern boundary.

Sano was such an enthusiast of mountaineering that on one occasion he formed a Yosemite team that traveled to Nepal and Tibet in 1983 with the goal of putting the first United States woman on the summit of 29,035 feet Mt. Everest. Chas and Anne Macquarie were among the team participants. Sano was the expedition leader and Chas fulfilled the important role of climb leader. Dangerous

Donnie Priest Rescue Site, 1983

storms on Everest caused the team to abort its summit attempt, but not before one of its climbers, Annie Whitehouse, set an American woman's altitude record at 28,000 feet. Some members of the team suffered injuries, but no life was lost. And, as Sano said subsequently, "We all remained friends," a fact not necessarily true of all Everest expeditions.

Nurse Scholzen, who worked with Dr. Jim Wurgler at the Yosemite Medical Center, was an equally important addition to the search team contingent. Dr. Wurgler and his small staff cooperated with park rangers in all kinds of emergencies. Wurgler was a true general practitioner, handling everything from heart attacks, illnesses, and severe trauma caused by accidents in the park to routine sniffles. The medical center often had the appearance of an emergency room and family practice all rolled in to one. He and his small staff were highly regarded by the Yosemite community and considered "A-team" by the rangers.

Dill asked the Angel Three team to investigate the terrain in the vicinity of White Mountain, an 11,000-foot crag north of Tuolumne Meadows. Sorties already had been flown over the area but with no results. Dill was not satisfied; he wanted a search crew to look again. In first early morning light, Angel Three lifted from the valley, made a quick landing in Tuolumne Meadows to pick up Anne Mac-quairie, another terrain expert, and then flew over the High Sierra crest between Mount Conness and White Mountain. Sano said of the aerial leap over the crest, "This search was one of the hairiest I ever experienced because the wind was howling." The chopper was being whipped by turbulence, but crew and observers were afforded excellent visibility left in the wake of the passing storm. Once over the crest, Pilot Ellison swung Angel Three into a 90° turn to fly parallel to the easterly facing High Sierra escarpment. Sano reported that, "We were seeing the tops of yellow white bark pine sticking out of the snow lower down. Higher up toward the crest there was what looked to be a dark tree. As we approached from the south and closed in on the 'log' I pointed it out to Anne and Dave saying into the intercom this could be it!"

On the second pass, all eyes were riveted on the blotch. The "log" proved to be the dark shadow cast by the Grumman's vertical stabilizer protruding just above the snowline, apparently uncovered by swirling winds that had blown during the night. The rest of the Grumman's fuselage was invisible beneath the snowpack. The aircraft was in a precarious position, encased in unstable snow on a sharp gradient under the face of White Mountain where avalanches threatened. Sano asked Ellison to fly back to Tuolumne Meadows to pick up Chas Macquarie who had in his emergency equipment signaling devices of the type used by skiers in deep snow country. If a skier is overwhelmed by an avalanche, the device can pinpoint where searchers should begin to dig. When the helicopter landed at Tuolumne, Sano reluctantly jumped out to reduce payload weight and Chas climbed in.

Back at the snowfield, Ellison found a touch-down location on a ridgeline above the crash site. He put the skids of Angel Three gently into the snow, keeping the engines running near full power to fight wind and altitude. The Macquaries climbed out, strapped on their skis, and started for the crash site. Ellison controlled the chopper, keeping the two park rangers in sight, ready to swoop toward them if events dictated. The Grumman had been missing for about one-hundred hours. For obvious reasons, the Macquaries thought of their risky mission as one to confirm that the Grumman had been found and that three bodies were in the wreckage. When they reached the plane, Chas began to dig.

"The shovel hit the fuselage and I heard a whimper," he later recalled. He broke through a Plexiglas window and looked inside. The bodies of Vaughn and his wife were in the front two seats, likely having died on impact or soon thereafter. But huddled on the back seat, semi-conscious and partially covered by a sleeping bag pad was Donnie Priest. The fact that the cockpit of the aircraft had remained generally intact as the Grumman tore into the snowfield had been Donnie's salvation. Even when surface temperatures are subzero, the insulating quality of snow can maintain temperatures two or three feet below the surface near the 32° freezing level. Just such an insulated cocoon of snow enfolded the little aluminum compartment in which Donnie was trapped. By the time Chas's shovel clanged against the aluminum hull, the boy was hypothermic and dehydrated, close to death. Still, the one-note symphony of metal striking metal brought a response. Macquarie heard the sob.

The Macquaries radioed Angel Three. Avalanche threat or not, Donnie had to receive immediate medical attention if his life was to be saved. Angel Three lifted off from the ridgeline and came to a hover directly over the crash site, Ellison handling the controls while his co-pilot, Dave Urban, kept an eye on a flickering instrument panel light that warned of low fuel. Angel Three, like all Navy rescue helicopters, was equipped with a powerful hoist mechanism that allowed loads to be lifted from ground or water and swung right into the rear passenger compartment of the chopper. Hoist equipment included a "vest" made of interlaced nylon webbing and various metal snaps and locks that allowed a crewman to descend and ascend on the hoist cable for up to 250 feet. Crew Chief Jerry Balderson had the vest on as Ellison put Angel Three into hover. The Macquaries managed to extract Donnie from the cockpit and were waiting, snow swirling in the downdraft caused by the chopper blades. In moments Balderson was beside the Macquaries. Donnie was clipped into the vest and, with an added bear hug from Balderson, the crew chief and the boy were reeled upward together. When they were swung into the helicopter, Donnie was crying. His body temperature was a dangerously low 84°.

With Angel Three in the air and headed toward the Yosemite Valley Medical Center, the Macquaries were left in sudden quiet. "I could tell it was on the edge of going," Chas said, referring to the precariously balanced tons of snow surrounding him and his wife. There was no need to linger at the Grumman. The bodies would be retrieved later, in more benign weather and snow pack conditions. The Macquaries made a careful exit on their cross-country skis from the crash site. Sano says, "Anne and Chas made a humongous effort because they had to break trail through thigh-deep snow. I vaguely remember that they stayed at the Tioga Pass entrance station that night. The total distance was about twelve miles, a herculean effort." The next day the Macquaries reached their base at Tuolumne and a greatly relieved Sano returned to Yosemite Valley via a helicopter airlift.

Donnie Priest lost both his feet to frostbite, but for those involved in his rescue, his survival seemed astounding. We later learned that when Donnie was not sleeping, the young boy had busied himself reading the Grumman radio and flight manual, a booklet full of details about engine performance, maintenance requirements, and aircraft flight characteristics. To quench his thirst he had eaten the snow that sifted into the cockpit through a crack in the fuselage. Despite his terrible losses, Donnie was lucky. Even in the winter season when search emergencies are few, the Yosemite's practiced core staff of search-and-rescue experts was in place with lines of communication open to the Navy fliers.

Years later, in an email message to Jim Sano, Donnie Priest said of his airborne rescue, "it definitely was an E-ticket ride with lots of heroics—with a phenomenal crew. Dan Ellison, the pilot, earned and was awarded the Distinguished Flying Cross. From my research, it appears that 99% are earned in combat, with most of them in hard flying conditions, lots of enemy fire, and many hits to the plane, but the pilot finishes the expected mission with the mission being the high priority. Some of the other non-combat (Flying Cross awards) would be the likes of Charles Lindberg and Admiral Byrd. Chief

Balderson, who came down on the hoist, earned the Navy and Marine Corps Medal, which is the second highest medal one can earn in peacetime. Co-pilot Dave Urban and Reg Barnes earned the Air Medal."

For the NPS half of the team, the award simply was respect from other search-and-rescue professionals and Yosemite staff in general for a job well done against very long odds. Donnie Priest went on to beat other odds as well. He learned to ski on water and snow and in 1993 won first place in the Disabled World Water Ski Tournament, held that year in France. He has become a successful businessperson who constructs, fits, and markets prosthetics for amputees.

In the same year that Priest was rescued, 151 search-and-rescue operations were conducted in Yosemite. All told, 162 people were rescued, 96 of them injured. Eighteen people lost their lives. Not included in these statistics are the scores of children who wander off momentarily from parents or guardians and are found by park rangers. On an average summer day in the park, multiple searches may be underway simultaneously. The sheer SAR caseload at Yosemite, and therefore the deep experience of Dill and others, meant that Donnie Priest had a chance despite the almost impossible odds against him.

But the accidental tragedy suffered by Donnie Priest and his family, and the statistics each year at Yosemite that record other harrowing moments, are the exceptions to a generally stellar safety record. National parks are high on the list of the nation's safest places, and that includes the most wildly rugged sections of parks that hold such fascination for so many. My respect for the rangers and maintenance personnel who keep it that way is immense, and so should be the respect afforded them by every park visitor.

HER ROYAL HIGHNESS, QUEEN ELIZABETH THE II OF ENGLAND

In early 1983, while routine preparations were underway in anticipation of another heavy travel year, an entirely different demand on the park staff suddenly popped up out of the blue, or, more

Queen Elizabeth II of England, Superintendent Robert Binnewies, 1983

accurately, out of the tricolor. My office assistant alerted me to a telephone call from the White House. "THE WHITE HOUSE?!" I asked. The caller was an Air Force Colonel assigned as liaison to the White House staff wanting to know if "forest rangers" might be available to help provide security for an unnamed high level dignitary who wished to visit Yosemite. I confirmed that we were staffed with park rangers highly competent in security procedures. Soon after, the telephone rang again. This time the call was from the NPS Regional Office in San Francisco. The message was that Her Royal Highness, Queen Elizabeth the II of England, and her husband, Prince Philip, the Duke of York, intended to visit the park during a trip to California in March. Moments after this call, Ed Hardy telephoned to confirm that he, too, had learned of this pending, extraordinary visit.

Celebrity visits to Yosemite are quite common, many occurring without fanfare. Movie stars and politicians, sports heroes and pop

Yosemite Photo Archives

Queen Elizabeth II and Prince Philip, meeting Dr. Julia Parker and her daughter, Lucy, 1983

     Your Yosemite: **PROTECTING A PUBLIC TREASURE**

idols, protégés of science and the arts, esteemed writers, radio and television performers—unusually successful people from all walks of society regularly are counted among Yosemite's annual visitors. Recently, Oprah Winfrey came to Yosemite Valley on her first-ever camping adventure. She was followed into her tent by a television camera technician and, metaphorically, by thousands of her loyal viewers.

Several United States presidents have come to visit. James Garfield (1875), Rutherford B. Hayes (1883), Theodore Roosevelt (1903), William Howard Taft (1909), Herbert Hoover (1927), and Franklin D. Roosevelt (1938) are on the list. While still serving as Commander of the North Atlantic Treaty Organization (NATO), Dwight D. Eisenhower visited Yosemite just before he was elected President in 1952. In 1962, John F. Kennedy stayed overnight at the Ahwahnee Hotel and was treated to an especially vigorous display of burning "fire fall" embers pushed from Glacier Point. While serving as Governor of California, Ronald Reagan, accompanied by his wife, Nancy, rode their horses into the backcountry and, much more recently, Laura Bush and some of her friends were escorted on a High Sierra hike by Park Ranger Laurel Boyers. As a gesture of thanks, Mrs. Bush later invited Boyers and her spouse to a White House dinner, a considerable change in menu from backpacker food.

In mid-June, 2016, President Barack Obama, his wife, Michele and daughters Malia and Sasha made a three-day visit to Yosemite. In addition to his official duties, including comment on the threat posed by climate change and emphasis on the need for renewed attention to the nation's conservation agenda during the National Park Service centennial year, the President and his family hiked to the summit of Sentinel Dome, passing close to the campsite used by Theodore Roosevelt and John Muir more than a century earlier, down the Four Mile Trail from Glacier Point to the valley, and up the Mist Trail that leads past Vernal and Nevada Falls. They were, for these personal moments, typically enthusiastic park visitors.

The NPS and concessionaire staffs become conditioned to adjustments when celebrities visit the park, ranging from brief reconfiguration of priorities to assure as much leisure and privacy as possible for special guests to full-blown safety precautions and crowd-control procedures. Many celebrities just want to enjoy the park like any other visitor. When I presided in 1984 at the dedication of the Ansel Adams Wilderness on a gorgeous day at Tuolumne Meadows, one of the featured speakers was Robert. He knew the park well, first visiting with his mother as a 10-year-old, and, in the summer of 1951, at age 15, working briefly in the park as a waiter/dishwasher, with emphasis on the dishes. He has kept his eye on the park ever since, crediting Yosemite with his keen and activist environmental awareness. Just before the appointed time, Redford, almost unnoticed, eased through those in attendance and stood off alone for a moment admiring the view. Later he told me that he was just happy to be back in the park, his moment of return only slightly unsettled by the speeding ticket he had received from a highway patrolman on the east side of the Sierra Nevada en route to the event.

By comparison to other celebrity moments at Yosemite, the royal visit was at the high end of intensity. Queen Elizabeth and Prince Philip were coming to the United States to officially express gratitude for President Reagan's support during a brief but sharp territorial dispute in 1982 between England and Argentina. The conflict was over control of the remote Falkland Islands in the South Atlantic Ocean.

For the royal visit, California was the primary destination. Yosemite was included on the itinerary at the request of Prince Philip who especially wanted to see the celebrated park. As preparations began at Yosemite, the first order of business was contact between United States Secret Service agents, their British counterparts, National Park Service law enforcement personnel, and select members of the Yosemite Park & Curry Company concessionaire staff. Security would be paramount. In any such visit, everyone involved has to assume that someone out there might, for whatever reason, attempt to do harm to the dignitaries.

The agents and park rangers were obligated to review a host of contingencies, trying to imagine possible attack modes and how to take the necessary steps to prevent them from happening. Communications procedures were confirmed, surveillance locations identified

Your Yosemite: **PROTECTING A PUBLIC TREASURE**

Robert Redford and Bob Binnewies, Dedication of Ansel Adams Wilderness, 1984

and assigned, patrol routes analyzed, scheduling coordinated, and site safety critiqued, especially at the Ahwahnee Hotel where the royal couple would be staying. Only hours before their arrival, special identification buttons would be issued to those who were to be in close proximity to the Queen and Prince to assure that no imposter spoiled the event. All roadways were examined to determine the best access options and to identify possible alternative emergency routes. Background checks were run on NPS and concessionaire employees. Individuals in surrounding communities with known records of criminal violence or histories of mental instability were given special scrutiny.

The Queen's traveling party numbered fifty-six, a diverse group which included the British Secretary of State for Foreign and Commonwealth Affairs, the British Ambassador to the United States, the Mistress of the Robes, the Master of the Household, the Equerry-in-Waiting to the Duke of Edinburgh, the Flag Officer of the Royal Yachts, the Captain of the Queen's Flight, the Private Secretary to the Minister-in-Attendance, the Queen's Page, the Lady Clerk to the Assistant Private Secretary to the Queen, the Sous Chef, the Queen's Hairdresser, the Page of the Presence, and the Medical Officer to the Queen, to name a few. One of the visiting dignitaries was listed as the Right Honorable Sir Philip Moore, K.C.B., K.C.V.O, and C.M.G. His initialed titles never were explained to the park staff, but we gathered that he was important.

The party would also include footmen, porters, cooks, secretaries, and personal traveling-companion friends of the royal couple. President Reagan would be represented on the Yosemite leg of the trip by John J. Louis, United States Ambassador to the United Kingdom and Northern Ireland, Michael Deaver, Reagan's Chief of Staff, Selwa Roosevelt, U. S. Chief of Protocol, and her spouse, Archibald Roosevelt, Jr., the grandson of Theodore Roosevelt. This was definitely not going to be a normal park event.

Preparations were made for media coverage. We were told that privileges would be given to a "pool" of reporters assigned by the White House and that local media representatives would be confined to a secondary status, apparently a standard security precaution in metropolitan areas, but unusual at Yosemite. Gene Rose of the *Fresno Bee*, who frequently covered Yosemite issues and was highly respected for his devotion to the park subsequently had to scramble under the imposed media constraints, but nonetheless got his story including excellent photographs.

Beyond the control of anyone involved during the visit was a rowdy and uninvited phenomenon known as El Niño, a major weather disturbance in the North Pacific Ocean periodically caused by an unusual rise in surface water temperature. The result is disruption to overlying air pressure that pumps one moisture-laden storm after another into southern California, causing flooding in the lowlands and heavy snowfall in the Sierra Nevada. On the occasion of the Queen's visit, Yosemite was right in the El Niño bull's-eye. Two days prior to the Queen's anticipated arrival, park visitors and non-essential employees were encouraged to voluntarily leave the park for their own safety due to flood and road-closure threats.

The official visit by Queen Elizabeth to the U. S. began on February 26 in San Diego. After a star-studded gala in Los Angeles, the Queen and Prince originally planned to travel up the coast aboard the royal yacht, *Britannia*, a 412-foot ship manned by 19 officers and 27 crew members, but El Niño was right there to greet them, making the prospect of travel by ocean going vessel too risky. The yacht churned north toward San Francisco with only British officers and crew on board while the royal visitors traveled by car to the Reagan Ranch outside of Santa Barbara and then by air to San Francisco.

With the weather-beaten *Britannia* now safely tied up at a Bay Area dock, President and Mrs. Reagan were welcomed aboard by Queen Elizabeth and Prince Philip, along with two hundred additional invited guests, to celebrate the Reagans' 31st wedding anniversary. The next morning, as reported by Catherine Wilson of the *Associated Press*, the Queen and her group left San Francisco after a dockside celebration attended by several thousand people: "Caterers dressed in Elizabethan costumes dispensed Cheerios cereal and doughnuts to those who braved rain to say 'Cheerio' to the royal couple." A spokesperson for the Queen said that the next stop, Yosemite, was for the purpose of "rest and relaxation," echoing the wish expressed eight decades earlier by Theodore Roosevelt. Air transport was provided to Castle Air Force Base in the Central Valley near the town of Merced.

Due to the storm, Secret Service agents made an abrupt, last-minute change in the road route that would be used to reach Yosemite. The original route was to have been along Highway 140 through the Town of Mariposa, then down the winding road into the Merced River Canyon, and into Yosemite via the Arch Rock Entrance Station. After quick consultation with local officials, the Secret Service agents chose to avoid the narrow Merced River Canyon, infamous for its rock slides when heavy rains create instability on the steep canyon slopes. Instead, the agents chose a narrow two-lane country road that wiggles up into the Sierra foothills from the Central Valley until it intersects with Highway 120, a more northerly course at higher elevation that provides entry into the park via the Big Oak Flat Entrance Station. This change in plan sent local law enforcement officers who were to help provide security for the Queen's fifteen-car motorcade scrambling to their new posts.

Mariposa County sheriff deputies Rod Sinclair and Rod McKean were racing down into the foothills to intercept the motorcade and provide escort service when Sinclair's patrol car rounded a curve just as a Secret Service vehicle was approaching from the opposite direction. In the resulting head-on collision, agents George LaBarge, age 41, Donald Bejeck, age 29, and Donald Robinson, age 38, instantly lost their lives. The main convoy of vehicles, including the Queen's limousine, was several miles behind when the accident occurred. When the motorcade drove around the scene of the accident a few minutes later on a quickly arranged bypass through a rancher's field the mangled vehicles were visible 100 yards away.

At the Big Oak Flat Entrance Station to the park, the Queen and Prince Philip were informed of the calamity. After some hasty discussion among White House and British officials, the decision was made that the Yosemite visit should proceed as planned, in part, as an expression of respect for the agents who had been doing their duty. Ranger-Naturalist Bob Rooney joined the royal couple in their limousine for the drive into the park.

At Inspiration Point, a classic viewpoint at the Wawona Tunnel, Assistant Superintendent Bill Burgen and I were waiting with umbrellas to officially welcome the Queen and Prince while simultaneously processing the awful news of the Secret Service Agent tragedy. A small bleacher had been erected to accommodate the thirty or forty media representatives awaiting arrival of the motorcade. Several dozen reporters and photographers, who had not yet learned of the tragedy, were adjusting and readjusting their equipment to compensate for wind noise and changing light patterns in the swirl of patchy clouds that had descended below the valley's rim. El Capitan was partially obscured by mist. Flood-swollen Bridalveil Fall had exchanged its usual lacy appearance for a plunging torrent. Off in the far distance, Half Dome kept appearing and disappearing in the clouds. Fortunately, no rain was falling. Burgen and I were standing by a small stone wall at the edge of the Inspiration Point parking lot when the Queen's limousine appeared.

The arrival was carefully orchestrated. When the limousine pulled to a stop, Burgen and I took a few steps forward, about halfway to the automobile, and stood while the Queen and Prince were escorted to us for introductions. The mood was somber. Graciously reserved, the Queen seemed entirely in control of the moment, certainly a reflection of the countless times she had been greeted under all kinds of circumstances around the world. As coached in advance, I escorted the Queen to a predetermined spot only a few steps away, then we turned slightly, our backs to the view that makes Inspiration Point so famous. With the scene as backdrop, I pointed up toward the far less impressive tree-shaded slopes above. The Queen, knowing her part exactly, followed my gaze with apparent rapt interest, prompting a veritable cacophony of shutter-clicking cameras erupting from the nearby media bleacher. The resultant photo images captured a weather-washed Yosemite Valley with Bridalveil Fall and El Captain prominently on display. Queen Elizabeth was resplendent, her ever present purse in hand, and I was armed with a furled umbrella. These images soon would be on the wire services, racing around the world. After this brief photo opportunity, the next destination for the royal couple was the Tresidder suite at the Ahwahnee Hotel; the entire hotel had been reserved exclusively for the Queen and her traveling party.

Ranger-Naturalist Ginger Burley was not in attendance among the spectators at Inspiration Point. Her duties were down in Yosemite's ranger ranks as a "fulltime-subject-to-furlough" employee. In essence she was a bargain-basement employee, a person of proven skill and experience who could step in seamlessly in the busy seasons and disappear quietly when the budget purse was empty again. Burley and her peers, living this subject-to-furlough lifestyle, might have felt like fiscal victims, but accepted a routine that included roughly coequal parts of cherished work in Yosemite and opportunities to travel, explore, and pursue educational interests or avocations in the off seasons.

Sometimes, when budget dollars allowed, Burley's work year was extended by assignment in Yosemite Valley before moving to her regular summertime post at Tuolumne Meadows. By chance she was on the payroll during the Queen's visit and found herself sitting on the rear seat of a van that had been dispatched from park headquarters to the Ahwahnee Hotel to provide transportation services for the visiting royal party. Word had it that some of the special visitors had requested an afternoon valley tour. Two vans were sent to the hotel, both driven by security officers unfamiliar with the park. Burley's supervisor, Jim Sano, was in the lead van, she in the second.

Neither of the rangers expected to have any contact with the Queen since their duties were to provide regular informational services for park visitors and media representatives who remained in the valley despite storm warnings. But when the unscheduled request was made for tour vehicles, Sano and Burley, knowledgeable and adaptable, were nearby and in uniform. Their supervisor, Chief Naturalist Len McKenzie, assigned them to the task.

Rangers must learn to adjust quickly to everything from medical emergencies and scheduling mix ups to inebriated adults and gifted children. They learn to handle the exuberant, the officious, the befuddled, the combative, and pretty much everything in between. Requests for educational services are part of the mix, so Sano and Burley were trundling along in their vans not knowing exactly what services were being requested or by whom. At the hotel, the lead van with Sano aboard was waved away because it had tinted windows, apparently not to the liking of the waiting passengers. The driver of Burley's van pulled up in front of the Ahwahnee's porte cochére. "They both got in," Burley later said, the "both" referring to Elizabeth and Philip Windsor, the Queen and Prince. No one else climbed aboard. Apparently all other members of the royal group were finding the hotel so comfortable that they had opted to bypass the tour.

The Queen and Prince settled into the middle seat of the van. Burley was sitting behind them. As the van pulled away and started meandering along the park road network, the Prince asked the driver questions while Burley remained silent, as instructed. She described the awkward situation: "After about five minutes of confusion, the driver could not drive and look at the park map at the same time, I spoke up and said that I was their guide, but that Secret Service agents had told me not to speak unless spoken to, so I was sorry, but I really needed to speak. The Queen and Prince looked around at me for the first time and smiled."

Burley took control and made sure that the royal couple had a slow and satisfying drive-by view of El Capitan. When the van looped around past Bridalveil Fall, Burley directed the driver to stop at a pullout along the roadway so that the Queen and Prince could step out of the vehicle, enjoy the scene, and hear the roar of the waterfall.

On Sunday morning the royal couple attended church service at the little New England-style Yosemite Chapel, the oldest structure still in use in Yosemite. The chapel was constructed in 1879 close to the base of the Four-Mile-Trail and then moved some years later to its present location, a photo-perfect setting near Sentinel Bridge. That Sunday morning, the sun shone intermittently and when the royal couple stepped out after the service onto the lawn sprinkled with pine needles, Julia Parker was there to greet them. Julia Parker is a Kahia Pomo/Coast Miwuk who visited the park throughout her childhood. In 1948, she settled in Yosemite at age seventeen as the bride of Ralph Parker, a member of the park maintenance staff and a Mono Paiute. Julia began to master the art of weaving baskets by learning from her paternal grandmother, Lucy Telles, and weavers Mabel McKay and Elsie Allen. The making of baskets is a precise and eloquent act of marrying a cultural practice to earthly gifts. In the Sierra Nevada region, grasses and twigs have long been gathered by Native American women for use in weaving the baskets that become both practical containers and finely crafted works of art. Not content just to meet utilitarian needs, they wove intricate designs into their baskets that tell of the history, traditions, legends, and hopes of their people. Many of these baskets have found their way into museums and private collections.

Julia Parker learned well the skills of basketry, so much so that she is an acclaimed master of the art who, in 2006, received an honorary doctorate degree from the California College of the Arts in recognition of her work. For many years she demonstrated her skills and described meanings hidden in basket designs to audiences at the park Visitor Center, and, in so doing, brought Native American history alive. Parker's philosophy is: "Take from the earth and give back to the earth, and don't forget to say please and thank you."

On the morning that Parker met the Queen in front of the chapel, she was holding a large basket made of plant materials carefully gathered in the valley, the product of many hours of her crafting skill. In a fine moment of honored history, Julia Parker presented this basket to Queen Elizabeth II. The gift was graciously accepted. It was a dreamlike and touching moment, this meeting of two important women at Yosemite, each representing customs and times past, cultural pride, lessons taught and learned, conflicts subdued, and human dignity celebrated. More cameras clicked and this image, too, went round the world.

Later that day, Queen Elizabeth and Prince Philip specifically requested that Ginger Burley accompany them on another outing, this time to visit Mirror Lake, a small wetland tucked neatly between the bases of Half Dome and Basket Dome where Tenaya Creek, tumbling down from the High Sierra, changes from a whitewater cascade into a stately mountain stream. This time there was more enthusiasm for the tour among members of the royal traveling party and three vans were required to carry the group. Burley led her visitors on an easy walk to the upper end of the wetland, describing geological and biological phenomena as she went, and answering questions that are typical on a Yosemite nature stroll. On these occasions, Burley keeps in mind the lessons taught to her by Bob Fry, one of her favorite ranger-naturalist mentors: "He could talk about details of the life cycle of moss and intertwine humankind's connection to the whole universe."

After the guided walk at Mirror Lake the visitors clambered back into the vans for the ride back to the hotel, one person the exception. Prince Philip wanted to walk back and so he did, Ranger Burley at his side continuing to comment on the intricacies and delights of the park and answering his questions during the two-mile saunter, security agents trailing closely behind. She said later, "He would make a pretty good naturalist."

Ironically, it was El Niño that nudged Queen Elizabeth and Prince Philip a few inches closer to life as it is lived by the rest of us, not simply by introducing unexpected changes into their schedule, but by upending it altogether. The next leg of the royal trip was cancelled, giving the royal couple an extra, unscheduled day in Yosemite Valley. Suddenly, there were no places that they had to be or people they had to meet; no clock ticking away toward the next event. On this extra day, the royal party was treated to occasional rays of sunshine peeking through the overcast to light up the valley. The Queen and Prince took full advantage of the unanticipated freedom to go for leisurely strolls, relaxed security agents tagging along at a discrete distance. Or, on one occasion, in panic. The Queen went on a bird walk and, in good birder style, wandered off for a moment on her own, out of sight. The park radio network came alive with the voices of secret service agents and park rangers in frenzy until the Queen reappeared.

At dinner that evening at the Ahwahnee Hotel, she told me that she almost never had such opportunity except on her private estates in England where she enjoyed "putting on my rubber boots and being a farmer." She seemed to relish the feeling, too, of being almost an "average visitor" at Yosemite and asked thoughtful questions about how the park functioned, even suggesting good-humoredly that she might do well as a host at the park's information desk. Across the table, Prince Philip and my wife, Midge, fell into long conversation about horses as only the equine-addicted can do. Part of the conversation that evening focused on the historic visit by Theodore Roosevelt to the park, obviously of interest to Archibald Roosevelt, who, along with his wife, Selwa, and Ed and Jackie Hardy, sat at the table-for-eight. The dinner and conversation lasted for about two hours. The following morning, after the Queen and Prince formally expressed their gratitude to park and concessionaire staff members in a receiving line at the Ahwahnee, they departed the park, leaving in place the melancholy of the loss of the Secret Service agents, an easing of tension among the park rangers that no security breach occurred, a high-profile mark on park history, and a return to business as usual. El Niño stayed right where it was. By late spring, snow depths near Tuolumne Meadows reached eighty feet.

13

Mr. Rent-A-Riot

PENCILED ONTO MY CALENDAR two days after the royals left was a meeting with Charles Cushman, "Mr. Rent-A-Riot." Ironically, this meeting was to lead to my downfall from Yosemite. Journalist Margaret L. Knox, later describing in *Wilderness* the man with whom I was about to meet, said, "Big Chuck Cushman paces the stage like the huggable host of a kiddie TV show. 'I generally just like to have a good time with people,' he booms, spreading his hands and rocking back on his heels with a gravely laugh. 'I'm not trying to scaaaaaare you.' This is the Captain Kangaroo of the movement against public lands—he pushes away from the pesky podium, scratches his beard with a hand the size of a catcher's mitt, leans forward, all 270-jean-clad-towering pounds of him oozing sincerity."

The American Land Rights Association that Cushman founded is described as "a public interest advocacy organization that works to protect landowners across America who are affected by various growth management schemes as well as the Endangered Species Act, Clean Water Act (wetlands) and other Federal land use regulatory laws." The roots of this organization trace back to 1978 when Cushman gave up his job as an insurance salesman and formed the National Park Inholders Association. When I met with him in 1983, the name of his organization had changed to the National Inholders Association, representing the wide net he tossed across the nation to people who were aggrieved by government land issues. He also served at the time of our meeting as a Reagan appointee to the National Park System Advisory Board, an entity established in 1935 under the Historic Sites, Buildings, and Antiquities Act to provide expert advice to the NPS Director on matters of history, archeology, anthropology, historical and landscape architecture, biology, ecology, geology, marine science, social science, and management of national and state parks, protected areas, and cultural resources—certainly a full plate. My impression is that Cushman viewed himself as a highly knowledgeable expert on most if not all of these subjects.

The genesis of the National Park Inholders Association was Cushman's reaction to a forceful effort in 1972 by the NPS to acquire private properties in "Section 35" in Yosemite's Wawona District. A cabin there that had been owned by his father now was his. Section 35 had not been acquired by the NPS in 1932 when over 8,000 acres, including the nearby hotel, was added to Yosemite holdings. The section land, about 640 acres, was originally patented in the late 1800s by Albert Bruce and a few other early pioneer settlers and eventually subdivided into 240 small parcels completely surrounded by parkland. It was a somewhat self-contained mountain community similar to others scattered through the Sierra Nevada where early ramshackle cabins had given way for the most part to more substantial weather tolerant structures. Predominantly the properties were used for vacation purposes, but some residents lived there year around either as owners or renters. Section 35 was labeled an "inholding," a term commonly used to describe islands of private property encompassed by federal, state, or local public holdings.

Cushman had stepped forward among his apprehensive Section 35 neighbors as a staunch defender of their property rights. There was deep suspicion among the lot owners that NPS tactics to acquire inholdings might include the use of eminent domain (condemnation) authority, a federal government means to acquire privately owned land despite owner objections. This authority has been widely used throughout the nation to create highway and utility corridors, airports, military installations, water reservoirs, canals, and educational and medical institutions. When eminent domain is used, private property owners are compensated at "fair market value," but cannot decline to sell. In the National Park Service, this authority was used to acquire holdings of the Gettysburg Electric Railroad Company that led in 1933 to creation of the Gettysburg National Military Park. Other Civil War battlefield sites, similarly acquired, include Chickamauga, Shiloh, and Vicksburg. The immensely popular, 1,700-acre Rock Creek National Park in Washington, D. C., was acquired in the 1930s in part by using eminent domain authority, as were portions of Shenandoah, Great Smoky Mountains, and Mammoth Cave National Parks. More recently, a significant portion of Cape Cod National Seashore was so obtained. Use of this authority was also considered, but ultimately not required for establishment of the National Memorial in Stonycreek Township, Pennsylvania, to honor victims of the September 11, 2001, terrorist attack on United Airlines Flight 93.

At Yosemite in 1972, eminent domain authority was recommended for use in Section 35 as one means of acquiring private property, prompting Cushman to rally owners in protest. The NPS backed off, continuing to rely, instead, on volunteer willing-seller transactions. I favored this approach or, even better, donation of property to the NPS. For example, Acadia National Park, a fabulous 47,000-acre unit of the NPS is created entirely by donations of private land. Acadia is atypical in that many of the donors, Including John D. Rockefeller, Jr., were exceedingly well to do, but donation of inholdings in any park always is an option and possibility if the owner is looking for a good tax benefit, wants to support the purposes of the park, or both. My view, shared by the NPS hierarchy in the 1980s, was that the use of eminent domain in Section 35 was not justified. But suspicion was entrenched and fear of eminent domain was used as rhetorical fuel for the property rights flames. Cushman had positioned himself as the unwavering guardian of inholders and, by the time of our meeting, had made a career of demonizing government land conservation initiatives.

I assumed that Cushman asked for the meeting with me to measure my attitude about current acquisition efforts in Section 35. I knew him slightly, and knew of his reputation as a super-salesman for his cause and of his habit of lambasting public agencies, "preservationists," and "subversive" environmental organizations. He would become very adept at orchestrating vocal protests at press events and public forums, thus his moniker, "Mr. Rent-a-Riot." Prior to the meeting, a park ranger who I held in the highest regard (and still do) suggested that a tape recording be made of the discussion with Cushman so that an accurate after-the-fact transcript of the proceedings would be in hand. Translation, we did not trust Cushman. In hindsight, I realize that I should have either declined this suggestion or, if a tape was to be made, asked in advance for Cushman's permission. I did neither. Instead, without giving the suggestion the thought that it deserved, I contacted Yosemite's senior law enforcement officer who assured me that such a recording would be entirely legal. Regardless, had the tables been turned and I walked into a meeting without knowing that a tape machine was running, I would have been insulted and angry, yet I kept Cushman in the dark. This was a gross lapse on my part. The meeting took place, the recording was made, and Cushman did nothing afterwards to misrepresent our conversation.

I never listened to the tape, just tossed it in a desk drawer and almost forgot about it. I did not see Cushman again until many years later at a Congressional hearing in Washington, D. C., when I was working to acquire 20,000-acre Sterling Forest that became a state park in New York. He was at the hearing on other matters and we very briefly acknowledged each other. But the tape made that day in my office unknowingly marked the midway point in my tenure at Yosemite and would come to light three years later, used as a blunt instrument that caused my abrupt departure from the park. My suspicion of Cushman prompted the stumble on my part, but he had nothing to do with the blunt instrument. That was left in the hands of a park ranger right there on the Yosemite staff.

LOOKING FOR MONEY

With the Queen on her way and the Cushman meeting concluded I turned my attention back to the daily park challenges, including the snow piled high in the mountains. The rule of thumb for park snowplowing crews is to open the cross-Sierra Tioga Road to public travel on the Friday before Memorial Day weekend. Vendors in the tourism-dependent eastside Sierra Nevada communities of Lee Vining, Bridgeport, and Bishop are so anxious for the road to open that they recruit local pilots to monitor the snowplows' progress. In 1983, the winter's accumulation of snow was so deep that bulldozer operators, positioned in their machines atop the snow pack, struggled to push snow down into the jaws of the snowplows. Giant spinning blades in the jaws of the snowplows would blast the snow back up, out, and sideways in a brilliant arch, a literal fountain of white pouring into the tree line parallel to the road. The result was a continually extending roadway chasm, framed by vertical walls of snow that did not melt away for weeks. That year, Tioga Road did not open until the Friday before the 4th of July weekend, stretching patience in the small communities on the east side of the High Sierra and the dollars in our operational account.

Yosemite was not destitute; sufficient funds were being provided to keep staff in place and maintenance standards adequate, but in terms of seeking a better future for the park through a refined human presence, we were spinning in place. Then a serendipitous opportunity presented itself from a resource close at hand. The not-for-profit Yosemite Association, founded in 1923 at the urging of Stephen Mather, was the first of scores of such entities now operating in areas of the National Park System. This public-private alliance has proven to be a great success. By 1983, these associations principally functioned as publishing houses, producing and marketing high-quality, well-vetted books, maps, and informational materials in support of NPS educational needs. Profits from the sale of these publications allowed most associations to be self-funded, with enough money left over each year to distribute to the host park in support of various laudable projects.

Over the many years of its existence, the Yosemite Association had generated hundreds of thousands of dollars that were reinvested in the park, affirming Mather's vision. The Yosemite Association was also a membership organization that counted close to 11,000 active participants who especially valued Yosemite. The annual park membership gathering was a time to hear from renowned speakers, learn more of the human and natural history of the park, exchange ideas and concerns with park executives, and rekindle Yosemite-inspired friendships.

A Board of Trustees, elected by the Association membership and on which the park superintendent and Yosemite's chief of interpretation served as ex-officio members, met quarterly to guide the affairs of the organization. At my first such meeting with the trustees in 1979, Henry Berrey, the Association's executive director, asked the Board for permission to raise money for the construction of a cabin at Tuolumne Meadows to house summertime Association employees. Despite the close working relationship between the Association and the park staff, housing at Tuolumne Meadows was always a problem. When staff counts ballooned during the months of heaviest visitor travel, the scramble for housing was intense. The available tent cabins at Tuolumne Meadows were barely sufficient to meet NPS needs. Yosemite Association employees were in competition for even the most meager spaces. Another concern was temperature. Most Association employees arrived as soon as the road opened in the spring and stayed until snow started to fly in the autumn. In the high alpine setting of Tuolumne Meadows, the tent cabins assigned to staff for the season could be very chilly. A snug cabin would be much better.

Berrey knew of the interest among park managers for a year-round cabin at Tuolumne so that a patrol ranger could live there and keep an eye on the ski-borne adventurers who reached the meadows in the depths of winter. He reasoned that a new cabin could fulfill a dual purpose, providing winter quarters for the ranger and housing for YA staff members the rest of the year. Berrey proposed that half the money needed for the cabin project might be obtained through fundraising efforts by the Association and the other half squeezed from the NPS budget. At first, the Board members were wary. They were not accustomed to fundraising other than the low-key variety occasioned by unsolicited donations from grateful park visitors. Dependent almost entirely on book sales for financial stability, they were not at all sure that such deliberate fundraising, or "begging," as one of the members expressed it, would be good for their small, stable, and uncontroversial organization.

Berry was only asking for a small cabin at Tuolumne, but as the debate continued the initial kneejerk reaction against fundraising began to change and his idea started to expand to include other much needed park renovation and educational projects, including reenergizing the School of Field Natural History, absent from the park

    Your Yosemite: **PROTECTING A PUBLIC TREASURE**

scene since before World War II. Although new to the Y. A. Board, I was already well aware of the chronic limitations of the park budget. Jumping at the chance provided by Berrey's initiative, I was among those who urged that we should up the ante and go for a fundraising program to benefit the entire park. This was a leap in strategy that pushed the usual one-hour meeting well toward three hours. There was talk of deteriorated trail systems, struggles to acquire and protect historic objects and art works, lack of maintenance of historic structures, and a general consensus that the natural values of Yosemite were in need of much more scientific and recuperative attention. Finally, the Board members agreed that if a bold fundraising effort was to have any chance of success it should be tied to the park as a whole, not just to the cabin project.

They still worried about entering into fundraising that might be a distraction from the organization's core sales activities, but as defenders of their beloved Yosemite first and foremost, they took a deep breath and, led by their chairperson, Dana C. Morgenson, agreed to further explore the idea. Others serving on the Board at that time were Thomas J. Shephard, Dr. Harvey S. Rhodes, Jeannie Falk Adams, Gene Rose, Dr. Frederick Harper, and Sterling C. Cramer, all highly knowledgeable of the history of Yosemite and concerned about the park's future well-being. The ebullient and very able attorney, Tom Shepard, who would succeed Morgenson at the helm of the Association the following year and serve onward for many years, proved to be especially supportive. My own earlier fundraising experiences with the National Audubon Society and Maine Coast Heritage Trust probably caused me, on that day, to be the most comfortable person in the room about the idea.

More discussion followed at subsequent Board meetings, and, despite inevitable changes in Board membership, the Association remained steadfast, finally retaining the services of David Rice, a professional fundraising consultant from the San Francisco Bay Area. Rice became a regular at Board meetings, listened carefully, provided encouragement and solid advice, and proposed the *Return of Light Campaign* for Yosemite, a catchy play on the words of John Muir, who referred to the High Sierra as the "Range of Light." Berrey and Chief Park Interpreter Len McKenzie collaborated on putting together a wish list of projects that totaled $52 million, a leap upward of considerable height, one might say, from half the cost of a small cabin.

This was to be the first major organized fundraising campaign in a national park, a fact not lost on some in the NPS hierarchy in San Francisco and Washington, D.C., who took a dim view of such a tactic. They worried that charitable giving might result in demands by private donors to dictate how the money should be spent in the park. To safeguard against this tail-wagging-the-dog concern, a mechanism was set up whereby the park Superintendent would annually submit a list of projects to the Yosemite Association for funding consideration. The projects and cost estimates would be prioritized in advance by the superintendent, leaving the Association Board to determine how far down the list it could stretch any charitable dollars that might be available. While this discussion was still in its infancy, and to our collective surprise and delight, employees of American Savings & Loan, Inc., a financial services company based in Stockton, California, contributed $150,000 to the *Return of Light Campaign*, no strings attached, and pledged even more.

Building on the momentum of such a pleasantly surprising start, Rice counseled that prominent individuals who had a special affinity for Yosemite should be recruited to serve voluntarily on a fundraising committee. He put me in contact with his associate, Dr. Herbert Moffitt, who lived on Nob Hill in San Francisco, just across the street from the Pacific Union Club, a bastion of high achievers and comfortably wealthy heirs. Moffitt was a well-connected member of the club who was not shy about explaining the Yosemite fundraising initiative to his associates.

In a series of luncheons at the club and through telephone contacts with other businesspeople in the Bay Area known to have a strong interest in the park, the committee was formed. Typically, Moffitt and I would be at the club during the lunch hour. In laser-like fashion Moffitt would spot a potential committee recruit and drag me over to be introduced. At the first mention of the word, Yosemite, most would smile and begin to reminisce about trips to the park.

Usually only a verbal nudge was required to move from reminiscence to a willingness to help, either by joining the committee or signaling readiness to write a check, or both.

One example was a project high on the park's preferred list to try to reintroduce Sierra Nevada Bighorn Sheep into the Yosemite ecosystem. In the High Sierra, especially in the Lee Vining Canyon region just east of Tioga Pass, bighorn sheep once had numbered in the hundreds, but hunting during the gold rush and disease transmitted from domestic animals had been ruinous to the species. In all of the Sierra Nevada mountain range only two small herds, about 250 animals in total, still existed by the mid-1980s, but none in Yosemite. Wildlife biologists were anxious to establish two or three more herds to increase population numbers and ensure the species' survival. From an aesthetic perspective, the reappearance of bighorn sheep in and near Yosemite would offer park visitors an especially memorable experience should they be lucky enough to catch glimpses of these agile animals on the high mountain slopes.

During the early stages of the campaign, I telephoned Richard N. Goldman, who was the founder of Goldman Insurance Services in San Francisco. Goldman was known to be a keen environmental advocate and admirer of wildlife. Only one short telephone conversation with him was required to win his enthusiastic pledge of financial support to bring back the bighorns when the time was right. That time would not arrive for another three years, but Goldman was steadfast.

At the first official gathering of the *Return of Light* committee, hosted in 1983 by the Yosemite Association at the Wawona Hotel, David Rice had a surprise. Byron Nishkian, a prominent member of the committee, was a highly successful consulting engineer in San Francisco known particularly for his expertise in the use of concrete and steel in major construction projects. He and his wife, Ellie, had a strong allegiance to the park that was confirmed when, prompted by Rice, the Nishkians stepped forward and announced a $200,000 gift to the fundraising campaign, thereby implicitly challenging fellow committee members to do the same. The list of donors, large and small, began to grow. Among them, Ed Hardy handed over a

$500,000 check on behalf of the Yosemite Park & Curry Company. In a sense, fundraising took on a life of its own at Yosemite, so much so that the Association agreed that the effort should be spun off into a separate entity in 1988 that became the Yosemite Fund, a charitable nonprofit organization with offices in San Francisco. This led, finally, to an outright merger between the Fund and Association in 2010, prompting another name change to the Yosemite Conservancy, bringing full circle a connection begun almost thirty years prior when a few Yosemite old timers voted to raise charitable dollars with the hope of building a cabin, having no idea what the response would be.

The Conservancy has chalked up millions of dollars in donations to the park, and still counting. In just one year, for example, the audited Conservancy financial statement showed over $14 million in revenue and aid to Yosemite of more than $130 million. The large Conservancy staff is a far cry from Berrey's day when he counted himself among his staff of four tucked in cramped space at the park Visitor Center. Charitable giving for the park has funded hundreds of worthy projects so far, including a major reconfiguration of facilities and improved pedestrian access at Glacier Point, realignment of the foot-trail approaches to Yosemite Falls, and habitat restoration of valley meadows. Support also flows to scientific research, preservation of cultural and historic objects, acquisition of rare books, paintings, photographs and related Yosemite reference materials, and protection of archeological values. Backcountry trail maintenance has benefitted and even the old water fountain in front of the Wawona Hotel, moribund for many years, spouts happily again just as it did when Theodore Roosevelt's traveling party happened by. The Conservancy partnered with the Trust for Public Land to acquire 400-acre Ackerson Meadow and added it to park holdings. Ackerson is a vibrant wildlife area that had been on the park's wish list for years.

The Conservancy is a mirror image of the larger NPS program at the park, perhaps best viewed as the polish put on a gemstone. It is a lively example of how government and its citizens, united together in a worthy cause, and with private purse strings loosened, can provide a strong vote of confidence for the future wellbeing of a place like Yosemite or for that matter, any urban, suburban, or rural setting where wildscapes and manufactured America shoulder against each other in competition for prized open space. When individuals donate to the Yosemite Conservancy, they are signaling a trust in astute custody of a national park by our government that is bright with promise. When the few of us were sitting at the Girls Club that day to launch fundraising, we certainly had in mind the pocketbook, but the larger benefit is proving to be a constancy of support for the national park concept, bringing fresh strength to this "best idea."

The risk, though, in private fundraising for national parks is that success might give a tightwad Congress even more excuse to cut park budgets. There is a disconnect between the increasing popularity of national parks and miserly keepers of the purse strings in Congress. Maintenance backlogs are huge and growing. No fundraising organization ever will be capable of meeting basic operating needs in parks—maintaining the roads and utility systems, providing for safety and education, refining resource stewardship, serving generations yet to come. The Yosemite Conservancy is a bright asset, but no substitute for Congressional responsibility for the public's parks.

On a daily basis, the test in any national park is to work through a maze of contradictory demands to conserve environmental treasures while at the same time nourishing memorable, perhaps once-in-a-lifetime recreational experiences for visitors that bring personal meaning to the "best idea." One example is that for the last century-and-a-half, humans, fearful of loss of life and possessions, have routinely suppressed forest fires in the Sierra Nevada. When wildfires blast from control in combustible California the result can be shattering. A recent example in the Yosemite region was the horrific "Rim Fire," brought to roaring life in August, 2013, by the senseless human folly of an untended campfire. The small circle of flame and embers got a monstrous grip on drought stressed vegetation and did not let go until it became the third largest forest fire ever recorded in the state's history. The fire started in the lower foothills outside of Yosemite and burned for weeks, incinerating over 400 square miles of timbered and meadowland habitat, including more than 60,000 acres when the unstoppable fire front crossed the boundary into

Yosemite. No human was burned to death, but the cruel impact on wildlife was immense. The permanence of rare species in the region, such as the Great Gray Owl, Sierra Nevada Red Fox, Pacific Fisher, and Black-backed Woodpecker, is severely threatened as a result. Bobcats, mountain lions, deer, bear, chipmunks, squirrels, frogs, turtles, butterflies—innocent wild victims of all kinds—were destroyed along with cattle grazing on nearby national forest lands. The watershed was left raw and highly vulnerable to flooding. The Rim Fire stands in the record book as a devastating example of why the red lights go on, the sirens scream, and trained crews, often at military strength, rush to suppress forest fires in the Sierra Nevada as soon as they are detected.

But wildfire also is a life-sustaining force in the natural environment. The Giant Sequoias in Yosemite have survived for centuries by being incredibly fire-resistant, their thick, dense bark adapted to act as insulation against flames and heat. Wildfires that historically passed through the groves kept undergrowth at the base of the trees in check, allowing tiny sequoia seeds to flutter down, find nourishing soil and germinate. But in the 19th and 20th centuries human suppression of wildfires in the groves, aided by better trained manpower and more effective mechanical equipment, allowed undergrowth to flourish and become increasingly dense, forming a human-induced barrier to the lifecycle of the sequoias. The undergrowth captured the seeds in a bushy net, preventing them from reaching ground. The heavy undergrowth fuel load also was a ticking time bomb, awaiting only a spark to explode into atypically fierce fire that adolescent sequoia trees, struggling to join their ancient elders, could not withstand. Evidence became clear that well intended human interference was preventing regeneration of the groves.

To safeguard and perpetuate the sequoia groves, specially trained park crews began deliberately to set fires that were allowed to creep along at ground level, so-called "cool" fires, in imitation of the natural conditions of old. The tradeoff was that unlucky park visitors found portions of the Giant Sequoia groves temporarily off-limits and smoke-filled while NPS crews went about their flaming ecological work. "Prescribed burning" has gone well beyond the sequoia

*Park Rangers Laurel Boyers and Ginger Burley leading
backcountry hike, Yosemite*

groves to include thousands of acres of oak and conifer habitat. The program was initiated at Yosemite in the 1970s through the watchful leadership of Dr. Jan van Wagtendonk, a careful student of the technique during his university years and a person willing to take the risk of putting theory into practice. He was mentored by Dr. Harold H. Biswell, a pioneer educator in fire ecology at the School of Forestry, University of California, Berkeley. A burn "prescription" is a measurement of several factors including moisture content in forest fuels and soil, weather patterns, terrain, and density of undergrowth. The trained crew that carried out the program in the park was small compared to the much larger contingent of fire suppression crews stationed in Yosemite Valley and elsewhere to instantly respond to structural fire emergencies and out-of-control forest fires.

There was a definite stress point between the two programs; even a physical separation. Yosemite Fire Chief Don Cross maintained his substantial cache of large fire trucks, emergency generators, chain saws, breathing apparatus, protective clothing, communications equipment, and tools at the park maintenance yard. His proud crews were easily identified by their vivid yellow shirts and hardhats. The handful of nondescript prescribed burn experts, equipped with a couple of pickup trucks capable of carrying slip-on water tanks and some hand tools, operated from the superintendent's old house far from Cross's domain. Even when prescribed burns were underway, flames crawling along, the "turf problem" persisted. Woe to a prescribed burn person who might need to borrow a piece of equipment or ask for additional help from the Fire Chief. Cross made crystal clear to me and others that his job was to put fires out, not nursemaid them. I had to step in more than once and order cooperation.

In microcosm, Cross represented a split in attitude that exists in many land management agencies. Prescribed burning has had its ups and downs, sometimes tragically so when control has been lost. Specialists in fire suppression often take a dim view of other specialists who deliberately walk through the forest with dripping fire torches. But at Yosemite, van Wagtendonk, Steve Botti, Charisse Sydoriak, and their like-minded contemporaries were immensely successful, so much so that we started referring to the "asbestos forest," those portions of the park wildscape where the combustible underbrush fuel load had been set back through cautious "cool" burning. For several years thereafter, any subsequent fire that might be caused by lightening or human error in the prescribed burn zones could not grip enough fuel on the ground to gain hazardous momentum. In the meantime, the natural cycles of the forest were renewed and energized. Over the years, more than 55,000 acres of forest habitat in Yosemite have been successfully burned under prescription control, bringing laudable health to the park's ecosystem.

NPS personnel also must be sensitive to the competing demands of visitors and wildlife. More than 250 wildlife species are found in Yosemite, absent one magnificent creature, the California Golden Bear (grizzly bear), resplendent on the state flag but eliminated by the gun. The last known grizzly in California was shot and killed in the Sierra foothills in the 1920s, not far from Yosemite. Other species cling to tenuous existence aided by the safety of parklands. They are susceptible to habitat disruptions and lethal practices unconsciously or consciously brought into the mountains by humans.

     Your Yosemite: **PROTECTING A PUBLIC TREASURE**

NPS resource managers try to restore and maintain suitable habitat for wildlife, attempting to enlist park visitors as their enlightened partners.

The Yosemite Conservancy is proving to be an active pathway for volunteer involvement as are nature programs, museum displays, literature, and volunteer projects oriented toward the need to help nurture and perpetuate indigenous species. Richard West Sellars, in his book, *Preserving Nature in the National Parks*, reports that Dr. Carl Russell, Yosemite's superintendent from 1947 to 1952, called for a "full understanding of our responsibilities as trustees." Implicit in Russell's plea was strong recognition that hardheaded, objective scientific inquiry is essential if the National Park Service is to determine "what it is protecting, and what it must protect against."

Russell and his scientifically inclined colleagues were keenly aware that several of the NPS's prewar policies were difficult to defend in the name of park conservation. In Yellowstone, bison and elk had been fenced in so that visitors could readily see them. NPS-sanctioned "reductions" of wolves, mountain lions, and coyotes were routinely implemented in many national parks on the mistaken premise that predators must be eliminated in order to allow more attractive, less frightening, visitor-worthy species to thrive. One of these predators, a mountain lion cub that survived the extermination of her family in Yosemite by a government-paid hunter, was kept on display in the park for several years. Her cage and the cages of several other incarcerated species, including unlucky bears, deer, and other lions, made up a small zoo, fortunately closed for good in 1932.

BEARS AND THEIR NEIGHBORS

The mosquitoes in Yosemite probably are more aware and appreciative of human visitors than any other of the hundreds of wildlife species that are found in the park. Black bears and jays, known respectively for their food-raider prowess, are inclined toward similar near encounters with humans, although not quite so close as mosquitoes. Deer are adaptable to the nearby presence of humans and frequently provide photo opportunities, but they are wary and ready to flee if humans intrude too abruptly into their personal space. Hawks, eagles, falcons, and owls surely take note of human interlopers and make strategic avian adjustments to their hunting territories if humans become too disruptive. The raptors and owls seem to conclude that humans are too heavy to carry away for dinner and, therefore, they are uninteresting. Fish and frogs scatter and hide if a human presence is detected, and even the tough species—badgers, mountain lions, bobcats, coyotes, rattlesnakes—avoid what they sense to be the extreme and threatening danger of humans. At Yosemite, and in any nature preserve, the living creatures that humans judge to be "wild" are trying to mind their own business, defend themselves and their young against predation, find food, shelter, and comfort, and rest when they can. The best wildlife news at Yosemite is that most park rangers and visitors have come to understand that they are safe in the company of the homegrown beings that share the park with them. Ferocious beasts can be left in comic books, video games, and movies. In the real world of Yosemite wild creatures and tame humans have found a truce, and the park lives.

Within the wilderness concept, visitors to our national parks are expected to respect and accommodate the many wild species, but adaptability flows both ways. Other species adapt themselves to our curious habits. The champion among them is the lovable black bear. The omnivorous bear diet consists of roots, berries, bugs, carrion, nuts, fish, and the occasional unlucky small mammal. Black bears easily learn and are always willing and eager to supplement this menu with the exotic foodstuffs many humans believe they must have to thrive—chips, tuna fish, soda pop, pizza, marshmallows, peanut butter, jam, eggs, bacon, and all the other good stuff in the human larder. By contrast, grizzly bears and their impressive cousins, the Alaskan brown bears, barely tolerate human interlopers in their realms and in some cases tolerate them not at all. In the lower forty-eight states, grizzlies are rare and found only in a handful of national park environments, primarily at Yellowstone and Glacier National Parks. They were eliminated from Yosemite country and throughout California decades ago when gunned down in a grossly uneven match by anxious humans with powerful rifles. Black bears are more ubiquitous, playfully at home in many parks and known to

 Your Yosemite: **PROTECTING A PUBLIC TREASURE**

happily ignore the official legislative line that separates designated wilderness from developed areas.

For many years, bears in the parks were treated almost as circus animals. Open-pit garbage dumps became theaters for the daily bear performance, complete with bleachers and platforms for the convenience of spectators who came to watch the show. Just such an open pit dump existed in the west end of Yosemite Valley until the 1940s. Visitors were encouraged to watch the bears, especially those cute little fuzzy cubs, feed on garbage. Park rangers were on hand to act as masters of ceremony, describing bear habits. The eventual discontinuation of the shows, and the much more delayed closing of the dumps, surely must have come as a disappointment to the generation of bears accustomed to these sites. But human food is still in the parks and bears are still tempted to try to get their share.

There is good reason why bears historically have been so popular in circuses. They are intelligent and trainable, and in the wild they have been known to train themselves. Snappy automobile convertibles are a case in point. In national parks like Yellowstone, Yosemite, and Glacier, bears learn that by placing their three or four hundred pounds of weight on a fabric top, often enhanced by a few tactical claw incisions, the result will be a quick, gravity-induced entry into the car's interior. Then the treasure hunt for that stray apple or bag of chips begins. If nothing of interest is found in the initial search, the trunk space often holds real promise. For a bear in the interior of an automobile the challenge is to rip out the back seat in order to gain access to the trunk. This can be an untidy business, but not an insurmountable test of skill. The real disappointment usually comes when a human appears on the scene and starts yelling at the bear to leave. Bears, frightened of people, typically retreat.

My wife and I had exactly this experience with a black bear when I assumed my first park ranger duties in Yellowstone. We had arrived in the park in our canary-yellow 1955 Ford Fairlane convertible, not exactly the kind of car for Yellowstone country. On an autumn day, we parked along the edge of a park road and hiked into the woods to a small pond known for its aquatic beauty. On return, using a different trail route, we reached the roadway about a half-mile from where the car was parked. In a light rain, we started walking toward the car. Just then a motorist happened by. He slowed to a stop, rolled down his window, and asked, "Do you own that car up the road?" I said, "Yes." "Well, there's a bear in it," he reported, then rolled up his window and drove off. When we reached the car, the bear was gone, leaving only the evidence behind, a caved-in convertible top, claw marks on the black-and-yellow pseudo-leather seats, and puddles of rainwater on the floor boards.

A modern national park campground in bear country is equipped with chest-sized, bear-proof iron lockers strategically located for use by visitors. The lockers are supplemented by garbage containers with heavy iron lids and mailbox-style pivoting deposit slots that prevent bear-paw entry. When visitors are away from their campsites, they are directed to put their excess food in the lockers for safe-keeping and not to leave garbage lying around. The campground at White Wolf in Yosemite on the road to Tuolumne Meadows and Tioga Pass was known during my tenure as a particularly favored location for bear invasions. After the park maintenance workers put the iron food lockers and bear-proof garbage cans in place, the calculating bears decided to spend their time elsewhere. Similarly, backcountry trekkers have learned to use portable, pipe-like canisters that, on a much smaller scale, serve the same purpose as the campground food lockers.

Rangers at Yosemite perform a kind of wildland ballet with black bears that too boldly cross into the developed portions of the park. The live trap commonly used to incarcerate troublesome bears is a large piece of culvert pipe equipped with fragrant bait and mounted on a trailer chassis. When the bear crawls into the culvert and pulls on the baited trigger, a heavy metal door at the entrance to the trap, held in place by a rod attached to the trigger, is released and slams down to block escape. The captive bear is then usually hauled off to a remote corner of the park, sedated, equipped with a high-tech tracking collar, and turned loose. The hope is that the bear will find succor in natural habitat far from its former raiding territory, or at least not get back to the point of capture before the ranger does.

     Your Yosemite: **PROTECTING A PUBLIC TREASURE**

In designated wilderness areas, the bears and other wild creatures and plants within are judged by humans to be at home. Humans have placed themselves outside the perimeter, defining their status when visiting as that of a guest. Former Secretary of the Interior Stewart Udall (1920-2010) made a salient point about inscribed naturalness when he said, "Plans to protect air and water, wilderness and wildlife are in fact plans to protect man." Within this context, it can be said that if allowed to falter, national park areas across the country and around the world, these bastions of wildlife almost free, will signal a danger to all of us that may prove irreversible.

The call by Dr. Russell and other ecologists for more science-based decision-making as a professional salute to the natural landscape and its wild, indigenous residents has been taken up vigorously by the NPS. An article of professional faith is that the national parks can serve as vital "field laboratories" for the study of natural processes, not only what was happening within the parks, but also what was taking place around them. A 1961 report by Howard R. Stagner (chief of the NPS Branch of Natural History) entitled "Get the Facts, and Put Them to Work," captured the anxieties of Russell and others by contending that the parks were "rapidly becoming islands" in a developing landscape of logging, mining, hunting, grazing, water control, farming, and swelling rural settlement. Park perimeters were no guarantee that environmental threats could be held at bay or, for that matter, entirely understood.

During the Mission 66 era, even as the battle was being fought over the Tioga Road, park crews were instructed to spray the toxic poison, malathion, in Tuolumne Meadows to control mosquitoes and the invasive needle miner insect that was attacking the Lodge Pole Pine. Malathion is considered by scientists to be a low-toxicity pesticide that may be used in areas of human habitation, but it eventually breaks down into malaoxan, which is sixty times more toxic. Use of Malathion in urban centers is suspected to cause high mortality in aquatic species once it enters the water supply. Tuolumne Meadows is a water-supply sponge in the high headwaters of the similarly named river, and the source of San Francisco's Hetch Hetchy water. At the time, pesticide poisoning was a popular tool throughout the United States and routinely used in the national parks. Park crew members who were assigned the spraying task were issued no protective clothing or respirators. As Jay Johnson, one of my colleagues at Yosemite who had worked as a young man on one of the Malathion crews, reminisced, "We walked through clouds of the stuff."

The entire nation would learn in Rachel Carson's seminal book, *Silent Spring*, how we were poisoning ourselves. Within its pages rested a stunning indictment of chemical industry officials and their surrogates in the U. S. Department of Agriculture for ignoring scientific proof that the nonchalant use of the long-term synthetic pesticides DDT, Dieldrin, Toxaphene, and Heptaclor were poisoning life forms dependent on the sanctity of the land. Carson said of the message in her book, "What I discovered was that everything which meant the most to me as a naturalist was being threatened, and that nothing I could do would be more important." A *Time Magazine* report stated, "Carson was violently assailed by threats of lawsuits and derision, including suggestions that this meticulous scientist was a hysterical woman unqualified to write such a book." This particular "hysterical" woman kept going, delivering scientific facts in a manner that swept the nation with her message. Other scientists supported Carson and use of many of the severe poisons so casually at hand is no longer permitted. There is very good reason why these substances were marked with a skull-and-crossbones. I wonder what Carson would be saying today about global warming.

A WILDERNESS QUOTA

Women have not had an easy time finding their qualified places in natural resources stewardship positions, an exclusive domain of assumed male ruggedness for many decades. When I attended university in the 1950s studying to become a park ranger there was one brave woman in my freshman class. She did not return the following year. In my first posting to Yellowstone, there was one woman in the ranger ranks, a scientist who worked almost solely by herself. Park Ranger Laurel (Munson) Boyers was not going to let this habit of maleness stand in her way at Yosemite. A proud graduate of the Castle horse patrol school, just not quite in the dramatic style of Tom Smith, her preference was to find her NPS career journey in the Yosemite wilderness, more often on foot than on horseback carrying essentials in a backpack, and finding the miles of trails to be "a match for me in a matchless place." She did not worry about being alone, enjoying the trust she placed in herself, pitching camp, protecting her health, sharing space with resident wildlife, and enjoying the goodwill among trekkers she met along the way. Only on a few occasions did Boyers experience "freaky" moments, sometimes weather-related, once or twice when she got lost, and sporadically when a man might pay too much unwanted attention. Mostly she enjoyed the kind of friendly, informal, and satisfying alliance commonly shared in the outback among those eager to exchange information about trail conditions, good camping locations, special wilderness features, and news of the outside world.

Mentored by her supervisor, Park Ranger Ron Mackie, she, in turn, advanced in rank to become a supervisory wilderness specialist. In this management role, she supervised seasonal rangers assigned to the park's most remote outposts, worked with the park-staff-at-large to improve safety and resource protection in the hundreds of thousands of acres under her purview. She also monitored concessionaire performance in the High Sierra Camps, contended with the mischievous humor of trail crews, and cheered their remarkable achievements. She often worked with little sleep, much practical judgment, and strong determination when emergencies, primarily caused by lost or injured people, took place within her territory. In so doing Boyers put many miles on her boot soles and left a figurative trail for other women to follow.

An oddity of the Yosemite wilderness is that, despite its vastness, overuse can occur. The backcountry permit system that was in place when I arrived at Yosemite in 1979 was judged by those on the NPS staff who had to administer it to be cumbersome and ineffective. Visitors who wanted to camp overnight in the backcountry were required to provide rangers with a detailed itinerary of their planned routes of travel through various "zones" within the backcountry that had been administratively designated by the NPS. Within these zones, the hikers and equestrians were directed to specific campsites. The concept was that the permit system would spread out use and reduce risk. In theory, the rangers would have some sense of where to begin looking if a backcountry trekker failed to return as scheduled.

In practice, however, rangers found that by designating campsites, they were in effect focusing human impact. The most favored campsites suffered the result, both in trampled down ground and messy waste. Professional pack outfitters were also returning again and again with their clients to the campsites that best fit their commercial needs, and the most popular trails were receiving an annual pounding. Many visitors felt the permit system to be overly restrictive by robbing them of the freedom and spontaneity that wilderness is supposed to offer.

Dr. Jan van Wagtendonk and his in-park scientific teammates, particularly Jim Benedict, P. R. Coho, and Charisse Sydoriak, decided to apply statistical Wilderness Simulation Modeling to the Yosemite backcountry in an attempt to match the expectations of wilderness trekkers with the ability of the landscape to withstand them. Van Wagtendonk had access to scientific findings from colleagues around the nation who were trying to solve similar problems in places like the Boundary Waters Canoe Area, Minnesota, and the Desolation Wilderness Area further north in the Sierra Nevada near Lake Tahoe. Laurel Boyers and Ron Mackie were responsible for the practical on-the-ground application of these statistical signals and worked closely with the scientists to develop an alternative administrative approach to Yosemite's wilderness.

After many months of analysis, including detailed interviews with backcountry users, the team developed a simple and elegant alternative to the permit system. Quotas would, instead, be established at the trailheads, thereby shifting emphasis from the heart of the wilderness to its entry points. Now visitors who intend to spend one or more nights camping in the backcountry may make reservations for use of a given trailhead or take their chances on a first-come, first-serve basis when they arrive in the park. Reservations are available for 60% of each trailhead's quota capacity. The remaining 40% is a daily up-for-grabs offering to the quickest of the wilderness clientele. If a quota has been reached at a particular trailhead, rangers

   Your Yosemite: **PROTECTING A PUBLIC TREASURE**

can often refer prospective trekkers to alternate entry points where quota slots are still available.

The quota system has proven to be simple to understand and easy to use. Although viewed skeptically in the beginning by some park visitors, it has also found wide acceptance among those who venture forth. Once across the wilderness line, the adventurer can go where she or he chooses, stopping to camp wherever fading daylight and muscle fatigue suggest, changing routes as desired, and wandering back to civilization when so inclined. The zones and specified campsites under the old permit system have been replaced by more freedom of choice and a strong dose of individual responsibility that is in keeping with the whole idea of wilderness. This solution also proved that park visitors are more than willing to join in partnership with rangers and scientists in finding the balance between preservation and use in national parks if the mechanics are judged to be fair and beneficial.

Hikers who step across the wilderness line only for the day and those who have reservations at the High Sierra Camps are immune from the quotas. Many of the beaten-down backcountry campsites have been relieved of the pressure of constant use and are recovering to a more natural state. The trailhead quotas have effectively added freedom and softened use in the backcountry. Boyers described the issue succinctly: "Yosemite is so heavily used, but it's resilient if given a chance."

14

Not So Great

IN EARLY 1986, Yosemite was functioning as usual. The wilderness was closeted again in winter's grip, no one was missing, fundraising results were amazing, and we were planning the next mini-steps to implement the 1980 plan. The only exception to the routine was a complex and lengthy investigation by law enforcement rangers into rumored trafficking and persistent illegal use of drugs in the park, a reflection of this corrosive problem in society-at-large. Arrests were being made and the investigation was on-going.

That January, I was attending a meeting at the NPS design and engineering center in Denver, Colorado, when my boss, Western Regional Director Howard Chapman, informed me that I was being reassigned "immediately" to a desk job in San Francisco. The genesis for this order, I learned, was the recording I had made three years earlier at the Cushman meeting.

A park ranger named Paul Berkowitz, who I did not know at the time of the recording, had handled the tape equipment. Subsequently, in succeeding years, he had become dissatisfied with law-enforcement activities at Yosemite, so much so that he asked to testify in October, 1985, at a Congressional subcommittee fact-finding hearing held in the park. The hearing was intended to invite comment on general park management issues, including law enforcement activities. At the hearing, Berkowitz alleged possible misuse of funds and tampering with evidence within Yosemite's law enforcement structure, singling out his supervisors. The chairman of the subcommittee, Congressman Bruce Vento, was so startled that he promptly adjourned the hearing and called for an immediate investigation of the allegations by the federal General Accounting Office. A few weeks after the hearing, in January, 1986, Berkowitz felt compelled to send letters to NPS Director William Penn Mott and members of Congress tying my lapse with Cushman to his other severe criticisms of park investigative activities. He claimed that he was forced by his supervisors to handle the recording equipment, adding the specious claim that the recording had been illegal. For me, the result was swift and blunt. When NPS Director Mott learned of the recording incident, he ordered my immediate transfer from Yosemite. The newspaper headlines were sensational. One example was a *Los Angeles Times* headline proclaiming that, "Yosemite Chief Firing Tied to Ranger Morale, Crime." I was in shock and so was my family.

A few days after I cleaned out my office, a subsequent McClatchy News Service headline, dated January 20, 1986, read, "U.S. Clears Yosemite Drug Probers": As reported by Gene Rose, "Federal investigators have cleared Yosemite law enforcement officers of allegations they acted improperly while probing illegal drug activities in the park between 1982 and 1984. A General Accounting Office investigation found there was no basis to any of the 11 allegations made in October by Yosemite Ranger Paul Berkowitz, said Representative Bruce Vento, Chairman of the Subcommittee on National Parks and Recreation. The General Accounting Office has spent considerable time looking into Mr. Berkowitz's charges, particularly the five specific charges of possible criminal misconduct, Vento said. The GAO found no evidence of criminal conduct, but more importantly no basis to support such allegations."

For me and most of the park ranger corps at Yosemite, the result of the investigation was welcome, restorative news. Unfortunately, I was receiving this news at my desk in San Francisco. Some months after my abrupt exit from the park, Mott, having learned more of the facts about the Berkowitz allegations, and as a gesture of support, offered me the superintendent position at the Santa Monica National Recreation Area in the Los Angeles basin, or, alternatively, said he would urge California Governor Pete Wilson to appoint me as Director of the California State Park System. I considered the state park opportunity and was interviewed by Governor Wilson, but, instead, and still in a twit, decided on early retirement from the NPS in order to take my chances outside of government. That did not last long. My wife and I were soon on the move again, this time all the way back across the country where I was to serve as Assistant Commissioner in the New York Department of Environmental Conservation in the administration of Governor Mario Cuomo. From there, I received the honor of succeeding Nash Castro, a highly regarded conservation leader, as Executive Director of the Palisades Interstate Park Commission.

POLITICAL DRIFT

Yosemite's centennial year in 1990 was supposed to be a milepost year marking the attainment of many of the goals identified in the publicly endorsed *General Management Plan*. Park use was at an all-time high, reaching the amazing level of four million visitors per year, double the number of only a decade earlier when I arrived in the park. Miserable crowding in Yosemite Valley on the busiest days had become a given. Better news was that people of all ethnic backgrounds were coming to the park, including thousands upon thousands of visitors from other nations. The park's popularity was evidence that Yosemite is firmly woven into America's cultural fabric, so much so that many who visit the park assume that the preservation experiment started there in 1864 to be successfully concluded.

A signal to the contrary was a 1989 "Examination Report" issued by the NPS that called into question some of the planning assumptions for the park. The report hinted that restrictions on commercial development might be softened, a contradiction to the publicly supported effort to reduce development in Yosemite Valley. A front page article in the Yosemite Association newsletter called the report "disturbing" and charged that it "effectively repudiated" the 1980 GMP. In a *Los Angeles Times* article entitled "Who Owns Yosemite," Maura Dolan reported that "conservationists had assumed that the 1980s plan eventually would be enacted once funding became available, so the report stung like a broken promise." Although this "examination" vaguely claimed that "the Yosemite National Park of the future" would reflect earlier planning goals, Gene Rose, writing for the *McClatchy News Service*, pointed out that the "Examination Report" also claimed in seeming contradiction that many of the 1980 goals could not be achieved because they were unrealistic or too expensive.

Just as he had a decade before, Ed Hardy tried to tip the scales in favor of the Yosemite Park & Curry Company by urging that its customers make their opinions known about the need for more and better accommodations, but once again he did not get the result he was hoping for. Of the 4,250 public respondents, 87% supported the 1980 GMP; 2% thought that lodging in Yosemite should be increased from the existing 1,770 units while the rest were evenly split on whether accommodations should remain the same or be decreased; 65% thought employee housing should be decreased; 78% thought traffic should be limited.

Echoing these sentiments, journalist Kevin Roderick, also writing for the *Los Angeles Times*, quoted the superintendent in charge of the park during the centennial year, Michael V. Finley, as saying, "I think that the plan [the GMP] was developed with the greatest sincerity, but some things that seemed simple 10 years ago were not really so simple." Roderick commented that lack of action on the plan had resulted in "a storm of protest from conservation groups, lifelong hikers, and cliff-scaling daredevils who keep a close eye on anything that happens here—and who spent the 1980s confident that Yosemite would become more wild, not more commercial." In counterweight to the protest, spokespeople for the Yosemite Park & Curry Company echoed Superintendent Finley's contention that "the goals of reducing overnight accommodations and tearing out parking lots are out of date." The article concluded that "the bold plan has been left mostly on paper—and the future of Yosemite Valley left not much clearer today that it was 100 years ago." Yosemite National Park arrived at its centennial much as it began: in controversy.

BUSINESS UPHEAVAL

The most significant change in the valley during the centennial year was not initiated by the NPS, but came entirely from an unexpected direction. Matsushita Electric Industrial Company announced that it was in the process of acquiring the MCA Corporation. Matsushita employed more than 300,000 people worldwide and counted

Panasonic among its many subsidiary assets. If approval by financial regulators could be achieved, the $6.59 billion deal to purchase MCA would mark the largest Japanese acquisition of an American company on record.

Although the Yosemite Park & Curry Company was the largest concessionaire operation in the National Park Service, it was a very small part of the pending buyout, with an estimated book value of between $100 and $300 million. Nevertheless, the historic relationship between the NPS and the concessionaires was suddenly shaken by the image of foreign commercial dominion over Yosemite. The Secretary of the Interior, Manuel Lujan, Jr., serving in the administration of President George H. W. Bush, publicly stated that he did not stay in foreign-owned hotels or buy foreign cars. He warned that a transfer of Yosemite concessionaire services to a Japanese owner without government authorization might result in cancellation of the contract.

In the face of this challenge, MCA and Matsushita agreed to put the Yosemite concession into escrow and sell it within twelve months to an American buyer. Lujan was not satisfied: "I thought that was very arrogant of them. They have the attitude that they are bigger than the government." As it happened, Lujan had some leverage on his side of the argument because the NPS contract with the YP&CC was due to expire on September 30, 1993. The Secretary of the Interior could either obstruct the MCA/Matsushita transaction by withholding approval if the YP&CC was part of the deal or cancel the YP&CC contract outright, as he was threatening.

Lujan made clear that he did not want "this Japanese company" to gain exclusive rights under the existing concession contract "to do business in Yosemite." "I don't want foreign ownership," he said, prompting an observation in the *New York Times* that Lujan might be "flirting with racism." The larger question, of course, was whether any new concessionaire should have exclusive rights to such a lucrative contract.

In January, 1991, Matsushita agreed to sell the YP&CC to the National Park Foundation, in those years a little-known charitable arm of the NPS, at a bargain price of $49.5 million when the existing contract expired. During the remaining three-year term of the con-tact, Matsushita-MCA would donate $6 million to the Foundation from Yosemite profits. Using these donated funds as collateral, the Foundation would finance the purchase at 8.5% interest over fifteen years. A key factor was that so-called "possessory interest" in about 800 YP&CC buildings would be transferred through the Foundation to the NPS, thus breaking a hold on MCA's claim of outright own-ership of commercial facilities in the park. In essence, the National Park Foundation was being used as a conduit for this complicated transaction. After Matsushita was out of the picture, the assumption was that a new concessionaire with American credentials acceptable to Lujan would step in to take control at Yosemite, relieving the foundation of its debt in the process.

Many of us felt that this unexpected turn of events was an excellent opportunity for the National Park Foundation to simply hold on to the YP&CC after the transaction was completed, employ experi-enced business people to operate the company, and plow the prof-its, estimated to be $10-$15 million per year, back into stewardship needs at Yosemite and other parks. Here was a chance for commer-cial Yosemite and preservation Yosemite to find a creative merger opportunity. After all, large charitable corporations successfully operate throughout the nation. This would be a radical departure from business-as-usual in the national parks. Lujan was not wresting the YP&CC contract from Matsushita in order to convert Nation-al Park Service concession activities to not-for-profit status. He was simply eager to pass along those activities at Yosemite to the next private vendor and the next group of stockholders.

Still, the not-for-profit idea was sparked to life in the buyout deal by the involvement of the National Park Foundation. What better result than to allow millions of dollars in commercial income to be reinvested on behalf of those who spent those dollars, the members of the public who are the true owners of the park? If the National Park Foundation was not going to claim the prize, perhaps another nonprofit group could do so, thereby causing a mighty shift that would benefit park stewardship by creating a fusion of commercial and conservation practices at Yosemite.

     Your Yosemite: **PROTECTING A PUBLIC TREASURE**

As other potential investors were lining up to bid on the Yosemite contract, Steve Medley, the Executive Director of the Yosemite Association and a fervent believer in the national park ideal, telephoned me and suggested that I have a conversation with William Alsup about the nonprofit possibility. Alsup was a San Francisco-based attorney and a highly skilled landscape photographer. He had spent many hours roaming the High Sierra, camera in hand, capturing images that were reflective of one of his role models, Ansel Adams.

Alsup agreed that a not-for-profit bidder for the Yosemite contract was a superlative idea and he took the lead in organizing a consortium to make it possible. The group included investment banker Bernard Butcher, Executive Director of the Wilderness Society George Frampton, the philanthropist Richard Goldman, Peter Dangermond, a former Director of the California Department of Parks and Recreation, Dr. Richard Martyr, the Executive Director of the American Youth Hostel Association, Dr. Edgar Wayburn, physician and former President of the Sierra Club, Attorney Sarah Rockwell of the firm Morrison & Forester, Joan Reiss, Regional Director of the Wilderness Society in California, Alsup, and me. The nonprofit company was named the Yosemite Restoration Trust. Steve Medley could not participate due to an obvious conflict of interest, but he cheered us on from the sidelines.

A strong subsidiary organization, entitled the Yosemite Restoration Trust Services Corporation, was poised to step in and run day-to-day operations at the park should our not-for-profit initiative prevail in the bid process. Dr. Martyr was selected as chairman and CEO of the subsidiary corporation and was backed by highly experienced board members including Stuart Cross, former president of the Yosemite Park & Curry Company and chairman of the Conference of National Park Concessioners; Robert Maynard, president of the Aspen Ski Corporation; Frank Wells, president and CEO of the Walt Disney Company; Michael Glennie, former manager of the Waldorf Astoria Hotel and president of Rockresorts, Boca Raton, Florida; Nancy Glaser, a specialist in equity financing in the retail industry; Thomas Klutznick, chairman and CEO of the Urban Investment and Development Corporation; and Jim Sano, who had stepped away from his duties at Yosemite to become Vice President and CEO of Innerasia Expeditions, a San Francisco-based company that specialized in hosting trips to the Himalayas.

The test for competitors who wished to bid on the Yosemite contract was to prove financial viability and professional capability. The NPS rightly established a businesslike framework for bids that would avoid haphazard or purely speculative ventures. Our group knew the rules and tried to comply by confirming access to $12 million in minimum working capital, as required by the NPS. This capital was pledged by several California banks and would be made available within 30 days should we be notified that we were the successful bidder. Accordingly, we submitted written documentation to NPS decision makers, including a guarantee that the expected millions in profits generated from sales would be reinvested in park stewardship projects at Yosemite and, if sufficient, in other national parks as well. We contended that experienced business people could be put in place to run the company, including veterans of the YP&CC with established track records who could be recruited to the cause. Our access to the lines-of-credit could be activated immediately should we win the bid.

When the final list of "qualified" bidders for the Yosemite contract was announced by NPS personnel in Washington, D. C., six for-profit corporations were approved. The Yosemite Restoration Trust Services Corporation was found "not qualified" and summarily dropped from consideration, supposedly due to a lack of sufficient cash in the bank and no prior resort-management experience. This seemed to us to be very hazy logic on the part of those at NPS headquarters in Washington, D. C., who had evaluated our bid. Our board members obviously had excellent business, fiscal, and legal credentials and we were ready to step in on day one to meet our management and financial obligations. Nonetheless, we were disqualified.

Our consortium had little recourse other than to engage in a brief legal tussle to try to regain a position in the bid process. That possibility fell beyond our reach when a judge made a preliminary review of the circumstances and advised that, in her view, we could not prove "overwhelmingly" that we had been wrongfully treated. Sad-

   Your Yosemite: **PROTECTING A PUBLIC TREASURE**

ly, right before our eyes, had been the possibility that commercial revenue generated in parks by concessionaires could be reinvested in the parks on behalf of the users. This was a notable opportunity lost. The Yosemite Restoration Trust, designed to channel commercial activities to the park's well-being, instead would become an advocacy group, keeping a watchful eye on events to come, and, as these events unfolded, forced to become a defender of Yosemite Valley against even more commercial abuse.

At the conclusion of the bid process the Delaware North Corporation based in Buffalo, New York, was declared the winner, picking up its first-ever national park concession contract. After seventy-five years, including twenty years as subsidiary of the MCA Corporation, the Yosemite Park & Curry Company, was no more. Delaware North received a fifteen-year contract with projected gross income of $1 billion. Tucked into the details was the proviso that the new concessionaire agreed to remove twenty-seven derelict underground fuel tanks left behind by the YP&CC, an unexciting but important step toward reclaiming environmental health in the park.

The upset precipitated by the Matsushita buyout brought about several positive changes at Yosemite. Delaware North was required to pay a 4.5% franchise fee for the privilege of operating the business monopoly in Yosemite, more than four times the 0.75% fee paid by the YP&CC. The newly empowered company also agreed to forego "preferential rights," theoretically opening the door for fresh and vigorous competition when the Yosemite contract again would come up for renewal. Specialists on the NPS staff in Washington, D.C. judged that these changes were more in keeping with resort industry standards and Delaware North accepted.

In a stroke of good management judgment, Delaware North selected Dan Jensen as the chief operating officer for its Yosemite operation (he would later be promoted to president). Jensen formerly had been the controller (account executive) for the YP&CC. He was a native of Visalia in the nearby Central Valley, a "local boy" who first saw Yosemite at a young age. Like so many before and since, Jensen was captivated by the grandeur that surrounded him. He was obligated to watch the bottom line for Delaware North and seek profits wherever possible, but Jensen also was more of the "old school," a Yosemite devotee, who, with his family, sought a lifestyle as well as a job in the park.

THE FLOOD

Delaware North settled in and it was business as usual until 1997 when the park's fortunes were altered by a commanding presence, Mother Nature. When atypical weather patterns combine to dump heavy early-season snow in the High Sierra followed by unseasonably warm rain, humans in the valley must scramble to elevated ground where they can only watch, marvel, and wait. Flooding has been part of the Yosemite Valley scene for eons, long before people were around to record these events. When people did finally take note, major floods were documented in 1889, 1937, 1955, and 1964. Then came the flood of 1997. Four feet of snow piled up in the High Sierra during December, 1996. Heavy rain followed, beginning on New Year's Day. Unpoetically speaking, Yosemite Valley is a giant tub fed by many spigots, but with only one drain, the Merced River. When a combination of early snow saturated by warm rain occurs, these spigots, Vernal and Nevada Falls, Tenaya Creek, Yosemite Falls, Bridalveil and their many lesser kin are turned on full force. That January, the spigots overwhelmed the valley.

As the flood waters swept through before plunging into the constricted downstream exit toward El Portal, roads were obliterated, the sewer system that connects the valley to the treatment plant in El Portal was severed, all three water wells in Yosemite Valley were damaged, and support legs for the towers that feed 69,000-volts of electricity into the valley were undermined. Three hundred guest accommodations at Yosemite Lodge filled with five-to-eight-feet of water and 250 units at the housekeeping camp near Curry Village did the same. Nine hundred campsites were inundated while picnic tables and garbage cans disappeared down the Merced River. The historic Yosemite Chapel held tenuously to its foundation, water splashing through the building. A grinding swirl of trees, rocks, and debris of all types churned along in the flood.

When the floodwaters receded, the initial estimate for damage repair ranged from a low of $10 million to a high of $100 million, depending on the degree to which structures, utility systems, roads, campsites, and parking lots were included in the assessment. (One insurance adjuster placed the cost of repair to commercial facilities at $4 million, perhaps assuming that squeegees and paint would suffice.) Special funding was obviously needed to restore visitor and administrative services in Yosemite Valley, but logic suggested, too, that the moment finally had arrived to honor the basic findings of the 1980 *General Management Plan*, at least to the extent of eliminating buildings from the valley's flood zone.

Instead, the NPS found itself in the almost unprecedented position of receiving millions of dollars in authorized funding from the U.S. Congress to actually expand development in the valley. The power behind this generous windfall was Congressman George P. Radanovich. Radanovich is a genial man born in the Yosemite gateway community of Mariposa, who, after briefly serving as a County Commissioner, was elected to the House of Representatives in the "Republican Revolution" of 1994 as representative of California's 19th Congressional District, a slice of foothill and agricultural lands extending from Yosemite to neighborhoods in Fresno. He proudly claimed to be the "first full-time winemaker elected to Congress since Thomas Jefferson" and won an impressive majority of votes using the campaign slogan, "Run, George, Run."

At the time of the flood, only in his second term but soon to become Chairman of the House of Representatives Subcommittee on National Parks, Radanovich was in a key political position to seek maximum support from his congressional colleagues for Yosemite flood repair monies. He was a businessman whose hometown had been heavily dependent on Yosemite-generated commerce since the gold rush days. Similarly, the gateway community of Oakhurst, also in his district, was thriving on Yosemite traffic.

Commercial development within the park has had obvious trickle-down economic benefit for the gateway communities, but a reasonable assumption is that wise limits on these services within the park would encourage millions of visitors to become better acquainted with the towns they now only hurry through to reach the valley. My own view has long been that the gateway communities of Mariposa, Oakhurst, Fish Camp, Lee Vining, and Groveland would benefit enormously if they became the predominant overnight destinations for Yosemite-bound visitors rather than second cousins to the park's business monopoly. These communities have repeatedly demonstrated their ability to provide quality services and they certainly are integral to the history of the Yosemite region. But habit is hard to break. Behind the inflated appropriation of monies for Yosemite was the attitude that a bigger trickle was preferable to a shift in policy.

This attitude is somewhat understandable. Far less understandable was the sudden new level of development being proposed and bankrolled in Yosemite Valley after so many years of seeking to soften development. In addition to urgent repair of roads, utility systems, and campgrounds was a project to smoother Camp 4, the climber's campground, with three-story dormitory buildings to house concessionaire employees. Tom Frost, a respected photographer, equipment specialist, and rockcrafter who had climbed in Yosemite and elsewhere with such luminaries as Royal Robbins, Yvon Chouinard, and Sir Edmund Hillary took a very dim view of this gambit and brought a law suit against the NPS to stop it. In short order, he was joined in protest by the American Alpine Club. The dormitory project was dropped and, in 2003, Camp 4 was added to the National Register of Historic Places. Yosemite Lodge, hard hit by the flood, was to be expanded by one- hundred rooms. In the west end of the valley, at Taft Toe, a "temporary" parking lot for 1,800 cars was proposed. This was the same Taft Toe that had been so threatened eighteen years earlier when a similar proposal was considered and thankfully rejected. In an astonishing exercise in reverse logic the flood was being used as a reason to enlarge infrastructure in the valley.

   Your Yosemite: **PROTECTING A PUBLIC TREASURE**

Coincidentally, the NPS had begun work a year before the flood on two new plans, the *Valley Plan* and the *Merced Wild and Scenic River Comprehensive Management Plan*, to supplement the original 1980 GMP as the guiding blueprints for future park development. The 1980 plan had been 81 pages. The *Merced River Plan*, when first offered for public scrutiny, was a forbidding 1,300 pages and weighed 14.5 pounds. It focused on the entire 122-mile length of the Merced River and its tributaries from the headwaters in the High Sierra, through Yosemite Valley, past El Portal, and down the Merced River Canyon to the Don San Pedro Reservoir on the edge of the Central Valley.

Its thesis was that for planning purposes the entire river ecosystem must be considered as a robust natural entity, an assertion that prompted little fundamental disagreement among those who debate the future of Yosemite. In the eyes of many, the plan as presented for public review was heavy on new structures, tepid on traffic control, and silent on use capacity. Some thought it might even be intended as a smokescreen to justify a thrust toward more development in Yosemite Valley in conjunction with Radanovich's funding initiative.

The ever-watchful Jim Snyder was dismayed by the "planning frenzy" prompted by the flood, writing, "For all the talk of restoration, flood response and planning signaled the demise of the ability to take things as they come, to recognize human frailties as part of the landscape, and to live with the landscape's processes. The 1997 flood marked the end of an agency conception of people and rivers as inseparable elements of the Yosemite landscape, supplanted with a domineering, polarizing view of people and the land as competing, even conflicting elements of the world." The NPS's new vision, apparently buttressed by the irresistible lure of Congress's promised millions, suggested a detour, if not a complete course reversal, on the path toward eased crowding in Yosemite Valley.

The Yosemite Restoration Trust, under the leadership of Janet Cobb, Dr. Hal Browder, and Walter Kieser stepped forward to urge renewed public dialog in the Yosemite planning process. Buoyed by financial support from the David and Lucile Packard Foundation, the Trust commended the NPS "for its continuing efforts to work with the public to develop lasting and enforceable protection for Yosemite," but also lamented the "unrealized" promise of the "shelf-dweller," the 1980 GMP. The Trust Board of Directors worried about the threat to the valley "glutted with more than $177 million in new visitor facilities and employee housing." These messages had teeth. The Trust had found allies in nine other organizations including the National Park Conservation Association, the Natural Resources Defense Council, and the Wilderness Society collectively representing over one-million members. Cobb, Browder, Kieser and their Board colleagues brought particular focus to creation of "a transit-based system for day-use visitors to Yosemite Valley during the peak visitation months of June through September," and urged a "day-use reservation system" to mitigate overcrowding. A grant of $300,000 was provided by the California Department of Transportation in support of the transit system initiative.

THE NPS TAKEN TO COURT

On another front, the Sierra Club joined with the locally organized Friends of Yosemite Valley and Mariposans for Environmentally Responsible Growth, made up primarily of residents from the gateway communities and, in August, 1998, filed a lawsuit to stop the proposed expansion of the park's commercial facilities. On the Mariposans board was Len McKenzie, the retired Yosemite Chief Naturalist. The Friends group also included a Yosemite NPS retiree, backcountry Supervisory Park Ranger Ron Mackie.

The following year, in a hearing before Federal District Judge Joseph Breyer, National Park Service representatives wisely rescinded the proposal to add rooms and buildings at flood-prone Yosemite Lodge, but otherwise reserved the right to proceed with repairs and new construction in the park. They also refused to define how these projects related to an overall visitor capacity for Yosemite Valley. Soon after, sixty-one organizations represented by the public interest Western Environmental Law Center issued another legal challenge, asserting that ever more people cannot be crammed into seven-square-mile Yosemite Valley as though the valley had infinite

          Your Yosemite: **PROTECTING A PUBLIC TREASURE**

space. The litigants contended that the National Park Service was obligated under existing law to define logical use limits for this precious piece of public real estate as an essential part of any new planning initiative.

Before long, legal proceedings to determine the parameters for future planning and development in Yosemite were in full swing, with the National Park Service on the defense. Government lawyers were in place to argue the merits of *Merced River Plan* findings that seemed to support large expenditures of funds to rehabilitate the flood-damaged park without grappling with the knotty use-capacity question. Lawyers representing the alliance of plaintiffs wanted the NPS to

Russell Tanaka photo

Park Ranger Ron Mackie

draw a bright and clear planning line and say "no development beyond here." The agency's refusal to do so meant that many of the very individuals and organizations that normally cheered and supported the National Park Service found themselves in the position of fighting against it.

Ron Mackie did not expect to find himself actively involved in the legal proceedings against his former employer. He had served in Yosemite for thirty-seven-years, starting on a trail crew before finding his first ranger job at the South Entrance to the park near Wawona. He subsequently moved up through the ranks until he was exactly in the right place at the right time to secure what he describes as "the best job in the world" when he succeeded his mentor and friend Roger Rudolph as Yosemite's wilderness park ranger. Mackie held that position for twenty-two years.

When he retired in 1997 he assumed that he would maintain a general, arm's length interest in National Park Service activities until he learned that the flood was being used as an excuse to push more development into Yosemite Valley. The unwritten NPS protocol has always been to voice concerns from within and be deferential from without. The "old guard" should defer to the new generation of managers, give advice when asked, volunteer if help is needed, provide institutional knowledge if sought, enjoy alumni gatherings, golf outings, and picnics with old friends and otherwise stay out of the way. Certainly, that was Mackie's intent, but he decided that he could not just stand by and watch his park be damaged by good intentions gone wrong.

Many were surprised when Mackie joined the legal challenge against the NPS, but he understood that his detailed knowledge of the park would be useful in the legal proceedings and he did not hesitate. He explained that he had taken to heart the language in the 1916 Act of Congress requiring that national parks be left "unimpaired for the enjoyment of future generations." Expanding the resort infrastructure in Yosemite was not Mackie's idea of leaving the park unimpaired.

Others of course had contrary views. Congressman Radanovich held a field hearing in the park on Earth Day, 2003. He made clear that efforts to reduce facilities, relocate campsites, or boost public transit as an access alternative for the car-infested valley did not have his support. Charles Cushman, now the founder and executive director of the American Land Rights Association, was back in the valley with a group of demonstrators. Ever the showman, he provided black-and-white striped prison costumes for some of the demonstrators apparently to imply that park visitors were captives in an environmental jail. Radanovich followed up the hearing by introducing legislation in Congress to "block plans to slash day-use parking by one-third and encourage the public to swap private cars for clean-air buses to reach the valley," as reported in the *Los Angeles Times*. The NPS was caught between Yosemite's rocks (and floods) and the hard spot of spiraling demand, trying on the one hand to reorient toward more use control while at the same time attempting not to tread on free-choice access to the park.

The legal challenge to the *Merced River Plan* eventually moved to the Ninth Circuit Court of Appeals in San Francisco. In October, 2003, the court ruled in favor of the plaintiffs, finding that the absence of defined use capacities in the plan was a major flaw at odds with federal environmental requirements. The judge ordered the NPS to prepare a new and revised plan based on a transparent and well-reasoned analysis of limits that must be imposed in order to maintain an acceptable balance between use and preservation at Yosemite.

When the court finding was announced, Mackie was quoted as saying, "this ruling is the greatest thing which ever happened to Yosemite. For years we have been fighting this concept of planning without first determining user capacity to protect the park's natural environment." Even then, however, the NPS was unwilling to back down. The legal proceedings subsequently entered that dark labyrinth of appeal that only judges and lawyers cherish, not to surface again for three more years.

National Park Service planners, responding to the court's initial ruling, began to crunch numbers yet again in a complex process of public input and data analysis. In 2004, "specific measurable limits on use" in Yosemite Valley were defined and submitted for further consideration by plaintiffs, defendants, and the public-at-large. These limits were remarkably similar in scale and intent to the numbers produced a quarter century earlier in the 1980 plan, the amount of lodging to be maintained in the valley was almost identical, total number of campsites somewhat reduced, and day-use parking numbers considerably higher. Unlike the 1980 plan, there was no call for elimination of automobile congestion, but otherwise the idea of significantly expanding commercial development as a peculiar cure for flood damage had been replaced by the goal of slightly reducing the human footprint and emphasizing environmental compatibility and safety.

In the meantime, the legal proceedings continued to drag on. In 2008, Federal District Judge Anthony Ishii issued a decree that found additional fault with the *Merced River Plan*. He announced that legal environmental procedures had not been adequately followed, even as the plan was being revised in response to the earlier Circuit Court of Appeals finding, now dated by three years, and almost a decade after Ron Mackie and his associates had stepped forward to challenge plan assumptions.

In a July, 2009, article in the *Fresno Bee*, Mark Gross reported that, "Nine years after creating a plan to limit crowds in Yosemite Valley, National Park Service officials are starting over again. Fresno will be the first stop on a tour from Sacramento to Pasadena where officials will seek public comment about protecting wildlife and the banks of the Merced River from crowds." In fact, the NPS was starting over again after thirty years, reaching out once again to connect with the true owners of Yosemite, the public-at-large.

It was not until October 1, 2009 that an *Associated Press* article appeared in the *Los Angeles Times* and other news outlets headlined, "U. S. To Delay Development in Yosemite Valley": "Ending a lengthy legal battle with environmentalists, the federal government agreed Wednesday to halt all commercial development in Yosemite National Park's most popular area and to consider limiting access to its wilderness. The settlement was reached by the National Park Service and two small environmental groups that sued the federal government in 2000. Under the agreement, the Park Service will delay all planned construction until at least December, 2012, when officials are expected to finish a far-reaching plan to manage and protect the [Merced] river. The settlement lays out a new process for park managers, consultants and the public to determine the maximum number of people who can visit certain areas in Yosemite."

Those not involved in this lengthy legal process are forgiven if their eyes roll at the thought of yet another round of planning for Yosemite. During the succeeding process the NPS suggested a use capacity in Yosemite Valley of 19,900 visitors per day controlled by traffic diversions when this maximum was reached. In an attempt to emphasize low impact non-commercial uses in the valley, the artificial swimming pools at Curry Village and Yosemite Lodge, as well as raft, bicycle, and horseback rentals, were proposed to be shut down, as was the ice rink at Curry Village. The NPS proposals were backed by 2,500-pages of details that the public was encouraged (once again) to critique.

One person not impressed with the renewed planning effort was Tom McClintock, representing California's 4th Congressional District that, when gerrymandered in 2011, encompassed Yosemite. McClintock claimed that some recommendations in the plan represented the "most radical and nihilistic fringe of the environmental left." He sits on the House of Representatives Subcommittee on National Parks, Forests, and Public Lands, and, as a member of the Republican majority, is in a powerful position to influence the plan's survival as was George Radanovich who retired from Congress in 2011.

In February, 2014, Yosemite Superintendent Don L. Neubacher announced release of a final plan for the park based on "rich collaboration between scientists, planners, American Indian tribes, stakeholder groups, and members of the public." Resting like a boulder within the plan is a daily "user capacity" for Yosemite Valley, pegged at 18,710 visitors. Of these, more than 15,000 could be staying overnight. The plan allows for a substantial increase in camping, a modest increase in parking, and a slight increase in overnight accommodations. Much attention is paid to flood plain and rock fall safety.

Congressman McClintock issued a statement in support, saying that, "The NPS has come a long way toward meeting the concerns expressed by park visitors, recreational groups, and local business and community leaders." He added, "I am particularly gratified that the final report has rejected radical proposals to close many traditional tourist amenities at the park, including swimming pools, raft and bike rentals, horseback riding stables, and ice skating and lodging facilities."

 The use capacity numbers are reflective of the most crowded summer days in the valley, and, on this, the NPS has taken a firm stand; enough is enough! After years of trying, the plan formalizes the simple notion that Yosemite indeed is finite, and that cramming its famous valley evermore with people and facilities would be a grievous quality defeat for everyone. The capacity number, large as it is, has given all visitors a victory; a chance to befriend Yosemite and to let the park give back genuine gifts of itself that are beyond purchase.

The view forward is toward better traffic control and an increasing acceptance of alternative transportation, restored habitat, better-quality facilities, and, finally, to a bright line that guards Yosemite from being overwhelmed by its very celebrity.

In the newest version of the plan, the superintendent's old house (Residence #1) that I refused to occupy in 1979 is slated, still, to be removed from the flood plain before it finally washes away down the Merced River in some big storm. That finding gives me a buzz of fiendish delight, but not so the fact that much of the maintenance, housing, and administrative imprint will remain in the valley. Regrettably, the ponderous NPS maintenance yard, tucked right under the base of Yosemite Falls, is slated to stay in place, including the jail which might better be consolidated with the county facilities in Mariposa. Still, after years of court battles and mulish development pressures, the words of Frederick Law Olmsted, written in 1865, have finally found anchor in a contemporary Yosemite plan, that "the rights of posterity as well as contemporary visitors" should be guarded, and that the park should be treated as "a trust for the whole nation."

OLD GUARD ON GUARD AGAIN

If, in the process of all this plan debate, Ron Mackie once seemed the exception for taking what seemed to be a lonely stand against the agency he cherished, he soon found out that he was not so lonely after all. Other NPS employees became so indignant about the environmental mischief surrounding the parks that custom gave way to the urgent need for advocacy to prevent the NPS from being driven into a ditch. In 2003, Bill Wade, former superintendent of Shenandoah National Park, was, like Mackie, so aghast at shenanigans aimed at the national parks that he and a handful of likeminded colleagues formed the Coalition of National Park Service Retirees (Coalition to Protect America's National Parks) and convinced more than six hundred of their contemporaries to join in defense of the agency. The organization's membership now exceeds eight hundred.

     Your Yosemite: **PROTECTING A PUBLIC TREASURE**

The Coalition's five guiding principles are:

1.	Provide a sustained level of investment of public funds that will insure preservation of the national parks.

2.	Heed and incorporate science in management decisions and planning.

3.	Insure the highest degree of protection of national parks consistent with the law.

4.	Preserve the uniqueness and special role of units of the National Park System.

5.	Respond with urgency to the growing impact of climate change on these units.

In this age of government-bashing, there is a strong message of hope in Wade's coalition, a signal that the fight for the national parks is not over and that even the grizzled park rangers whose faded uniforms now hang in the back of the closet have not relaxed their vigilance. This speaks volumes about the importance of the parks to those who have lived most closely with them. The existence of Wade's coalition is also a clarion call to others that national parks are still threatened, sometimes even by the very agency in charge of their protection.

An indirect warning for all of us who cherish public parks used to hang on the wall of architect Edward Larabee Barnes' office in New York City, a graphic of Central Park. On this graphic, penciled to scale, were most of the buildings ever proposed for construction within Central Park limits; art centers, educational facilities, theaters and amphitheaters, restaurants, athletic amenities, charming shops, places of worship, zoos, museums, children's playgrounds, libraries, parking. Had all those structures been built, Central Park would have been reduced to pleasant green strips between buildings. The graphic provides a stark illustration of humankind's desire to have its parks and abuse them too. The salvation for Central Park is that millions of city dwellers pay close attention, defending their rights to this touchstone of green expanse amid the metropolitan canyons.

Keeping the American public aware of the multiple and various threats to our national parks and icons like Central Park is a constant need. If manipulators of the park concept are allowed to nibble at the fringes and try to cash in when they sense moments of political opportunity, they will eventually undermine the very foundation of park purposes.

PARKS AT RISK

There are people in our society who, if they had enough political power, would do away with our national parks, Yosemite included. They do not represent the majority, but it is important for those of us who value the parks to remember that opponents to the concept are often extremely vocal, highly motivated, and organized. In a libertarian sense, these Americans contend that almost all "rights" of land ownership should rest in private hands.

Their version of an ideal nation is where individuals and corporations own and use land resources as they so choose, unrestricted by public controls. They tend to label our democratic government as an intransigent monolith that tramples on citizens' property rights; the rights to fence, dig, build, cut and chop, shoot, defend, dump, graze, dam, trap, and control. In some instances of mixed preferences, these "rights" are even championed in the form of privately held nature preserves where seclusion and bliss are carefully secured for the favored few. Generally missing from this philosophy is a land ethic tied to the conservation of wildland resources protected by law to insure that what John Muir called nature's "good tidings" can be heard by everyone.

And yet even in the face of such opposition, a century of vigorous political debate and legislative action has led to the existence of national parks and forests, wildlife refuges, protected grasslands, shielded wilderness, outdoor recreation areas, and historically significant sites. This evolution suggests that the benefits of the public estate have become obvious to the majority of Americans, a legacy of noble thinking and majority rule to be handed on year-by-year as society's gift to itself.

But the history of Yosemite teaches us that rants against this type of public gift have been part of our political dialogue from the start, and are still a strident voice in politics today. If Americans value their national parks and public spaces, they must continue to defend them vigorously.

An example is that, in 2005, Paul Hoffman, an assistant to Secretary of the Interior Gail Norton, attempted a stealthy attack on the NPS by attempting to alter its stated mission, prompting the *New York Times* to publish an editorial entitled, "National Parks Under Siege." "In the past two months," said the editors, "we have seen two proposed revisions. The first, written by Paul Hoffman, was a genuinely scandalous rewriting that would have destroyed the National Park System."

The *Times* declared that Hoffman wished to establish "essentially political screening" for NPS personnel who sought to advance their careers beyond middle management. He also tried to edit from the agency's mission statement the finding that "conservation is to be predominant" when the hard management choices are made between development and protection of natural, historic, and cultural resources. Todd Wilkinson, writing for *New West Magazine*, delivered his message under the headline, "National Park Service is being Skinned from the Inside-Out." A headline in *Vanity Fair* asked, "Who's Running Our National Parks?" Blowback against Hoffman from many media sources and the public forced him to back off.

That same year, seven-term Republican Congressman Richard Pombo, representing a district in the Central Valley of California, tried to use a deficit-reduction bill to "privatize" thousands of old, moribund claims on public lands left over from an 1872 mining law. His idea was that any "valid, existing" mining claim on federal land, even if such a claim had been abandoned for years, could be "patented to facilitate sustainable economic development," meaning handed over to private speculators and developers. The National Academy of Sciences estimated that 350 million acres of public land would thus be thrown up for grabs, including large chunks of national parks, forests, and wildlife refuges.

President Obama and family visiting Yosemite in 2016

Yosemite, born in the California gold rush and the search for silver that followed, includes within its boundaries several obsolete mining claims. Pombo actually won approval of his provision in the House of Representatives, but the language he had inserted in the Deficit Reduction Act of 2005 was dropped from consideration when the bill reached the U. S. Senate. Oregon's *Ashland Daily Tidings*, covering the story, headlined its article, "Pombo's Land Grab: It Doesn't Get Any Worse Than This."

But "worse" is in the eye of the beholder. Congressman Duncan Hunter, also of California, had his sights set on the Channel Islands National Park just off the California coast near Santa Barbara. The park is made up of five islands: Anacapa, Santa Cruz, Santa Rosa, San Miguel, and Santa Barbara. Hunter had never set foot on these islands, but he got the idea that the second largest of the group, 53,000-acre Santa Rosa, would make an ideal hunting preserve for military veterans. As Chairman of the House Armed Services Committee, Hunter had wide legislative discretion and significant influence among his colleagues. He used the 2006 Defense Authorization Bill, which provides funding to the military, to insert language that would permanently open up Santa Rosa to hunting for disabled veterans and restrict general public access during hunting seasons.

The Defense Authorization Bill, passed in the House of Representatives, moved with equal success through the Senate, and was signed into law by President George W. Bush. Congresswoman Lois Capps, in whose district the Channel Island National Park is located, said, "It is simply outrageous that this deeply misguided proposal has been inappropriately included in the Defense Authorization in an act of pure congressional hubris." She added, "Kicking the public off a national park it paid more than $30 million for in order to continue indefinitely a lucrative private hunting operation is not good use of public land and sets a terrible precedent for the use of our national treasurers." Even the Santa Barbara County Republican Party opposed Hunter's maneuver.

When representatives of the Paralyzed Veterans of America visited the island, they found the terrain intimidating, likely to be used only with great difficulty or not at all. Noam Levey, writing for the *Los Angeles Times*, observed that "Hunter's ability to push his proposal this far vividly demonstrates how a single member of Congress can muscle a pet project through the legislative process despite widespread opposition." Ninety years of restriction against hunting in national parks was severely weakened.

Fortunately, Congresswoman Capps and her California colleagues in the United States Senate, Dianne Feinstein and Barbara Boxer, fought to repeal Hunter's amendment. Taking a page from Hunter's playbook, Feinstein and Boxer attached the repeal language to an Omnibus appropriations bill passed by unanimous voice vote in the Senate in late 2006. Capps made sure that the repeal language remained intact in final negotiations between the Senate and House of Representatives before the bill was sent forward to President Bush, who signed it in 2007. On Santa Rosa Island, NPS management initiatives were reinforced to assure that the island would blossom once again as an ecological shelter open always to its public owners.

In 2014, only a month after the final Yosemite plan was announced, the House of Representatives, by a 221 to 201 vote margin, approved HR 1459, the "Ensuring Public Involvement in the Creation of National Monuments Act." This mouthful is an attempt to sweep away authority of the President of the United States to establish national monuments to protect the nation's cultural, historic, and scenic treasures, an authority first used by Teddy Roosevelt and by sixteen Presidents in all, eight Republicans and eight Democrats. The 108 national monuments that grace our land include Fort McHenry where, during the War of 1812, Francis Scott Key wrote the Star Spangled Banner; the birthplaces of George Washington and his namesake, George Washington Carver; the site of the 1876 Battle of the Little Bighorn; the volcanic Mount St. Helens; half of the Giant Sequoia Trees on earth; and the Statue of Liberty.

The Grand Canyon was declared a national monument before it became a national park. President George W. Bush proclaimed a sweeping national monument to preserve millions of acres of oceanic marine resources, one of five national monuments he established during his tenure in office. But when President Barack Obama used the same authority to elevate protection of 1,660 acres of supreme habitat along the northern California coast—land already owned by the federal government—the current class of Republicans in the House of Representatives reacted by trying to severely inhibit this

Buffalo Soldiers on patrol, Yosemite, 1890s

authority for all future Presidents. Maurine Finnerty, speaking for the Coalition of National Park Retirees, said that the House action would "make Teddy Roosevelt weep." The bill had no chance in the U. S. Senate, and President Barrack Obama, a frequent visitor to national parks beginning at age eleven when he traveled with his mother to Yellowstone, has won the media tag, the "Monuments President." He has proclaimed at least twenty-three national monuments ranging from vast marine sanctuaries to cultural sites honoring Cesar Chavez, Harriet Tubman, and U. S. Cavalry Soldiers, the very type of soldier once among the cavalrymen on patrol in Yosemite.

A living example of great hope for the national parks are the Sierra Nevada bighorn sheep released into Lee Vining Canyon near Yosemite's eastern boundary. Beginning in 1986, thanks in large measure to financial support pledged by Richard Goldman, twenty-seven bighorns were released into the canyon by wildlife experts. More bighorns were released in following years. Don Banta, owner of the Best Western Motel in the village of Lee Vining, an occasional constructive critic of park management policies and my personal friend, helped the dream thrive. He became such an enthusiast for protection of the bighorns that he voluntarily journeyed up into the canyon almost every day, weather permitting, to monitor the condition of the herd. Goldman and Banta never knew each other, but their shared personal commitment to the bighorns has passed into the hands of other equally determined human allies. They would be pleased to know that in March, 2015, twelve quizzical bighorns were released into the Cathedral Range right in the heart of the Yosemite backcountry. These bighorn sheep join others in fragile, but growing herds in the Sierra Nevada. The numbers overall have increased from 125 to about 600, suggesting hope for continuing recovery.

TRADEMARKS

Just as the park contingent of bighorns were beginning to explore its new home on the Cathedral precipices, the National Park Service in June, 2015, selected a new company to provide commercial services in Yosemite. In the bid competition, the Delaware North Company, holder of the contract since 1993, lost to Philadelphia-based Aramark, the same company that twenty-three years earlier had lost a shuttle bus contract in the park through political shenanigans. The value of the new fifteen-year contract is estimated at $2 billion. Within this financial lump are 1,543 guest rooms, 25 food and beverage outlets, 19 retail stores, and various other lesser venues. Aramark, a company with 270,000 employees scattered in 21 countries around the world, and holder of concession contracts elsewhere within the National Park System, took over at Yosemite on March 1, 2016.

But "a funny thing happened on the way to the bank," as the saying goes. Delaware North executives brought a lawsuit against the National Park Service contending that their company is owed about $50 million for "intangible" property rights at Yosemite, including trademarked names. These names, quietly trademarked by Delaware North in 2002, include "Yosemite National Park" as used by Delaware North on T-shirts, coffee mugs, and various other assorted commercial products, and the historic names, Ahwahnee Hotel, Curry Village, Yosemite Lodge, Badger Pass ski area, and the Wawona Hotel. Delaware North contends that Aramark, the winner of the new contract, cannot use these names unless it buys the trademarks.

In the absence of binding arbitration, which was not required by the NPS to settle the dispute, Delaware North turned to the courts to try to win a favorable judgment, but the clock was ticking toward the March 1 deadline and resolution of exactly what "intangible" rights were owned by Delaware North at Yosemite, and how much they were worth, seemed a long way off. Faced with the pending deadline, the NPS responded in January, 2016, to Delaware North's claim of ownership of trademarked names. If Delaware North would not give up its demand for millions of dollars in compensation for the names, the NPS simply would change the names. The Ahwahnee Hotel would become the Majestic Yosemite Hotel; Curry Village would become Half Dome Village; Yosemite Lodge would become Yosemite Valley Lodge at the Falls; Badger Pass would morph into the Yosemite Ski and Snowboard Area, and the Wawona Hotel

   Your Yosemite: **PROTECTING A PUBLIC TREASURE**

would be reborn as Big Trees Lodge. Michael Doyle, reporting on these details for *The Fresno Bee*, reminded his readers that the Delaware North Corporation also holds a concession contract at the Kennedy Space Center in Florida and is applying for trademark ownership of the name, "Space Shuttle Atlantis."

The claim of ownership of historic names at Yosemite created a furious backlash. Protest poured into newspapers and onto the internet, and voices of shock are heard on radio talk shows and television programs. Cartoonist Mark Fiore, capturing the mood, has suggested alternative names: Yosemite becomes "Yousueme," El Capitan, "El Counselor," the Ahwahnee, the "Grand Litigious Hotel," Half Dome, "Corporate Profits Dome," Glacier Point, the "Intellectual Property Overlook," and Bridalveil Fall, the "Veiled Threat Falls." The historic names Delaware North claims in Yosemite date to the Wawona Hotel, 1884, Yosemite National Park, 1890, Camp Curry, 1899, the Ahwahnee in 1927, and Badger Pass during the Civilian Conservation Corp era of the 1930s. The two contending private companies and the NPS tried to avoid litigation in favor of the jawbone, attempting to hammer out a fair agreement that would perpetuate the historic park names, but this attempt failed and the name brouhaha has drifted into the court labyrinth, finally coming out the other end when a $12 million settlement was reached in 2019, allowing the historic names to be restored.

FERDINAND

The "best idea" of national parks is "sustained and fortified by public sentiment," as the author, Freeman Tilden put it. Without this sustenance and defense cattle might still be grazing in the meadows of Yosemite Valley. Instead, these meadows are being carefully restored to their natural splendor and the park in general, including the peregrines and bighorns, is receiving increasingly sensitive care. The NPS management trajectory often zigs and zags between society's complex demands, but very steadily over the many years, step by step, Yosemite is being taken toward to a level of safekeeping that "matches people with a matchless place." This is true of all national parks. Tilden uses just eight words to capture the essence of why national parks are so treasured: "They add to the joy of our living."

At Tioga Pass, not far from where the bighorn sheep roam, is a small stone and log structure perched at 9,945-feet. This is the entrance station on Yosemite's eastern boundary where Ferdinand Castillo, otherwise known as "Mr. Yosemite," held forth from his podium for thirty-six summer seasons delivering his messages to incoming visitors. An orphan raised by Albertinium Dominican Sisters, Castillo was a former Marine who held college degrees in history and physical education. He was a swimming coach during school terms and, most of all, a fixture on summer days at his elevated entrance station. Theoretically, his job was to collect money, hand out brochures, answer a question or two, and speed visitors on their way so that the next car in line could be processed with equal efficiency.

These basic job requirements seem to have escaped Castillo almost from the first moment he was hired. No amount of coaxing or coaching by his supervisors could convince the self-described Aztec-American that his primary task was to collect entrance fees, with emphasis on the word "entrance." For unsuspecting visitors, arrival at the Tioga Pass gate could be a surprise when they were greeted with a vintage Castillo monologue.

 "Welcome. Where you from? Chicago? Do you know that in the Chicago zoo they have the healthiest animal in the world, the anteater, full of antibodies. You are looking very healthy yourselves, and beautiful too. While you are driving watch out for the lady bighorn sheep. She's known for making illegal ewe turns. Here's your brochure, all about magnificent Yosemite. You kids in the back seat, memorize every word because I won't let you out of the park until you pass my quiz. This is your park, you own it, and that means you have to take care of it, no littering, no chopping on trees, leave footprints, take pictures, don't try to catch skunks, protect the wildflowers. I'm putting you personally in charge of park protection. Remember, there are lots of you but only one Yosemite. You have arrived at the castle. You are royalty. Have a fine visit."

Castillo prided himself in his rock-hard memory and he often greeted regular visitors to the park by name. He also attempted to converse with foreigners in their native tongue, even if some of the words were garbled and brought puzzled looks to the faces of these visitors. When park employees passed through his gate, Castillo treated them like famous celebrities, announcing their presence to anyone within earshot, eliciting more puzzled looks.

Peter King, reporting for the *Los Angeles Times*, described the ranger who stopped traffic to allow toads to cross the road and coaxed tourists into singing the national anthem when he raised the flag: "He gave impromptu lectures on the secret lives of bears, the characteristics of native wildflowers, and the urgent need for nature preservation. He also could be cranky, scolding drivers of smoky diesel vehicles and pedestrians who strayed off the footpaths threatening alpine blooms with clumsy footsteps. He regularly backed up traffic, while lecturing, informing, and telling jokes, prompting some of the more frantic seekers of relaxation to lean on their horns."

Castillo thought that for most visitors he was the first and perhaps the only park ranger they would see. This was his one chance to make a difference, and so he seized it. He learned to be an expert judge of the moment. He knew all the questions: Where is the campground? How do I get to Yosemite Falls? Where are the bears? How far to San Francisco? Where is the bathroom? Where is the restaurant/gas station/grocery store? Can we still see the fire fall? His answers were accurate and rapid-fire.

On a busy summer day, about 2,000 cars would pass Castillo's entrance station. He could not perform for everyone but he could sense openings, especially when children were part of his audience. He would plunge in, trying to make a difference on behalf of the park he cherished. In a surprisingly effective manner, he complemented legendary ranger-educator Carl Sharsmith's careful tutelage of visitors with his own startling approach, a sort of blunt ranger instrument urging visitors to be alert and grateful. Many of Yosemite's returning visitors made a point of entering or exiting the park through Tioga Pass just to enjoy the full Castillo treatment. He tried never to disappoint, delivering his favorite message whenever he could: "Take good care of *your Yosemite!*"

Over the years, thousands of park visitors heard this message. My fervent hope is that they have taken Castillo's phrase, "Your Yosemite," to heart. Those two words are a poem, the first encapsulating all the responsibilities we share for our inherited ownership of revered precious places and the second giving congratulatory identity to one of the most enchanting among them. All we have to do is make sure that those words are proudly handed forward to the next generation.

RESERVATIONS

In the current era, Superintendent Cicely Muldoon and her staff are struggling to implement use capacities for Yosemite. From April to October, reservations are required on many days to enter the park. The limit for Yosemite Valley is about 5,000 cars daily. Similar reservation programs have been implemented or are planned for many areas of the National Park System. There is hope, yet, that the vexing challenge of preservation, public use, and the right of future generations to enjoy priceless national treasures, unimpaired, can be overcome—that this right is inalienable.

Bibliography

Adams, Ansel, *Ansel Adams: An Autobiography*, Little Brown and Company, 1985.

___________. *The Eloquent Light*, Sierra Club, Exhibit Format Series, 1963

Alsup, William, *Such a Landscape: A Narrative of the 1864 California Geological Survey Exploration of Yosemite, Sequoia and Kings Canyon from the Diary, Field Notes, Letters, and Reports of William Henry Brewer*, Yosemite Association, 1999.

Barrett, Bob, *Yosemite, Where Mules Wear Diamonds*, Loose Change Publication, 1989.

Bingaman, John W., *Harry Coupland Benson, Pathways: A Story of Trails and Men*, Chapter VII, *www.yosemite.ca.us/library*, 1968.

Botti, Stephen J., *The Illustrated Flora of Yosemite National Park*, Yosemite Association, 2001.

Carr, Ethan, *Wilderness by Design*, University of Nebraska Press, 1998.

Clark, Lew and Ginny, *John Muir Trail Country*, Western Trails Publication, 1977-78.

Clark, Lew and Ginny, *Yosemite Trails*, Western Trails Publication, 1976–79.

Dilsaver, Larry M., *America's National Park System: The Critical Documents*, Roman & Littlefield Publishers, 1994.

Ditton, Richard P. and McHenry, Donald E., *Self-Guiding Auto Tours in Yosemite National Park*, National Park Service, 1965.

Farabee, Charles R. "Butch," Jr., *National Park Ranger, An American Icon*, Roberts Rinehart Publishers, 2003.

Fouts, William, *Yosemite Packer*, Spurs Publishing, 1987.

Green, Linda Wedel, *Yosemite Historic Resource Study, Volumes 1, 2, & 3*, National Park Service, 1987.

Huntley, Jen A., *The Making of Yosemite, James Mason Hutchings and the Origin of America's Most Popular National Park*, University Press of Kansas, 2011.

Hutchings, James, *In the Heart of the Sierra,* Pacific Press Publishing House, Oakland, California, 1888.

Johnson, Hank, *Ho! For Yosemite,* Yosemite Association, 2000.

————, *The Yosemite Grant 1864–1906,* Yosemite Association, 1995.

Johnson, Paul C., *Sierra Album,* Doubleday & Company, 1971.

Jones, Johnny, *Following the Bells,* Dwight H. Barnes, 1994.

Maharidge, Dale, *Yosemite: A Landscape of Life,* Yosemite Association, 1990.

McCracken, Harold, *George Catlin and the Old Frontier,* Bonanza Books, 1959.

Medley, Steve, *Guidebook to Yosemite,* Yosemite Association, 2004.

Merced Wild and Scenic River Draft Comprehensive Management Plan and Environmental Impact Statement, National Park Service, 2013.

Neihardt, John G., *The Splendid Wayfaring,* University of Nebraska Press, 1920.

O'Neill, Elizabeth Stone, *Mountain Sage: The Life Story of Carl Sharsmith,* Yosemite Association, 1988.

Proctor, Alexander, *An Ascent of Half Dome in 1884,* Hester Proctor, 1979.

Report of Yosemite Park Commission, Secretary of the Interior, United States Senate, Washington, D. C. 1904.

Reynolds, Annie and Gordon, Albert, *Stage to Yosemite,* Big Tree Books, 1994.

Runte, Alfred, *Yosemite: The Embattled Wilderness,* University of Nebraska Press, 1990.

Russell, Carl Parcher, *One Hundred Years in Yosemite,* University of California Press, 1932, 1947.

Sargent, Shirley, *The First 100 Years, Yosemite 1890 –1990,* Yosemite Park & Curry Company, 1988.

Sellars, Richard West, *Preserving Nature in the National Parks,* Yale University Press, 1997.

Shankland, Robert, *Stephen Mather of the National Parks,* Alfred A. Knopf, 1951.

Smith, Thomas A., *I'm Just a Seasonal,* Productivity Publications, Thomas A. Smith, 2005.

Stebbins, Cyril, A. & Robert, *Birds of Yosemite,* National Park Service, 1954, 1962.

The Wild Muir, Yosemite Association, 1994.

Tilden, Freeman, *The National Parks,* Alfred A. Knopf, 1951, 1968.

Trexler, Keith A., *The Tioga Road: A History 1883 –1961*, Yosemite Natural History Association, 1961, 1975, 1980.

Walklet, Keith S., *The Ahwahnee, Yosemite's Grand Hotel*, Yosemite Association, 2004.

Watkins, T. H., *Righteous Pilgrim: The Life and Times of Harold L. Ickes, 1874 –1952*, Henry Holt & Company, 1990.

Yosemite General Management Plan, National Park Service, 1980.

ARTICLES

A Blueprint for Beauty, Editorial, Los Angeles Times, 12/02/2000.

A Brief History of the Anti-Conservation Movement, www.colorado.edu/ AmStudies/lewis/anticon.htm

A Comprehensive Study of Visitor Safety in the National Park System: Final Report, Tuler, Seth and Golding, Dominic, The George Perkins Marsh Institute, Clark University, Worcester, MA, 04/15/2002.

A Hefty Price Tag on Restoring Hetch Hetchy, Bailey, Eric, Los Angeles Times, 07/20/2006.

A Historic Act of Faith in the Land: Ansel Adam's Romantic Roots, Wilson, William, Los Angeles Times, 04/29/1984.

A Jewel Worth Protecting, Editorial, Los Angeles Times, 06/05/2004.

A Life of Peak: Warren Harding, Editorial, Los Angeles Times, 03/08/2002.

A More Natural Yosemite, Editorial, Los Angeles Times, 12/01/2001.

A Nation of 'Scenic Lovers', Editorial, San Francisco Examiner, 05/26/1996.

A New Conservation Ethic, Babbitt, Bruce, Los Angeles Times, 06/01/1994.

A Photographic Look at the Early Careers of Theodore Roosevelt, Theodore Roosevelt Association, www.theodoreroosevelt.org

After the Flood in Yosemite, Editorial, Los Angeles Times, 02/18/1997.

Aiming for Trouble in Our National Parks, Editorial, Los Angeles Times, 03/03/2009.

America's Best Idea, Born in Yosemite, Yosemite: A Journal of the Yosemite Association, Vol. 73, No. 3, Fall 2009.

American Paintings, Charles Dorman Robinson, Arader Galleries.

An Official Report That Is Full Of Falsehoods, MacKenzie, George, The New York Times, 09/13/1890.

An Overland Journey from New York to San Francisco in the Summer of 1859, Horace Greeley, New York, C. M. Saxton, Bakker & Company, San Francisco, Bancroft & Company, 1860.

And the Bronze Goes To …, Downes, Lawrence, Editorial, New York Times, 06/06/2009.

Aren't There Enough Trails? Editorial, New York Times, 11/14/2008.

Astoundingly Flawed, Editorial, New York Times, 04/15/2009.

Busing To Beauty, Editorial, Los Angeles Times, 08/15/1998.

Capps Seeks to Repeal Santa Rosa Island Hunting Law, Michael, Joe, Medill Reports, Northwestern University, 04/27/2007.

Clinton and the Environment: A Good Record May Improve, Editorial, Los Angeles Times, 11/18/1996.

Closing of Yosemite Renews Debate Over Fire Policies, Bishop, Katherine, New York Times, 08/16/1990.

Congestion Plan: Yosemite Tries Again, Yosemite River Plan Could Limit Access, Cone, Tracie, Associated Press, 10/30/2011.

Could Tourists Pack Heat With Cameras? Lee, Carol E., Politico.com, 05/22/2009.

Court Halts Yosemite Development Projects, Eden, Joyce M., Friends of Yosemite Valley, 04/22/2004.

"Dam Hetch Hetchy! John Muir Contests the Hetch Hetchy Dam, History Matters/The U. S. Survey Course on the Web.

Defending Grave Abuses, The Yosemite Commission Makes a Report, MacKenzie, George, New York Times, 04/06/1891.

Defense Authorization Act of Fiscal Year 2007, Vote Smart, 09/29/2006.

Despoiling the Yosemite, MacKenzie, George, New York Times, 08/20/1890.

Developments at Yosemite, Editorial, Los Angeles Times, 05/08/1989.

Don't Derail Yosemite Plan, Editorial, Los Angeles Times, 09/24/2002.

El Capitan Climb, Various Articles, Yosemite Research Library, 1958.

Eleventh Congress, 1ˢᵗ Session, H. R. 1684, 03/24/2009.

Elk Hunting In the Badlands, Editorial, New York Times, 07/08/2009.

Eminent Domain, Legal-Explanations.com, 07/14/2011.

Environmental Concerns: Babbitt Says President Has Rolled Back Landmark Laws: Spokesman for Administration Defends Record, Rogers, Paul, San Jose Mercury News, 10/06/2004.

Environmentalists Seek Yosemite Contract: Dolan, Maura, Los Angeles Times, 09/25/1990.

Fair Perk? Island Eyed as Hunt Club for Soldiers, Associated Press, 05/03/2006.

Falling Boulders Endanger Lives at Yosemite, Cone, Tracie, Associated Press, 11/17/2006.

Falling Rock Closes Part of Yosemite Campground, Surdin, Ashley, Washington Post, 11/21/2008.

Farewell to Ferdinand, Yosemite Association Newsletter, Winter 1994.

Federal Appeals Court Declares Merced River Plan Illegal, Wild and Scenic Rivers Initiative, 06/28/2005.

Ferdinand Castillo, King, Peter H., Los Angeles Times, 02/18/1996.

Ferdinand, Roknic, Dave, Review-Herald, 06/09/1988.

First Ascent of Half Dome, First Grade VI in the USA, Green, Stewart, About.com, Climbing, 1957.

For Rock-Climbing Guru, the Sky is His Roof, Brick, Michael, New York Times, 09/30/2008.

Forest Fire As A Friend, Editorial, Los Angeles Times, 09/23/1996.

Foundation to Buy Yosemite Concession, Dolan, Maura, Los Angeles Times, 01/09/1991.

Free to Flow, Editorial, Los Angeles Times, 11/29/1987.

Giving A Dam: Congress Debates Hetch Hetchy, History Matters/The U. S. Survey Course on the Web, 04/07/2009.

Going Wild, Seideman, David, Time Magazine, 07/25/1994.

Gun Rights in NPS and Wildlife Refuges, H. R. 1684, House of Representatives, 04/01/2009.

Guns Are Now Permitted—But Not Necessarily Welcome—in National Parks, Cart, Julie, Los Angeles Times, 02/22/2011.

Guns At The White House? Lee, Carol L., Editorial, Politico.com, 05/22/2009.

Harriman Alaska Expedition of 1899: North to Alaska, Smithsonian Magazine, 2003.

Here's One For Nature, Editorial, Los Angeles Times, 11/06/1997.

Hetch Hetchy Reclaimed: A Special Pulitzer Prize Reprint, The Sacramento Bee, 04/10/2005.

Historian Charts Changing Ideas About U. S. Wilderness, Environment, Mills, Kay, Los Angeles Times, 06/30/1985.

Honoring Our Legacy: Shaping the Future Yosemite, Yosemite Association, Spring 2010.

House Passes Santa Rosa Island Hunting Provision, Ferry, David, Daily Nexus, 10/04/2006.

House Votes to Boost Merced River Water Storage Despite "Wild and Scenic" Status, Doyle, Michael, McClatchy Newspapers, 06/19/2012.

How Not to Honor the Dead, King, Peter H., Los Angeles Times, 02/18/1996.

John Bachar Dies at 52: Rock Climber Specialized in Free-Solo Ventures, Obituary, Los Angeles Times, 07/09/2009.

John Muir Writings, The Treasures of the Yosemite, Century Magazine, Vol. XL, No. 4, 08/1890.

John Muir, Aged Naturalist, Dead, Obituary, New York Times, 12/25/1914

John Muir, An Appreciation, Roosevelt, Theodore, Outlook, Vol. 109, pp.27-28, 01/16/1915.

Josiah Dwight Whitney, 1819 –1896, Bourgoin, Suzzanne Michele, Encyclopedia of World Biography.

Judge Considers Yellowstone Snowmobile Cap, Neary, Ben, Associated Press, 08/19/2009.

Judge Curbs Snowmobile Use, Cart, Julie, Los Angeles Times, 12/17/2003.

Judge Halts Raft of Yosemite Upgrade Projects, Bailey, Eric, Los Angeles Times, 11/07/2006.

Judge Halts Rule Allowing Guns in Parks, Los Angeles Times, 03/20/2009.

Land Grab, Editorial, Los Angeles Times, 02/15/2005.

Letter: Ansel Adams to Norman Livermore, Jr., Administrator, The Resource Agency of California, Bancroft Library, University of California Berkeley, 02/18/1968.

Letter to Supporters of Yosemite Restoration Trust, Kunofsky, Judith, 04/22/1992.

Letter to the New York Times: For Mr. Hecht to Dwell Upon, Johnson, Robert Underwood, 07/29/1890.

Life Buoy for the Parks, Editorial, Los Angeles Times, 04/23/1999.

Lujan Pressures Matsushita on Yosemite Pact, Dolan, Maura, Los Angeles Times, 01/01/1991.

MCA Agrees to Sell Interest in Yosemite to End Dispute, Reinhold, Robert, New York Times, 01/09/1991.

MCA, Matsushita To Meet On Merger, Chicago Tribune, 11/15/1990.

Mission & History, American Land Rights Association, www.landrights.org/mission.htlm

Mission 66 Proposal To Eisenhower Cabinet, January 27, 1956, America's National Park System: The Critical Documents, Chapter 4, Ed. by Dilsaver, Lary M., Roman Littlefield Publishers, 1994.

Mount Whitney-The Early Climbs, Farquhar, Francis P., "History of the Sierra Nevada," University of California Press Berkeley 1969.

Mr. Pombo's Map, Editorial, New York Times, 10/19/2006.

Mr. Lewis Refuses to Listen, Editorial, New York Times, 11/22/2008.

Muir Biography: Re-Walking John Muir's Trip from San Francisco to Yosemite, a Trans-California Ramble, 04/2006-05/2006.

National Park Backers Call for Creation of a Service Corps Similar to Depression-era CCC, Cart, Julie, Los Angeles Times, 02/01/2009.

National Park System: The Critical Documents, Dilsaver, Lary M., Ed., 03/15/2011.

National Parks a Bargain Even With Higher Fees, Editorial, Los Angeles Times, 11/28/1996.

National Parks: Issues Involved in the Sale of the Yosemite National Park Concessioner, 09/10/1992.

National Treasure Hidden Away at Park, Nolte, Carl, San Francisco Chronicle, 09/04/1993.

Negotiating Away the Environment, Editorial, Los Angeles Times, 10/30/2001.

New Hope for a Better Yosemite, Editorial, Los Angeles Times, 10/17/1999

New Tack in Assault on Yosemite Commercialism, Reinhold, Robert, New York Times, 09/23/1990.

NPS Housing Plan Calls for New 'Foresta City' Inside Yosemite National Park in Endangered Owl Habitat! Sierra Club, 09/1992.

Our Fading National Jewels, Editorial, Los Angeles Times, 07/20/2002.

Paiute Indians: Yosemite's History Wrong, Burke, Garance, Associated Press, 12/24/2011.

Parks or Parking, Editorial, Los Angeles Times, 08/30/2005.

Pathways: A Story of Trails and Men, Bingamon, John W., Yosemite Research Library, 1968.

Plan for Yosemite Seeks Restoration, New York Times, 12/18/1991.

Removal of Yosemite Dam to be Studied, Romney, Lee, Los Angeles Times, 11/12/2004.

Restore Hetch Hetchy, Restore Hetch Hetchy.org

Robbins, Royal, Middendorf, John, Big Wall Climbing, www.bigwalls.net/climb/royal.htm.

Royal Robbins-Spirit of the Age, Ament, Pat, Yosemite Research Library, 10/1992.

Scalpers Flipping Yosemite Reservations, Lundstrom, Marjorie, Sacramento Bee, 04/18/2011.

Schwarzenegger Administration Will Study Restoring Hetch Hetchy Valley in Yosemite, Wolk, Lois, Assembly Member Newsletter, 11/11/2004.

Senate OKs Bill to Block Big-game Hunting on Santa Rosa Island, Los Angeles Times, 11/15/2006.

Settlement Blocks Yosemite Commercial Development, Burke, Garance, Associated Press, 10/01/2009.

Sierra Nevada Bighorn Sheep, Yosemite National Park Newsletter, 08/2007.

Solo Climber Reaches New Heights, Neville, Tim, New York Times, 06/15/2012.

Some Sense at Yosemite, Editorial, Los Angeles Times, 12/08/1998.

Spokesman for Administration Defends Record, Rogers, Paul, San Jose Mercury News, 10/06/2004.

Stephen T. Mather, 1867–1930, Sierra Club Bulletin, Vol. XV, No. 1, 02/1930.

The Mystery Buried in Bridalveil Meadow, Johnson, Hank, Yosemite Annual Review, Yosemite Association, Vol. 54, No. 2, Spring 1992.

The National Park Service Organic Act, U. S. Congress, 1916.

The National Parks: 1864 –1880, Introduction: A History of the Park System, Johns, Joshua S., 05/05/1990.

The Price of Great Beauty: Yosemite Falls Access, Editorial, Los Angeles Times, 05/27/2002.

The Report of the Yosemite Park Commission Appointed to Ascertain what Portions of Said Park are Not Necessary for Park Purposes, and also at What Place a Substantial Road can be Built from the Boundary of Said Park to the Yosemite Valley Grant, Together with Maps, Etc., Senate, 58th Congress, 3rd Session, Document No. 3, 1905.

The Sagebrush Rebellion, U. S. News and World Report, 12/01/1980.

The Story of the Sierra Club, Colby, William, Sierra Club Bulletin, 12/1967.

The War and Postwar Years, 1940–1963, Preserving Nature in the National Parks: A History, Chapter Five, Sellers, Richard, Yale University Press, 1997.

Timetable Set For National Park Transit Plan, Los Angeles Times, 12/26/1997.

Trio High on Life In Sierra, Rose, Gene, Fresno Bee, 08/19/1991.

Trouble in Paradise, Roderick, Kevin, Los Angeles Times, 02/05/1990.

U. S. Clears Yosemite Drug Probes, Rose, Gene, McClatchy News Service, 01/20/1986.

U. S. To Delay Development in Yosemite Valley, Los Angeles Times, 10/01/2009.

Warren Harding, Obituary, Los Angeles Times, 03/08/2002.

Waving Points of Order against Conference Report on H. R. 5122, National Defense Authorization Act for Fiscal Year 2007.

When Corporations Sponsor Parks, Editorial, San Francisco Chronicle, 02/20/1994.

Who Owns Yosemite? Dolan, Maura, Los Angeles Times, 09/30/1990.

William Whelan III, 66, Ex-Park Service Director, Dies, Hevesi, Dennis, New York Times, 10/11/2006.

With Theodore Roosevelt and John Muir in Yosemite, Kimes, William F., Westerners Brand Book No. 14, Los Angeles Corral, 1974.

Yosemite and Yellowstone, 1864 –1877, Johns, Joshua A., xroads.virginia.edu. 05/15/1996.

Yosemite Managers Ask For Help Deciding Future of Historic Cabins Closed After Rock Fall, Cone, Tracie, Los Angeles Times, 02/22/2010

Yosemite Officials See Fresno's Input on Merced River Plan, Gross, Mark, Fresno Bee, 07/07/2009.

Yosemite Rock Fall Forces Ahwahnee Evacuation, Associated Press, 08/26/2009.

Yosemite: Lodging Won't Be Cramped, MacLean, Alexander, The Union Democrat, Sonora, California 06/15/2012.

Yosemite Overhaul May Hit Troubles, Fimrite, Peter, San Francisco Chronicle, 01/11/2013.

Yosemite Plan Calls for More Campsites and Parking Spaces, Los Angeles Times, 01/11/2013.

Yosemite, Where To Go and What To Do, MacKenzie, George C., C. A. Murdock & Company, 1888.

Yosemite's High Sierra Trail Loop Makes Hiking Accessible, Clifford, Frank, Los Angeles Times, 03/21/2011.

Index

A

Abraham Lincoln 90

Acadia National Park 10

Adams, Ansel 66, 71, 132, 183, 185, 186, 197

Adams, Michael 72

Adams, Virginia 71

Ah'wah'nee'chee 51, 56, 59, 61, 64

Ahwahnee Hotel 5, 112, 183, 273, 281

Albright, Horace 167, 171, 174, 180, 188, 193

Alder, Jack 139

Alsup, William 313

American Alpine Club 318

"America's best idea" 65

Ancestral lands 51

Anderson, Captain George C. G. 104, 105, 107

Andrus, Cecil 111, 115

Ansel Adams Gallery 13

Appoinments
    Acadia National Park 10
    Yellowstone National Park 9
    Yosemite National Park 12

Arnberger, Leslie P. 5, 15, 74, 75, 250

Ashburner, William 95

Ashley, William 21

Astor, John Jacob 19

"A Way Across the Mountain" 36

Ayers, Thomas 84, 86

B

Bachar, John 213

Balderson, Jerry 262

Ball, George 188

Bard, Dale 203, 215

Barnett, Bob 113

Barrett, Annie 222, 224, 226

BASE (Building-Antenna-Span-Earth) 233

BASE Jumping 234, 235

Bautista, Chief 50

Beatty, William H. 129

Bechtel, Stan 238

Beeler, Madison 57

Bejeck, Donald 276

Benson, Major Harry C. 149–164, 150–164

Berkowitz, Paul 307, 308

Berrey, Henry 71, 288

Beveridge, Charles E. 95

Bidwell, Jim 203

Bierstadt, Alfred 92

Bingamon, John 152, 153

Binnewies, Bob 222, 273

Binnewies, Doug 222

Binnewies, Midge 9, 12, 201

Biswell, Dr. Harold H. 295

Blinn, Karen (Donaldson) 69

Board of Park Commissioners 109

Boenish, Carl 233

Boling, Captain James 60, 61

Bonneville, Benjamin Louis Eulalie de 18, 22, 38

Botti, Stephen J. 35, 296

Boyers, Laurel (Munson) 6, 70, 302, 303

Bracebridge Celebration 185

Bradshaw, Captain John 37

Bridger, Jim 23

Browder, Dr. Hal 319

Brower, David 190, 197

Brown, Sue 224, 226

Bryant, Dr. Harold C. 177

Bryce, Lord James 65

Bunnell, "Doc" Lafayette 52, 53, 57, 61

Burgen, Bill 68, 276

Burley, Ginger 70, 277, 280

Burnett, Babe 80

Burney, James 49

Burroughs, John 130

Burton, Philip 232

Bush, Laura 271

Bush, President George H. W. 311

Butler, Nicholas 138

Butler, Walt 223

Byrne, John 69, 201

C

Cabrillo, Juan Rodriguez 1

Caine, Captain Joseph E. 130

Calderwood, Richard 209

California Gold Rush 4, 45

California Predatory Bird Research Group 203

California Wilderness Act 233

Camp A. E. Wood 149

Camp Curry 172, 176, 178

Capps, Lois 331

Carpenter, Scott 41

Carr, Jeanne 98, 118, 119

Carson, Rachael 202

Carter, Hugh and Lou 200

Carter, President Jimmy 8, 12, 112

Castillo, Ferdinand 336

Castle, Walt 69, 244, 246, 247

Chapman, Howard 112, 307

Chief of the Ah'wah'nee'chee 53

Chief Tenaya 63

Chorove, Jon 222

Chouinard, Yvon 213, 214, 318

Civilian Conservation Corps 189

Clark, Galen 95, 96, 106, 107, 109, 129

Climbing 106, 204, 206, 207, 209, 213, 214

Cobb, Janet 319

Cody, William (Buffalo Bill) 102

Coelho, Congressman Tony 252, 255

Conway, John 103

Cosmopolitan Hotel 102

Coulter, George W. 95

Cross, Don 295

Curry, David A. 132, 133, 171, 173

Curry, Foster 176, 177

Curry, Jennie 132, 175, 176, 180

Curry, Marjorie 178

Curry Tent Camp 131

Curry Tresidder, Mary 178, 191, 193, 194, 199, 248

Curry Village 14

D

David and Lucile Packard Foundation 319

Deering, Alexander 95

Desmond, D. J. 172, 173, 174

Dickenson, Russell E. 111, 113

Diegelman, Dave 203

Dill, John 261, 262, 264

Dingler, Bill 68

"Does It Pay To Visit Yo Semite?" 77

Dorr, George 176

Drake, Sir Frances 1

Duncan, Dayton 65

Dutcher, Sally 106

E

Early Explorers

    Benjamin Louis Eulalie de Bonneville 18

    John Sutter and James D. Savage 43

    Joseph Walker 18

    Russians 42

    Spaniards 42

Eaton, Lewis 255

Eisenhower, President Dwight D. 195

Ellison, Dan 262, 265

El Portal 200, 201

Emerson, Ralph Waldo 103

Erickson, Lynn 222

Everhardt, Gary 82

F

Fall, Albert 180

Farabee, Charles R. "Butch" 240

Feuter, Bill 209

Field School of Natural History 177

Fillmore, President Millard 49

Finley, Michael V. 310

"Following the Bells" 113

Fort Ross 43

Four-Mile-Trail 103

Frampton, George 313

Frederick Law Olmsted, Jr. 169

Frémont, John 51

G

Gallwas, Jerry 204

Gardner, James 95

Garfield, President James 102

Gaylor, Andrew Jack 151

General Management Plan (GMP) 75, 83, 112

Giant Sequoias 36, 120

Gillespie, Bright 138

Glacier Point Hotel 250

Goldman, Richard N. 291, 313, 333

Grant, President Ulysses S. 101, 102

Great Depression 187

Greeley, Horace 87, 88, 89, 100

Green, Stewart M. 208

Griffin, B. J. 164

Grosvenor, Gilbert 169, 187

Grumman American AA-5B Tiger 258, 260, 262, 265, 266

H

Hall, Ansel F. 177

Harding, President Warren 208, 210

Hardy, Edward C. 72, 249, 251, 254, 255, 281

Hardy, Jackie 281

Harriman, Edward H. 130

Hartzog, George P. Jr. 104, 248, 254

Hayes, President Rutherford B. 102, 271

Hearst, William Randolph 102, 121

Hecht, M. H. 125

Heritage Foundation 114

Hetch Hetchy 155, 156, 159, 162

Hillary, Sir Edmund 318

Hite, Gustavus 89

Hodges, Clare Marie 175

Hoffman, Paul 329

"Ho For Yo-Semite" 79

Holden, E. S. 95

Horse Creek Rendezvous 21, 22

Hummel, Don 229, 230, 231

Hunter, Duncan 330

Huntley, Dr. Jen A. 86

Hutchings, Gertrude 104

Hutchings' Illustrated California Magazine 86

Hutchings, James Mason 85, 89, 97, 99, 100, 102, 118, 129

I

Indian Appropriations Act in 1851 50

Indian Village 70

Irish, J. P. 124

J

James, Les 41

Jefferson, President Thomas 317

Jensen, Dan 315

Johnson, Hank 79

Johnson, Jay 42, 70

Johnson, Lyndon Baines 227

Johnson, Robert Underwood 122, 125, 129, 160

Jones, Holway 147

Jones, Johnny 113

Jones, William R. "Bill" 219

Jordan, David Starr 129

K

Kate-the-Mule 223

Keith, William 128

Kieser, Walter 319

King, Clarence 95

King, Thomas Starr 90, 92

Krumholtz, Dan 222

L

LaBarge, George 276

Lamon, Robert B. 86, 88, 96, 100

Land and Water Conservation Fund 114

Lane, Franklin 168

Langtry, Lillie 102

Laura Spelman Rockefeller Memorial Fund 178

LeConte, Dr. Joseph 129

Leidig, Charles 139, 143, 143–148

Leonard, Archie 139

Leonard, John 222

Leonard, Zenas 24, 29

Lewis, Washington B. 173, 174, 185

Lincoln, President Abraham 2, 3

Lippincott, Oliver 73, 79

Livermore, Norman "Ike" 113

Locomobile 80

Logan, Olive 76, 77, 78

Lowe, Frederick G. 95

M

MacKenzie, George G. 121, 123, 124, 129

Mackie, Ron 303, 304, 320, 321, 322

Macquarie, Chas and Anne 263, 265, 266

Mahalik, David 164

Maine Coast Heritage Trust 11

Manda, Mark 222

Mariposa 48

Mariposa Battalion 49, 51

Mariposa Grove of Giant Sequoias 93, 98

Mariposa Indian War 49, 85

Marshall, James 44

Marshall, Mike 164

Martin, Dick 236

Martyr, Dr. Richard 313

Mather, Stephen T. 5, 165, 165–191, 176, 182, 183, 184, 187, 193

McCauley, James 103

McClintock 325

McClintock, Tom 325

McDougal, John 49

McFarland, J. Horace 168, 169–191

McGregor, Bob 69

McKay, Douglas 195

McKenzie, Len 203, 278, 290, 320

McKinley, President William 135

McLaughlin, James L. 182

Medley, Steve 313

Memorial Day weekend, 1970 239

Merced River 12

Merry, Wayne 209

Millard, Walter 86

Miller, Adolph 167

Miller, Frank 180

Mills, Enos 169

"Mission 66" 195, 196, 198, 199

Mission of San Juan Bautista 38, 50

Moe, John 223

Mono Paiute 62

Moore, Army Lieutenant Seymour Treadwell 62

Mott, William Penn 308

Mountain States Legal Foundation 114

Muir, John 36, 97, 98, 118, 122, 126, 129, 131, 136, 137, 141, 155, 156, 160, 162, 163, 167

Muldoon, Cicely 338

Murphy, Jim 225

Music Corporation of America 74, 249, 251, 254

N

National Geographic Society 187

National Park Service

Establishment of 170

National Park System

Size 65

Vision 66

Neubacher, Don L. 325

Nidever, George 31, 36

Nishkian, Byron 291

Nixon, President Richard 202

Noot'chu 52

Norton, Gail 329

NPS Concessionaire Contract

Camp Curry 179

O

Obama, President Barack 271, 332

O'Keeffe, Georgia 189

Olmsted, Jr., Frederick Law 94, 95, 170

Olney, Warren 128

O'Neal, John 57

O'Neill, Elizabeth Stone 217

Operation Bootstrap 209, 211

O'Shaughnessy Dam 154, 162, 164

P

Pardee, George 138

Parker, Dr. Julia 41, 270, 280

Parker, Lucy 270

Parker, Ralph 279

Peregrine Falcons 201, 203, 213, 215

Perkings, George 129

Phelan, James 159

Pinchot, Gifford 157–164, 158–164, 170

Political Unrest 239

Pombo, Richard 329

Powell, Mark 209

Pratt, Beth 221

President Woodrow Wilson 161

Preston, John 198

Priest, Donnie 258, 259, 266, 267, 268

Prince Philip 270, 280

Proctor, Alexander Phimister 107

Q

Queen Elizabeth the II of England 269, 270, 276, 278, 280, 281

R

Radanovich, Yvonne (Bustillos) 69, 322

Raganowicz, Marek 211

Raithel, Kenneth Jr. 112

Raker, Congressman John 158

Raymond, Captain Israel Ward 92, 93

Reagan, Jr., Ronald 113

Reagan, Nancy 113

Reagan, President Ronald 112, 113, 117, 249, 253, 271, 272, 275

Redford, Robert 272, 273

Reid, Wallace 209

Reynolds, John 74

Reynolds, Nancy 113

Rice, David 289, 290, 291

Robbins, Royal 215, 318

Robinson, Charles Dorman 121

Robinson, Donald 276

Rockefeller, John D. Jr. 188

Rockefeller, Peggy 11

Rockwell, Sarah 313

Roderick, Kevin 310

Rooney, Bob 276

Roosevelt, Archibald 281

Roosevelt, President Franklin Delano 189

Roosevelt, President Theodore 135, 136, 137, 139, 144–148, 145, 153

Roosevelt, Selwa 281

Rose, Gene 274, 289, 308

Russell, Carl 44, 297

Russell, Edward 79

Rust, Rusty 71

S

Sabo Arch 221

Sabo, Bill 219

Sampson, Alden 107

Sano, Jim 263, 267, 278

Sargent, Charles 137, 144

Sargent, Shirley 150

Savage, James 44

Savage, James D. 43, 47, 49, 51, 52, 53, 58, 62, 63

Schelhas, John 222

Search-and-Rescue 258–282

Seaton, Fred 198

Sedergren, Oscar 211

Sellars, Richard West 297

Senger, Joachim H. 128

Sentinel Hotel 181

Shankland, Robert 176

Sharsmith, Dr. Carl 217, 218

Sheinberg, Sidney 249

Shenton, Mike 222

Sherrick, Mike 204

Sierra Club 129, 145, 162, 167, 197

Sierra Nevada 32

Sierra Nevada Mountains 57

Smith, "Borax" 166

Smith, C. E. 102

Smith, Jedediah 22

Smith, Tom 247

Smith, Tom (Smitty) 244

Snyder, Jim 69, 219, 220, 222, 223, 226, 228, 230

Society, National Audubon 7

Sovulewski, Gabriel 149, 169

Stagner, Howard R. 301

Stair, Alexander 86

Stebbins, Cyril 147

Stebbins, Robert 147

Steck, Al 209

Stegner, Wallace 65

Stevens, John 144

Stine, Scott 36

Stoneman Meadow riot 239, 242, 244

Strentzel, Dr. John 119

Strentzel, Louisa 118

Sutro, Adolph 129

Sutter, John 43, 45

Sutter's Mill 44

Swartz, Andy 152

Swift, Bryan 233, 236, 237

Sydoriak, Charisse 296

Sydoriak, Walter 35

T

Taft, President William Howard 157

Taft Toe 81

Taylor, Mrs. H. J. 186

Telles, Lucy 47, 279

Tenaya, Chief 53, 55, 56, 61, 62

Tenaya Lake 61, 197

"The White Hills, their Legends, Landscapes, and Poetry" 90

Thickstun, Carole ..35

Thompson, Lynn 246

Tilden, Freeman 141

To'tu'ya 186

Trail Design 220

Treaty of Camp Frémont 51

Tresidder, Donald 178, 181, 184, 186, 187, 188, 191

Tresidder, Mary Curry 189, 199

Turtleback Dome 56

Twain, Mark 122

Twenty-Mule-Team-Borax 166

U

Udall, Stewart 301

Underwood 156

Underwood, Gilbert 182

Urban, Dave 262

U.S. Army
Presence in Yosemite 127
Sixth U. S. Cavalry 149
U. S. Cavalry 169

V

Vandever, William 124, 127

van Wagtendonk, Dr. Jan 201, 228, 230, 231, 296

Vaughn, Ronald 258, 266

Vento, Bruce 307, 308

W

Wade, Bill 326

Wagtendonk, Dr. Jan van 295

Walker, Capt. Joseph R. 16–19, 24, 27, 32, 40, 41

Walker Party 25

Walklet, Keith 183

Walton, Brian J. 203

Washburn, Henry 80

Washington, President George 17

Wasserman, Lew 249

Watkins, Carlton 92

Watt, James G. 113, 116, 117

Wayburn, Dr. Edgar 313

Welch, William 169

Wendt, Bill 76, 81

Wheeler, Benjamin 138

Whelan, Bill 7, 11, 75, 85, 111, 200

"Where To Go and What To Do" 122

White House 274

Whitehouse, Annie 264

Whitmore, George 209

Whitney, Josiah 95

Widen, Jeff 206

Williams, Robert 178

Wilson 170

Wilson, Pete 308

Wilson, President Woodrow 4, 169

Winfrey, Oprah 271

Wirth 195

Wirth, Conrad L. 194, 195, 198

Woessner, Chuck 71

Works Progress Administration
    (WPA) 189

Wurgler, Jim 71

 Y

Yablonski, John "Yabo" 213

Yard, Robert Sterling 169

Yellowstone National Park 9

Yosemite Association 71

Yosemite Commissioners 96, 121,
    123

Yosemite Field School of Natural
    History 190

Yosemite Grant Commission 135

Yosemite Grant, The 3

Yosemite Museum Association 177

Yosemite National Park

Establishment 127

Yosemite Park & Curry Company
    5, 14, 72, 74, 181, 184, 189,
    194, 199, 229, 248, 255

Yosemite Plan, The

Implementation 112

master plan 5

Public Involvement 74

Yosemite Restoration Trust 319

Yosemite Stage & Turnpike Compa-
    ny 138

Yosemite Valley Railroad 171

Yosemite Village 13, 14

Young, Harold 9